THIS SIDE OF PEACE

A PERSONAL ACCOUNT

HANAN ASHRAWI

Simon & Schuster
New York   London   Toronto   Sydney   Tokyo   Singapore

SIMON & SCHUSTER
Rockefeller Center
1230 Avenue of the Americas
New York, NY 10020

Copyright © 1995 by Hanan Mikhail-Ashrawi
All rights reserved,
including the right of reproduction
in whole or in part in any form.

SIMON & SCHUSTER and colophon are registered trademarks
of Simon & Schuster Inc.

Designed by Meryl Levavi/Levavi & Levavi

Manufactured in the United States of America

1   3   5   7   9   10   8   6   4   2

Library of Congress Cataloging-in-Publication Data
ᶜAshrāwī, Ḥanān.
This side of peace : a personal account / Hanan Ashrawi.
    p.   cm.
Includes index.
1. Jewish-Arab relations—1973–   2. Israel-Arab conflicts.
3. Palestinian Arabs—Politics and government.
4. Israel. Treaties, etc. Munaẓẓamat al-Taḥrīr al-Filasṭīnīyah, 1993 Sept. 13.
5. ᶜAshrāwī, Ḥanān.   I. Title.
DS119.7.A68938   1995
956.953044′092—dc20
[B]   95-1793
CIP
ISBN 0-684-80294-5

A leatherbound signed first edition of this book has been published by Easton Press.

Photo Credits

1, 13. AP/Wide World Photos   **3.** Les Stone/Sygma   **7.** Schlomo Arad   **8, 9.** Moshe Milner/Sygma   **10, 11.** David Rubinger/ABC   **16.** White House Press Photograph   **19.** Tom Stoddart/Katz/SABA   **20.** Emile Ashrawi   Photos 2, 4, 5, 6, 12, 14, 15, 17, and 18 from the personal collection of the author.

ACKNOWLEDGMENTS

———◆·✦·◆———

Too many people have been part of both the narrative and the narration for me to mention by name; they know, as I do, who they are. I am profoundly grateful to each one of them.

The principles of selectivity and order as well as the first-person point of view and personal perspective have imposed their own restrictions on the scope of this work. This book does not pretend by any means to tell the whole story, the overwhelming epic of the Palestinian people. It is by necessity the tale of one participant, neither heroic nor villainous, but with a genuine commitment to the truth, however lacking in omniscience. To all those who played a significant role in the shaping of this reality but who are not mentioned in this particular narrative, I extend my acknowledgment and my apologies.

Edward Said, friend and mentor, has often lamented the lack of a Palestinian narrative to reveal in human terms our side of the truth. To him I owe the initial impulse to embark on this revelation. Mahmoud Darwish, poet and friend, has always called for the integrity of the Palestinian utterance. This is one modest attempt. Akram Haniyyeh, writer of fiction, politician, and friend, was the first to discern the new language and the emerging reality behind and beyond words. Perhaps this account will begin to convey his truth and my indebtedness. Faisal Husseini, Jerusalemite, friend, and politician, has taken risks and kept the faith where others succumbed to self-interest and trepidation. In part, this is his narrative. It is also a selective narrative of the Palestinian delegation/ team whose own chapter in history remains a luminous embodiment of dignity, courage, and integrity. To all the members of the political/diplomatic/information committee, whether mentioned by name or not, I owe the shared courage to speak out. They urged me to preserve our little-known chapter in the larger history; in the collective memory of a nation, nothing is lost.

Robert B. Barnett, tireless lawyer and discerning critic, started out as agent and became a special friend. Alice Mayhew, more than editor, sensed both substance and style and exercised the rare combination of sensitivity and skill. Eric Steel put up with my insane schedule with patience and persistence. Barbara Feinman, craftswoman and friend, understood both structure and substance. Linda Michaels represented me internationally with enthusiasm and energy. Victoria Meyers transformed publicity into human relations. All were indispensable at the human and professional levels. I am deeply indebted to them all, and personally grateful for their friendship.

All my assistants, at one time or another throughout the period covered by this work, have valiantly tried to inject some order and sense into my life and work. Sisters by choice, they are: Nuha Awadallah-Musleh, Suhair Taha, Farida Salfiti, Nadia Rahman, Rula Kort, Rula Dajani, and many volunteers during the hectic days and nights of negotiations. Ours remains a true bond of warmth and understanding. Two special men share this bond and I am privileged to be able to call them brothers and guardians, Bashar Masri and Hamdallah Alul. It has been my privilege as well to work with Penny Johnson and to call her friend. Whether in legal aid, human rights, negotiations, or in drafting documents, Penny has been a constant source of encouragement, warmth, well-being, and undaunted good humor.

Many Arab-American organizations and individuals rallied in support of the Palestinian delegation and the negotiations. Khalil Jahshan and the staff of the National Association of Arab-American Anti-Discrimination Committee deserve special recognition. George Salsm, in particular, continues to be a source of quiet support, generosity of spirit, and selfless dedication. Cousin, lawyer, friend, and colleague, he played a crucial role in Palestinian-American negotiations as well as in the entire process. Never seeking recognition or gratitude, he has earned both. His is also my affection and appreciation.

Above all I am forever indebted to those closest to me—my human "power base"—my husband, Emile, and daughters, Amal and Zeina. When all is said and done, what we have is what remains. Their unquestioning love and trust, their faith and courage, as well as their strength and support sustained our togetherness and my determination. They "lent" me to the peace process and made no claims in return. To them, I owe everything, and this book is the beginning of a testimonial. To them, I pledge everything, and this account is the memory and promise of a better future. They gave me my peace, and I shall always endeavor to reciprocate. As for my love, it remains boundless.

To Emile, Amal, and Zeina—
husband and daughters

To the memory of Daud and Wadiᵓa Mikhail
and Hanna Mikhail (Abu Omar)—
parents and cousin

To Muna, Abla, Huda, and Nadia—
sisters and friends

To the Palestinian people—
the rest of the family

With love and *amanah*

AUTHOR'S NOTE

On Friday, October 14, 1994, Yasser Arafat, Shimon Peres, and Yitzhak Rabin were nominated to receive the Nobel Peace Prize. To most people, a more unlikely trio and a stranger combination would be hard to find. In fact, until eighteen months ago, such a development would have been inconceivable. To the Israelis and the West, Arafat had been portrayed as the archetypal terrorist, while to the Palestinians and our friends, Rabin was the bone-breaker, the architect of the brutal "iron fist" policy of repression. Palestinian-Israeli enmity had been taken for granted as an ongoing fact of life, and violence was the daily fare.

It was not a miraculous transformation that had bestowed the title of "peacemakers" on these erstwhile enemies who had exchanged bullets and bombs instead of handshakes and smiles. It was a committee of Norwegian men—one of whom later resigned in protest.

The struggle for peace has been long and difficult. Officially it was launched on October 30, 1991, in the Spanish city of Madrid. Its origins and gradual evolution could be traced as far back as the Arab-Israeli war of June 5, 1967, with Israel's occupation of the Egyptian Sinai, the Syrian Golan Heights, and the Palestinian West Bank (from Jordan) and Gaza Strip (from Egypt). In fact, the origins of the Palestinian-Israeli conflict go back much further, even before the "disaster" of 1948 and the establishment of the State of Israel on most of the land of historic Palestine—but that is a tale too long and complex to fall within the scope of this book. In the aftermath of the 1967 war, the United Nations Security Council met and adopted Resolution 242, which subsequently became the basis of the Madrid peace process. It reiterated and reaffirmed the organization's basic tenets: the inadmissibility of the acquisition of land by war and the right of all states to live within secure and recognized borders, thus calling for a just solution to the Palestinian refugee problem. Another war in 1973 brought forth another resolution, number 338, which led, ultimately, to the American-brokered Camp David Accords between Egypt and Israel and the peace treaty of 1979. In the meantime, individuals on both sides made tentative and exploratory moves to assess the chances of a negotiated settlement, and many good people lost their lives (or at least their good name) in the process. Gradually a new discourse emerged, primarily among the Palestinian political and intellectual elite, with the cumulative effect of forming a linguistic and conceptual framework for an eventual peace.

The 1982 Israeli invasion of Lebanon, the trauma of the Sabra and Shatilla massacres in which hundreds of Palestinian refugees were murdered in cold blood by Lebanese Phalangists in full sight of (and collusion with) the Israeli army, and the expulsion of the PLO from Lebanon all added another tragic chapter to our region's history while, ironically, drawing it closer to peace. The Palestinian *intifada* transformed the concept and practice of Palestinian resistance from armed struggle to popular, and largely civil, disobedience. The focus shifted from a leadership in exile to a people under occupation, and rebellion began to take on the shape of nation building.

The *intifada* gave the Palestinian political agenda the momentum necessary for the peace "offensive" or peace "initiative" as it was then called. On November 15, 1988, the Palestinian parliament in exile, the Palestine National Council or PNC, met in Algiers and declared statehood; it adopted a resolution that in effect accepted the "two-state solution"—implicitly recognizing Israel as one of these two states alongside the state of Palestine. The way to achieve this solution, it was proposed, was through negotiations in a UN-sponsored international conference. Thus the "military option" was laid to rest and the political alternative became a viable and legitimate endeavor. A series of exploratory rehearsal dialogues were held all over the world, hosted by a variety of third parties, to "normalize" the negotiations option and to set its terms of reference.

Several initiatives were attempted to formalize the talks. Although none succeeded, all contributed incrementally to identifying the basic issues and creating a pool of possible approaches and agendas. In January 1991, the Gulf War struck the Arab world with the force of a major earthquake, leaving it politically, economically, and spiritually devastated. President George Bush and Secretary of State James Baker decided to take advantage of this collective shock to reorder the region in a way that would safeguard American interests (particularly the oil) and the security of its allies (mainly Israel). The Palestinians, as the major cause of instability in the region, had to be brought in, and the Palestinian question—the major Arab grievance—had to be resolved somehow. Thus began the Madrid peace process, which brought us to our current state of affairs and won our leaders the Nobel Peace Prize.

On September 13, 1993, a Palestinian-Israeli Declaration of Principles was signed on the White House lawn, and a famous handshake between the Palestinian Chairman Yasser Arafat and Israeli Prime Minister Yitzhak Rabin signaled to the world a new beginning. The agreement had been worked out in secret in Oslo, Norway, away from the public eye and without the knowledge of the Palestinian delegation that had been negotiating in earnest with the Israeli delegation in Washington. It was followed by what came to be known as "the Cairo Agreement," a more detailed elaboration on the implementation of the Declaration of Principles. As a result, the PLO leadership was allowed to return to the Gaza Strip and the town of Jericho in the West Bank, and a whole new dynamic developed in internal Palestinian realities as well as in Palestinian-Israeli relations. A transitional phase had begun, with all the uncertainty, pain, and volatility of a passage into the unknown. It unleashed forces that threatened to make peace even more destructive than war. It also signaled to the Arab world that other separate bilateral deals were permissible and that normalization (particularly economic) with Israel could commence.

On Wednesday, October 26, 1994, Jordan and Israel signed the first peace treaty between Israel and an Arab country since the signing of the Egyptian-Israeli treaty. The symbolism of the setting and the context was not lost on the audience: a minefield in the Jordan Rift Valley, the lowest spot on earth, was cleared for the ceremony and a sandstorm blew dust in the eyes of the signatories, who were already suffering from the heat and glare of the cruel sun. The only shadow was that of the latest suicide bomb attack by Hamas, the Islamic Resistance Movement, carried out exactly one week earlier, in which a bus was blown up in the busiest street of Tel Aviv resulting in twenty-three deaths and scores of injuries.

The Tel Aviv bombing on Wednesday, October 19, came as an escalation of an already sinister spiral of violence and revenge in which innocent civilians were paying with their lives for the political/ideological statements that extremists on both sides wanted to make. The peace process itself was the ultimate target and human beings were the unwitting victims.

On Friday, November 11, a young Palestinian carried out a suicide bombing near an Israeli settlement in Gaza, killing three Israeli soldiers and wounding six other Israelis and six Palestinians. A Palestinian opposition Islamic organization, Al-Jihad Al-Islami, claimed responsibility and declared the act as a response to the killing of one of their leaders, Hani al-Abed, whose booby-trapped car had been blown up nine days earlier. It was widely believed that the Israeli authorities at the highest level were responsible for Al-Abed's assassination in retaliation for his alleged involvement in the killing of two Israeli soldiers.

The peace process seemed to sink deeper into the quagmire of violence and revenge as it sought to make progress in the domain of negotiations and reconciliation. The Israelis demanded a crackdown on the Palestinian opposition groups, particularly Hamas and Al-Jihad Al-Islami. In order to cater to his own constituency, Rabin demanded of Arafat precisely those steps and measures that would undermine the latter in the eyes of his own constituency. Security, as defined by the Israelis, meant repression and human rights violations in the Palestinian dictionary. Alleviation of economic suffering and deprivation would have eased the transition and defused the anger and discontent of the Palestinians, particularly in Gaza. In the service of "security," Israel, on the other hand, closed off the Gaza Strip and intensified the pressure-cooker effect, which led to even greater suffering and violence.

Violence erupted in the Gaza Strip on Friday, November 18, 1994, and resulted in the death of fifteen Palestinians and the wounding of over two hundred. Members of the Islamic Jihad and Hamas, emerging from Friday prayers at the mosque in Gaza, clashed with the Palestinian police, which ignited a crisis of national dimensions and brought out into the open all the contradictions inherent in this precarious peace. Urgent attempts to contain the violence through mediation and the establishment of judicial and national investigation committees succeeded at the time in putting a halt to inter-Palestinian fighting. However, the underlying causes and long-term preventive and remedial measures required a more sober and comprehensive program.

The most pressing Palestinian call was for establishing the mechanisms of a democratic national dialogue to allow the peaceful and constructive expression of the various political platforms and positions, in order to achieve a new national consensus and permanent channels of coordination and debate. Of equal urgency was the need to undertake a thorough reassessment of the peace process, particularly the Oslo and Cairo agreements, which seemed to be the major sources of contention and internal friction. These agreements had painted the PLO and PNA into a corner and placed them on a direct collision course with many of their people.

Israeli control of the crossing points, security arrangements, economic constraints, restrictions on legislative authority and jurisdiction all formed the sources of Palestinian self-negation and led to further erosion in the support for the peace process and the PNA. Israel's patronizing and humiliating tone and attitude fed Palestinian discontent and accelerated confrontation. So did Israel's continued holding of thousands of Palestinians captive in Israeli jails. The PNA was losing credibility, and the opposition forces painted it as an instrument of Israeli security and a surrogate occupier. Israeli statements inciting the Palestinian Authority to crack down on Hamas and Al-Jihad Al-Islami and prove that it could deliver for Israel widened the internal Palestinian rift. The sealing off of the Gaza Strip undermined the PNA even further and created greater economic deprivation. The Israeli settlements were expanding and Palestinian institutions in Jerusalem were being strangled. New Israeli regulations raised serious doubts about the Israeli government's intentions and the Palestinian leadership's will to resist.

Needless delays and complications plagued the negotiations, and the Palestinian elections, which the Israelis had agreed to, were nowhere in sight as Israel repeatedly imposed more obstacles and preconditions. Palestinians who had looked forward to elections as a means of establishing the foundations of a genuine representative Palestinian democracy grew disillusioned with the process and began to articulate their skepticism publicly. The opposition, particularly Islamic Jihad and Hamas, stepped up their violent attacks on Israeli soldiers, settlers, and civilians in an attempt to capitalize on Palestinian discontent and thus challenge the PNA and the peace process. Polarization within the Palestinian population was on the increase, and with the escalating rhetoric the atmosphere became more charged. In addition, the Jordanian-Israeli peace treaty was perceived as a weakening of the Palestinian side and as a source of greater Palestinian-Jordanian mistrust and rivalry. Issues like Jerusalem, refugees, water rights, borders, and trade, which should have been worked out bilaterally prior to any agreement with Israel, became the source of Palestinian-Jordanian suspicions.

Funds and assistance promised by the donor countries, to be administered by the World Bank, resulted in no more than a trickle, and Gaza's standard of living deteriorated by 50 percent from an already intolerable low. In the absence of laws and regulations, as well as the necessary professional and accountable institutions to regulate and responsibly handle the economic development and reconstruction program, the donors held back and the Palestinian people were made to pay the price. Private investors stayed away, afraid to take risks in this unstable environment and also as a protest against what they perceived to be the leadership's unprofessional economic practices and policies. To build institutions and systems, the Authority needed funds for start-up and running costs and blamed the donor community and the private sector for their lack of responsibility and commitment. Another deadlock was emerging.

Internally, the Palestinian house was shaky, not just politically and economically. The political and security structures took precedence over institution building and the enhancement of civil society. The legal system remained fragmented and contradictory and the judiciary incomplete. So did the regulations and work systems that were badly needed to create professionalism and accountability as the procedural requirements of nation building. Political patronage and inefficiency seemed to prevail, which led to greater alienation. Self-censorship, reticence, and deliberate detachment prevailed among the political and intellectual elite. The people whose skills and expertise the Authority needed to extricate it from its dilemma stayed away.

Against this backdrop, the clashes of November 18 seemed inevitable. The intensity and magnitude of the violence, however, left the Palestinian people in a state of shock. They had reached the brink of an abyss, but a common resolve emerged not to commit collective suicide. Avoiding open and violent clashes was an immediate imperative, but more long-term strategies and steps were needed for a genuine process of rectification and reform. The building and governing of a nation required a historical vision with an active commitment to inclusive democracy and participatory representation based on the rule of law and respect for human rights.

Each side of the precarious Palestinian-Israeli peace had become dependent on the other to sustain its political investment in peace; yet the leadership of each side seemed to have to negate the credibility of the other to maintain support for the process within its own camp. We had exchanged the "fatal proximity" of the occupation with the "fateful embrace" of the process. Neither could afford the price of failure, but the price of its success was threatening to become too steep. With no alternative in sight, Palestinians and Israelis doggedly pursued their commitment to peace in a minefield of violence and pain.

As I sit in my office in Jerusalem as Commissioner General of the Palestinian Independent Commission for Citizens' Rights, I too try to steer clear of the mines. I am not a politician by choice. I pursue the objective of institution building as an essential component of the reconstruction of a nation. Looking back at the developments over the last seven years, I feel a sense of responsibility and apprehension. In my own modest way, I have contributed both to the achievements and ills of our present condition. Motivated neither by guilt nor by pride, but by a sense of responsibility and the exercise of honesty, I feel compelled to narrate that side of peace which the standard textbooks of history and political science tend to ignore—a personal account of one player and the human dimension of an impersonal process. While the fate of nations and the course of global politics are generally perceived in abstractions and sweeping moves, something remains to be said about the view from within.

From such an angle and with such proximity, this side of peace may reveal the unnoticed smile or the hidden grimace which makes the pursuit of peace such a frail and human endeavor. A compilation of individual tales could be the only way to convey the full truth of the narrative in its entirety. This little tale can claim a small space in the consciousness of those who seek to see through and beyond the Grand Peace into the human components of peace. If I have taken the liberty of using my own story as a vehicle to convey a reality much larger than myself, I ask for indulgence. The narrative cannot be detached from the narrator. Nor can the first person singular pronoun replace the plural in the composite experience of a nation. Such is the human context, and therein lies the substance.

Hanan Mikhail-Ashrawi
Ramallah
December 1994

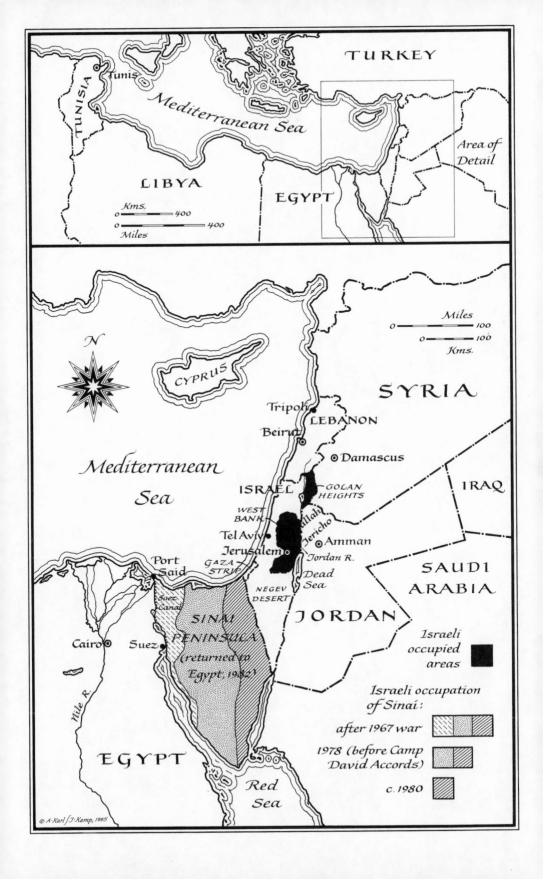

TURKEY

Mediterranean Sea

TUNISIA

Tunis

LIBYA

EGYPT

Area of Detail

Kms.
0   400
0   400
Miles

Miles
0   100
0   100
Kms.

N

CYPRUS

SYRIA

Tripoli

LEBANON

Beirut

⊙ Damascus

Mediterranean Sea

ISRAEL

GOLAN HEIGHTS

IRAQ

WEST BANK

Ramallah

Jericho

⊙ Amman

Tel Aviv

Jerusalem ⊙

Jordan R.

SAUDI ARABIA

Port Said

GAZA STRIP

NEGEV DESERT

Dead Sea

JORDAN

Suez Canal

SINAI PENINSULA
(returned to Egypt, 1982)

Cairo ⊙

Suez

Israeli occupied areas

Israeli occupation of Sinai:

after 1967 war

EGYPT

1978 (before Camp David Accords)

c. 1980

Nile R.

Red Sea

© A·Karl / J·Kemp, 1995

CHAPTER ONE

———◆◆◆◆◆———

On June 5, 1967, I was sitting at my desk in the student residence at the American University of Beirut, writing a research paper on James Joyce's *Ulysses*. My sister Nadia and I were students there in Lebanon while most of our family was back home in the West Bank, which was then that part of Palestine still annexed to Jordan. A series of events, including Israeli raids and culminating in Gamal Abdel Nasser's closure of the Straits of Tiran and the expulsion of United Nations troops, had left the whole region in a state of suspense and agitation. I turned on the radio to listen to the BBC's early morning news, and discovered that we were at war. Another Arab-Israeli military confrontation was at hand. Nadia and I immediately set about trying to find a way to return home. But airports, roads, and borders were closed, and Beirut succumbed to all the precautions and preparations of a war situation without being at war itself. The next few weeks were a succession of nightmares, disasters, and absurdities that shattered my protected universe and irrevocably altered the course of history in our region.

Facts were an elusive commodity, and there were as many versions of the truth as there were newspapers and radio stations, and as many rumors as there were people receiving and transmitting inside information. Later that day, Beirut declared a war blackout, and we turned off the lights, painted all windows black, and descended into underground shelters. The basement of our residence, the University Christian Center, was the dining hall, and all the students huddled there for several days with blankets and transistor radios. The Arabs won the war, lost the war, liberated Palestine, lost the rest of Palestine, invaded Israel, and were invaded by Israel numerous times daily. Someone whispered in my ear that my family's house on Radio Street had been shelled/bombed/destroyed and that all/most/some of my family had been killed. With equal cruelty, the same message was whispered to my sister Nadia. In reciprocal consideration, or perhaps fearing that the mere articulation of the horror would give it substance, neither told the other.

At the end of the week, an American graduate student, Thomas Green, came to see us, underground and in the dark. He had just been to the American embassy. "Stop listening to all those lies on the radio. The war has been over for days," he informed us. "Israel destroyed the whole Egyptian air force before it even took off on the first day. The war ended before it really started." In shock we turned against the messenger. "What about our homes, our families? What's happening on the West Bank? On the other fronts? You're just saying these horrible things to demoralize us." He remained calm, but sad. "You have to face facts. The Arabs have lost the war. The West Bank, the Sinai, and the Golan Heights are under Israeli control." He left us in silence.

Among us were three Lebanese brothers from the Haidar family. The oldest was a graduate student in English at the American University of Beirut, a colleague, scholar, and friend. The youngest was an active member of the resistance who had succeeded in hijacking a plane and then coming back to classes with a business-as-usual attitude. The middle brother was the one who broke the silence that day. He laughed. "Good," he said. "This will solve the domestic help problem. My mother has been having a hard time finding a maid, and now with all the Palestinian students stranded here, she can have her pick." For a moment everyone froze, staring. Then my close friend, Adnan Bader, a Syrian student, reached across the table, picked up the only nearby object, which happened to be a sugar canister, and hurled it at the Lebanese boy. The projectile seemed to fly slowly through the air, sprinkling sparkling white sugar granules everywhere, then hitting its intended target smack in the face. Ever since then, the dominant image I have of those days is of sugar flying everywhere and landing in our clothes, our hair, on the table, and all over the floor.

My sister and I tried to be useful. We spent two days working on camouflage nets for the Lebanese army before the absurdity got to us. I took intensive first-aid classes and kept trying to find a way home. Day after day my sister and I stood in line before the Red Cross office trying to get word about our family. While standing in one of those interminable queues, Nadia and I finally shared our horrible secret, that we feared the worst. In those hours, standing, waiting, praying that my family was unharmed, but not knowing if they were even alive, I began to undergo a transformation. Up until that point I had largely been protected from the pain experienced by my people, having only digested in small servings the horror that had become their daily fare. Which is not to say that I had up to this point ignored our history or our legacy. I knew about Palestinian deprivation and suffering; my father, among others, had made me aware, intellectually, if not emotionally. But this was different, this was visceral, and there was no turning back.

Nadia and I returned to the residence with our shared burden. The moment we walked in the phone rang. It was my sister Muna calling from Washington. The family was unhurt; the house was shelled but no irreparable damage was done. We broke down and finally cried. Someone made me swallow a sedative and I slept for twenty-four hours.

At home my parents and Muna's children, ten-year-old Fuad and eight-year-old Samar, had weathered the storm. Following the death of her young husband, Elias, my sister Muna had gone to the United States to start a new life, while both her children had stayed behind temporarily with my parents. My sister Abla, her husband, Alfred, and their four children were living on the first floor of the family home. All had huddled together in the dark hallway near the kitchen while the house was being shelled. They had their first glimpse of the occupation when Israeli soldiers banged at the door demanding "whitesheez." Abla, having difficulty understanding their accent and wondering at the strange priorities of this enemy, ran to the kitchen and got them a plate of white cheese. Every Palestinian house stocks this kind of home-preserved goat's milk cheese, boiled and kept in salt. Maybe it was a peace offering, Abla figured—a variation on breaking bread. Instead of the expected conciliatory response, the soldiers grew more and more frustrated, repeatedly shouting, "whitesheez," and pointing at the roof. Then they added "blue" to their demands, and Abla finally understood that they wanted white sheets and blue coloring to prepare a makeshift Israeli flag to hoist on top of the building across the street from our house, which was the prison and Jordanian officers' club. Abla found one of her daughter's large cloth diapers and dug up some laundry blueing. The soldiers drew two blue parallel lines and a Star of David in the middle, then placed their artwork on a broomstick and announced their occupancy of the place across the street. The metamorphosis of the first Israeli occupation flag in Ramallah has, till now, remained a family secret.

• • •

When I was born, the state of Israel had not yet been created. Thus my birth certificate, like my parents' marriage certificate, was headed by the word "Palestine." But I was born in time to include in my unconscious biography the end of the British mandate over Palestine, the United Nations partition plan of 1947, and the establishment of the state of Israel on most of our land in 1948 by the time I was nineteen months old. Thus the most significant developments that shaped the rest of my life, as well as the life of a nation and the realities of the whole region, had taken place before I had even gained awareness of my own being. As a medical officer in the Palestine army, my father, Dr. Daud Mikhail, had taken the family to a succession of cities and towns in Palestine, from Majdal to Jerusalem to Hebron to Nablus to Tiberias. Born in Nablus on October 8, 1946, I was taken to Tiberias as an infant in time for the latest breakout of Jewish-Palestinian hostilities and the mass expulsion of Palestinians sometimes referred to as the Exodus of 1948. Life in pre-Israel Palestine, the struggle of the Palestinian rebels, the circumstances of our evacuation, and the reality of my family's temporary exile in Amman, east of the Jordan River, remained fragments of an incomplete memory to be gradually rediscovered and pieced together in agony and awe.

Awareness came to me in Ramallah, my father's ancestral home. Two parts of Palestine remained outside Israel, known as the West Bank and the Gaza Strip; the former was annexed to Jordan in 1951 and the latter was placed under Egyptian custody. Ramallah was in the West Bank, and I grew up under Jordanian rule. Mine was a sheltered life, protected by privilege and a loving family, rooted in the certainty of my origins and the recognition of numerous relatives and friends. Even when external reality intruded, it did so sporadically and hesitantly. In 1956, I remember my father bringing in workmen to dig and prepare a shelter in our garden in anticipation of war. My mother, Wadiʾa, made lists of essential supplies and equipped our war shelter with basic provisions, including canned foods and kerosene lanterns. When the Suez Canal war broke out as the trilateral (French-British-Israeli) attack on Egypt, a total blackout was declared and we went into the shelter. War remained an abstraction and the shelter was a temporary adventure. Whether in the memory of my parents as the War of Palestine or in my childish memory as the Triple Aggression on Egypt, war was a distant and indefinable state—the responsibility of an older and wiser generation.

The word "Palestine" was then taboo, and I remember my father telling us that we were Palestinians and not Jordanians, but cautioning us against saying it out loud. It was safe to whisper the word at home and to listen to Sawt al-Arab (the Voice of the Arabs) radio station broadcasting from Gamal Abdel Nasser's Egypt, provided the volume was low and the windows were closed. Even as children, we harbored sinister political secrets and words to be whispered. Only when my father came out into the open following the Triple Aggression and King Hussein of Jordan's legalization of political parties did I understand the enormity of the secrets the grownups had kept hidden. Instead of surreptitous meetings and cryptic messages from visitors or dread documents to be locked up, Palestinians now had public marches and demonstrations. Some men came to the house and put up a sign declaring this to be the headquarters of the Nationalist Socialist Party, which, like all parties, hitherto had been illegal. My father and his friends wrote leaflets and gave public speeches and we, their children, were filled with pride and admiration. Things changed one day in 1957 when my uncle came from Amman where he had gotten wind of the fact that the Jordanians were clamping down on Palestinian political activities. In an effort to prevent this from happening in our home, in the dead of night, documents were burned. The next day, a group of uniformed soldiers appeared, riddled the party sign with bullets, and ransacked the house looking for the documents. My father was nowhere in sight. Instead, my mother told me that I would be able to visit him in jail. Prison was for criminals, I thought, and my father was an honest and gentle soul.

My sisters and I went to school in shame and anger. My social studies teacher started class by asking me to stand up and face my classmates. Then she addressed us all: "In this unjust world of ours, only the good and the brave go to political prison. We are all very proud of Hanan's father, who has just been arrested, because this means that he is a man of principle and courage. Hold your head up high, Hanan, for prison is an honor that is bestowed only on the worthy." She began clapping and the rest of the class joined in. I returned to my seat, head held high, tears streaming down my cheeks.

Prison visits became a source of excitement, an occasion to look forward to, to dress up for and put a ribbon in my hair. Prison became a motif running throughout my life, linking one compartment to the other with uncanny persistence.

In Ramallah the school I attended was Quaker, the Friends Girls School, and there was also of course its counterpart, the Friends Boys School. It was a family tradition, my parents having attended, as well as my sisters, daughters, nephews, and nieces. It was established in the mid-nineteenth century, and the students were a mixture of Muslims and Christians, but we did not know who was what, and it was not an issue. It was not until later that I became conscious of my Christianity and how it was part of my authenticity as a Palestinian. I had inherited from my mother a deep sense that those in the West had appropriated Christianity, acting as though it were their own religion.

My mother, who is Lebanese, has been devout her entire life. I can remember when I was maybe nine or ten and some missionaries came to our home. My mother told them, "You didn't have to come here. We don't need missionaries to come all the way from the United States to Palestine. We are the ones who know Christianity directly, culturally, historically. Jesus was born here," she reminded them, "right next door." My maternal grandmother herself, in a way, was a missionary, always going around and spreading the Gospel, and my grandfather was an Episcopalian minister. My father, though also Christian (originally Greek Orthodox), was not raised in an atmosphere as religious as his wife's. I remember him regularly driving my mother to church and then returning to pick her up, but rarely joining her.

One day my father and I stood on the western balcony of the house he had built on Radio Street, and we could see off in the distance the shimmering lights of Jaffa and Tel Aviv along the coast. As though speaking to himself he noted that one day Israel would take over the rest of Palestine, and that "the Arabs are not ready and will not be ready then." I was shocked. Israel was an unimaginable aberration out there, while the Arabs were a large nation with many armies and governments that had vowed to liberate Palestine for us. Most Palestinians lived in anticipation of the fulfillment of that promise. Two trends in Palestinian political realities, however, were emerging. The Palestinian National Liberation Movement, Fateh, was slowly growing in exile (the Gulf countries and Egypt), mainly among students and young professionals, while the Palestine Liberation Organization was being set up in Palestine to be officially announced in 1964. As I was preparing to go to college during my last year of high school, I noticed that more visitors were coming to the house without much fanfare or commotion. Later, I found out that consultations were taking place for setting up the PLO and that my father was also involved in recruitment and field surveys.

From the Friends Girls School to the American University of Beirut was my transition into adulthood and an exposure to a different reality. I took with me memories of my mother picking flowers from the garden and creating exquisite flower arrangements that turned our house into a celebration of color and fragrance. I also took memories of family picnics, of games and jokes, and a special reverence for words. In that enchanted circle, all was well with a world that had been protected from the outer world by a deliberate exercise of love. Initially, I wanted to study medicine but my mother succeeded in dissuading me. "There are only two types of doctors," she said. "Good ones who are selfless and dedicated like your father and therefore never get an uninterrupted night's sleep or a complete meal with the family, or bad ones to whom medicine is a good source of income and a nine-to-five job. If I know you, you will be the former, and you will not have a life of your own. You will be consumed by your calling." I gave up medicine and went into physics and then English because of the abstraction of the former and humanism of the latter. My mother's counsel on the subject of medicine, in retrospect, is the essence of irony in light of the all-consuming "calling" I have taken upon myself.

•   •   •

After the 1967 war, the "Palestinian Question"—whether we would ever have our land restored to us, or at least a portion of it—had become a personal issue. With the occupation of the West Bank and Gaza, it had hit home, literally. It was no longer my parents' legacy or an abstract historical or political concept. It became my burden, my responsibility. Overnight, I had become an "exile," and most of my family remained under occupation. The urge to go home became my overriding motivation. The era of resistance had taken on a new urgency and momentum. Thus began a momentous transition in my life in which activism was the key. I became involved in the growing Palestinian revolution. All around the entire region, as the initial shock of the Israeli occupation began to wear off, resistance activity stirred and recruitment efforts swelled into the ranks of organizations of armed struggle—primarily Fateh. The battle of the Karamah (one of the first military clashes between the Palestinian resistance and the Israeli army in Jordan, east of the river) brought a new surge of enlistment by eager young men and women who felt that they could take part in shaping their destiny. Sacrifice and the *feda'yeen* (the freedom fighters—"those who sacrifice") were the operative words as the new generation of Palestinians embraced the struggle for the liberation of Palestine. That phase of Palestinian activity in a way foreshadowed the *intifada* with its exuberance, drive, vision, and sense of invincibility and essential *rightness*. Like the *intifada,* it too ultimately underwent excesses, distortions, and convolutions that turned it against itself.

At that station, I learned the meaning of organization, resistance, discipline, and self-criticism as a means of reform, and participated in the first cells of underground activity. Jihan Helu, one of the active women in the resistance, was in charge of our group. Together, we worked in refugee camps, digging shelters and trenches, and teaching consciousness raising. Jihan later married my cousin Hanna Mikhail (Abu Omar), the purest, most idealistic Quaker academic-cum-revolutionary. He left behind a promising academic career at the University of Washington, put away his Princeton Ph.D., and joined the revolution to live in the camps and often going hungry. When I first saw him in uniform, I could not believe that this pacifist Quaker, brilliant intellectual, and most idealistic of visionaries had joined the revolution. But I discovered that it was precisely these qualities that had driven him to renounce the comforts and acclaim of a life in exile as an intellectual and take up the self-denial and deprivation of a purist revolutionary in desert camps. To him, revolution was the ultimate in asceticism and the essence of service. He never fired a gun; his weapons were his brains and words. The French philosopher Jean Genet captures the enigma of Abu Omar in his personal account of the Palestinian revolution, *The Prisoner of Love*. In 1976, when the boat he was on just off the coast of Lebanon was blasted out of existence, and Hanna was declared missing, presumed dead, Jihan lost her equilibrium and spent the next twelve years in an obsessive, though futile, quest. His death remains a mystery; versions ranged from Israeli bombardment at sea, to capture by the Syrians, to torture by the Lebanese Phalangists. Jihan's search for Hanna lasted more than a decade, and the PLO declared him martyred. In spirit, Hanna lived beyond his brief life, and as Edward Said described him in an article in August 1994, he represented the best in all of us. As Hanan Mikhail, I often had a difficult and exasperating time explaining to security officials in airports all over the world that Hanna Mikhail was a different person who was beyond their reach.

During that time, in the aftermath of the 1967 war, I also worked on setting up women's revolutionary structures, wrote leaflets, and talked to reporters, escorting them on camp visits. In this capacity I made friendships that have remained a solid part of my life, particularly with Peter

Jennings and Charles Glass of ABC. While I learned the basics of political organization and information in Beirut, the thin protective walls that had sheltered my life until the war continued to be torn down. I learned that the precious word "Palestinian" was a controversial one, evoking a whole range of reactions. Gradually, I acquired the awareness that to be believed and accepted, we had to speak for ourselves, not be typecast, and to present ourselves directly to the world. Only then would we be able to begin the transformation of the word "Palestinian" from one that was to be whispered to one that could be uttered in normal tones. But to get there, we had to go through a stage of shouting it in defiance. Only in retrospect could we reach the conclusion that the silence of denial and the din of defiance were equally deafening.

In 1969, when I was an increasingly idealistic, radical student, I found myself standing beside a legend, at a meeting of the conference of the General Union of Palestinian Students in Amman, Jordan. Yasser Arafat to the rest of the world, Palestinians know him as Abu Ammar, a name adopted for the revolution. To acquire an alternate name was not unusual; in fact, a whole culture of pseudonyms was born out of our situation, imposed by the necessary secrecy of our circumstances.

I was awed that day; Abu Ammar was only forty years old then, but he seemed somehow to transcend age, by this time having gradually become, at least within the revolution, larger than life. My first image of Abu Ammar is of him standing among us in the audience. I was struck by how human and down-to-earth this legendary leader really was in person.

At this particular conference, I was the sole elected female delegate among about two hundred males. There were other women, but only in the role of observers. Some conservative boys tried to force me to wear long sleeves and a scarf but our delegation resisted, refusing to make me comply. This was among my early encounters with the more overt aspects of traditional Arab male-dominated attitudes. A song written by a friend of mine called "He Brought Me ꜣAkkoub and My Hands Are Bloody" says it all. ꜣAkkoub, a special food that grows in rocky, barren land as a wild thorn, is very delicious but difficult to prepare. The delicacy is gathered, then women spend hours cleaning the stems and heads and removing their thistles, bloodying their hands in the process. Out of a whole bushel a woman is left typically with just a handful of edible ꜣakkoub, which the man then consumes in five minutes.

As I stood talking among the group with Abu Ammar, I became aware that pictures of us were being taken, and this had very dangerous implications for me. Soon I hoped to be returning home to the occupied West

Bank, and there were now in existence pictures of me and the man who was becoming the symbol of what the Israelis were trying to quash. Not surprisingly, one of the pictures turned up in a Lebanese paper.

After that I had occasion to communicate with Abu Ammar over the years and on a variety of issues. I could not meet with him openly because Israel had declared all Palestinian political parties illegal and had banned any communication with the PLO. "Membership"—as a legal offense— carried the penalty of a long jail sentence, and the Palestinian flag itself was outlawed. All along, I saw the side of Abu Ammar that was not visible through television or print reports. The Western media refused to look beyond the image, and he was reduced to outlines rather than substance. The manner of presentation was confused with the reality; it was much easier for the West to deal with Abu Ammar as an archetypal terrorist, an archetypal villain, and a revolutionary leader—but never the simple essence of what makes a person a human being. This one-dimensional image of a bogeyman was taken as representative of all Palestinians.

•   •   •

When I received my master's degree from the American University of Beirut in 1970 I had nowhere to go. I could not remain in Lebanon because I had neither a visa nor a work permit, and I could not go home to Ramallah because of the Israeli occupation since the 1967 war; when I applied for a permit to return I was denied. I had planned to go home and teach, but this was not to be, at least not then. Fate intervened. The head of the English Department called me to his office and said that the department had a doctoral scholarship for its top student and that the Faculty Graduate Committee had selected me. Within a week my papers were prepared and sent to the universities of my choice. A month later I was on my way to the University of Virginia at Charlottesville, to become a graduate student and Ph.D. candidate in English literature. I called my parents from Washington, D.C., and informed them of this sudden shift in the course of my life. It was my first opportunity to call them with my news, as there were no direct telephone links between the Arab world and Israel or the Occupied Territories.

After Beirut, my initial impression of the United States was that of isolation, provincialism, and newness. How protected and innocent were the Americans I met, how removed from the pain and complexity of life beyond their continent despite the collective trauma of the Vietnam War. How untouched and yet how open. How powerful and yet how vulnerable. It was, however, refreshing to see how un-Byzantine their scheme of things was, and how novel. But I longed for history and permanence. I craved my familiar time frame in which one century was piled on earlier centuries to form a comprehensible and assuring chronology and perspective. All of Palestine could be gift-wrapped and deposited in the corner of one American state. Yet in all the vastness of that geography, I could not locate my layers of archaeology to give me my bearings, to reassure me that the here and now coexists with the there and then, and that the stone I have used for the foundation of my house was once chipped by a Roman mason. Contemporary America appeared to me to be precariously painted on top of the earth, not yet fully engraved or sculpted to completeness. And in my innocence, I worried about its vulnerability. It took time for me to recognize the nature and components of contemporary power, and to understand that its freedom from a cluttered past could be a form of release for the future.

The anti–Vietnam War movement and the end of the Nixon era was the political backdrop of my academic pursuits. My cultural legacy included the singers Fairouz and Muhammad Abdel-Wahab, the poets Badr Shaker As-Sayyab and Mahmoud Darwish, and the Eastern Muslim and Christian philosophy and continuum of history. But it also included the Beatles and the Rolling Stones, Bob Dylan and Dylan Thomas, Simon and Garfunkel as well as the counterculture of flower power. As the founder and only member of the Charlottesville branch of the Organization of Arab Students and as head of a group called American Friends of Free Palestine, I formed coalitions with the Charlottesville Resistance (an anti–Vietnam War group), women's groups, the Virginia Collective (a 1960s cooperative), the Appalachian mine workers, and the Black Students Alliance. The organizers of the mineworkers, I quickly discovered, knew more about Palestine and had a stronger global awareness in general than the professors, hidden away in their ivory towers. To show my support as a Palestinian sister, I attended the Black Students Alliance meetings, the only nonblack student to participate. In between, I attended seminars, wrote papers, and taught American students English. I found myself equally at home in radical political activism and in esoteric pedantic pursuits. My home became a refuge and meeting place for advocates and practitioners of both. I myself felt equally awed and at ease in the Library of Congress and the coffee shops of Dupont Circle in Washington.

While I made a place for myself in this new world, acceptance by all was not automatic. But as soon as people realized I was not going to jump up and start belly dancing between the salad and the main course, nor was I going to toss a grenade into the dessert, I began to make friends. At that time the word "Palestinian" meant terrorist or nothing at all. There was a group of students who believed that I should not be allowed to teach, that if permitted, I would teach world revolution. The graduate committee just laughed off their letter of protest.

One time during that period I was on a plane and found myself next to a historian working on a medieval thesis. Soon we were engrossed in a conversation about medieval literature. He noted my accent and asked where I was from. "I'm a Palestinian," I replied. He blanched and then muttered, "Do you think we're going to get there?" The man clearly thought I was going to hijack the plane!

My studies were going very well at UVa and before long it came time to begin a dissertation. When I applied for a dissertation scholarship, I came up against one of the more irritating moments of discrimination in my life, and this had to do with gender rather than geography. A very powerful scholar in the department was against giving me the scholarship because I was a woman, explaining that women get married and have children. Pointing out his specious logic I retorted, to no avail, "In my experience, men get married and have children too. Does that exclude them from becoming good scholars?"

Throughout my stay in the United States, whenever someone asked me what I wanted to do, "To go home," was my instinctive response. My return journey was another passage and a "pilgrimage of woe." When I left Beirut for Washington, the lyrics of the song that accompanied me, with the jasmine garlands my friends had strewn and worn, kept echoing: "I'm leaving on a jet plane/Don't know when I'll be back again." When I left the United States it was "Homeward Bound." My first stop was Paris where I was detained and questioned for twenty-four hours as a potential terrorist in what turned out to be a case of mistaken identity; they thought I was Leila Khaled, a famous member of the Popular Front for the Liberation of Palestine (PFLP), a group that had carried out many hijackings. Having settled that, I stopped in Cairo next. There I was detained for forty-eight hours for no apparent reason other than my national identity. In Beirut, Abu Jihad (or Khalil al-Wazir, one of the top military leaders, who was later assassinated in 1988) came to see me and asked me to pursue my work at home through my academic endeavors—the revolution must be served in a variety of ways. In Amman, I finally discovered that I actually did have a permit for a family reunion, and taking advantage of what a Jordanian intelligence officer told me was a general amnesty for Palestinians, I crossed the bridge over the river Jordan for the first time since the 1967 occupation and I went home.

• • •

One day, not long after I had returned to Ramallah, an elderly Jewish gentleman came to our home to visit my father. I was horrified. "How could you receive an Israeli in our home?" I questioned my father. "We go back a long way," he answered. "Hear him out first." It turned out that the gentleman had been a prisoner of war in 1948 and my father had been among the doctors who had treated the Jewish prisoners, including this man. "He was so human and kind to us," said the Israeli, "that we never forgot him. You could say that his gentleness kept us alive. I've been looking for him for a long time to thank him. And now I'm here." My father had always taught us not to hate anyone, including our enemies, and now I could see that he had practiced in his own life what he had preached to his daughters.

From the outset, the occupation and I did not get along. I became a faculty member and head of the English department at Birzeit University, settling into the academic life. I nevertheless found myself closely involved with student activities. Following a few demonstrations and protest marches, I received a summons, underwent questioning by the Israeli police, was arrested, fingerprinted, released on bail, and a trial date was set. During this time I attended a pop concert in Jerusalem. I was moved by the fact that the band, Baraʾem (blooms), used Arabic lyrics with contemporary music. Standing in the back of the crowded concert hall, I noticed the band's long-haired drummer, impressed with his natural stage presence and obvious deep connection to the music.

His name was Emile Ashrawi and in addition to his rock band he was a force of creativity in Balaleen, an irreverent, contemporary theater group that had placed modern Palestinian theater on the cultural map, as well as a gentle mentor of children in the voluntary community work project. One of my sisters was also a member of Balaleen, and in light of the fact that our community was a tightly knit group, it was perhaps inevitable that we would meet. Soon after the concert we talked on the phone. He had heard that the Israelis had charged me with a whole list of violations —incitement, threatening the security of the state, etc.—because I had participated in demonstrations. One day a group of people gathered at my parents' home to discuss strategies for my trial, and Emile and his brother were there. While everyone else was busy giving advice Emile sat quietly, taking it all in. I thought to myself that this was a man who truly listened.

My trial was set for December 25. It was a somber Christmas, spent in court. When it came time for me to state my case to a military judge, he asked if I wanted to take my oath on the Koran, the Old Testament, or the New Testament. "The New Testament," I answered solemnly.

He paused, the significance of the day apparently registering, and then he asked, "What are you doing here today?"

"That's a good question," I replied evenly. "A very good question. Maybe you can answer it."

My Christmas present that year from the Israeli government was the choice of a prison sentence or a substantial fine. The faculty members of Birzeit University paid the fine on my behalf.

In 1974, I established the University Legal Aid Committee to provide legal defense for Palestinian students. My university career alternated between being an administrator and member of the University Council or being an activist and a member of the Faculty Union. Outside the university framework, a group of women and I started feminist study groups and held consciousness-raising sessions to try to work out an appropriate gender agenda that would address a whole different set of Palestinian realities. At that time as well, we began the first tentative contacts with Israeli activists seeking to end the occupation and to bring about a settlement on the basis of the two-state solution (an idea the United Nations proposed in 1947). It was then that we formed the first Palestinian-Israeli underground political organization.

While this was a period of my life filled by political and academic work, it was also the time when Emile and I fell in love.

One of my greatest desires upon my return from the United States had been to join Balaleen. My sister Nadia and Sameh Abboushi (an architect and writer who had married Nadia in 1973 in a joint Christian-Muslim ceremony), as well as Emile and his brothers, had established this unprecedented drama movement for social change. I longed to be part of that drive toward hope and joy, that expression of youthful confidence. I joined the group, and subsequently Emile and I worked on several plays together.

Although Emile was not a political activist, he was already involved with the left-wing Israeli and Palestinian groups that had begun forming by the early 1970s. In fact, many of the political meetings I attended took place in his home with the participation of his brother Ibrahim and other friends. Emile's vehicle of expression and change was consistently music, theater, children's projects, and a pacific counterculture that defied all types of provocation and meanness of spirit. This sense of largesse, of generosity and gentleness, continued to be Emile's trademarks as husband, father, and friend. With an abundance of love, patience, and tolerance, Emile has steadfastly remained a constant "bridge over troubled waters." His is the quiet confidence of a man secure enough in his manhood not to have to prove his masculinity by oppressing women or by entering into marriage as a relationship of competition and domination. Many of my women friends jokingly ask me where I had found him. "He's one of a kind," I always reply, "and I found him waiting for me to return home!"

On February 14, 1974, I told my father that Emile and I intended to get married.

"Are you asking for my permission or advice?" he asked.

"Your advice," I answered.

"Good," he said. "You don't need anyone's permission. I brought you up to rely on your own judgment. Emile is a good man, and you made the right decision. I know it must have been difficult, and the future won't be easy."

"I know, Papa, and I'm grateful for your confidence and support. Emile and I love each other very much."

"I have eyes. I saw this coming, and I confess I've been preparing for it. You know that this won't be a conventional marriage, and you'll face opposition. Ours is not a traditional family, but his is. You have to be prepared for trouble from that direction. You're older than he is, better-educated, and from a different social background." Emile's father, who had been a salaried employee, had fewer resources from which to draw upon, but somehow managed to stretch what they did have to send his six children to private schools.

"Your mother and I went through something similar when we got married. She was older and from a feudal family who thought she was marrying beneath her. But we won, and things turned out well for us. You'll have the additional responsibility of having to work for the rest of your life. He won't be able to support a family." (Until her death in September 1994, my mother never revealed her true age, having adopted my father's year of birth, 1909, as her own.)

"I know, and I don't mind," I told my father. "You know that I didn't get my Ph.D. to frame the degree and hang it in the kitchen. You were the one always urging us to be independent, and not to rely on anyone else financially, including future husbands. It was you who told us that the only thing you take for granted is that all of us would get a higher education. So now you have five independent, educated daughters and you can't complain."

"I'm proud of all of you. You know how fond I am of Emile, and I will stand by you the way I stood by your sister Nadia when she and Sameh got married and the whole extended family was against it because he's Muslim. It seems unconventional marriages run in this family; that's what makes us original and diverse. Emile is special because his goodness comes through. I can sense it. And he really loves you. You won't have the choice of not working, but you've already made that commitment. Go for it, and make it work."

On August 8, 1975, we had an unusual and wonderful wedding that was an accurate harbinger of the marriage to come. We had called our friends on the phone and said, "We're getting married, would you like to come?" We chose not to have fancy invitations or a reception, and I wore a champagne-colored dress, and Emile a beige jacket and brown pants. The cathedral was full as I walked down the aisle on my father's arm. I looked ahead at the man who was to be my husband waiting at the altar. I was simultaneously filled with love and apprehension. The whole idea of marriage had been foreign to my vision of the future as an independent woman, bent on defying the constraints imposed by a traditional society, determined not to be owned in holy matrimony, and committed to proving that a woman was perfectly capable as a human being of claiming a distinct role and place of her own away from patriarchy and patronage. Then I had met Emile. He had reached out with his gentleness and quiet confidence to my deepest fears and wiped them away; his humor, assurance, and creativity overcame the strongest barriers of defensiveness and defiance that had made me look upon marriage as a form of organized captivity.

When we decided to get married, Emile and I dreamed of having two daughters. I had grown up with four sisters and no brothers and if I had had a son I would not have known what to do with him. Emile too had always wanted daughters, which was very unusual for a man in our society. He always dreamed of walking down the street with daughters with long hair flowing behind them.

For our first, we prepared the room, toys, clothes, and name in full confidence that it would be Amal. Faithfully, we went through the exercises and training for natural childbirth, and only as I was going into the delivery room did I remember to ask Emile, "Suppose it's a boy? What will we do?" He answered in good humor, "We'll have to come up with a name and clothes real quick, but we'll be just as happy. The next one will be a girl." Amal, our hope, brought not only fulfillment and wonder into our lives, but a sense of imagination and creativity that made us see the world afresh. She "ordered" her sister, Zeina, who would bestow on us her gifts of vitality and daring and even greater reservoirs of unquestioning love.

My life has been taking shape as a Palestinian, as a woman—as mother, daughter, wife—as a Christian and a humanist, as a radical and a peace activist, as an academic and a political being. And as a composite of all these constituents, I am hopeful that one day I shall attain the only identity and name worth seeking—that of human being.

•　•　•

It was the Saturday before Easter in 1981, and I was pregnant with Zeina. My three-year-old daughter, Amal, my parents, and I were out in our garden, which was in full bloom, enjoying the day. Since the early Middle Ages, the Saturday before Easter has traditionally been the day of the holy fire ceremony, called the Saturday of Light. The ritual celebrates the Marys' and other women's visit to the tomb of Christ and their discovery that it was empty and the dazzling light associated with that discovery. Every year appointed runners carry the miraculous flame that is supposed to have emanated from the Holy Sepulcher from town to town, greeted by a gathering of people in each place.

On this particular day, as the runner carried the flame to Ramallah, the religious procession turned into a demonstration. Nationalistic chants were recited, flags were raised, and tires were burned in the streets. Of course, the Israeli army soon appeared on the scene, arresting everyone in sight, including shopkeepers minding their stores. From the garden we did not know what was happening; all we could hear were the sounds of the demonstration, and then the silence. The next noise we heard was the pounding of boots against the road. As the pounding grew louder, we could see Israeli soldiers marching toward our house, shepherding the men of Ramallah, who were shirtless and sooty, having been ordered to use their clothes to clean the burned tires from the streets. There I stood, pregnant with one child, holding my other, watching as friends and neighbors were beaten and taken off to jail. I was furious and hurt. It was as though the holy fire had been turned into ashes. Little Amal, in my arms, mirrored my fury. After a moment she began to yell at the soldiers, *"Naughty soldiers!* You cannot do that. *Naughty soldiers!"* I joined her, shouting, "You are behaving like animals. No, animals don't behave like this, animals don't indulge in gratuitous cruelty." As infuriated as I was I could not bring myself to say anything stronger due to my rather puritanical upbringing. Our mother had never allowed us to use invective, and there was an intense sense of propriety regarding the use of language in our home.

I remembered my father telling me a story from my own early childhood in Tiberias. The British soldiers had marched by, beating the Palestinians they had just rounded up to cart off to prison. As we stood by, helpless to do anything, one of my sisters had scolded the soldiers, "Naughty uncles, naughty uncles." "Uncles," because this was the word we used to address my father's various male friends. This memory struck me as sad and funny, this syntax of "naughtiness" passed down through the generations. So little had changed from one generation to the next.

That night Leah Tsemel, a close friend and Israeli attorney who was among the first to take up the defense of Palestinians, managed to have the men released, after an all-night session. Emile took photographs of the men in the compound waiting to be let go. Then we all went home to get a few hours of sleep before celebrating Easter, which was a holiday that Leah and her family had joined us in celebrating one year. Once again, another holy day had been tainted, and there was nothing we could do but try to make the remainder of it as happy as possible for Amal, with the traditional Easter eggs and holiday meal.

This was just one of the indignities we endured as a people under occupation. Each incident was like a pebble, then a stone. Placed one atop the next they would form a wall of wounds between us and our occupiers. We did not know when or how that wall of anger and frustration would get so high that we couldn't bear it; we only sensed that it would. Six years later, in late 1987, that wall did in fact reach its maximum height and we were ready. Stone by stone, pebble by pebble, we dismantled it, transforming the stones of anger into the stones of action. We used those stones to throw at our enemy, to get their attention, and ultimately that of the rest of the world, in an uprising that would come to be known as the *intifada*.

CHAPTER TWO

———◆·✕·◆———

"I t's happening, Hanan, and nothing can stop it!" Leah Tsemel and I are working on the cases of the latest batch of Birzeit University students arrested by the Israelis during the months of November and December 1987. She is the defense attorney and I am head of the University Legal Aid Committee, later to become the Human Rights Action Project. We are going through charge sheets and statements spread out on the dining room table at my house in Ramallah.

"What's happening that nothing can stop?" I asked my Israeli friend.

"Gaza is in revolt. The people are going out into the streets spontaneously. They've had enough. They're not willing to put up with things anymore—their options are clear: end the occupation or death."

"But things have been brewing for some time now all over the Occupied Territories. People are being killed every day—last month Bethlehem University students shot by soldiers, a few days ago Gaza pedestrians run over by an army truck. Why do you think this is any different? We've had demonstrations and strikes before."

"I can feel it. I sense it in the air, in the way people move and speak. It's all spontaneous, nobody's telling them to go out and protest. They just do it—men, women, children. They walk out of their shops, homes, and schools and pour out into the streets. There is a spirit of determination and defiance that I hadn't seen before. Yes, and the anger. Believe me, they've had enough. They will not be stopped."

Pushing back a few strands of her straight, dark brown hair as she is wont to do when excited, Leah straightens up, her eyes flashing almost as brightly as the many silver rings on the fingers of both her hands. I have seen her hazel, green-speckled eyes undergo many transformations: from sorrow over the pain of her Palestinian clients and their families, to exasperation and anger at the injustice she witnesses every day, at her sense of helplessness before it, to the laughter of her undefeated sense of humor, to the gentleness of a mother deeply concerned at the heavy price her children are being made to pay—both for being part of a system of occupation and conflict as well as for being the children of Leah Tsemel. One image I can never erase from my memory is that of her deep hurt and bewilderment at her son's denial of her when taunted and threatened by his classmates as the son of "the Arab-loving traitor."

Our special friendship is no secret. We are a strange combination: this fierce yet gentle Israeli woman who early on took a moral and legal stand against cruelty and injustice, and her academic Palestinian counterpart who recognized in her a kindred spirit. Ours is a bond of sisterhood and instinctive recognition that defies history and national boundaries, or perhaps is the outcome of precisely these forces; in our own way, each of us is the product of the unique experience of her race. Our daughters, Zeina and Talila, are "milk sisters," for I breast-fed Talila along with my Zeina when Leah had to go to court on behalf of my students. Neither child speaks the verbal language of the other, but on family picnics they hold hands and go off merrily in search of wildflowers or muddy streams.

Leah is right, of course. Her antennae homed in early on the first expressions of the outbreak of the *intifada,* the Palestinian uprising that began on December 9, 1987, and took most of the world by surprise. We found ourselves wrestling with a reality that could tolerate no illusions.

• • •

Even, or perhaps specially, those of us who live in medias res, in the eye of the storm so to speak, were uncertain whether the rumblings were a portent of an impending explosion or part of the ongoing activity of a dormant volcano. At the weekly meeting of the Arts Faculty Council at Birzeit University in the second week of December 1987, I was desperately trying to find ways to salvage the semester by holding makeup classes before Christmas vacation. Curfews, strikes, and military closures

had taken their toll on the academic year. Counting calendar days, calculating class hours, and checking course outlines, we took the sound of
shots and explosions in stride as part of the backdrop against which we
usually conduct our business. The sounds drew closer, and whiffs of tear
gas began to invade the meeting room.

The old campus of the university, home of the Faculty of Arts, is
located on a hilltop in the middle of the village of Birzeit (olive oil well).
Deceptively pastoral, the village and campus seem to grow organically
from the terraced hills among the rocks and olive trees, the major features
of the Palestinian landscape. Both village and university grew into and
out of each other, though never really merging. When I first joined the
university as head of the English Department, I had to weave my way
between and under the neighbors' dripping laundry hanging out to dry
on clotheslines to reach my office. A daily morning greeting and exchange
of views was the proper way to begin the day. Good neighborly relations
also demanded that they send me a sample of everything cooked, baked,
or boiled in their kitchen—the enticing aroma turned the whole department into gluttons. When the neighbors' goat sauntered into a senior
seminar, the students adopted her as an honorary English major. When
she started nibbling at their papers and literally eating up the books,
however, we were compelled to send her on her way.

In this setting, meeting on this December day in 1987, in an old stone
house with a domed roof and gracefully arched ceilings and windows,
the Arts Faculty Council turned its attention to another confrontation
with the Israeli army. Often when there was a demonstration in town the
army would then come to the university. With practiced skill, we went
through the usual crisis procedure: check the emergency first-aid stations
for the standard supplies of antiseptic, cotton wool, local anesthetic, ban-
dages, oxygen canisters and respirators, stretchers, splints; check the stations for personnel, including doctors, nurses, early-warning scouts,
runners, volunteer witnesses and guards; close down all gates and alert
all gatemen to admit only students and university personnel; send faculty
members to each building; alert Human Rights Action Project members,
the public relations office, hospitals, and press; inform the university
administration on the new campus. Then we all poured out to perform
our standard tasks—heads of departments, assistant dean, dean, and staff
—to protect the students in case of a clash with the army and negotiate
on their behalf should the need arise. Years later, Albert Agazarian, head
of the university's public relations office, was heard remarking to the

press at the Madrid Peace Conference that I had gained my negotiating experience after seventeen years of negotiating with the Israeli army every time they raided the university.

I took my position at the gate of the parking lot behind the dean's office. This was the largest gate, strategically located on a steep incline and affording a view of the entrance to the dorms and to two possible approaches the army could take. The shooting grew louder, and the tear gas tore through my lungs like a hundred sharp knives. Stomach lurching and face burning with a searing itch, I fought to keep my eyes open, peering through the thickening cloud for the first signs of the approaching army. Students began emerging from the mist, vague outlines approaching swiftly and soundlessly as in an old black-and-white horror movie. Gradually, the ghosts took flesh and color as they drew nearer, the rhythm of their pounding feet beating in the primeval dance of survival, a new variation of the *dabke,* our ancient dance/ritual. I opened the gate and they swept in. Ahmad Harb, the assistant dean, helped the stragglers and directed them to the dining room and assembly hall in the main building, then closed the heavy oak doors and asked the students to secure them from within. I stepped outside the parking lot gate and closed it behind me. Then a different host of phantoms emerged from the mist.

• • •

I was engulfed by a deep sense of déjà vu. I had stood like this before, almost a year before, in a state of dreadful anticipation, looking mortality in the eye. Stealing in behind my back, it had lurked in the winding recesses of the walled-off passages and claimed two students for its own. I could still see the blood, the sightless eyes. I could still feel the cold lifeless hands and the pain of the mother, father, sister, brother. They had been loved, but could not be saved. We had snatched up four wounded. Racing through student barricades and army checkposts, amid bullets and sirens, we drove with headlights blazing and horns blaring to the Ramallah hospital emergency entrance. The doctors saved them. The Israeli army arrested them. Hence our famous saying: It is a crime for a Palestinian to obstruct the free passage of an Israeli bullet.

Ahmad had saved me that day in 1986. A group of soldiers had forced their way into campus in pursuit of the students. Having closed the gates, I was running toward the main building. Coming from the opposite direction, Ahmad saw them standing on top of the caretaker's shed and taking aim. He bellowed, "Hanan, *stop!*" and I did. The bullet struck the cobbled stone a step ahead of me. I turned and looked at the sniper-soldier and saw the barrel of his gun aimed at me. I jumped back and hugged the wall of the shed right below him. A second bullet struck where I had stood the moment before. Another groove in another stone. The soldier yelled in fury, "You Arabs are all animals! You should all be slaughtered!" He drew his hand across his throat to drive his point home. Ahmad and I tried to reason with him; finally, Ahmad succeeded in bringing an Israeli officer, who escorted his trigger-happy soldier away. I picked up the spent shells and added them to my collection of the bullets that had been meant for me, gathered at previous campus confrontations with the Israeli army or during demonstrations. I threw them out four years later, right after Madrid. My daughters insisted that we did not need such morbid souvenirs of death at home. I agreed. For them, that day, the sight of blood from the wounded students, which I had neglected in my agitation to wash off the back seat of our car, was the horror itself. Seeing the anguish in my husband, Emile's, eyes, I made a silent pledge. It was to him and to our daughters. I committed us all to life.

· · ·

But here I was standing again, a year later, bracing for another bout. How many times should I, should we be tested? Who will have the courage to break away from the seemingly endless cycle? This time the pounding of military boots was intercepted by the irregular beat of explosions, gunshots, and the rapid fire of Uzis. I took a few steps. The university gateman panicked.

"Dr. Ashrawi, come back! It's too dangerous," he yelled.

"Just keep the gate closed. Don't open it for anyone." I willed myself to move forward, head high, eyes looking straight ahead. Don't panic. Don't show any signs of fear. The soldiers stopped; I stopped. We looked each other in the eye. Silence stretched between us like a taut spring. I could sense Albert rounding the corner and coming up on foot behind them. Ahmad made a slight movement behind me as he slowly opened the gate and closed it behind him. They and I were frozen in a time lock.

Suddenly there was a look of recognition between me and the officer in the front line. He was my neighbor from the military governor's office across the street from my house in Ramallah. I also recognized the soldiers for what they were: kids, teenagers, some of them even younger than my students. Their eyes held a host of uncensored messages—apprehension, fear, mistrust, sadness, hostility, violence, anticipation, questions, longing, disbelief, and even mindless blankness. I knew them too.

"Don't come any closer. I want to speak to the officer in charge."

"I'm in charge," responded the officer. "We must go in and arrest the students who were demonstrating and throwing stones. Besides, we have a list of wanted people and we believe that some of them may be inside."

"You can't go in. This is a university campus and the army has no business on university campuses. You must respect that."

"Who's in charge here? Call the president of the university."

"You deported the president fourteen years ago. I'm the dean of arts and I'm in charge of this campus."

"This campus always gives us a lot of trouble. Some students have been killed here. We must close it down."

"Instead of closing down the university, stop shooting students. You've already closed down the university sixteen times, and your soldiers still kill students."

"They invite trouble. They go out and demonstrate and disturb the peace. They force us to shoot them."

"They're no different from students all over the world. They want to protest and to express their opinions freely. That's no reason to kill them. Do you shoot Israeli students when they demonstrate?"

"That's different. Don't try to play smart with me. Your students threaten the safety of our soldiers."

"Then your soldiers shouldn't be here. They provoke confrontations. Besides, if they would leave the students alone, then the demonstrations would end peacefully and no one will get hurt."

"It's our job. We have to maintain law and order. Now we have an unfinished job; either you bring out the students one by one for us to identify or we shall force our way in and arrest them ourselves."

"There's no way we'll set up a lineup for you. And no, you can't go in. Storming the campus could lead to a massacre."

Albert and Ahmad joined us, and the usual negotiations commenced. The campus remained under military siege all day. Just before midnight, we reached an agreement that the army would withdraw and the students would get on the buses to be driven straight to their homes. Faculty volunteers got on each bus to make sure that the army did not intercept it and that the students arrived home safely. Death withdrew empty-handed that day. It was merely saving its strength.

The next day the campus was declared a "closed military area." For four and a half years, the university would remain closed and the campus off-limits. For four and a half years, we would devise alternative curricula and classes. We taught in our homes, in the fields, in abandoned buildings, in churches and mosques. The small and run-down building of the YMCA in Ramallah became our substitute offices. We were engaged in the subversive activity of underground education. The *intifada* had begun, and we were in the middle of it.

· · ·

Despite the pain, the anguish, the breaking of bones, the beating, and the killing that was endured by the *intifada* Palestinians, there was a sense of exhilaration that charged the atmosphere. We relished our power, the strength of our will, which drew us together. The word itself, *intifada,* means uprising or a shaking off, as if all of a sudden one wakes up and shakes something off. This massive and spontaneous popular uprising released our hidden or suppressed resources and energies and transformed them.

When it started, the *intifada* brought together seemingly irreconcilable components of Palestinian society, charging them with creating an alternative social, political, and national order, free of the distortions of the Israeli occupation. We had a simple message: let there be freedom! We had a direct approach: neutralize the Israeli military machine by confronting it with a human spirit that rejects intimidation and defeat. We faced the monster and forced it to face itself. The army was not Medusa; it did not turn to stone. It fought back, claiming many victims. But it was only when we refused dehumanization that we placed the occupiers on a course of recognition. We hoped that ultimately it would understand that its freedom lay in affording us ours.

· · ·

"I don't understand why we can't go to church with you," six-year-old Zeina protested. "And if we're Christians, how come you've started going to the mosque every Friday?"

With the infinite wisdom of a ten-year-old, her sister, Amal, explained. "You're really dumb, Zeina! Mama, Aunty Abla and Najwa [Abla's daughter] don't go to the mosque or the church to pray. They go to demonstrate." Turning to me, she implored, "Please be careful, Mumsy. We can't stand it if anything should happen to you. The soldiers shoot real bullets."

Bending down to tie the laces of my sneakers, I froze. Was I being selfish? Was I taking risks that no mother had the right to take? Did I have the right to expose my daughters to so much anxiety and fear? But suppose all of us said the same thing, who then would take the risks? There are no lives more dispensable than others. There is no scale to measure human value in relative terms; each life is unique and irreplace-able. Amal and Zeina deserve a mother who is safe and available, whom they can take for granted. Emile deserves a wife who is not always tempt-ing fate. We all deserve a life in which our choices do not have to be of tragic dimensions. Is it hubris then for me to go out daily and test the gods?

"Do you have an extra pair of running shoes?" Abla asked. She had come back from Amman only two weeks before and had immediately caught the fever. It became the antidote to the Israeli deportation of her husband, Alfred, back in 1974, a dentist who had been suspected of being politically active. Her children had chosen to stay in Ramallah, and Abla was torn. Amman represented an artificial life of forced exile, but one that her husband was compelled to endure. Ramallah was her ances-tral home. On this Sunday, she was getting ready to go to church with me to take part in a distinctly Palestinian form of secular communion. Her daughter Najwa, an undergraduate English major and student of mine, was also a regular participant, and a more reckless risk-taker in these ventures.

"I want to go to the demonstration too," Zeina insisted.

"You can't. It's too dangerous." I thought I was being logical.

"If it's that dangerous, then why are you going?"

"Because I know how to take care of myself. I know what to do when the army comes."

"I know what to do when the army comes. I will make the V sign and chant 'PLO.' " She had been watching the television news attentively.

"You have to study the location beforehand and prepare escape plans. You also have to know safe places for hiding. It's not easy. I'll tell you what—you can go on demonstrations when you grow up."

"But by the time I grow up the occupation may have ended and there'll be no more demonstrations."

How I wished for her prediction to come true. Abla, Najwa, and I put our scarves around our shoulders (to be used to cover our heads and faces to prevent identification), and stuffed our pockets with onions (an antidote for tear gas). We all wore jeans and neutral colors in order not to attract attention. We drove to a side street a few blocks away from the church and walked the rest of the way. Women were converging, slowly, silently, from all directions. All wore scarves around their shoulders and good walking shoes. We nodded in cautious recognition, but avoided speaking. A hush enveloped the street. The shopkeepers started closing their doors and pulling down their metal shutters. The church courtyard was rapidly filling with women. Some went in to pray. Others waited outside for the prayers to end and the congregation to emerge. There was no sign to distinguish Christian from Muslim. The church bells rang, and the faithful filed out. We mingled and walked out with them. Still, we walked up the street leading from the old city of Ramallah to the center of town. Many watchful eyes witnessed our advance from behind closed windows and partially drawn curtains. Soldiers on the rooftops tensed and pointed their guns. We reached the *manara,* the town square. A Palestinian flag was unfurled by a woman up front. The voice of Amal Khreisheh, a feminist activist, always daring and creative, pierced the silence, followed by a collective intake of breath:

> National unity once and twice
> Muslims and Christians alike
> The West Bank and Gaza too
>
> From Ramallah to Jenin
> We're a people who won't give up
> We're the people of Palestine
>
> Openly, we'll spell it out
> Occupation we don't want
>
> Rabin, go tell Shamir
> We're the PLO
> Shamir, tell Rabin
> We're the people who won't surrender
>
> Grow and forge ahead
> Our popular *intifada*
> We want our state and identity
> We've never accepted a life of humiliation
> We want to live in freedom

In choral unison we repeated the chant after her. Linking arms, the women surged ahead in a procession. Suddenly, the air was filled with explosions. Rubber bullets hailed down on us; a girl named Leila and another high school student screamed. A group of women picked them up and put them in one of several waiting cars, on alert by prearrangement specifically to transport the injured to the hospital. Following a particularly loud detonation, a revolving tear gas grenade landed right in front of me, spewing smoke. I willed myself not to pass out. Two friends came to my rescue, one kicking the grenade away and the other pulling me by the arm in the direction of Midan al-Mughtaribeen, Expatriate Square. We had agreed earlier on an alternative reassembly site should the army disperse us in the town square, a normal modus operandi for the army and women alike. Our lungs almost bursting with the effort and the tear gas, we clambered up the steep incline of Hospital Street.

Once again, from all directions, the women reconverged. Across fields and backyards, over stone walls and fences they emerged, a fusion of the furies and the "kindly ones," seeking both retribution and a new system of justice. On the hilltop, across from the Arab Orthodox Club, we started building our stone barricades. Teenage girls in jeans, middle-aged women in embroidered traditional gowns, middle-class women in stylish Western dress, professional women in suits, older white-haired women in a variety of garb—we formed a chain, passing stones and stacking them up in a version of the ancient stone walls that encircle our terraced hills. Each woman had a family to go home to, and an experience of discrimination and oppression that had brought her here. Each kept her demons to herself as we all prepared to face the army that approached.

The faces were familiar on both sides: Imm Khaled (Leila Ata), Maisoon al-Wheidi and her daughters, Jamileh Bakr, Islah Abdel Jawad, Amal Khreisheh, Jamileh Kassis, Imm Khalil (Feiruz), Abu Nahleh, Abla, Najwa, myself, and many more. Maisoon had a tragedy that continued to unfold. In 1992, her daughter, ʿAbir, in her early twenties, was arrested for being the head of a cell, an underground military group. She was sentenced to seventeen years in prison. The day after the trial of ʿAbir, the Israeli army demolished the family's new home, claiming that they suspected there was someone hiding within. The father, a doctor, had said, "Come and search." But the army was intent on destroying the building. Family, friends, neighbors—we had all come and surrounded the house. But they brought in antitank missiles and blew it up. Nothing was saved. One could see the children's toys in the rubble, the garage folded in on their car. They wouldn't allow Maisoon to retrieve documents such as birth certificates or even her wedding photographs. Each name had a story connected to it, and there are so many names, too many to recall here.

We never knew the soldiers by name, but their faces had become recognizable. My husband, Emile, used to say that should anyone from either side not show up, he or she would be missed by the other. The shooting, the tear gas, the stone throwing, even the face-to-face skirmishes formed a pattern. Perhaps more than the men, the women embraced the *intifada* in every possible way. We adopted every prisoner and detainee, claimed as our child whoever was being beaten, arrested, or harassed. Our rescue missions often succeeded in literally snatching the victim from the back of a jeep or the clutches of a patrol. With the *intifada*, Palestinian women had come into their own. In every confrontation, committee, project, or enterprise women took the initiative, stood up and stood out. Neither kitchen nor prison could contain or intimidate them. The first-person pronoun was no longer the sole domain of the masculine.

I had grown up with this sensibility on a personal level, unlike most of my Palestinian sisters. In my home, equality reigned, and female children were cherished and brought up to believe in their power and value as human beings. When I was born, my father had gone through the hospital in Nablus, Palestine, distributing the Arabic sweet *knafeh* to staff and patients alike. "This must mean that now you have your longed-for son," they all said. "No," he replied. "Wadiᵖa and I have just received the gift of our fifth daughter. But she's the one we've been waiting for. Now our family is complete." He later told my mother, "I'm glad she's not a boy. How would we treat him after four girls? Would we be able not to discriminate? And in this culture, he's sure to be treated differently and that wouldn't be fair to his sisters." And all my life he made me feel that I really was the one they had been waiting for. In fact, every one of my sisters was made to feel special. It was neither the fact of his unusual marriage, nor of his fathering five daughters that made my father an advocate of women's rights. As a young student in Terra Sancta College in Jerusalem during the 1920s, my then young single father had written: "Women deserve equality by right, and not as a gift condescendingly bestowed by men. And if the men do not realize this fact and rectify the injustice willingly, then women will rebel and violently demand and attain what is rightfully theirs. Once they do, then I advise the men, beware of the injustice of the oppressed once they take over power." His early writings also attested to his daring candor and self-criticism: "Liberate yourselves first and you'll liberate the land." "Internal reform is the key to real freedom," he wrote. "We always blame the British mandate for all our ills; that's a convenient excuse. Real slavery comes not from colonialism but from our own attitudes and internal disunity and corruption. We must have the courage to free ourselves from within as we struggle to free ourselves from external oppression." The words he had written then still have the same ring of truth today.

. . .

As the *intifada* gathered momentum, we knew that we had to reach the world not just by confronting Israeli soldiers with our stones of defiance, but by confronting the world with our reality. And so, we started a campaign of information. Ted Koppel's *Nightline* was a turning point in that drive. In early 1988 Betsy West, an ABC producer, and John Cooley, an old friend who was working for ABC and *The Christian Science Monitor,* came to my house to explore the possibility of a televised "Town Meeting," which would have a mixture of Palestinians and Israelis not only on stage but also in the audience. My immediate response was, "You must be crazy!" No Palestinian had ever addressed an Israeli in a public debate. Our contacts were limited to dialogue and street action with like-minded Israelis or to interrogation sessions with the military and intelligence in Israeli prisons. As a matter of policy, Palestinians refrained from any official communication with the Israelis as a way of withholding recognition or legitimacy. Thus the Israelis gained an exclusive access to the media, while the absent Palestinians were simultaneously blamed and misrepresented. It would be ironic later on to see the Israelis adopt our futile attitude of evading and rejecting any public engagement or debate, when we took the initiative to challenge. But such was not the case then. Reticence and boycott had been our tradition, and I knew that to change all that, a very dramatic and public display—such as an appearance on ABC's *Nightline*—would be a strong signal.

Gil Pimental, a young ABC producer, was sent in rushing where angels feared to tread. For two weeks in April 1988, I dragged Gil around to meet all the local political leadership to persuade the various factions that such an event could be carried out without conceding the "normalization" of relations between occupier and occupied. He had been told to set up a credible Palestinian panel to debate a group of seasoned Israeli politicians —in the middle of the *intifada.*

"It cannot be done. It is entirely against our policy, and no Palestinian must participate in such an event," was the reaction from the representatives of the Popular Front for the Liberation of Palestine (a PLO faction), who had gathered for a meeting in my home. "Separate panels without direct contact or interaction may be possible. But with a joint format we will not participate and will discourage others from taking part. We will take a public stand against it."

"We think it is important and it should be done," Ghassan al-Khatib of the Communist Party (later to become the People's Party, another PLO faction) responded. "I shall try my best to make it succeed." I found out later that Ghassan had taken the initiative and had committed his party before consulting with the rest of its leadership.

"Things are not clear, but we'll consult," said the representative of Fateh, the largest PLO political faction. "However, your judgment in this case is important. It also depends on the composition of the panel."

"We're against it, but won't attack it," was the position of the Popular Democratic Front for the Liberation of Palestine.

The independents and intellectuals had mixed reactions.

At one point, Gil exclaimed, "Take me to the Unified National Leadership of the *intifada*. Perhaps they can be persuaded. You can blindfold me. You can take me through circuitous routes. You can disguise their voices. I don't care, just get me to them! Take me to your leader!" Ali and I laughed. Without realizing it, in the course of the last two weeks, Gil had actually met all the members of the UNLI in addition to those who gave them their instructions.

By April 24, Gil was muttering, "Credible panel, Panel A, Panel B, Panel C." He was sitting in my living room when Rick Caplan called. The American producer did not display much patience.

"We are now dealing with three possible panels," Gil began. "Panel A is the credible panel, which will have Haidar Abdel-Shafi, Saeb Erakat, Mamdouh al-Aker, and Hanan Mikhail-Ashrawi. Panel B is the American Connection and will have—"

"Don't give me any of that A, B, C crap," Rick shouted. "Either you have a list of four Palestinians by tonight, or you're fired!"

"But Hanan says that we cannot mix any of the panels, and I have twelve names on hold . . ."

Rick had hung up.

Throughout, Haidar remained constant. "I'm committed and I will do it regardless of what the political factions say. It's preposterous. You have a way of complicating things in the West Bank." With his usual understatement, Haidar, an older man, one of the PLO founders, was an unwavering reference point.

"I leave the decision up to you," Saeb said. "If you're in, I'm in. I trust you to get all the political clearance needed."

That left Mamdouh, a doctor and human rights activist, who remained uncertain to the last night but finally agreed.

"The good news is that we finally have a full and credible Palestinian panel," Gil informed ABC. "The bad news is that we have to put up a barrier between the Palestinian and Israeli panels."

We were supposed to meet at the American Colony Hotel in Jerusalem at 4:00 A.M. Emile decided to drive me, defying the curfew the Israelis had predictably imposed, counting on our yellow license plates—a color reserved for Israeli and Jerusalem cars as opposed to the blue of the West Bank. At the checkpost, the soldiers stopped us, saluting Emile, spoke a few words in Hebrew, and stood at attention as we drove off. Emile explained that they had mistaken him for General Amram Mitzna, his look-alike who was then the military commander of the area! When we described the incident to Ted Koppel, he thought it would make good television to have a special show featuring Palestinian and Israeli "twins." The drama continued: following Mitzna's election as mayor of Haifa, Emile had to shake many Israeli hands and accept congratulations and advice as the new mayor of the city.

Soon after we arrived at the hotel we received a message from Mamdouh's wife informing us that he was unable to participate. So the three of us, Haidar, Saeb, and I headed over to the Jerusalem Theater where we debated the four Israelis: Ehud Olmert, Eliahu Ben Elissar, Haim Ramon, and Dedi Zucker. In that Town Meeting we sent out multiple signals: to the world—that we wanted to be heard directly; to the Palestinians—that it was time to take the initiative and speak out; to the Israelis—that we were ready to take them on.

The formation of the Political Committee was the next move in that direction. The Occupied Territories were being flooded with visiting politicians, diplomats, and journalists as well as with Israeli political groups who wanted to talk. They all needed someone to talk to. Many of us were inundated with invitations to participate in international conferences and to address a variety of audiences. The *intifada* had opened many closed doors. Still, if it were to succeed, we needed an address, and we needed a mechanism to coordinate all the individual efforts on behalf of the *intifada*. A group of political "independents" including Mamdouh al-Aker and I decided to take the initiative. Khalil (Charley) Mahshi, an ex-colleague at Birzeit University and principal of the Friends Schools in Ramallah, was also a major driving force. We enlisted the support of Sari Nusseibeh, a brilliant and controversial academic/politician. We invited a representative from each political faction as well as a number of nationalist academics and professionals.

After several meetings at my house, the membership (loosely defined) included Riad Malki, Ghassan al-Khatib, Zahira Kamal, as well as Khalil, Mamdouh, Sari, and myself. Faisal Husseini joined after a stint in jail under administrative detention, and as time went on the number of participants expanded and we defined our objectives: formulating an analysis and political presentation of the *intifada;* gathering and organizing ideas and creative options for implementation and having them somehow filter to the UNLI; creating a pool of speakers with an accredited voice to participate in conferences and seminars all over the world; becoming the core of political and diplomatic activity in the Occupied Territories chosen to meet regularly with the diplomatic representatives of the international community in Jerusalem and to receive visiting official envoys; addressing representatives of the media, both locally and internationally, and shaping a coherent information campaign; working out strategies for reaching Israeli public opinion and dealing with Israeli political activist groups. The atmosphere was charged with excitement and a sense of purpose, despite the differences in our political positions. We felt in control, one body of like-minded friends. Such work was illegal then, and the Israeli military was constantly asking questions, trying to learn the composition of the group. Most of the meetings took place in my house under the eyes of the Israeli military authorities. The danger spurred us on.

. . .

Echoes of the past frequently crossed my mind during the long meetings laced with coffee, tea, cigarettes, and cookies. I tingled with the excitement and furtiveness of earlier clandestine meetings in Jerusalem and Ramallah in 1974, when a number of Palestinians and Israelis formed the first underground political organization that brought together Israeli radicals and Palestinians from the Occupied Territories. Neither workers nor communists, nor a league, we called ourselves the League of Communist Workers and issued one underground leaflet announcing our political platform and our acceptance of the Palestine Partition Plan of 1947 as the basis of our agenda. Our cell was comprised of four Palestinians and Ilan Halevi, who had just left Mavak (a small radical Israeli anti-Zionist group), which was an off-shoot of Matzpen. We used to meet at odd hours in private homes in the Old City of Jerusalem and out-of-the-way places in Ramallah. But publicly we acknowledged each other silently. During negotiations in Washington, Ilan (who had subsequently become the PLO representative at the Socialist International) and I often shared reminiscences. One scene we both remembered well was the night he and Katherine Levi, a French Jewish woman whom he later married and who had helped the Palestinians, hid in our house in 1975, the year Emile and I married. It was a night made for a thriller movie: dark (with a power failure to boot), angry (with howling winds and a brewing storm), and misty (the fog had rolled in with vengeance). Katherine was wanted by the Israeli authorities, and we had to smuggle her and Ilan out. Their ancient car wouldn't start. As the searchlights of the Israeli military post bounced off the thick fog, Emile, Ilan, and I pushed the stalled car with Katherine inside. Subsequently she was arrested and deported and Ilan followed. We would meet later at different times in different parts of the world, but never at home.

• • •

We pursued peace only as those who had lived in its absence could. We shaped it in words, carried it in our briefcases in seminar papers, political proposals, public exhortations—tools of persuasion to employ with our leadership, our people, our friends, and our enemies. It was then that Zeina announced, "I have lent my mother to the peace process. She is going off to make peace for all of us, so that she will come back and spend more time with us at home."

But it was my older daughter, Amal, who questioned me. "You've been going all over the world telling people about us, about the injustice of the occupation and what it does to the Palestinian people?"

"Yes, I have."

"And you've been telling everybody the truth?"

"Of course."

"And they listened?"

"Yes, they did."

"Then how come we're not free yet?"

How do you explain to your child that the truth alone was not enough to set you free. How do you justify to her that the adult world, with its knowledge of good and evil, was just as comfortable with injustice as it was with its opposite, provided it kept its distance. We had the unenviable task of shaking the world's complacency and comfortable ignorance. We could do it. We had to do it. But we knew that the price was going to be high. I am not sure when I made the commitment or whether it was simply the inevitable outcome of the life that I had led (or that had led me) up to this point. When an ancient biblical prophet first spoke of "the land of milk and honey," he began spinning the fate of my people and the plot of my life. But it is up to every one of us to untie the knot.

When the Palestine National Council (our parliament in exile) met in Algiers in November 1988, it did so to signal a historical intrusion, to herald the end of an era and the beginning of another. The context was set to accommodate the Palestinian acceptance of the "two-state solution" —Palestine and Israel—on the land of Palestine. Thus when, on November 15, the highly emotive and poetically charged Declaration of Independence was announced, Palestinians all over the world wept. The reasons were complex and paradoxical—some having to do with the validation and denial of our past, and others with anticipation and apprehension about our future. By taking the first step, or what seemed like the first step, the Palestinian legislature accepted as inescapable the process of mutual recognition, mutual legitimization, which played itself out five years later, in September of 1993, in a famous handshake on the White House lawn between Yasser Arafat and Yitzhak Rabin.

There was a lot of media, many meetings, but also action since the *intifada* had begun. In my own neighborhood, a relatively affluent community of professionals, there had been a flurry of activity all related to the *intifada*. A neighborhood committee met in the backyard of the Khoury family down the street. The doctors formed a medical committee and carried out a survey of the neighborhood and maintained full data on blood types and cases requiring special and/or ongoing medical attention. They also set up a communication system for emergency contacts and for getting donors to hospitals requiring blood donations. I headed the educational committee and conducted a survey of school students of all ages, diagnosed their needs, and tabulated the number of potential volunteer teachers and their fields of specialization. Over the course of one weekend, our committee set up a whole alternative educational system for the neighborhood, covering the entire range of classes from preschool to graduating class, for a total of eighty-two students and nineteen teachers. With the schools closed down by Israeli military orders, it was up to us to prevent the forced illiteracy of our children. In closing down the schools, one military governor boasted, "We know the importance of education to the Palestinians; that's why we hit hard where it hurts most." That is how the education of our children, like their childhood, was held hostage by the Israeli occupation. But we prevailed. Not only did we teach them science and math, Arabic and English; we had extra activities in theater (which Emile held, sometimes even acting the clown), in art (which my niece Faten taught using home materials), in dancing (a communal activity in which we all became children again). In spite of the occupation, we tried to teach our children how to laugh, to create, and to maintain a sense of joy in their souls.

It was not always easy. We did not want to inhibit them, yet at the same time, we had to be realistic about the day-to-day dangers of living in an occupied territory. For a long time we could not allow them to walk to school. Like many parents, Emile and I insisted on driving the children or making special arrangements with a taxi. In a short story I wrote called "A Pair of Shoes," the main character is a pampered woman who is sheltered from the harsher realities of living in such a world. She is extremely reluctant to allow her daughter to walk to school although the child wants so much to be afforded this one small act of independence. One day the mother finally gives in, but insists on driving behind the group to make sure they arrive at school safely. Suddenly, the group of schoolgirls comes upon a demonstration, and before the mother can step in, the girl is clubbed in the head and tear-gassed by the army, winding up in the hospital.

Amal and Zeina will look back on their childhood later and realize just how different their experiences were from those of many children elsewhere. They share a strong sense of Palestinian pride and identity, and have always supported my efforts. Neither has met Abu Ammar, but both have a phone relationship with him, and over the years while he was headquartered in Tunis he invited them to visit. But Tunis, so politically charged, was not a family atmosphere and I did not feel comfortable bringing them along on trips. Abu Ammar has sent my children little presents and has corresponded with them. Zeina would ask me to deliver letters to Abu Ammar occasionally and would not allow me to read them. Soon after he married, I was having lunch with him in Amman. I had given him a letter from Zeina. He looked up laughing: "What are people saying about me?" I could not imagine what Zeina might have heard and written; Abu Ammar had recently married a much younger Christian woman, and everybody had an opinion. Zeina had written: "Don't worry, I know you have a difficult task. But don't worry about what people are saying about you and the marriage. It's all right. This is your business. This is your life. You shouldn't listen to what they say about you."

Like Palestinian children all through the land, Amal and Zeina wanted to be involved in the *intifada*. They joined the voluntary work committee, running errands for elderly people who lived alone, planting the communal "victory garden" of the whole neighborhood, maintaining our provisions, and keeping watch to alert the neighborhood of any impending army attack. Najwa, my niece, headed this committee assisted by a group of youngsters including fourteen-year-old Raja Salah. Raja, with his ever-ready smile and mischievous dimples, became the neighborhood favorite. His light brown hair and greenish eyes gave him an impish look, and he seemed to radiate a glow of his own as he worked in the sun, clearing another field for a community victory garden. Forming an escort group to make sure that the younger children moved from house to house safely between classes, he taught them how to sing nationalistic songs on the way. The echo of these childish voices still seems to haunt our neighborhood, and from time to time I catch myself frozen in the middle of my work trying to recapture their lost songs. Death struck Raja down from the back.

He was fifteen on June 10, 1989. His best friend, Yasser Abu Gosh, was shot in the middle of the town square. A plainclothesman from an Israeli undercover unit recognized him, and knowing he was a student activist, called out his name. Yasser turned and a soldier aimed, shooting him in the thigh as Yasser tried to run off. He fell to the ground and attempted to crawl away. The soldier came up to him and shot him repeatedly in the head. A doctor tried to reach him but was pushed back. Yasser was dumped in the back of an open jeep and paraded around Ramallah. For days afterward, his mother would get up at dawn and stand in the same square where her child had been killed, and, bearing a bunch of seasonal wildflowers, she would stare at the Israeli soldiers on their dawn patrol. It is still a wonder how the whole Israeli occupation did not crumble and fold upon itself before such a silent accusation.

Raja lost his smile along with his best friend, and the glow seemed to abandon him as well. He arranged the symbolic funeral for Yasser. No real funerals are allowed by the Israeli military for those who are killed during a confrontation with them. The bodies are confiscated for a postmortem, and only much later given back to the families surreptitiously, in an unholy midnight ceremony (or transaction), provided the body is buried immediately. From my bedroom window, i had witnessed many such a furtive deal and had heard the wails of bereavement. When all the preparations had been made, Raja came to Najwa and asked her to take care of his mother.

"Try to ease my death for her," he said. "I know she will take it the hardest."

"Don't be morbid. Don't invite death; it has the habit of turning up unexpectedly." Najwa was alarmed.

"The moment I saw Yasser dead, I knew it was my turn next. We were inseparable."

"These premonitions are superstitious and melodramatic. Just take care of yourself, and don't be too visible at the funeral."

"Still, I know it in my heart. I know I'm not coming back. Just don't say I didn't bid you good-bye."

The symbolic funeral was held in the nearby village of Betunia. The Israeli army viewed these sorts of funerals as protest marches and always dispersed those in attendance, targeting individuals they believed to be threats to their "national security." Soldiers chased Raja through the fields. With five bullets in the back, Raja lay dying for two hours before help could reach him. By the time I reached the hospital, he was dead and Najwa was sitting at the door outside the emergency room holding his mother's hand. When we went to her house, empty of Raja though full of mourners, she seemed like a Palestinian Niobe, a stone statue weeping for all eternity. Only much later did she speak: "Just don't let his death go for nothing." What is the price of Raja's death? What is the price of all our dead? What can we demand in return? What have we demanded?

CHAPTER THREE

———◆◆◆———

There were two men who became my allies and partners in this unfolding quest for peace—different from each other in temperament and experience, but alike in their commitment to the Palestinian dream of statehood. And each belonged to a distinct major component of the Palestinian political movement: the "inside" and the "outside." The *intifada* was carried out by those who lived within the Occupied Terrorities, but of course we were acting (resisting) not only for ourselves, but also on behalf of those who had been forced to leave Palestine. Those on the "inside," such as myself, were strictly forbidden by Israeli law from associating with the PLO. Those on the "outside," deportees and refugees, were forced to live apart from their homeland. The leadership found refuge in Tunisia, the country that had graciously hosted the PLO since 1982, following Israel's invasion of Lebanon and the subsequent expulsion of the organization from that country.

My ally on the inside was Faisal Husseini, who was born in Jerusalem, and was among the original PLO founders back in the mid-1960s. In fact, though I had no memory of meeting Faisal, he told me that he had visited my house back then on PLO-related missions, and met with my father. Faisal and I did not actually meet face-to-face until 1988 when he was released from prison, although we had talked to each other and communicated previously. The son of a famous freedom fighter/mountain rebel killed in a battle in 1948, Faisal grew up in the shadow of a Palestinian legend, but never allowed himself to be overpowered by the memory, finding his own immutable place in the history of our people. Faisal is gentle and kind, an asthmatic who endured my cigarette smoking with the utmost of grace.

Our other significant ally, Akram Haniyyeh, I had known a decade longer, since the late 1970s. Akram was born in Ramallah, and was deported on December 28, 1986, taking up residence in Tunis, where he devoted himself to the PLO. A writer and Fateh leader, Akram is extremely intelligent and creative, with sharp political insights, and is not one to make a move unless he considers all the implications. His personal reserve and economy of words set him apart from the other advisers to Arafat. Uprooted from his home, his equilibrium had been thrown, although to the casual observer he appeared calm. But the manner in which he smoked cigarettes, taking just a few puffs and then putting them out, as well as the constant clicking of his worry beads, revealed an inner turmoil.

These two men became friends and colleagues, and during the next several years were able to personally stave off and transcend the growing internal tension and artificial rift between the "inside" and the "outside." We (the "inside") became the umbilical cord of the PLO, at once linking it to the rest of the world, while granting it the legitimacy of a constituency on the land of Palestine. Yet the "outside" often questioned our motives, concerned that we were trying to set up an alternative authority that would ultimately usurp their power.

A Palestinian-Israeli dialogue was being developed with the help of third parties. By establishing a dialogue within an international context, with other countries hosting the talks, we were able to get the lines of communication moving more smoothly. Having informed Akram of my plans to visit Washington on the periphery of a Palestinian-Israeli "dialogue" meeting, I was asked by Abu Ammar to meet with State Department officials and make a plea for the upgrading and normalization of the U.S.-PLO official dialogue. That was the beginning of a role that was to run my life during the next six years in a drama that ranged from high tragedy to soap opera, with a predominance of the element of the absurd. The idea, initially, had been that of the Political Committee. The Egyptian Ten-Point Plan of July 1989, and the Baker Five-Point Framework of October 1989 were the subject of intensive discussion and scrutiny by both the "inside" and the "outside." The Palestine National Council resolutions and Arafat's Geneva speech before the United Nations as well as his public Stockholm statements at the instigation of the then Swedish foreign minister, Sten Andersson, had all culminated in the opening on December 14, 1988, of the U.S.-PLO dialogue in Tunis. In all likelihood, never in the history of "dialogues" had communication been as absent as it was in these official Palestinian-American encounters. The American ambassador to Tunisia, Robert Pelletreau, and the Palestinian member of the Executive Committee, Yasser Abd Rabbo, each brought his insulating bubble to the meetings to make sure that their voices were garbled and that they never made any human contact. Reciting from prepared scripts, neither listened to the other as both were captives of the stilted discourse of rigid officialdom.

Because of the history of impressionistic and doctored reporting that had clouded Palestinian perceptions of international politics and relations for a long time, I took two minute-takers with me to that first meeting at the sixth floor of the State Department. I met with Dennis Ross, Dan Kurtzer, and Aaron Miller and we established a tone and attitude that set the course and tenor of Palestinian-American meetings (of the unofficial kind—with the "inside") for the next six years. Being, and perceiving myself to be, of the people and not officialdom, an envoy though not a diplomat, I exercised my option for directness and honesty. I brought with me an aspect of the innocence of the *intifada,* its willingness to confront, to take the initiative, to assert itself, and not to succumb to intimidation. But most of all, I brought to that encounter, and subsequently to all others, that one essential sine qua non that was to become the most salient quality of Palestinian political discourse: the human dimension. When Baker used that expression a few years later in his closing Madrid speech in 1991, a Palestinian journalist turned to me and said, "That's your doing." An accident of history had sent me as a reluctant and ambivalent envoy to the United States; another had made the "inside" boycott official U.S. contacts; a third had suspended the official dialogue "outside." I think it was a direct result of the inclusion of the "inside" into the diplomatic conversation that a new idiom was weaving its way into the tapestry, its details to emerge fully only at a later date.

· · ·

All the while, a different set of encounters was unobtrusively changing the discourse. Palestinian and Israeli women had once again decided to explore uncharted terrain, armed with a map of joint gender concerns and a dedication to save, rather than to sacrifice, lives. During one of the early dialogue meetings in 1988, at The Hague that time, I had met the Belgian couple Simone Susskind and her husband, Davide. Both committed to the cause of Palestinian-Israeli peace, Simone was of the conviction that women would have the vision and courage to take the first step as well as the will and temerity to make a difference. After several trips to the region, she made contact with a number of women on both sides in preparation for a women's meeting in Brussels under the title "Give Peace a Chance." Notwithstanding the cliché of the heading, the enterprise was essentially innovative in the history of the Middle East.

The Palestinian women at that time were in the midst of an internal debate and transition—an inevitable outcome of the *intifada* and the new modes of perceptions, attitudes, and priorities that were superseding the behavioral and work patterns of the traditional women's organizations. The older and previously undisputed leaders of women's charitable organizations were being challenged by "upstarts," the younger women who were emerging on the political and feminist scene armed with a political agenda and gender agenda, eager to lay claim to their territory and power. The women's committees began to encroach on the turf the women's organizations had reserved as their sole domain, particularly in the areas of political action, social programs, and women's representation. Trying to set up a Higher Council for Women, we were ferociously attacked by the General Union of Palestinian Women, which had existed only through the charitable organizations. It seemed that the grassroots groups and action committees had momentum on their side. However, without realizing it, they had incorporated the same factional rivalries and disputes that had troubled the political groups from which they had evolved and to which they still remained attached.

Following several coordinating meetings, the committees and independent women (later to become known as the professional women) decided on a list of participants (with the exception of the PFLP women, who decided to boycott). Shulamit Aloni was to speak on behalf of the Israeli delegation, and I was to give the opening address on behalf of the Palestinian side. Sent by the PLO in Tunis, Sulafa Hijjawi insisted that she had to give the "official" Palestinian address, and in the interest of "peace" the organizers added an "official" speaker to each side. Totally oblivious of the "outside's" sensitivities and their need for public legitimization and recognition, the women from the "inside" found the situation rather comic. We even had jokes about who was sitting in Sulafa's seat, and Suad Amery (who later became a member of the Washington delegation), had been made to give up her chair to the woman official several times during the conference. When we visited her at home later, she had put a sign on her favorite chair declaring: "Suad's Chair. Not Sulafa's, not the PLO's, exclusively mine!" We all laughed, until we found out that the question of "whose seat" was one of major political significance that dominated Palestinian politics and strategies throughout the peace process, and is still with us today.

At that Brussels conference, a path of mutual recognition and identification was charted very tentatively, both internally within each side and externally between both. The women from the "outside" were an invigorating revelation to most women on our team from the "inside," who had been deprived of the tremendously rich human resource and experience of the exiled Palestinians. How clearly they embodied the historical dimension and the trauma of displacement. And they in turn remarked on the degree of awareness and sisterhood displayed by our group. We provided not only the witness account but also the moral and contemporary context for the Palestinian women's movement, constantly evolving within occupied Palestinian land. A woman named Mariam Mirʾi presented the concrete dilemma and paradox of the "Israeli Palestinians," who, in their ancestral homeland, found themselves bearing the citizenship of a state that not only was established on their own land, but denied their very existence. With all of the layers of occupation, exile, and national alienation, the quest continued. How do you join together what man has torn asunder?

As for our Israeli counterparts, they too had their own house to put in order. They were trying to come to grips with their "in-gathering," to come to terms with their multicultured communities composed of Jewish immigrants from all over the world. At the meetings, it seemed we were united; they were disjointed. Nevertheless, we spoke to (and not at) each other, and dared to reveal our mutual fears, hostility, distrust, anger, and recrimination. Having done that with sincerity and vigor, we turned to the task at hand. Drafting a joint political statement proved to be a challenge. Naomi Chazan, an Israeli political intellectual, and I, who had previously drafted political statements during dialogue meetings, were chosen to work out the formulation and the political substance of the agreement. Since then, Naomi and I regularly found ourselves cast in that role with such predictable frequency that we shared a tacit smile and a silent knowing laugh each time we were called upon to rescue a deadlocked dialogue or create a compromise text. In addition to her dedication to peace, I appreciated Naomi's wry sense of humor and sardonic candor. Her integrity and discretion led us, a few years later, to resort to using her as a channel to Prime Minister Rabin when Faisal and I needed to reach him directly. Both Naomi and I shared the joy and affliction of having teenage daughters (Tali and Amal) who ran our lives as benign dictatorships. Our discussions ranged from the latest impasse in the peace talks, to the future of Zionism and Palestinian nationalism, to pierced ears and the maximum time allowed for a teenage phone conversation. Our passion for Belgian chocolates remained a firm constant in our long friendship, while cigarettes and coffee were a matter of indulgence and defiance. The one unanimous resolution adopted by the Brussels participants was a pledge to stop smoking with the establishment of the Palestinian state.

The fate of the political declaration was not so fortunate. Having drafted a text we were sure was acceptable to all participants, Naomi and I were defeated by the Israeli version of the Rock of Gibraltar. Nava Arad of the Labor Party would not sign because the statement referred to Palestinian statehood. The other members of the Israeli delegation begged, entreated, cajoled, and threatened to no avail. Tearfully, Simone Susskind insisted on trying again for a new approach. Both sides consulted. Sulafa "officially" announced that we had reached a decision. I announced that we would go for a statement of principles. The Israeli women agreed. Naomi and I went to work again and produced a statement, a declaration of principles, which was signed by both parties at a press conference in Brussels. We also announced the establishment of the Palestinian-Israeli Women's Network, a significant and ongoing enterprise. At times the whole peace process and the September 1993 signing of the Declaration of Principles on the White House lawn seemed like a glorified replay in slow motion to me, because there had been so many rehearsals. We celebrated over dinner that night. Rita Giacaman, one of the Palestinian participants, played a mixture of Western, Arab, and Jewish music on the piano and we danced.

• • •

From Prague to London, from Paris to New York, from Stockholm to Jerusalem, from Milan to Helsinki, we met, debated, agreed, and argued how to untie and resolve the Gordian knot of the Palestinian-Israeli conflict. We approached it from different angles and with a variety of tools, knowing full well that we were the advance team carrying out preliminary explorations and trial runs in preparation for the real event. International conferences like these generally identified the major issues, isolated and defined major areas of potential agreement and of conflict, suggested possible solutions and follow-up mechanisms. But most importantly, for us these meetings provided opportunities for human interaction and identification on neutral territory and with well-meaning third parties.

As a result, new language emerged and eventually found its way into our negotiations and political platforms. Taboos were broken, such as the ban on the PLO and on the issue of Jerusalem, while long-held antagonisms and fears were uncovered. Gradually, we came to understand and to distinguish the sacred from the profane, the meadow from the minefield, the scar from the wound, and the human being from the stereotype. But all that was not enough to make peace. I once said, we could not afford to wait until every single Palestinian recognized and trusted every single Israeli and vice versa before we made peace. What was needed was the mind-set, the commitment, and the political will to take the necessary and painful decisions and to make the inevitable and critical compromise. It was inevitable, for we had unleashed historical forces that were beyond containment. The question was when, and at what price. Time became our enemy, stretching almost beyond the limits of human endurance, and the price it exacted was beyond value.

I was adamant, like many others, that these encounters would not become psychotherapy sessions or degenerate into a redundant routine. Thus, when the Italian women, Louisa Morgantini and Chiara Ingrao, first suggested a popular celebration of peace involving Palestinian, Israeli, and European NGOs (nongovernmental organizations), we responded enthusiastically. Feverishly trying to achieve consensus on the heading and slogans of the three-day endeavor, we finally agreed on the basic principle of "Two States for Two Peoples." Somewhat optimistically, our banner headline read "1990: THE YEAR OF PEACE." The two most memorable events of that weekend were the Women's March and the Human Chain. Women from all over the world linked arms and marched through Jerusalem, the City of Peace, chanting international songs of empowerment, freedom, justice, and peace. The power of our will and the excitement of the challenge seemed to hold the Israeli army at bay. We set off from the Green Line separating West and East Jerusalem, or No-Man's-Land as it used to be called, which we renamed later Women's Land at a March 8 women's rally. Descending the hill from Notre Dame, we marched through Salah Eddin Street and rounded the corner to enter the courtyard of al-Masrah, the Palestinian National Theater. A few women waved the Palestinian flag and the army charged like a bull. An

Italian woman lost her eye; another was shot in the arm; others required hospitalization due to tear gas inhalation; and there was the usual assortment of bruises, lacerations, and contusions.

The Human Chain also held a mixture of triumph and grief. Palestinians, Israelis, and representatives of international NGOs held hands and formed an unbroken Ring Around Jerusalem. Only such a chain, we felt, could free us from the recurring cycle of conflict and the bondage of violence. The elation and sheer joy at our success could not be dampened by the colored water with which the army tried to hose us down as if we were soiling the streets of the Holy City. That day I came close to being trampled by the horse of a mounted policeman. Still, disbanding, the links of the human chain felt a strange sense of triumph. We had set the future on course, and 1990 had been dubbed the Year of Peace. What could go wrong?

Everything. Too sanguine and enraptured by our own vision, we failed to hear the beat of distant drums or feel the earth begin to tremble beneath our feet. But who did, then?

• • •

"A hunger strike? What kind of a ridiculous idea is that?" Akram Haniyyeh shouted on the phone from Tunis, via the United States, because there were no direct lines between Israel and the Arab world. "If the whole political leadership and the prominent members of civil society go on a hunger strike, what have you left for the grassroots activists?" Gathered around Faisal Husseini and his cellular phone, we could hear Akram's words clearly. We were in the meeting room of the National Palace Hotel in Jerusalem trying to decide where to hold our strike.

It was May 20, 1990, the day of the massacre of seven Palestinian workers and the wounding of scores of others who were waiting for their bus at ʾIyun Fara (Rishon LeZion). The trigger-happy Israeli who had mowed them down was immediately declared "insane, unbalanced, driven to distraction because his girlfriend had left him." It was only on such occasions that the otherwise "sane" Israeli society brought out into the open its "insane" elements. Every time a "distracted" Israeli translated the slogan "death to the Arabs" into action, he or she was assigned extra therapy sessions. Whenever a Palestinian was "distracted" enough to commit any act of violence against an Israeli, he or she was just another proof of the "terrorist Palestinian" stereotype. Obviously, the occupation was "disturbing" to the Israelis, and rather lethal to the Palestinians. We often wondered at all the psychological studies carried out to assess the impact of bone-breaking, beating, and killing on the sensibilities of the Israeli soldiers; nobody exhumed the bodies of their victims or visited the hospitals to assess the damage done to those on the receiving end. The solution was staring everybody in the face: end the occupation; spare your children and ours. But life is not so simple; both Israeli and Palestinian were locked in a process of learning and unlearning ourselves and each other— each driving the other to distraction. Ishmael (Isma'il) and Isaac (Yitzhak) engaged in perpetual sibling rivalry of a particularly lethal kind. Centuries later, in an equally punitive peace process, we sought "neutral" third-party intervention to help us disengage, each wanting to stay the other's hand.

The massacre was not only an echo and repetition of a series of previous massacres that had formed the chronicle of our existence, it was also (unbeknown to us at that time) a grim foreshadowing of other massacres yet to come: the al-Aqsa Mosque massacre on October 8, 1990, and the Hebron al-Ibrahimi Mosque massacre on February 25, 1994. A sinister chain was steadily linking one slaughter to another, leaving a bloody trail of victims in its course, but try as we may, the world was capable of perceiving only one link at a time and of giving it only a cursory glance. Had we known then what we know now, would we have chosen to intervene the way we did?

At the time, however, a hunger strike seemed an appropriate form of self-deprivation. Our idealism persuaded us that we could challenge the conscience of the world by visibly demonstrating that we were prepared to die rather than endure captivity and subjugation. Little did we know that at the same time, our counterforces were busily scurrying in the dark not only to negate our moral gesture, but to create an alternative reality —a moral vacuum that would absorb the luminosity of our act and hurl us back into a particularly sinful terrestrial Jerusalem.

Forty-four nationalists had gathered, to refrain from eating until our demands were met. "We have to keep them simple and attainable if we are to succeed," Faisal said, after deflecting the PLO's attempts to dissuade us. We were in a meeting room, people were walking in and out, several of us were sitting on the floor.

"First," I replied, "there must be a real investigation of the massacre, with the results made public and the perpetrator punished." Accountability has always been of particular significance to me.

"Yes," Faisal countered, "but we cannot trust the Israeli authorities to carry out an impartial investigation. They always manipulate the results or refuse to disclose them."

"Then let us ask for an international investigation by a neutral body—a third party is needed here. We also must demand international protection if we really want long-term results." Protection, as the other side of the coin of accountability, has also been a longtime favorite of mine.

"The U.N. is the only body capable of doing that. We must ask for a Security Council meeting as a priority; then the council must not only condemn the massacre, but also take steps to send a mission to investigate and to monitor. Why don't you call the people you know at the U.N., Hanan, and start the ball rolling. Tell them our strike will continue until they convene and respond to our demands."

I did. The PLO representative at the U.N., then Zuhdi Tarazi, called and protested that we had gone directly to the secretary general's office without going through him first. We defended our right to take initiatives and to act quickly. He wanted an official PLO decision. We emphasized the people's decision. Ultimately, the Security Council meeting was requested and scheduled.

We had organized ourselves into different committees: drafting, media, diplomatic contacts, technical and supplies, security, and so forth. We took the decision to hold our hunger strike on the premises of the International Red Cross, in Jerusalem—the usual site for many popular Palestinian protests. We took up the most mundane tasks with energy and zeal. In one night, we prepared official press releases, public statements, and letters to the U.N. and other organizations. The Israeli-Arab parties, being old hands at this, donated tents and canvas shelters, which we set up in the front yard to house the men protesters. The few women were allocated the damp basement of the building, where subsequently we made the acquaintance of numerous insects, of all sizes, shapes, and colors, whether of the creeping, flying, or jumping kind. Hospitals and hotels donated mattresses and blankets, as well as numerous cases of bottled mineral water. One hospital sent a volunteer medical team and their equipment, including thousands of salt sachets; then being nationalists themselves, the team also joined us in the strike.

Setting up shop, so to speak, we started receiving visitors, including solidarity groups from all over the Occupied Territories and Israel, in addition to diplomatic and international missions and envoys from around the world. Members of the press flocked to see us, and we were amazed at the amount of attention we had attracted until we discovered that having us grouped in one place was a tremendous convenience to them. After the first few days, the hunger strike ceased to be their primary concern, but we were all available for comments on a variety of issues.

One of our most endearing members joined us the second day of the strike, quietly pitching his tent on the side, hoisting a Syrian flag, and putting up a sign boasting: "THE EMBASSY OF SYRIA," and below that: "Representative of the National Institutions in the Occupied Syrian Golan Heights."

Day after day, we dutifully tried to imbibe the required volume of water with the right amount of salt dissolved in each bottle. We were losing weight, looking more gaunt and disheveled as we wandered about the grounds of the Red Cross, each carrying his or her own bottle of mineral water. I developed a strong aversion to water—particularly to lukewarm, salty water. Hunger was our constant companion. At first, it was mainly the physical hunger of bodies suddenly and rudely deprived of food. Actually, I suffered severe pains and nausea the morning of the third day only to discover later that they were withdrawal symptoms, mainly from the absence of caffeine, the doctor said. Coffee remained the only craving that stayed with me throughout: now I seem to drink coffee at every opportunity.

Every day, we wrote our press reports and public appeals. We sent letters to the Bush-Gorbachev summit, to Secretary General Javier Pérez de Cuéllar at the U.N., to the Arab Summit in Baghdad, and to all human rights organizations, under the delusion that they would make a difference. Instead, we received a U.S. veto at the Security Council—human rights issues not being a priority on their agenda at the time and certainly not on the list if it meant meddling in Israel's "internal" affairs. We also got the cold shoulder from the Arab Summit, the Palestinian *intifada* being at the bottom of the Arab leaders' list. Perfunctory moral support was extended by the human rights organizations. The then superpower leaders responded with utter silence. But the coup de grâce came from a Palestinian source: Abu Abbas, infamous for the *Achillo Lauro* incident.

Abu Abbas's failed attempt, while we were still on hunger strike, to make a landing on the Israeli coast and carry out armed attacks against Israelis plunged us into a new quagmire of confrontation and recrimination. Faisal described it as the stab in the back that was more painful than all the frontal wounds delivered by enemy arrows. Although no Israeli lives were lost, this attempt was perceived as the real test, which the PLO had failed, to demonstrate good behavior and the mending of their ways. It also happened to be a convenient excuse to suspend the U.S.-PLO dialogue (which had been largely formalistic anyway) and to vindicate all the "I told you sos." The PLO was reprimanded and instructed to denounce the failed attempt (emphasis on "attempt" not on "failed") and to discipline and expel Abu Abbas from the organization. International outrage was unleashed on the Palestinian "terrorists" who not only had planned to destroy Israeli life but who also failed to obey instructions as to the type of public penance they were asked to carry out. While none of us sympathized with Abu Abbas, all of us could hardly believe the high-handed presumption and the blatant double standard of the United States in particular and the international community in general. For thirteen days, we had been starving ourselves to protest a terrorist act that had destroyed many Palestinian lives, and the world barely nodded in recognition or compassion (although we did view the American veto as a punch below the belt). Yet at the prospect of potential harm to Israelis, all Palestinians were labeled, judged, and condemned. For thirteen days, we had laid claim to the higher moral ground by adopting nonviolent means of civil resistance, and by seeking protection for a vulnerable civilian population, only to be defeated by one act, one failed act, that reversed the roles of the sides involved. The victim was once again judged guilty. In the wake of the U.S. ultimatum to break off the dialogue (such as it was), the hunger strikers held a meeting and decided to boycott all meetings and contacts with U.S. officials. Such a preemptive move, we thought, would make the United States think twice about terminating the dialogue, as it would leave them with no Palestinian interlocutor.

Reduced by then to forty, we resolved to end the strike with a bang and not a whimper. We put on our "On Hunger Strike" ash-gray T-shirts and embarked on a procession through the cobbled streets of the Old City of Jerusalem. At our first stop, the al-Aqsa Mosque, we covered our heads, walked barefoot, and prayed reverently. At the Church of the Holy Sepulcher, we also covered our heads, but prayed at the tomb. We walked through the Stations of the Cross, on a *Via Dolorosa* of our own, and climbed the stairs to the Syrian Catholic Church where Bishop Lahham was waiting to receive us, ready to offer us our first meal in two weeks. We broke our fast together on communal soup. Our last stop was where it had all started: the National Palace Hotel. There, we held a press conference and announced the end of our hunger strike and our suspension of official U.S. contacts. Two weeks later, after the American-specified grace period, Secretary of State James Baker announced the suspension of the U.S.-PLO dialogue. Our hunger strike created an even greater hunger. One pilgrimage of pain ended; another began.

CHAPTER FOUR

"This is Hanan. I'm in Geneva. I must reach Abu Ammar."

"He's not here, Dr. Ashrawi. He's out of the country."

"Then give me Sami, please. It's important."

Dr. Sami Musallam was the head of Abu Ammar's office. An old friend and colleague from my student days at the American University of Beirut, Sami maintained his humanity and equilibrium in spite of difficult and dangerous turns of fate. I could count on him to reach Abu Ammar anytime, anywhere, and to reach responsible conclusions. It was August 2, 1990, and I was attending a meeting of the Welfare Association's Planning Committee. The association, a development foundation set up by wealthy Palestinians in exile, was reformulating its policies vis-à-vis the Occupied Territories in the context of *intifada* priorities and projects. I had gone to bed the night before planning an outline in my head for my particular assignment. I woke up to find out that Iraq had invaded Kuwait.

"Have you heard the news, Sami? It's shocking," I asked when Sami came on the line. "What do you make of it?"

"Yes, I've heard. It's unbelievable. No one knows what to make of it. Abu Ammar is on a plane right now, but everyone here is talking about nothing else."

"Do you have any information, any details? What made Saddam do it?"

"We don't have any more details than what you heard on the news. It's tough. What do the people there say?"

"Those who had come from Kuwait are busy calling their families trying to make sure they're all right. No one has made contact yet. Victor Kashkoush [another old American University colleague] is here and he's been on the phone since dawn trying to reach his wife and children. Victor finds himself a third-time refugee, albeit in Geneva this time. What's happening to the people there? Are there any casualties?"

"It doesn't look like there are many, but no numbers or names have been released yet. Many people are leaving, though."

"You must come up with a statement; we must take a public position against the occupation."

"The situation is too complex; there are many unknowns."

"What is there to know? Morally and politically, we as Palestinians must be the first to condemn occupation. Find Abu Ammar and ask him to issue an official release."

"There are political ramifications, and I'm sure he'll study the situation carefully before taking any steps."

"Forget the political fine print and deal with principles. The whole moral foundation of our case, particularly of the *intifada,* will be destroyed. We have to be consistent. We must take a position of integrity against occupation anywhere and whatever the reasons. Let's do that first and then try to play a constructive role in bringing this disaster to a peaceful end."

"Principles are fine, but Abu Ammar has to deal with realities. He has to study the whole complex situation within a comprehensive understanding and concern for the interests of the totality of the Palestinian people. It's not so simple. We have to tread slowly and carefully."

"But the absence of a leadership position will confuse our public opinion. The gap will be filled by a popular emotional reaction."

Which is precisely what happened. I rushed home from Geneva to a turbulent situation. Many of us, from the political committee, the intellectual community, and community leadership as a whole, held extensive meetings and seminars to formulate positions and reach out to the public. Whether at PASSIA (Palestinian Academic Society for the Study of International Affairs), at the different Palestinian universities, or in special seminars convened for the purpose, we were all, it seemed, sending out a consistent message: end the occupation of Kuwait; work out a negotiated peaceful settlement; solve the underlying grievances; maintain an Arab context to contain the conflict and effect a just solution; reject any military solution and particularly any foreign troop presence on Arab land. We stressed the need for consistency, for dealing on a level plain with all issues. As a people under occupation we must condemn and oppose occupation everywhere. Having accepted negotiations as a means of resolving peacefully the Palestinian- (hence Arab-) Israeli conflict, we could not condone a military solution anywhere, particularly in an inter-Arab conflict.

Mine was the task, as usual, of drafting memoranda to members of the international community, and I wrote many. We held several meetings with the diplomatic community in Jerusalem trying to drive home our message and to avert the disaster of war in our region. We held emergency meetings at Faisal's home and at mine urging the PLO to adopt the same position; we actually sent Akram a draft of what later came to be known as the PLO Four Point Plan, which never actually received the public attention it deserved. That notorious Abu Ammar–Saddam Hussein embrace/kiss seemed to have erased not only all other images, but also the world's sense of judgment. When we released a statement by "Palestinian Personalities and National Institutions," containing our principled position, we began to receive the first signs of public criticism. At one point, we were working on a draft leaflet and Tunis insisted on reviewing it; upon seeing the "official" revisions, we decided to ignore them and distribute the leaflet unrevised. To Faisal's credit, he took it upon himself to bear full responsibility for the "mutiny"—an act of honesty and courage that we had occasion to call on him to repeat a few times in the future. At that time, however, we felt as if we were attempting to hold back a global tempest with our bare hands.

Sensing the storm gathering in the distance, Faisal suggested that we work out an emergency organizational structure to cope with the difficulties ahead. We set up first-aid committees, supply committees, civil defense and public awareness teams, but these provided little security. The Israelis, with their army, institutions, and support systems, had declared an all-out alert to deal with the possibility of war. We had nothing. Actually, we were sitting ducks, facing double jeopardy. On the one hand, the Palestinians had become universally identified with Iraq, and a campaign of guilt by association cast us in the role of villain and aggressor even while we were the victims of a continuing occupation. On the other hand, we felt just as exposed to Iraqi attacks as the Israelis did. When asked about the safety of the Palestinians under occupation should he launch attacks on Israel, Saddam was reported to have replied, "I'm not separating lentils." In addition to the fear of Iraqi Scud missiles and chemical attacks, the Palestinians had a very real fear of a replay of the 1948 tragedy when so many of us were either expelled en masse or massacred. We expected a military clampdown on the Occupied Territories, which would provide a cover for the Israeli settlers to go on rampages against the defenseless population of the camps, villages, and towns. We also feared extremist elements in the army, having learned from bitter experience that a siege and a blackout can be very convenient cover for the army to carry out invisible atrocities.

The Palestinian state of mind was unsettled and insecure. In all popular meetings, one pledge was repeated: We will not leave! If they come to expel us, we'll resist. Between death and deportation, we choose death. Potential victims of multiple disasters, we were made to suffer the added indignity of being cast in the role of the evil aggressor. To compound the tragedy, our leadership in exile seemed to be doing everything possible to reinforce the distorted image, and an indignant and impassioned public was reacting to the history of injustice to them as Arabs, swerving toward a full and unqualified support of Saddam. Between Scylla and Charybdis, the political leadership of the "inside" was forced to steer a very careful course, indeed, while violent storms raged on.

• • •

"Bottled water, canned food, first-aid kits, dried nuts and fruits in airtight plastic bags, baking soda—lots of it in case of chemical warfare, thick plastic sheets, wide masking tape . . ." Emile was checking off the list of essentials as part of our wartime emergency provisions.

"Don't forget the chocolates, chewing gum, and cookies," Zeina chimed in.

"Can we get the piano into the sealed room?" Amal asked.

"No," Zeina volunteered. "We need to bring in Paddy the parrot. We don't have enough room. Mama, why can't we bring in the kittens? Please? If not all eleven, at least five, please?"

"Don't forget Paddy's seeds, Baba. If we bring in the kittens, we must get them their food and kitty litter," Amal reminded Emile.

"Which reminds me," I interjected. "We need a big sand-filled container to use as a makeshift toilet."

"Don't forget the television and radio," practical Amal added. "We must stay in touch with the outside world. Make sure the telephone is in the room too."

"We need lots of batteries, Emile, for the radio, portable television, and flashlights. Maybe you'd better buy candles also, even though they take up oxygen." I too was trying to be practical.

"No smoking in the sealed room." Amal and Zeina both detest our smoking.

"There's no limit on the number of books allowed." Unanimous decision.

Preparations were in full swing. A black market on masking tape and plastic sheets was making a few shopkeepers rich. We expressed our moral indignation, to no avail. Those of us who had Jerusalem IDs found ourselves in the middle of a moral dilemma. Should we go claim our gas masks, or should we boycott in solidarity with the non-Jerusalem Palestinians who were denied gas masks by the Israeli authorities. "Lethal gas and chemicals are not going to check ID's" was the Palestinian claim. "Our responsibility is toward the Israeli people," came the Israeli counterclaim. "Go tell your friend Saddam to protect you," was the more cruel Israeli response. Al-Haqq, the Palestinian Human Rights Organization and ICJ (International Commission of Jurists) affiliate, launched a campaign to obtain gas masks for the Palestinians. The Israelis found every possible excuse not to allow in the European-donated masks, while refusing to supply us with any. It was decided that the Jerusalem Palestinians should take their gas masks while stepping up the campaign to obtain masks for the rest.

I woke up the morning of my birthday, October 8, 1990, looking forward to the surprise party and gifts that Emile and the girls usually prepare for me. Birthdays at home have always been special occasions to be celebrated in their full glory. Instead, I was surprised by an urgent phone call from Ghassan al-Khatib.

"Hanan, can you make it to Jerusalem immediately? There's been a horrible massacre at Al-Haram al-Sharif [the al-Aqsa Mosque], and we have to act now!"

"I'll come right away. Did you get in touch with Faisal and the others?"

"I'm trying, but Faisal himself is in the mosque. It looks like a bloodbath."

"What happened? Who did the killing? Who's hurt?"

"The mosque was packed with worshipers for the Friday prayers, and the Israeli security forces stormed the grounds and shot indiscriminately inside the mosque and into the crowd in the courtyard. There are many casualties, scores of them, and the *haram* grounds are strewn with bodies, blood, and brains. It's a real slaughter. We must move immediately."

I spent the rest of the day desperately and unsuccessfully trying to get to Jerusalem. As usual, the Israeli authorities had imposed a very strict curfew and declared the Occupied Territories closed military areas. We were under siege, prisoners in our own homes, guilty of being massacred. Emile, Amal, Zeina, and I celebrated my birthday that year in tears. Since then, my birthday has been tainted with blood, and I feel robbed of my right to celebrate even that one day of the year I used to claim as my own.

Christmas 1990 was a somber affair. Some shops in Ramallah, in a desperate attempt to salvage a festive atmosphere, sent out some bell-ringing Santas. They were promptly arrested. We wiped the children's tears, trying somehow to rationalize the tragedy of Santa Claus's arrest and rescue him from jail in time for Christmas Eve. We managed to have a friend dress up for the occasion, but the questions he got were heartbreaking. We were already a vulnerable civilian population; the children's plight was the exposed heart of that vulnerability. As we sang Christmas carols and watched the midnight service from Manger Church in Bethlehem under the watchful eyes and guns of the Israeli soldiers, we recited silent prayers for peace knowing all the while that war was just around the corner. For years we had tried to teach a language of peace among our people, to generate a vision of the future in which yesterday's enemy would be tomorrow's negotiating partner and the next day's neighbor. Like Sisyphus we had laboriously rolled the rock of nonmilitary solutions uphill. Now, it seemed with the glorification of Mars, the rock was not only about to roll back, but to crush us in the process.

The tension was like the electric silence preceding a violent storm. The Cairo Arab Summit, with its either-or reductive options, ruled out a contained Arab solution. The boycott of Iraq was stepped up as one U.N. resolution after another was adopted in preparation for the inevitable outcome. An international alliance materialized as countries clamored to join the latest global club. Bush and Baker, the force behind that drive, solicited subscriptions and approved the membership. In the midst of the gathering gale, the Arab world (rather, people) held its breath and searched the horizon for the first signs of lightning. When Secretary Baker and Iraqi Foreign Minister Tareq Aziz met in Geneva, it looked for a second like war could be averted and we would be spared. It did not happen. The belligerent armies were assembled, and before their impending onslaught the voice of reason was reduced to a feeble whisper. Never before had there been such a war rehearsed ahead of time by public pronouncement.

A "state of the art" war was an anomaly to us. When asked by National Public Radio about the expression, I responded that to most Palestinians "state of the art" evoked allusions to poetry, music, and painting. I cautioned that the war was liable to unleash hidden historical and nationalistic forces and set them loose in a region whose memory stretched back to span centuries and whose current reality was no more than a flimsy layer concealing an infinite number of strata. From one interview to another, one public (and secret) meeting to another, we desperately sought to inject some rationality in the cacophony of war. Not only did we go unheeded, but some of us were accused of being alarmists and defeatists. The West had already decided that the Palestinian response was that one "embrace," no more, no less, and the Palestinian people under occupation began to read into the impending cataclysm hints about their own release. The whole "linkage" idea, the "one yardstick" call for even-handedness and uniform standards, and the reverence for "international legitimacy" and the "will of the international community," all seemed to inflame Palestinian expectations. The public thought was that Saddam would free us, either through the politics of uniformity in exchange for withdrawing from Kuwait, or through a military confrontation he seemed confident of winning. Any attempts to dissuade them proved futile. We waited.

● ● ●

"Hanan, wake up! It's started." A familiar voice was shouting through the phone receiver.

Barely able to gather my scattered wits about me, I sat up in bed. "Who is this? What has started?"

"This is Rana," came back the answer. It was Rana Nashashibi, who had been with us in Brussels. "I've just received a call from the States. It's on television there. The war has started!"

"What war?" I asked. Having spent the last few weeks in frenzied preparation precisely for such an eventuality, when it actually happened I was caught entirely off-guard.

"What's the matter with you? Wake up! The Iraqi war has started."

This time, it sank in. I shook Emile awake, blathering like an idiot. "Emile, the girls. It has started. Wake up! We must get the girls ready. My mother, upstairs, your family. Hurry."

Not knowing what to expect, it took us some time to decide on a plan of action. We turned on the portable radios, woke up Amal and Zeina, who had already sensed the excitement, turned on the television, and distributed tasks in order of priority. Zeina was making calls to family and friends, while Amal started checking the provisions. Should we go immediately into the sealed room (the girls' bedroom), or should we wait to find out what was happening. Should we move all the provisions, or wait for developments. Whom should we call; had we forgotten anybody. Will Saddam strike here immediately; if not, how long would he wait. Running back and forth between bedroom and living room, kitchen and storage room, the veranda and the sealed room, we finally settled down in the living room with the television turned on to the Israeli channel that was relaying the news on CNN and up-to-the-minute developments. Everything was set for a quick dash to the sealed room, the plastic and tape ready to seal the door from within, but in the meantime we sat huddled together before the television screen, taking turns answering the phone. Amal and Zeina finally pulled their mattresses into the living room, while Emile and I kept vigil all night. The Israeli authorities immediately announced a total curfew. We heard the announcements over the loudspeakers of their military jeeps as they drove through town warning people to stay indoors and that "whoever violated the curfew would be shot on sight." Emile and I exchanged looks of silent alarm. It had begun. We were under double siege.

The irony of Israeli army patrols broadcasting curfew announcements to Palestinians throughout the Occupied Territories and enforcing compliance, while refusing to set up an alarm system or sirens (as in Israel) to warn us about raids or Scud missile attacks was both obvious and painful.

However, we developed a quick and efficient network with Israeli friends. The moment they heard the siren, they would call a few key people and those in turn would call others, and so on. Since the system relied on telephones, we developed an alternative system of whistling to inform whole neighborhoods. Amal and Zeina, as well as my niece Najwa and the neighborhood kids, had become quite expert whistlers by then —the benefit of extensive *intifada* experience. Inept adults like myself were forced to resort to small plastic whistles. Although ultimately everybody ended up relying on television and radio warnings, the whistling never stopped. It became the Palestinian response to the Israeli sirens and the Iraqi attacks; but more than anything else, it seemed, it was the defiant response to the long incarceration, under the title "curfew."

Having decided to use the gas masks, we had to train Amal and Zeina. To make them less hateful, the masks were first tried on all the stuffed animals our daughters held dear, and gradually their standard location became the faces of Mickey and Minnie Mouse, whom the girls had brought back with them from Disney World. At first, with each raid, we would run into our sealed room and close it behind us until we got the all-clear signal from Israeli radio. Emile and I would take turns, one of us listening to the radio or television for the raid alert. Nahman Shai, the Israeli army spokesman, became as familiar to us as he was to the Israelis. One of the many war jokes then was that Saddam's code for ordering an attack was "Wake up Nahman Shai." After the first couple of weeks or so, we stopped going into the room. We discovered that we could actually see the Scud missiles as they came in, flying over Ramallah and heading toward the Mediterranean coast. We could even tell where they landed, first seeing the explosions, then feeling their vibrations. As we went up to our roof, we noticed that almost everybody else in town had had the same idea. Later, when the Patriots were introduced, we could see them fly up to meet the Scuds, miss, and fall back to ground. But no one dared say anything. Sari Nusseibeh had been arrested and accused of being an Iraqi spy for describing to someone on the phone where a missile had fallen. It was a fate we wished to avoid; so although we had a clear view of the whole Scud-Patriot drama, including how many hits, how many misses, and where, we feigned ignorance—particularly on the phone. Not that we could have told anybody anywhere else in the world. Israel had cut off all our links with the outside world by closing down the long-distance lines to and from the Occupied Territories.

The war continued, and with it the curfew. Distress calls were pouring in. In some places, army units had entered homes, destroyed property and provisions, and beaten up people. In others, Israeli settlers were doing the damage. And while in some towns the curfew would be lifted for an hour or two every few days, in other places it continued nonstop for six weeks. In this context, my additional personal tragedy was an excruciating toothache that had to go without treatment for weeks since Hala Hallaq, my dentist, was unable to reach her clinic or to make emergency house calls from her home in Jerusalem. My recollections of the war period are indelibly colored by that persistent piercing pain.

The impact of the curfew was particularly hard on the refugee camps. Several times I tried to get to Imm Youssef, our old family cleaning lady who lived in Jalazon camp, but was turned back each time. One day we found her at our doorstep, having exfiltrated and found her way across fields and hills to our home. She and her grandchildren had not eaten for days, and had been reduced to burning their old furniture and shoes just to keep warm. Medical emergencies reached a critical level, until gradually the Israeli authorities started granting permits to some individuals and institutions who were performing essential services. Some nights, perversely, at the oddest curfew hours—between midnight and 2:00 A.M.

—the Israeli prison authorities would release the Palestinian prisoners who had served their sentences. Most would find their way to our home, the closest house to the prison, where we tried to supply them with food and shelter for the night and undertook to inform their families whenever possible. Ever since I had founded the Legal Aid Committee at the university, my home had become a familiar refuge for prisoners and their families. That was how Amal and Zeina had gained their detailed and specialized knowledge of prison life and legal terminology at such a young age. Occupation had a way of invading not only your home and life, but also of imposing itself on the emotional health and education of your children. All our carefully woven shields of love and comfort were not enough to repel the knowledge or the pain.

Living in the midst of this, we watched the world applaud Israel for its bravery and restraint in not entering the war. We had tried hard to prevent this war, yet we became both victim and villain. Although tourism was hard hit, the political pilgrimage to Israel remained a steady stream in homage to the country's "heroism." Such an elusive and protean concept, this subjective behavioral attribute and abstraction—the heroic. Ed Bradley thought I was being heroic to defy the curfew and find my way to Jerusalem to do *60 Minutes*. I thought Imm Youssef, our cleaning lady, was heroic. All those thousands, tens of thousands, of Palestinian prisoners in Israeli jails and detention camps were the embodiment of heroism in our eyes. Our children were heroic to salvage remnants of their childhood in the midst of this adult insanity called war or occupation. Now Israel was being heroic for becoming an American protectorate and for accepting international compensation for the Scud damage and the trauma. Our unsung, unacknowledged, uncompensated silent heroes would have a hard time understanding that definition of the concept. They did. And in their resentment, they applauded the antihero and longed for the salvation of the counterheroic. For that, the whole Palestinian nation was made to pay the price. And still is.

We had our own battles to wage and monsters to confront. Palestinians expelled from Kuwait and other Gulf countries, many third-time refugees, found themselves destitute—not only stateless, but also homeless. Instead of the remittances from these expatriates, the Palestinians in the Occupied Territories accrued responsibilities and obligations. Our exports halted, and our modest industrial concerns were dealt a serious blow; agriculture ceased in the six-week curfew, and grants from other Arab countries were withheld. Almost 80 percent of the income of the "inside" Palestinians was lost. The great economic blockade had started, and with it the political blockade of the PLO. However, the largest wound was cut into the body of the Arab world—a great festering wound that sapped its resources and energies, and clouded its vision for a long time to come. Fragmented and dissipated, both "winner" and "loser" camps came out reeling from the ordeal, nursing their wounds and grievances, and harboring deep-seated resentments. The Palestinian-Israeli dialogue also sustained a severe setback as some Israelis, like Yossi Sarid, a left-wing member of the dialogue team, lashed out at the Palestinian political leadership in the Occupied Territories, accusing us of hypocrisy and moral cowardice. Such insensitivity and lack of a real understanding of our political realities, and even of the nature of the dialogue, undermined our trust and confidence in some of our counterparts.

In the midst of this bleak landscape, and coming from the far-off horizon, we could discern a distant rider approaching from the West. Whether he came in white shining armor or with a cloven hoof was not entirely clear—in all likelihood, both. Whether to rescue the region from the clutches of war, or to exploit our condition of utter exhaustion and fragmentation, or a combination of both, was not clear either. The claim was that he would "invest the credibility that the United States had gained in the war in order to bring peace to the region." We read that as claiming the spoils of war. The claim was that a "New World Order" was emerging with the end of the Cold War and that we were part of it. We read that as a reorganization of our world according to the American blueprint. The claim was that a window of opportunity was opening up for Middle East reconciliation. We read that as a peephole, a long tunnel, or a trap.

. . .

"Philip Wilcox has just called. He has an urgent message for us. Can you come over immediately?" Faisal sounded very serious on the phone. Wilcox was the American consul general in Jerusalem.

"Why don't you see him now; in the meantime I'll try to get the rest of the group together and we'll meet at my house," I replied.

By the time Faisal arrived, most of us had worked out the mystery. Public hints about the United States exploring prospects for a Middle East peace process left little room for conjecture. We, the Palestinians, were to be included. Did we want to be?

"Secretary James Baker is coming to the region, and Phil Wilcox wants to know if we would like to see him," Faisal reported.

"What do you mean if we would like to see him?" I asked indignantly. "Is he requesting a meeting or isn't he?"

"He will not ask for one unless we do. He wants it to come from us."

"Like hell he does," commented Ghassan. "He can request a meeting and we'll study it and give him our response in due time."

"He doesn't want to repeat the George Shultz experience. He does not want to be rebuffed." We smiled at the memory. I remembered the sight of Shultz addressing an empty room in East Jerusalem after the Palestinians had refused to see him in 1988. We had sent him the public message to go talk to the PLO. Only the Palestinians under occupation could be that rude, I thought to myself. And we always chose dramatic ways of driving home the message. No wonder Baker was being super-cautious.

"Of course we don't want to see him. He shouldn't be afraid of a rebuff. We'll make it known ahead of time that he's not wanted here." Riad Malki never minced words.

"Let's think about it," said Zahira Kamal. "We should consult Tunis before we take a position on this."

"Public opinion will be against it. People are still smarting from the Gulf War." Mamdouh al-Aker always had his ear to the street.

"Let's not take hasty decisions," Faisal urged. "Why don't you think about it and consult your people; we'll meet tomorrow and discuss it further."

After they left, Faisal and I called Akram. He promised to start discreet explorations with Abu Ammar and the Executive Committee. He wasn't very optimistic. We then called Wilcox and asked him to tread gently; the manner of presentation could be more important than the substance. We persuaded him that no one could invite Baker, but that we would let him know when to issue an invitation that would not be refused.

CHAPTER FIVE

While the Arab countries welcomed the prospect of Baker's visit, not one would accept a coordinating meeting with the Palestinians, especially with the PLO, to prepare for the visit. Isolated from the Arab and international communities, the Executive Committee seemed incapable of making a decision. Some saw the U.S. initiative as an opportunity to reestablish the PLO in the international political arena, and the potential peace process as the instrument. Others saw it as another attempt to delegitimize and exclude the PLO because there seemed to be an opportunity for an "alternative leadership" from the Occupied Territories. Clearly the *intifada* had shifted the focus to the "inside," more so after the double blow the PLO had received: in 1982 when they were expelled from Lebanon, and as a result of the Gulf War. The persistence of these divergent attitudes created internal tension and suspicion through the duration of the negotiations, and in turn distorted the decision-making process.

They deliberated in Tunis. We debated in Jerusalem. With the rare exception, most political factions and independents were inclined to accept an initial exploratory meeting with Baker. We had nothing to lose by meeting, was the majority Palestinian position, provided we held our ground. The PLO in Tunis was still thinking about it. Abu Mazen, a member of the Executive Committee, was in favor but Abu Ammar would not commit himself. The rest were still skeptical. Akram reported to Abu Ammar that the "inside" was in favor, which swayed some positions. The decision was a very sensitive and critical one, and we didn't want to usurp the "outside" 's power to make the decision. Faisal and I were told to proceed carefully, and that the mood of the "outside" was more positive. The PLO announced its positive decision on March 10, and we met with Baker on March 12. The Communist Party participated in the first meeting and boycotted the rest. Eleven Palestinians attended the first meeting, five attended the second meeting, and the rest of the meetings were restricted to three (Faisal, myself, and Zakariyya al-Agha of Gaza) or just Faisal and myself.

Such was the beginning of the often "strange encounters," otherwise known as the "Baker meetings," which helped launch the Middle East peace process, with the Palestinians on board. Whether we joined of our own free will or were taken for a ride summarized the controversy that emerged within the Palestinian camp as a result. Was it a sell-out or did we buy into a process to find a place in history for the maligned Palestinian cause and people? Undoubtedly, we had embarked on another transition—a journey into both unfamiliar and familiar landscape. For us, the task was twofold: to reach out to the enemy, and to the world; but also to reach inward and to heal the split within our heart.

Baker's most striking feature were those cold piercing eyes that seemed capable of looking straight into your mind and calculating alternative tactics for a mental assault. This is a no-nonsense person, I thought to myself. He's obviously defined his target and is figuring out the shortest and most direct way of reaching it. Would we be obstacles to be destroyed or brushed aside, or were we convenient allies—useful but dispensable. Were we the cost of his success or an essential component of it. Would we be able to reach the human being within, or would we remain the objects of his scrutiny. Obviously, he was not an easy man to fathom or to cross. At that first encounter, however, each side was maneuvering for position, all the while studying the adversary for signs of weakness or hesitancy and looking for openings in order to score. But first, we had to set the record straight.

"We are here at the behest of the PLO, our sole legitimate leadership," Faisal began. We were meeting at the West Jerusalem American consulate. Clearly prepared, Baker responded: "Whom you choose as your leadership is your own business. I am looking for Palestinians from the Occupied Territories who are not PLO members and who are willing to enter into direct bilateral two-phased negotiations on the basis of UNSC resolutions 242 and 338 and the principle of land for peace, and who are willing to live in peace with Israel. Are there any in this room?"

That was easy. Or so we thought. How did one identify a "PLO member"? The PLO did not issue membership cards. Besides, it was illegal to belong to any political party or organization according to Israel's military orders. So who was willing to confess before Baker what he or she would not confess to the Israeli interrogators? We were all "from the Occupied Territories," although some of us had originally come from that part of pre-1948 Palestine that had later become Israel. The idea of two phases was more difficult, but with a binding time frame and the logic of interconnected steps leading to the objective of ending the occupation and establishing the Palestinian state, we could ensure that the transitional phase would not become permanent. The basis could be acceptable: we wanted our land back, and we would give them peace in exchange, and the U.N. resolutions reinforced the inadmissibility of the acquisition of territory by war. Were we "willing to live in peace with Israel"? Was Israel willing to live in peace with us? Wasn't that the whole point—to create a just peace with Israel by solving the causes of the conflict? And how else would we do it if not by negotiations? Things did not turn out to be that simple, as the ordeal of the next three years of negotiations would prove. But we proceeded.

"We must remind you, Mr. Secretary, that we are a people with dignity and pride. We are not defeated, and this is not Safwan Tent," said Saeb Erakat, an editor of *Al-Quds* newspaper and a professor of political science at An-Najah University, getting straight to the point. Safwan Tent was set up to negotiate with the American military representatives the terms of Iraq's surrender at the end of the Gulf War.

"It's not my fault you backed the losing side. You should tell your leadership not to back the wrong horse; that was absolutely stupid. There's a big price to be paid." With that Baker made sure that the whole next hour was taken up in defense of the PLO. The long list of Israel's human rights violations took another hour. "That's why you should negotiate—to end the occupation and all its practices."

"I've agreed to come to this meeting to talk about one thing only," Haidar Abdel-Shafi announced in his deep calm voice. "Israeli settlement activities in the Occupied Territories must stop. There will be no peace process while the settlements continue. You can count on hearing this from me all the time." Throughout the negotiations, Haidar remained true to his word. As head of the Palestinian delegation, he never attended a session or a meeting without raising the settlement issue in a compelling and persuasive manner.

"How can you expect our delegation to negotiate with the noise of bulldozers in the background? We feel that they're digging our graves," added Elias Freij, the mayor of Bethlehem.

"Begin negotiations, and the settlements will stop," Baker responded.

"They must stop before, or we can't enter the process," was our reply.

"The status quo is not only painful; it is also untenable. How do you propose to deal with it?" I asked.

"Now you're talking business." Baker wanted to tackle practical issues. We knew he was a lawyer; he wanted to "make a deal." We also knew that he wasn't used to failure. But in addition, we had seen that coming too close to the Palestinian question had destroyed many political careers.

With resuscitated copies of the Camp David Accords, and talking points prepared by his team, Baker leaned on us hard. Faced as well with a hard-line Israeli Likud government led by the brittle and caustic Yitzhak Shamir, he thrust his energies full force toward what he considered the point of least resistance, the Palestinians. Any proposals that bounced off the Israeli brick wall, he would try to sell us as "the only way to get Israel into the process." It subsequently became clear to us that he thought that Likud would enter the peace process; Labor, led by Yitzhak Rabin, would negotiate; and a coalition government would sign. Unfortunately, reality refused to conform to his blueprint. It was his unstated belief as well that the negotiations would produce an alternative leadership from the Occupied Territories that, having the legitimacy of elections, would replace the PLO.

Faisal, who had the habit of illustrating every point with an anecdote, a parable, an analogy, or a homespun tale, illustrated to Baker our relationship with the PLO as follows: Our leadership was like a man standing in quicksand before a stone wall. In order to be rescued, he had allowed another person (us) to climb on his shoulders to try to scale the wall and reach the top. By doing that, the man ran the risk of sinking deeper into the quicksand under the extra weight he had taken on, but knowing all the while that the person on his shoulders stood a good chance of reaching the top of the wall. Once there, the person would reach down and pull the man out of the quicksand and onto the wall with him. Both then would come out on the other side, home free. Entrusted thus with the fate of the PLO, we took our duty as the instrument of its salvation very seriously.

Baker and his team shuffled back and forth between us and the Israelis carrying a carrot in one hand and a stick in the other. The Israelis were granted all their demands: a few of those being that the U.N. would be excluded, that there would be no participation by Palestinians from the "outside" or by Palestinian Jerusalemites. We were informed that this was the only way to stop the settlements and to begin the devolution of the occupation, although we knew the conditions were unfair and the restrictions placed on us were putting us at a severe disadvantage. Israel got all the carrots and asked for more; we got all the sticks in the form of morbid forecasts about the consequences of saying no.

Israel's hostility toward the United Nations was no surprise: historically Israel has refused to cooperate with the U.N., with the exception of U.N. relief efforts. It has publicly accused the U.N. of being anti-Israeli, and has refused to comply with all U.N. resolutions, insisting on a total exclusion of the U.N. from the peace process—which was rather ironic in view of the fact that two U.N. Security Council resolutions, 242 and 338, were the basis of the talks. U.N. Resolution 242 refers to the inadmissibility of acquisition of land through war and finding an equitable solution to the Palestinian refugee problem. U.N. Resolution 338 was adopted after the war of 1973 to reaffirm Resolution 242 and to call for a negotiated settlement by holding a conference under appropriate auspices. Finally, after much effort, we were told that a representative for the secretary general would be granted observer status. Israel demanded the exclusion of Europe as well, and the relegation of our regional neighbor, Europe, also to secondary status. We demanded co-sponsor status for the European Community, but the most we could get was that Europe "would participate alongside the co-sponsors."

Even that, however, was almost lost. It wouldn't be until October that we would even be allowed to catch a glimpse of the Letter of Invitation; the only document that was binding turned out to be something we had no hand in drafting. I quickly noted that the reference to Europe was changed to indicate the presence of Troika observers (the triple representation of the past, current, and future head of the European Community). I immediately called Robert Serry, who was representing the E.C. during the Dutch presidency and asked him if they had agreed to the changed formulation. He rushed to Washington the next day and met with Dan Kurtzer and succeeded in restoring the text to its original form. We persisted in pushing the cause of Europe until we were accused of being more European than the Europeans. Closer to the region, and with a longer history of involvement, in addition to its more even-handed policies—mainly as expressed in the Venice Declaration (which recognized the PLO and called for Palestinian self-determination), Europe, we felt, could play a corrective role to balance the pro-Israeli bias of U.S. policy. It was not to be. Repeatedly told by the Americans not to interfere because of the delicate nature of the talks, and not to upset the apple cart, the Europeans abrogated what we felt was their responsibility and went along with "the only game in town." We felt increasingly cornered and abandoned.

To get rid of the last vestiges of the "U.N.-sponsored international conference" to which we and the international community (we thought) had been firmly committed, Israel demanded that the conference be held only once as an opening ceremony to be reconvened only with the agreement of all parties—which guaranteed that it would not meet again. Only "direct, bilateral talks" would do, while the co-sponsors were not allowed to participate directly in the talks unless "invited by both parties." Israel got its wish. As part of its preconditions, Israel also demanded and won restoration of ties with the USSR/Russia and any other country wishing to enter the peace process. The embargo on the PLO was stepped up. The most excruciating constraints that topped Israel's shopping list were those imposed on the nature of Palestinian participation, although supposedly no preconditions were allowed. We called these preconditions Israeli "ostrich politics." By sparing Israeli negotiators from exposure to the PLO and East Jerusalem Palestinians, Shamir was under the illusion that he was dealing with a made-to-order situation that had no relationship to reality. In addition, the insistence on a "joint Jordanian-Palestinian delegation" format was also an Israeli way of avoiding the fact of a separate Palestinian identity, despite the fact that one whole track in the negotiations was supposed to be Palestinian and the other Arab. "Exclude us, ignore us, deny us—we won't go away," I told the press then, which was true of the whole Palestinian question.

Faisal had a perfect anecdote to describe the strange distortions imposed on the Palestinian delegation. "The Baker suit": Once there was an honest man of modest means whose generous friend had given him a piece of fabric with which to make a suit. He could not afford a tailor, but one claiming to be a tailor came to him and offered to make the suit for free. The man gave him the material. A few days later, the tailor came back with the suit. The man tried it on. One sleeve was too long, the other too short; the sides were twisted and the hem uneven; the collar was loose on the right and tight on the left; the pants legs were twisted.

"What kind of a suit is this?" asked the horrified man.

"What's the problem?" said the tailor. "Where the sleeve is too long, just push your arm out and your shoulder down: where it's too short, just pull your arm up and raise your shoulder. Where the sides are twisted and the hem uneven, just turn your upper torso to the side as you walk. To deal with the collar just turn your neck to the right all the time and the collar will loosen on the left side and tighten on the right. Where the pants legs don't fit just twist your legs with the line of the seam."

The honest man of modest means followed the instructions of his tailor. As he walked down the street contorted beyond recognition, people looked at him in wonder, in sympathy, or in disgust.

"Look at that poor man," said one passer-by to the other. "His must be the most distorted, contorted, misshapen figure in the world."

"But you must admit," said the other thoughtfully, "he must have the best tailor in the world."

Faisal told Baker this story, and concluded with a moral: "So, Mr. Baker, if you see us behave in a strange or unusual or inappropriate manner, it is not that we were born that way, or that it is our nature, or that we like to behave as such. It's just that the suit you have tailored for us does not fit!"

We held close to eighteen "Baker meetings," mainly in Jerusalem, with a few in Washington. All the meetings had the unusual flavor of Texas-Palestine (Texatine or Palexas?). We exchanged proverb for proverb, one cultural bias for another, and innuendo for insinuation. Baker downed many Dr Peppers, while we drank numerous cups of coffee. Baker's favorite expression to egg us on was, "Don't let the cat die on your doorstep!" On such occasions, I played interpreter for Faisal and for Tunis, often sharing an inside joke at some literal translations working both ways. Responding to reporters' questions at one briefing, I described the encounters as an "educational process." They asked, "For whom?" My answer was, "For Baker and the Americans, of course."

To prepare for the meetings, my tasks included drafting memos and official documents, reviewing the minutes of previous gatherings. Every meeting was followed by a hectic all-night work session; the oral reports to Tunis were followed by written documents. In my assessments I enjoyed filling in the meanings behind and between the lines, interpreting moods and body language, and charting possible courses and making recommendations for future action. At the same time, we held briefing sessions at Faisal's house for the political leadership and factions, and then gave summaries to the consuls general and members of international organizations in Jerusalem. Faisal always claimed he did the "hard part," welcoming the diplomats and giving them a general statement—leaving me the "easy job" of providing the details and evaluations. And Faisal signed all the official letters and memoranda, cracking jokes about having to do everything himself!

My most visible work, media and information, came as an addendum to an already long list. That is why when some of my critics tried to put me down by describing me as "Faisal's translator," or by claiming that I was chosen for my "good English," or that I was an inconsequential "media figure" and creation, those of us who knew better laughed. I never responded.

For these meetings we formed a strong, cohesive team. Faisal would present the major points and deliver any official message from the PLO (whom Baker consistently referred to as "your leadership" or "your people out there" or just simply "Tunis"). I would elaborate and present additional details, quite often playing the "bad guy" to Faisal's "good guy." Dr. Zakariyya al-Agha from Gaza (whom Baker referred to as "my good friend, the doctor") would maintain a deliberate silence until the spirit moved him (regardless of where we were in the discussion) and he would exclaim, "Now tell me, Mr. Baker, what are you going to do about the settlements?" Or, "Do you mean to tell me, Mr. Baker, that you cannot bring Israel to stop the settlement activities?" At one meeting in which Zakariyya's silence stretched beyond the usual time, as soon as Zakariyya started his "settlement speech," Baker exclaimed, "Thank God! I was beginning to worry that the good doctor was not going to speak. No meeting is complete without his reminding me of the settlements."

Baker had promised us that the peace process would bring the settlement activities to an end, but that could not be a precondition to the talks. At the same time, the issue of the American loan guarantees to Israel being linked to Israel's settlement policy emerged as a major issue in our talks. For the first time, an American administration was willing to impose conditions on loan guarantees to Israel. The stipulation that housing loan guarantees would not be used for funds spent on Israeli settlements in the Occupied Territories was one way in which the administration sought to curb the expansion of settlements.

The Baker team usually included Dennis Ross, then of policy planning; Baker's spokesperson and assistant, Margaret Tutwiler; Dan Kurtzer and Aaron Miller of the State Department (Edward Djerejian joining later); Edmund Hull and Richard Haas of the National Security Council. When Philip Wilcox was consul general, we developed a "political geography" of a sort, with a set seating arrangement on one side of the room in the

West Jerusalem consulate. Most of the time, the talks were conducted against the background of angry shouts and chants reaching us from the street where Israeli settlers and right-wing organizations were demonstrating. When Molly Williamson, a small, nervous woman, took over as consul general, the background din was the only factor in the setting that remained constant. We were moved to the other side of the room, with a whole new political geography, and a different tone and mood.

The meetings began to take on that sterile tone of diplomacy that seemed so far removed from the human condition I knew and saw each day. Finally, I felt compelled to change the nature of the discourse. I began: "To you this may be an exercise in political virtuosity or intellectual abstractions; it may be an objective requirement to enhance a political career; it may be pure self-interest or the thrill of exercising power. To us, it is the very substance of our lives. We are discussing the lives and future of our children—of a whole people. We are presenting before you the raw and painful substance of our humanity—of human suffering experienced and expressed concretely and directly by us, by those who are negotiating here with you as though their lives are just as normal or just as safe as yours. It is time for you to hear and witness what the occupation is really like. What it does to us, to our children, to friends and neighbors and relatives who have names and faces, hopes and fears, and who are made to lead lives of fear, insecurity, and humiliation." I talked about Amal and Zeina and their closed schools, their dead and wounded friends, and their exposure to the worst that the adult world had to offer in cruelty and repression. "No one has the right to rob our children of their childhood." I talked about our prisoners and deportees, not as abstract statistics but as identifiable people who were close to us and with whom we shared special relationships. I talked about demolished homes, and what a stone house meant to Palestinians: our past and future, our identity and security, our legacy to our children, and our mark in the world. (One of my earlier poems had a section about demolished homes: Have you seen a stone house die?/It sighs, then wraps itself/Around its gutted heart and lays/Itself to rest to become/One with the earth who's in/The process of giving birth to/Yet more stones.)

I could not be silenced. When I finished, I could almost touch the hush in the room. Our minute-taker and one of Faisal's staff, Akram Baker ("our Baker," or "Baker Jr.") later told me, "I live the conditions you described. I know all the facts; yet you brought tears to my eyes." His were not the only tearful eyes that day. I felt I had reached the human being behind the sharp cold eyes of the older Baker.

Faisal also managed to make the human connection. At one point, following death threats against Faisal and myself, he looked Baker in the eye and in a peaceful tone said, "You are talking to a dead man." The whole room tensed up. "I believe enough in the cause of peace to be willing to die for it." He continued. "But if I am to die, I must have accomplished enough to encourage others to continue and to make my death an inspiration for others to take up where I left off. But if I am killed with nothing pocketed, it will only scare the rest. I will have died for nothing and the process will die with me. The one thing I need in my pocket more than anything else is a piece of paper with one word written on it: 'Jerusalem.' " Each one of us had his or her obsession. Faisal's was Jerusalem. It is undoubtedly inscribed in his heart. It was more than a political issue for him, it was a personal, emotional commitment. He came from a long line of Jerusalemites who have held positions of authority—both secular and religious—for centuries. I once heard him declare: "I'm a Palestinian and I love Palestine. I'm a family man and I love my wife and children. But first and foremost I'm a Jerusalemite. For that I'm willing to die."

Some of the reporters traveling with Baker said to me following one of the meetings in Jerusalem, "You guys really got to Baker. He's definitely impressed with you. He actually said that the Palestinian delegation was intelligent and capable, and its members respect themselves. He actually likes you." I replied, rather flippantly at that time, "After a six-hour meeting with Shamir, he'll find anybody likable." We had the advantage of not being hampered by diplomatic niceties and the constraints of protocol. We had the advantage of exercising our humanity freely, and we indulged ourselves in behaving outrageously at times. We did not have to play games of power politics, the honest and direct human approach being the shortest distance between two disparate worlds.

In spite of all that, and in spite of Zakariyya's settlements and Faisal's Jerusalem and my human rights obsession, all were denied us. Many other rights and requests were denied us. We were accused of being "hung up on symbols"—minor things like the PLO, the flag, Jerusalem, statehood, freedom, human rights, and the land, to cite a few. Regardless of how much Baker may have "liked" or "admired" us, he felt that his historical duty as well as his processed talking points compelled him to deny us and to deliver us to Israel. The final blow came when after months of negotiations, he looked us in the eye and told us that neither Faisal nor myself would be allowed to participate in the negotiations, both having committed the major crime of carrying Jerusalem identity cards. Shamir, obviously, was too sensitive a soul to be exposed to the reality of such a horror: that there was a Palestinian Jerusalem with real live people in it, and that the Israeli annexation of Jerusalem was just another myth to be exposed by reality. By not acknowledging the existence of Palestinian Jerusalemites, it was one more indirect attempt to gain acceptance of Israel's illegal annexation of East Jerusalem and to predetermine the fate of Jerusalem.

Ironically, we were the side that had embraced peace and struggled for a Palestinian peace offensive; Shamir was the intransigent hard-liner who had to be dragged kicking and screaming into the process. His sins were rewarded, our virtue punished. All the morality plays I had read as a student certainly did not prepare me for this.

All the anguish, and all our meetings produced only two official U.S. documents: the Letter of Assurance and the Letter of Invitation. One that we had worked on for hours, days, weeks, and months, the U.S. Letter of Assurance (LOA), we were only to be told later when we wanted to cash it in that it was a worthless sham. The LOA articulated American policy positions and was given by the United States to each side to address issues of concern and to indicate that the United States would assure these to every participant. The other, of which we had only been allowed to catch a fleeting glance, was the Letter of Invitation (LOI), a brief letter stating the basis of the talks and formally inviting the proposed participants.

While we concentrated on the LOA not only as a statement of U.S. policy but also as a system of safeguards, carrying the full weight and stature of the United States and the credibility of its foreign policy commitments, the Letter of Invitation was being composed and structured somewhere else. The LOI became the sole reference and the bible of the negotiations; the omissions we thought were covered by the LOA were systematically used against us, while Israel was allowed to violate it at will or to refer to it selectively as it saw fit.

The evolution of the Letter of Assurance would provide rich material for a case study in diplomatic textual analysis. Word by word, comma by comma, sentence by sentence we pored over the document assiduously throughout the summer of 1991, producing no fewer than eight drafts with multiple layers of formulations and amendments. At one point I ran out of different colors of ink and pencil to indicate the different stages of production on a master copy and had to classify the document's evolution in phases and substrata on multiple copies. At first, I had insisted on drafting a Letter of Understanding to be signed by both the Palestinian and American sides. I gradually became convinced that the task would involve a vast and complex negotiating process equivalent to the whole peace process leading to a signed bilateral agreement between us and the Americans, an immense undertaking that would delay the process for years with no guarantee of success. By mutual consent, we opted for a letter that would describe U.S. policy and commitments vis-à-vis the Palestinians.

After the first exploratory talks, the American team was ready to get down to business. Dennis Ross called and told me that the group was ready to start drafting the next day. I called Akram and asked for PLO guidelines; they had none. "Just stick to broad principles," was the Executive Committee's response. I was frantic. I asked Faisal to prepare basic points, but he was busy elsewhere. Abu Ammar gave me his instructions: "Send a wise person and you don't need to give him advice." I was awed by the responsibility. We agreed that the team would come out to my house the next morning, which was a strike day, to avoid media attention and interference.

That marathon work session lasted for eight hours. Dan Kurtzer, Aaron Miller, Edmund Hull, and Deputy Consul General David Winn came fully prepared, while I had to produce the Palestinian position on the spot. I came up with the sixty-five points that I felt should be in the LOA, which I later sent to Akram in Tunis, becoming a significant document to those very few Palestinians who were in the know. At one point, having moved to the back veranda to work in the fresh air (in addition to the fact that Zeina had kicked us out of the living room where she was watching television), we noticed unusual activity in the backyard. Reporters had traced us to my house and had climbed the trees and stone wall of our garden to film our meeting! Emile told us that the whole house was besieged. The sight was quite amusing; more than a hundred reporters, cameramen, soundmen, radio and TV announcers were surrounding the house while the soldiers across the street looked on in puzzlement.

Several work sessions ensued. In most of them, I represented the Palestinian side alone. Faisal attended some, and Sari Nusseibeh joined us in some of the later ones. One evening we held a Baker meeting till 11:00 P.M., followed by an all-night session of checking minutes, briefing Tunis, and writing reports. I went home at 4:30 A.M. to shower and change and drive back to Jerusalem for a long session with the drafting team at 7:00 A.M., to be followed by a meeting with Faisal and one with the political leadership, to be followed by another long briefing on the phone to Tunis. Both Faisal and Akram started then the habit of teasing me that I was a workaholic who felt that a minute's rest was a minute wasted.

During one of our trips to Washington to pursue the talks on the American side's home turf, Faisal and I decided that it was time to put our interlocutors to the textual test. At the same time we wanted to force their hand and make them commit to paper issues that had become the subject of endless debate. We sat down and worked out in writing all the points of agreement and all the areas that we felt still needed resolution. They hit the ceiling (which was neither the first nor the last time). Faisal threatened to walk out on the issue of Jerusalem. A crisis developed. I called Tunis. Akram asked, "Did a hint of a smile cross Faisal's face during the meeting?" I replied, "A hint of a semi-smile could be discerned about to appear on his face, but he controlled himself at the last minute and managed to look appropriately tragic." Levity on such issues was not condoned, and facial expressions were the subject of many jokes and evaluations.

During the course of our meetings, it became clear to us that the American side had prepared a preset paradigm for what they thought to be successful and pragmatic negotiations. The components were clear. The Camp David Accords were to be the basis and the ceiling of the talks and the policy of the United States. The motivation was to do what was good for Israel, and peace was good for Israel in spite of itself. Peace could not be achieved without Palestinian participation, as we were the key to Arab participation. But the Palestinians had to be delivered in accordance with Israeli preferences and constraints, some of which were consistent with U.S. interests. In order to allow enough time for a period of adjustment, they would start with what was functional and postpone the difficult issues to a later phase. Our problem with such a reductive paradigm was that it overlooked those essential components necessary for a settlement. The complexity of the conflict with its historical, cultural, and existential dimensions was ignored in favor of the American pragmatic approach. Neither the Orientalist construct (Western stereotyped views of the Arab world), nor the Occidental mind-set was the appropriate apparatus to effect a solution. My constant refrain was "Don't wait till we're proven right to believe us. It might be too late by then. The price could be too high." I sought to create, legitimize, and transmit an authentic Palestinian language, to give voice from within our reality, rather than let others speak on our behalf.

Edward Said, a special friend and a unique intellect, had launched an unrelenting quest and campaign for this assertion of authenticity. He had often pressed upon me and other Palestinians the need to narrate, to make known the Palestinian narrative from within, and to gain it the legitimacy of human identification and recognition. When Edward described me once to the Council on Foreign Relations in New York as the creator and speaker of the "new language" of the Palestinians, I felt that he had bestowed upon me the supreme affirmation—that of validation. Others had done the same since, mainly non-Palestinians, for our cumulative experience had bred a defensiveness that produced a political culture suspicious of innovation, newness, and self-assertion. The recognition of world political figures or prominent members of the media, although gratifying, did not have the impact of the words of women from the refugee camps or men from the villages who often made a point of telling me, "You make us proud."

The Palestinian nation produced the Edward Saids, Mahmoud Darwishes, and Akram Haniyyehs of our culture, poetry, and politics. Each expresses the fusion of creativity and deprivation. When I write I am mindful not only of those three intellects, but of the many who remain unrecognized and unacknowledged. They are the narrators and the narrative.

CHAPTER SIX

———◆•✦•◆———

September 20, 1991, 1:00 A.M. The phone rang. I instantly resented the shrill intrusion into my sleep-induced state of unconsciousness.

"Hello. Who's this? What is it?" I mumbled into the receiver.

"Wake up, Hanan. This is Faisal. Are you with me?"

"For your sake this had better be important. I'm exhausted. I'd just gone to sleep. I hope this isn't another emergency." I had come to expect crisis calls at all times of day and night, mainly from Tunis.

"It is urgent. Are you fully awake yet?"

Used to my lifestyle, Emile got up to make coffee.

"Yes, I am up. I thought you were in London," I answered.

"I'm still in London. But you must get up and get ready to go to Amman. Abu Ammar has agreed that you meet Baker there."

"Wait a minute! I thought we told Baker only yesterday that we weren't going to meet him in Amman."

"I know. There's been a change of plans. Baker, the Egyptian president, Hosni Mubarak, the Jordanian prime minister Taher al-Masri, and even the Russians have launched a campaign to get a Palestinian-American meeting in Jordan. Abu Ammar wants you to go."

"No way! Abu Ammar has been dead-set against this meeting. It will be read as acquiescence to the joint Jordanian-Palestinian delegation idea. Remember how he reacted when we suggested a meeting with the Jordanians? He's still holding out for a separate delegation or one overall Arab delegation."

"He has given his word to Taher al-Masri. They've been on the phone all night. The details are being worked out."

"This is quite risky. We haven't prepared our public opinion. I don't want to be sacrificed as the Jordanian Connection. You know how this can backfire. Why don't you go? You're more protected than I am politically."

"I can't get there in time. The meeting is at 10:00 A.M. Baker has already finished his Jordanian meetings. He'll meet with you and leave directly for the airport."

"I can't get there in time either. The bridge opens only at 8:00. It takes hours to cross. Besides, I don't have a permit. There's no way I can get one in time. Just apologize to Abu Ammar for me. I'm going back to sleep."

I tried to get back to sleep. The phone rang fifteen minutes later. It was Amjad, the code name for our Cyprus contact.

"Akram wants to talk to you."

"Tell him no thank you. I'm not going."

"Hanan, this is Akram. Abu Ammar wants you to go meet Baker in Amman. Taher has been on the phone with him for hours. We've worked things out down to the last detail."

"Akram, I thought that the issue of the Jordanian meeting was linked entirely to getting an American recognition of our right to self-determination. Yesterday, Faisal and I told Baker that we couldn't see him in Amman. Now you want me to go alone!"

"Abu Ammar has given his word. We are in the middle of finalizing the details of your trip. The American consul general will pick you up at 6:00 A.M. and take you to the bridge. The Israelis will open up the bridge for you at 6:30. The American embassy and the Jordanian Prime Ministry have both said they will pick you up officially at the other side of the bridge. Do not, I repeat, *do not* get into any car other than that of the Palestinian ambassador. Tayyeb Abdel-Rahim will pick you up in the official embassy car hoisting a Palestinian flag. The car will be driven straight to the bridge. You get into the back seat on the right side. You will be driven straight to the embassy where you will meet with the officials and the press. The minute-taker will be waiting for you there. Then you will be driven to the hotel where you will meet with Baker.

Following the meeting, you will get into the car and drive straight back to the Palestinian embassy where you will hold a press conference seated on the ambassador's chair with the flag on your left and Abu Ammar's portrait on the wall behind you."

"Hold on! You're going too fast. I still haven't said I was going. First I need a written confirmation from Abu Ammar, and he has to announce this officially."

"Don't worry. It's on its way. Remember also not to hold any official meetings in Jordan. You are there only for the Baker meeting. You should start packing. You don't have much time to get to the bridge."

"I know. Since when have you ever given me enough time for anything. Why should I pack? It should be a one-day trip, or overnight at most."

"Pack enough for at least a week."

"Warm climate, I assume?"

Akram was probably the single most effective force behind the Palestinian participation in the peace process. From the beginning he was privy to all the talks and developments and documents that we participated in or produced, which he shared very sparingly and selectively with the Tunis leadership. Abu Mazen, the Executive Committee member who was the closest to us and most supportive of the peace process, often complained about Akram's excessive secrecy and concealment. Only Abu Ammar had all the information and documents. The rest saw my summaries, or even selections from them. I found out later that Akram was protecting us, for Tunis had always leaked like a sieve, and the opposition was liable to distort our position or quote excerpts out of context to incite against us. He played the buffer, but also knew that information was power, and his power grew.

A member of Fateh's Revolutionary Council, of the *intifada* committee, of the Occupied Territories Committee, and special adviser to Chairman Arafat—Akram was a man of many roles. Actually, I found out many of his titles and official positions from the Americans when I went to negotiate a U.S. visa for him. Unobtrusive, secretive, intensely suspicious of the spotlight, for years he was our political interlocutor (and interpreter) with the PLO in Tunis. He was able to bridge both worlds, the "inside" and the "outside," but his deportation had turned him into a creature of neither. The PLO viewed him as one of us, treating him often with suspicion and resentment for his special relations with us and for having gained Abu Ammar's ear and confidence. The "inside" automatically treated him as one of them since he was Tunis-based and held such an important position. His family and constituency were in the Occupied Territories (although a 1948 refugee), but his forced exile and alienation placed him alone in Tunis.

When he was in Ramallah and Jerusalem, I had recognized and appreciated the human being and the creative writer beneath the mask of the politician. Before Akram and I had even met in the late 1970s, I had admired his writing and had written analytical reviews of and translated his short stories. His work conveyed a compelling human experience with deceptive simplicity and aesthetic economy. When Israeli authorities deported him in late 1986, it was not only existentially and emotionally traumatic for him, but it also allowed the politician to entirely take over and supersede the writer within. We developed a friendship and trust that went beyond politics.

When Akram joined the Washington talks as part of the "invisible" PLO team and member of the Leadership Committee, a polarization was created that had Nabil Shaʾth on one side and Akram on the other. Most of us turned to Akram although Nabil was supposed to be in charge. Politically perceptive and cautious, a stickler for details (which used to drive Abu Mazen crazy), and reliable in the accuracy of his information and analysis, he was the foil to Nabil's excessive optimism and love of the spotlight. One critic described him as a spider, lurking in its dark corner, spinning webs of intrigue, and not missing a move. Capable of quickly and perceptively grasping the historic opportunity and identifying the first step, of delineating broad strategy outlines and defining its minutest component, of taking bold risks and exercising obsessive caution, he was an enigma to most. Some hated him, others feared him, most respected him.

I knew that the Palestine National Council would be meeting shortly, most probably in Algiers. Inasmuch as it was illegal for us to talk to the PLO, it was also illegal for us to attend any PNC meetings. A stiff jail sentence awaited those who dared to violate the Israeli ban. All our contacts were done in secret, and the trips that Faisal and I had taken to Tunis were undercover journeys through circuitous routes, with no evidence like visas or entry-exit stamps on our Jordanian passports.

Emile and I started a packing frenzy. Amjad kept calling every few minutes to check up on our progress, even during my shower. I told him that if he kept calling I would never make it in time. While I got ready, Emile pressed a few outfits and packed a suitcase haphazardly following my hasty directions. In the meantime, Abu Ammar called. He also faxed me written instructions (drafted by Akram, I was sure) that read like a military decree. Molly Williamson assured me she would pick me up around 5:30 A.M. I kissed Emile and the sleepy girls good-bye, promising to be back anywhere from a day to a week later.

At 5:30 Molly arrived wearing bright white freshly pressed jeans and spotless sneakers. We got into the heavy bulletproof consulate car, and drove off into the gentle dawn drizzle of the first autumn rain. The winding road to Jericho was wrapped in a misty haze. The bridge across the Jordan was deserted with the exception of one military vehicle quietly waiting at the main checkpoint. The Israeli bridge commander met us there and escorted us to the waiting lounge. Since I did not have the required permit, he stamped my Israeli travel document with an exit stamp. Molly and the commander drove me to the actual wooden bridge, where I left the car and walked halfway across to meet Tayyeb (our ambassador), who was waiting for me with the Jordanian commander at the halfway point. This is life imitating art, I thought to myself. Perhaps I dreamed myself into a Cold War film. There was too much drama and suppressed tension. How, and when, would I be able to return?

Everything went according to script, with three exceptions. The first appeared to be a technical snag that would prove to be of major political import. The minute-taker I was supposed to take with me turned out to be a PLO employee. Dennis Ross asked me not to bring her, as the secretary of state would not meet with PLO people—even secretaries. I said that if I had wanted to bring the PLO into the meeting, it would be through the front door, and at the highest levels. My condition, though, was that the American side would provide me with a copy of their minutes. It was already a sensitive enough meeting and I needed an accurate record of it. They agreed.

The second appeared to be of major political significance but turned out to be harmless. Baker began the meeting by conveying to me greetings from Queen Noor of Jordan and extending an invitation to meet with her later that day. While I actually did want to see Queen Noor, I knew that I could not afford the political implications. Fortunately, I was supposed to leave the country immediately after the press conference, so I took a rain check although I did not feel comfortable about it. Later, Baker was quite indignant. "I can't believe you came to Jordan and left without meeting one single Jordanian official!" I later saw Queen Noor on several occasions, in Amman and the United States, and enjoyed a delightfully informal candlelight dinner with her and King Hussein—an attractive royal couple with dignity, charm, and foresight.

The third exception had to do with the press. Throughout my public work, I had maintained excellent relations with members of the media based on honesty and mutual respect. I had been given a fair hearing, and got along with the press at both the personal and professional level. This was the first exception. As the press were about to come in for the standard photo opportunity, Baker turned to me and asked me for a favor. "Could you please not mention the PLO when the press people come in. At your press conference, you can say whatever you want, and you would anyway. But while we are seeing them together, it would be very awkward for me if you talked about the PLO." I replied that I was not in the habit of lying or taking instructions about my public statements from anybody. The situation appeared deadlocked. We finally found an honest compromise: the photo op would remain just that, a silent session for the visual media. If they asked any questions, we would refer them to the press conference to be held at the end of the meeting. Out of consideration for Baker, and respect for the reporters, I agreed that this would be the best solution. When they came in and started asking questions, both Baker and I gave them the agreed-upon response. They all took it graciously except for one CNN reporter who insisted on asking me personally whether I was sent by the PLO and did I bring a message from Arafat. When I repeated my statement, he looked at me venomously and said with contempt, "So much for Palestinian honesty and courage." That was the first time I was genuinely hurt. Baker noticed. He later apologized for putting me in such a situation and urged me not to take that particular reporter's insensitivity personally. I have had occasion to remember Baker's advice, every time the same reporter tried to pull a similar trick.

Back in Amman, the Baker meeting was proceeding. Of all three volumes of minutes of the U.S. meetings, this was the only meeting whose minutes were recorded by the American side. Reviewing them, I found the dominant themes to be the recurring issues of Palestinian self-determination, Israeli settlements, Palestinian human rights, and Jerusalem. Baker handed me the latest version of the Letter of Assurance—absolutely nonnegotiable. We ended up spending four more sessions on it. What the world (and certainly Shamir) never knew was that we discussed the upcoming PNC meeting. I told Baker that Faisal and I were on standby and that the chairman may want us to go and make the case for peace at that session. He asked for two things: first, that we would not make a media event of it, and second that we would not circulate the LOA draft there because it would leak to the press and create problems with Israel. I agreed that we would present a synopsis, but would not distribute copies. I assured him that he had nothing to worry about with the media because we had planned to go to Algiers secretly. The American minutes reflected this conversation.

Following the meeting, I held the famous press conference in which I announced that I had given Baker a message from Chairman Arafat, and that the chairman had asked me to hold the Amman meeting. As soon as the conference was over, I was whisked off to the airport. Five hours later, I found myself in London answering reporters' questions at Heathrow Airport. Somebody picked me up and deposited me at the Gloucester Hotel where Faisal, his wife, Najat, and our PLO representative in London, Afif Safieh, were waiting for me. A whole new episode of cloak-and-dagger and tug-of-war politics was under way.

First, I discovered that most of the clothes I had asked Emile to pack were light summer clothes. I was prepared for warm climates—it was still balmy at home. London was freezing. Faisal got his cousin Saʾida Dalloul to take us shopping. For a while, I felt like a schoolgirl on vacation—a rare and brief moment until somebody would recognize me at Harrods or Selfridges and I would be brought back to an uncertain reality. We were on call, waiting for the convening of the Palestine National Council, while conducting negotiations by phone with Washington. Baker had invited us to meet with him in Washington immediately following the PNC meeting, and I was working on LOA amendments while writing a political analysis for Tunis. The Israeli press discovered our hotel and were calling every day to verify our whereabouts. It felt as if the whole world had. We also spent quite a lot of time with the wealthy Palestinian expatriates in England who maintained their ties to the PLO and the Palestinian national movement, in different capacities at various times. They were supportive of the peace process and wanted the PLO to take a positive decision to participate. Those, however, who had felt that the PLO did them and the Palestinian people a disservice in its stance during the Gulf crisis were extremely critical of the PLO leadership.

Faisal and I were in a state of anticipation and apprehension. To meet with the PNC and present the case for peace was challenging and exciting. To take on a historical responsibility of this magnitude was sufficient cause for dread and trepidation. By then the PLO was no longer that unknown factor, the forbidden fruit out there wrapped in sheaths of mystery and danger, whose knowledge could lead to a fall from grace into exile or prison. We had been there before. Cloaked in secrecy and anonymity, our earlier visits to Tunis were secret adventures. Actually, we had been smuggled into Tunis as a bizarre kind of human contraband, just five months earlier, in the spring of 1991.

• • •

"You must get to Paris or to London," declared the male voice over the phone. "The pope and the cardinals are very pleased with your work and would like to see you in the next few days."

Amjad managed to sound both mysterious and ridiculous at the same time. His overdeveloped security sense led him to adopt the most transparent codes that I was sure must have entertained the Israeli telephone censors enormously.

"I appreciate their blessings!" I responded facetiously. "However, I still need an official invitation to show to the Israeli security officers at Ben Gurion Airport. I also need the appropriate visas and arrangements."

"Don't worry. I will fax you an invitation to an academic conference. Get the visa for the first station and we'll do the rest." The plot thickens, I thought.

I probably looked as guilty as I felt when two days later the Israeli airport security stopped me for a thorough questioning and search. The routine of taking my luggage apart and asking the most intimate and detailed questions took all of two hours, at the end of which I even convinced myself that I was going to Paris for a harmless meeting with the editorial board of a real journal.

At Charles de Gaulle Airport, I was met by two French security officers from the Foreign Ministry. With them came Ahmad in a raincoat, sent by the Palestinian mission in Paris. I was taken out of the line and outside the airport, and driven at breakneck speed across Paris to Orly Airport. All my documents were somehow "correct" and ready. Within minutes, I found myself in the first row of an already full plane heading for Tunis.

As soon as we landed, a small white minibus drove straight up to the runway and stopped at the bottom of the mobile stairway. Two men climbed up the stairs, boarded the plane, came straight to me and said, *"Al-hamdillah ʾa salameh, ukht Hanan."* (Thank God for your safe arrival, sister Hanan.) They escorted me to Abu Ammar.

Faisal and Akram got up as soon as I entered the room. (Faisal had preceded me to Tunis by a similarly mysterious route.) Around one dozen people were having lunch with Abu Ammar, seated around a large wooden table. After a round of hugs and kisses, I suddenly felt overwhelmed. Here I was with the Palestinian leadership in exile, people we had been forbidden to see or acknowledge, who were the guardians of our national cause and identity. Here I was, face-to-face with members of the Executive Committee, our very own cabinet, and they were warm and human and welcoming.

On the wall there was a mural of Jerusalem, and in another part of the room there was a television tuned to CNN, which was always on mute unless there was breaking news. Those of us who smoked would periodically excuse ourselves to an adjacent "smoking room," because Abu Ammar is very health-conscious and does not tolerate smoke. He also eats very carefully and sparingly, and the food that is specially prepared for him I found monotonous and bland. He does not eat much meat, and the vegetables are always steamed, never fried. The one constant indulgence he allows himself is honey in his tea. I would tell him whenever I came to meet with him in Tunis that the food was atrocious. He would always insist that I sit beside him at meals, and would choose specific items of food to share, making sure his guests got the best morsels or larger-sized portions. Typically he would be the one to ladle out the soup. I observed on many occasions how he used food to establish contact with someone. The chairman and I developed a ritual of sharing the custard that he habitually served after dinner. We would work away at the custard, from our respective sides of a single plate.

The afternoon lunch ended at 4:30 P.M. Akram and Faisal took me to my secret residence, my second home in Tunis during my visits for the next two years. It was the house of Salwa and Hisham Mustafa and their two lovely daughters, Badr (full moon) and Nada (dew). I had known Salwa and Hisham for some time, in the course of the numerous dialogue meetings and conferences in which we had participated. Both worked in Abu Mazen's office, having arrived in Tunis via Paris and Beirut as members of the Palestinian revolution. Our friendship was not only instantaneous, but of that rare durable quality often described unimaginatively as "a meeting of the souls." Salwa, a Tunisian woman who had embraced Palestine as her cause and the core of her being, literally radiated energy and passion. Daring, outspoken, and unrelenting, she had that unique blend of searing honesty and touching compassion. Her deep dark eyes and shiny black hair were those of a thoroughbred Arabian mare, as were her dignity and pride. The issues of gender, peace, and democracy were her triple energy source, always sparkling and tingling with electric conviction. I found in her a true sister and in her home a warm haven. She belonged to and in Palestine.

From Salwa's home I was driven to the chairman's home in Yaghurta. His intense eyes always sent signals of recognition and concealment. I know who you are, I acknowledge your role and importance, but I also know so much more that I won't reveal—at least not yet, they seemed to say. Somewhere at the back of his mind, there was always that larger map, and as you spoke he was busy placing you appropriately in that greater scheme of things. But you, nevertheless, held his complete and undivided attention. In all the years that I had known him, he was never condescending or insulting. He treated me with a mixture of respect and affection, devoid of any sense of patronage or affectation. I also knew that I served a purpose in that grand plan, and that he was not beyond manipulation or exploitation as required. But I was certain that he would never set out to cause me deliberate harm. After witnessing a particularly painful scene in which he deliberately tore apart one of his advisers and robbed him of his dignity in front of his peers, I told him frankly, "If you ever do that to me, I will walk out and you'll never see me again." He smiled. "I know who has self-respect and who doesn't," he said. I took him at his word. He never broke it.

"What's the agenda?" I asked Akram as we sat at the table waiting for the Executive Committee meeting to begin. He smiled.

"It's in his head," he said, nodding toward Abu Ammar, who was sitting at his desk facing the rest of us, but deeply engrossed in a pile of documents before him. In person he is smaller and thinner than he appears on television, and he is balding. His understated appearance belies the enormity of influence he has over his people, and the effect he has had on history at large. Only his intense, penetrating eyes reflect his unwavering strength and commitment. And the ever-present traditional kufiyya, the Palestinian scarf, which Abu Ammar wears draped about his chest in the shape of the map of Palestine.

"When do we start the meeting?" I persisted.

"When he decides it's time."

"Then let's start reviewing the minutes while we're waiting."

Sighing patiently at my naïveté, Akram whispered. "There are no minutes except for the notes that he keeps in his little notebook. And those are selective. You're not attending a meeting of the university senate or council, you know."

I was shocked. Coming from the orderly and rarefied atmosphere of academia, I wasn't adequately prepared for impromptu politics. More surprises were in store. The meeting was supposed to start at 8:00 P.M. At 9:00, people were still wandering in, while Abu Ammar was still going through the faxes and memoranda that his assistants were placing in front of him at regular intervals. He finally looked up, commented on the laxity of the latecomers, and began the meeting.

"We are all pleased to welcome here tonight our sister Hanan and our brother Abu al-Abed [Faisal] who came here tonight to brief us in person on the meetings with Baker and to give us their assessment as to where the Americans are heading with the talks. But first I want to tell you about my very successful trip to Yemen on a conciliation and mediation mission . . ." For the next two hours, Abu Ammar took us on a long journey through Yemen, the Sudan, and the past. The Beirut days and the Israeli invasion of Lebanon were prominent in the presentation, which concluded with a thorough survey of all the American promises, both kept and broken, and the unfortunate history of the U.S.-PLO dialogue. He often turned to a bald, bespectacled quiet man for verification of his narrative. His name, I found out later, was Muhsen Ibrahim, a Lebanese who was one of the chairman's closest allies, privy to all his secrets and welcome at all meetings. Muhsen had a twinkle of humor in his eyes and, while nodding in agreement with Abu Ammar, he would never let an opportunity pass without making a clipped and funny comment that revealed a critical ironic distance even from his own account.

Around midnight, we were asked to give our account. We fell naturally into our roles: Faisal began with an overall presentation; I was asked to supply the details. Then Faisal and I attempted a comprehensive evaluation and presentation of options, with all the positive and negative implications and consequences. From 1:30 to 3:00 A.M. we heard political speeches from the committee members, and Abu Ammar adjourned the meeting at 3:30 and we went to our respective homes.

• • •

So there we were in London, five months after that secret Tunis meeting, and Faisal and I were facing the prospect of another meeting—but this time with the entire Palestine National Council in Algiers. The phone call came. We were summoned, and were expected to be in Algiers by the twenty-seventh of September. The British Foreign Office was informed and started with the special preparations. Faisal and I then made reservations on several different airlines to various European destinations. Najat was supposed to keep up signs of occupancy in Faisal's hotel room, sleeping in both beds and making phone calls in Faisal's name. Saʾida was supposed to crumple up my bed and use my phone to keep a record of occupancy. On the morning of the twenty-seventh, someone from the office smuggled out two overnight bags and hid them in the trunk of a car parked a block away from the hotel. Faisal and I sauntered nonchalantly through the lobby, which was riddled with reporters, Mossad agents, and representatives of a variety of international intelligence services. We drove around London making several stops on the way, and finally got to the airport.

I stood in one line, Faisal in another. At the last minute we shifted to a third and picked up tickets to Paris. As usual, we were the last to embark and the first to get off the plane in Paris. Our tickets to Algiers were ready, and no one asked us for visas or identity verification. We sat in the first row. As soon as the plane landed, Algerian intelligence officers boarded the plane, escorted us out, and deposited us in government cars with blackened windows. In another replay of a by now familiar thriller, we were surreptitiously driven to a secret destination: the official government guest house for state visitors, a magnificent and gigantic structure dramatically located on top of a cliff with a breathtaking view. It was fully staffed, but the only guests were Faisal, myself, and Akram, with an official foreign ministry escort. After a quick dinner, we were spirited off to another location where we held a short meeting with Abu Ammar, who had preceded us. We were told we would address the Political Committee.

From the entrance, the conference grounds looked deserted, probably because they were off-limits to the press. In addition to the Algerian officers, a group of Palestinian security personnel surrounded us and propelled us through the dark grounds and long hallways until we suddenly found ourselves in an enormous meeting room, brightly lit and packed with hundreds of people, their faces turned to us. Suddenly, everybody stood up and started clapping. Abu Ammar advanced toward us, his arms outstretched, his eyes sparkling, and his face beaming. Tearfully, we embraced those members of the leadership sitting in the front rows of the auditorium, and climbed the steps to take our seats at the table onstage. I was asked to speak first.

I walked slowly to the podium. A hush descended on the room. The transition took interminable seconds. During that infinite moment, flowers blossomed over many graves in Palestine. I looked toward the women and willed them to be my allies. I looked at the men and willed them to join us. A life force swelled from their midst and reached out to me as I began to speak.

My voice seemed to take on a life of its own. At no moment in our history was the symbiotic relationship between internal healing and external reconciliation more apparent. Perhaps I was agitating, inciting, for peace—my words committed to the active not the passive voice: to intrude, confront, intervene, engage, challenge, participate, present our case, and shape our destiny. I incited the women and challenged the men. A genuine leadership does not disempower half its people, and real women do not accept exclusion and internal alienation. A genuine leadership draws its legitimacy from the people, and the people have the right to know and to participate. A healthy and confident nation does not allow the confiscation of its voice and will, and will not be absent from the assembly of nations.

But I could not publicly lay claim to a speech that was officially denied as having occurred. One newspaper called it the speech that I would have made had I been there. We were forced to render invisible a remarkable station on our journey, and to deny the very words that sought to safeguard the integrity of our utterance, whose whole purpose was to end the epoch of denial and usher in one of recognition. To give credence to our message, we had to deliver it in secret as the contraband merchandise of a forbidden people.

A restricted meeting followed. Abu Ammar, Mahmoud Darwish, Muhsen Ibrahim, Akram, and a few others brought us secretly to an informal session. We applauded Abu Ammar's speech. "The people created the PLO to serve them and protect their interests. If forced to choose between the organization and the people, we'll choose the people. Even if it is destroyed, if there's a need the Palestinian people will create another PLO the way they did this one," he had said. We then discussed the role of the leadership. "To protect and defend people's lives, not to sacrifice them," I said. They agreed. "Then allow us to grieve for our dead, not just to glorify them. When mothers ululate at the martyrdom of their children, they do so in heartbreak and sorrow. Heroism cannot take the place of a lost life." They agreed too. Mahmoud Darwish was close to tears. We spoke the same language.

Next morning, Faisal and I were placed on a plane to Rome. It appeared that we had been spotted at the Paris airport the day before, and Agence France Press had released a wire service report that excited the interest of hundreds of reporters who joined the game of hide-and-seek. The transit in Rome was supposed to be very brief, but as usual the plane was delayed for two hours. We went to the counter to check on the new plans and found ourselves surrounded by a large group of Japanese reporters who were quite worked up at having located the prize. We finally convinced them to agree that they actually had not seen us—in the interest of peace. They acquiesced, and we finally took off for London. The British Foreign Office officials were very discreet, and they got us to the hotel late at night and none the worse for wear. We walked in calmly, as though we had never left. Our dream journey was already relegated to that realm of proscribed experience where both knowledge and admission were dangerous.

As soon as I walked into the room, the phone rang. Akram wanted to make sure that we had arrived safely. The PNC was still meeting, and the drafting committee was preparing the text of the resolution. "You made a tremendous impact," Akram said. "Faisal's and your appearance and speeches are the talk of the council. We're sure that the vote will be positive." He promised to call the moment the vote came out and to fax us the text of the resolution. As soon as I hung up, the phone rang again. It was Dan Kurtzer inquiring whether the results were out. "The secretary is very anxious. He wants to know as soon as possible." I promised to let him know. The phone rang again and did not stop for the next week. The press were on the scent. Word was out also that we were going to head for Washington for the next meeting with Baker. But the explosion came when accounts of our Algiers trip began to leak. Shamir hit the ceiling and announced that Faisal and I were to be arrested and tried upon our return, and that the Israeli authorities had started their investigations looking for incriminating evidence. Faisal and I made sure that there were no ticket coupons, luggage tags, matchboxes, or any other form of proof. No pictures or recordings were available, and I doubted that the Israeli police would find any PNC members willing to testify against us.

"The situation is very critical, Hanan. The secretary is trying to keep things under control. He's called Shamir and asked him not to put you and Faisal on trial." Dennis Ross was anxious to contain the explosion.

"There is no evidence whatsoever. Besides, the whole law is unjust and illegal. Why should the Israelis prosecute us for seeing our own leadership or for attending a meeting of our parliament?" I was indignant.

"We're not here to debate the principle. You know the conditions. Besides, I thought that it wasn't supposed to be a media event."

"It wasn't. And we're sick of all these conditions. Maybe it's time to call Shamir's bluff. Let him arrest us and put us on trial."

"That would be very unwise. We're almost there with the conference. October is the month. Do you know what your arrest would do to the whole thing? You must not get back until we're sure that you won't be arrested. Shamir still would not commit himself in spite of all our efforts."

"Of course we're going to get back. Shamir isn't going to make us accept a self-imposed exile. But that's not an urgent issue yet. We will go back after our meeting in Washington, which is coming up in a few days."

"That's another thing I wanted to talk to you about. We don't think it's wise to have you come to Washington just yet. The issue is still too hot."

"What do you mean, not wise and too hot? That sounds like a flimsy excuse to me. Obviously Shamir got to you. Baker had officially invited us to meet with him in Washington, and we accepted. We don't see any reason to change our plans."

"Everybody knows you went to the PNC meeting. How can we receive you in Washington immediately afterward? We need an intervening event."

"Are you telling me we need decontamination? Baker knew that we were going to the meeting before he invited us. He cannot de-invite us now. It's a clear case of submission to Israeli blackmail. If Shamir intimidates you, he doesn't intimidate us. Maybe the best intervening event would be for us to go home and stand trial. We will turn it into a political trial; we have a good case, and we'll blow the whole thing wide open."

"You can't do that. It will have serious implications for us. Baker doesn't lie, and the whole issue of your trip must not become a public case."

"We don't lie, either. We discussed the PNC meeting in Amman, and I have the official U.S. minutes to prove that."

"Have you told the press?"

"No I haven't, and I promised I wouldn't. But when asked about the PNC meeting my response has consistently been that I won't tell the press what I wouldn't reveal to the Israeli interrogator. But if you cancel or delay the Washington meeting, then you would have gone back on your word. If you allow Shamir to call the shots on such issues, he would do that throughout the process. The tail must not continue to wag the dog."

"You're being very harsh. We're just trying to protect the peace process."

"And we're trying to get it off to a right start. As far as we're concerned, we have two options: either we go home and face trial, or we go to Washington for the meeting."

"There's a third option. Stay in London for a while, until we're sure you can go home."

"This would be self-banishment. We have the right to go home."

"At the right time. We'll be going out to the region mid-October. We'll have the meeting in Jerusalem."

"Give Baker this message from us: if you give in to the Israelis and go back on the Washington meeting, there'll be no meeting in Jerusalem."

• • •

"She actually said that to Ross?" Akram asked as Faisal gave him an account of the conversation.

"And more." Faisal was rather pleased with my mischief making. "You know how Hanan can be when challenged. She doesn't mince words. She is right, you know."

"And you support her in this ultimatum?"

"Yes, I do."

Both Faisal and Akram supported me, even when the State Department unleashed a multipronged persuasion campaign using all their contacts and intermediaries—Egyptian, Jordanian, Palestinian, and generally international. "The pressure's on?" I asked Dennis and Dan. "You know it, and it's legitimate," they answered. By now we were both familiar with each other's game. Abu Ammar and the Executive Committee were bombarded with "friendly calls" from "friendly governments" and individuals giving them "friendly advice" about how to and how not to speak to the Americans. "Those people from the 'inside' don't know how to behave diplomatically." Abu Ammar relished the moment: "She's an academic and not a politician, and you know how academics are." He often used this expression, whether as an excuse or as a form of disparagement. It was a convenient response to the frequent admonishment, "You must teach your people how to behave." We held firm, and behaved exactly as people should behave, with honesty and self-respect.

It was not just a question of principle or dignity; it was more of an ominous indication of a pattern of behavior that we had detected from the beginning of our American talks, and that did not bode well for future relations or the peace process. The Israelis, particularly Shamir, were stubborn, intransigent, tough, and uncompromising hard-liners; they must be indulged, pampered, cajoled, and bribed. The Palestinians were the weaker side; they must be bullied, pressured, persuaded, and sometimes humored into acquiescence. The Israelis drive a tough bargain and must be paid and accommodated. The Palestinians can be appeased and must be complimented while made to swallow the sugarcoated bitter pill. Hence the State Department's Orientalist "textbook" (which Molly Williamson applied literally and unimaginatively) often backfired with people like us. I had no patience with the formulae "saving face, preserving dignity, maintaining pride and honor, and keeping up appearances" if they meant losing the land, negating our rights, sustaining the shame and brutality of the occupation, and subverting the substance of our reality. We wanted to save lives, not to be patronized into submission. We did not want to be pacified with a kind word; the hard truth would have been kinder. But when it came to Israel, I often wondered if the United States would ever be free to shape its own policies. In another of my typically so-called rude conversations later on in Washington, I asked Dennis Ross and Ed Djerejian: "We're under occupation and we haven't surrendered our will; what's your excuse for surrendering yours?"

The London limbo dragged on. Baker was determined to prevent our return to Jerusalem to face a public political trial, which would embarrass him and hurt the peace process, and was equally determined to avoid the confrontation with the Israelis that would ensue if he met with us in Washington. Shamir's public pronouncements became increasingly portentous and menacing, depicting Faisal and myself as terrorists and security threats who must bear the full brunt of the punitive measures provided by Israeli law for our transgressions. Somehow, Faisal and I found it difficult to suit the image to reality, being a most unlikely pair of outlaws. The humor of the situation was not lost on us; if we were to be so severely punished for the heinous crime of actively seeking peace, what would be our punishment should we actually succeed?

My daily phone calls home, though, brought to me the increasing anxiety of Amal and Zeina, who still maintained the belief of children in their mother's sanctity and inviolability.

"Don't let Shamir scare you. He wouldn't dare touch you. I won't let him. You're my mother, how dare he say he'll arrest you?" Zeina's moral indignation and sense of bravado also incorporated an unquestioning and unquestionable proprietorship.

"Take care, Mumsy, and don't come home until you're sure it's safe." Amal's concern reflected her constant habit of careful reasoning and responsible assessment before every move.

"Don't listen to her!" Zeina interjected on the extension line. "Shamir won't get away with it. He's a nasty old man and I won't let him put my mother in jail."

"Don't be childish, Zeina," Amal admonished. "How can you stop him? He's nasty and mean and has done worse things and gotten away with them. You don't scare him. It's all right if you wait awhile to make sure it's safe, Mumsy. What does ʿAmmo Faisal say? Did you check with a lawyer?"

"Please don't worry about me," I pleaded, trying to reassure them. "I'll be careful, but I also want you to take care of yourselves in my absence. Shamir doesn't scare me, Zeina, but Amal is also right; there's no need to take unnecessary risks. But I do miss you two very much, and I want to get back to be with you as soon as possible. Wherever I am and whatever I do, I always think of you, and I love you very much."

"We miss you too, Mumsy. Take care of yourself, don't work too hard, don't stay up too late, and don't spend too much. I love you." Amal's list of don'ts was a constant throughout my travels. So was her gentle love.

"I love you, Mama," Zeina said. "Don't worry about spending too much! Buy us nice things, but hurry back."

My hostages to fortune. Wherever I go I carry their absence with me, heavier than any luggage, more painful than any unkind word, more forbidding than any threat. Amal, with her flowing hair and imagination, who writes poetry and plays the piano with vision and feeling, astounds and touches me with her gentle child/woman creative variations. Bouncy, cuddly, fearless Zeina, with curly hair and dimples, challenges both me and the world with her daring vulnerability. Motherhood is such a willful and willing act of subjugation that it takes my breath away at times. How else could such unhampered and unconditional loving and giving exist? Our fear for them makes us brave, and their vulnerability is our coward-ice. When they hurt we suffer beyond reason, and their joy is our elation. I have experienced and delighted in the full spectrum of parental idiocy, with its self-fulfillment and self-denial, and reveled in its vagaries with total abandon, committing all the sacrifices and follies that I used to mock in others who belonged to this exclusive universal club.

My seven-year peregrinations in search of peace have transformed the experience of parenthood; it has become a stroboscopic relationship with intense flashes interspersed with darkness rendered even blacker by the contrast. And in those intermissions my mind conjured up images, both of the past and the future, of such depth and sharpness as to challenge the reality of the present. I saw Amal as a baby "nicing" me (a verb of her own creation), softly stroking my cheek before going to sleep. I saw Zeina lay her head on my lap asking me to "nice" her hair as her way of going to sleep. I saw each one of them wrapping herself in my frayed wool peach robe, older than both of them, warmer than any heater, more comforting than any word of solace. I saw myself on every trip home wearing the peach robe or huddled under it with one or both of the girls, as it absorbed and transmitted the scent of family. I saw Emile, husband and father, secure in his love (both given and received), and at peace in his spirit, hence capable of a generosity and warmth that only the strong can afford. Where else would I obtain the fortitude and strength to endure and to persist in a quest that promised more deprivation than gratification? Without inner peace, is there any peace out there waiting to be captured? Without the "power base" that Emile, Amal, and Zeina formed to sustain my efforts and buttress my will would I have dared and endured?

· · ·

I went home from London on the sixth of October, determined to spend my birthday with my family, though not certain I would be allowed to. Emile and our good friend Leah were waiting at the airport; so were scores of right-wing Israelis who wanted to drive home a different message. Leah and Emile, as well as the Israeli police, were certain that Faisal and I could not pass through the crowd unharmed. As the shouts and threats increased in volume and menace, the police stepped up their vigilance. They surrounded us and hurried us through back doors and passages and into a waiting police van, but not before they handed us our summonses to appear the following day before security officials for interrogation and to respond to several charges already presented against us. We drove to a side road and transferred to Faisal's waiting car. As we took off, we noticed two cars in hot pursuit, but soon discovered that they contained members of the press—evidently more perceptive and persistent than extremist Israelis. We drove home with the realization that we had had two invitations we couldn't refuse: one for the following day to the division of serious crimes at Israel's police headquarters, and the other for two days later to meet with Baker in Washington. Criminals or peacemakers, Faisal and I knew that neither course was easy.

The next day, and amidst elaborate security precautions, we were driven to Petah Tikvaa, a suburb of Tel Aviv, to respond to charges whose nature we still did not know. As we drew near, the by now familiar sight and sound of Israeli settlers, Kach movement members (an extremist Israeli group later to be banned after the Hebron massacre of February 1994) and other such extremists assailed us. The Peace Now movement had also sent a group of its young members to counterdemonstrate. Police officers and the border police added to the strange medley. We got out of the car right in their midst, but managed to get safely to the building through two security cordons that blocked out pretty much everything except for some creative invective expressions—mainly borrowed from the Arabic, the Hebrew language being rather impoverished in that field. As it turned out, abusive language was not the only thing to break through and reach us.

We were taken up under police escort to the second floor where each was placed in a separate interrogation room. Faisal and I had agreed with our lawyers that we would respond to all questions with one answer only: "I have not broken the law, and I maintain my right not to answer any questions." From the outset, I warned my interrogator (who was of Iraqi origin) that this would probably be the most boring interrogation session of his career. He recited his questions; I reiterated my answer.

I discovered that at least four charges had been pressed by the notorious Elyakim Haʾetzni, an extreme right-wing politician, then a member of the Knesset from Hatihya, and another settler from the Gaza Strip settlement of Gush Katif. The alleged violations included contacts with a hostile and terrorist organization (the PLO), carrying messages to and from that organization to and from U.S. Secretary of State Baker (I wondered if they would detain him too), and threatening the security of the State of Israel (a recurring charge, reminiscent of my Christmas 1973 trial). I must admit I found it difficult to keep a straight face. The hyperbole was so preposterous as to deprive our little drama of any real meaning, let alone an illusion of reality. After inspecting my travel document with its colorful variety of international visas, my interrogator embarked on a long ironic lament of his own sad fate. As much as he longed to travel, he could not afford it on his meager salary, especially as he still had three children in school. After dutifully inquiring about their ages, interests, and academic specializations, I tried to comfort him by reassuring him that once they're out of school and gainfully employed, and true to long and honored Eastern custom, they were certain to treat him and his wife to a nice long vacation in foreign and exotic lands—probably even New York. Our bizarre interchange was rudely interrupted by a loud commotion in the hallway and the sudden entry of two bearded men armed with machine guns. During that split second I found time to wonder at the realistic disguises used by the Shin Bet, the Israeli secret service. Almost simultaneously, the horror of recognition hit me right in the stomach: these were the Kach thugs who constantly appeared on Israeli television either threatening Palestinians with doom, or having just attempted to carry out that threat. As I made eye contact with one of them, I jumped out of my chair, up against the wall, trying to get outside his immediate line of fire. He hesitated for a fraction of a second, and I could tell that he had expected to find Faisal, and was thrown to discover me instead. All hell broke loose. Emile and Tamar Peleg (who had replaced Leah as my lawyer for the occasion) had recognized the two men in the hallway and immediately sounded the alarm. My husband and lawyer were forbidden entry, while the would-be assassins stood before me fully armed, having made their way through police and border guard security cordons, an electronic gate, up two flights of stairs, and into the interrogation rooms of the maximum security police headquarters, division of serious crimes.

"What are they doing here?" I asked my interrogator.

"Don't be afraid. They're here for questioning," he answered.

"Fully armed?"

"They're taking them away." He stated the obvious as other police officers escorted the two outside.

"I hope they detain them or at least disarm them." I was thinking ahead.

They did not. As Faisal and I walked out to the parking lot flanked by police officers, lawyers, husband, and security personnel, our two Kach avengers attempted to break through, still brandishing their weapons. Jostled, pushed, and shoved, we were bundled into the car and we maneuvered our way among the spit and jeers of the crowd.

• • •

Two days later, we were on a plane heading for Washington to keep our next assignation. Even inside opposition had issued leaflets denouncing us and the Baker meetings. Both Hamas (the Islamic Resistance Movement) and the PFLP had described us as American agents and traitors and our preliminary peace talks as capitulation and a sellout. The Political Committee had disintegrated, torn apart on the issue of the proposed peace talks. The People's Party had refused to participate in the Baker meetings although they were kept fully informed of all developments. The PFLP came out solidly against, and were vocal in their opposition. The Democratic Front was in the middle of a painful split between the Nayef Hawatmeh and the Yasser Abd-Rabbo camps—the former opposed to the talks while the latter in favor (subsequently forming the Palestinian Democratic Alliance—FIDA). That left the largest faction, Fateh, and the independents—neither being a monolithic group or unanimous on the issue. Faisal and I felt vulnerable and exposed. We were negotiating with the Americans, trying to coordinate with the Europeans, maintaining talks with the different political factions, mobilizing public opinion, working with the PLO leadership in Tunis, and trying to get an Arab coordinating effort started.

Faisal often repeated his conviction that history would never forgive us if we abandoned or relinquished our rights in the process; but equally it would not forgive us if we saw a historical opportunity and failed to grasp it. We both knew that we would be blamed for any failure or pain, and that the credit, if we succeeded, would go elsewhere. Nevertheless we both consciously decided to take up the challenge and the risk. The only hope for peace lay in getting the PLO on board, to gain for them recognition, and ultimately to get them to negotiate directly and officially. We resisted every attempt to create an alternative leadership to replace the PLO, turning down many offers, some very tempting. It later turned out that we had many allies in this endeavor, some wittingly and others inadvertently.

Our own Palestinian opposition weakened the delegation's standing and its negotiating position. The Israeli government undermined us by maintaining a hard-line position and an entrenched delegation in the Washington negotiations; the Israeli military as a matter of policy eroded our popular support by stepping up its repressive measures in the Occupied Territories while the politicians offered human rights as a bargaining chip in the negotiations, something that should have been a given. Increased Israeli settlement activities struck at the very integrity and credibility of the process. And the United States in its role as co-sponsor—driving force—even-handed peace broker—catalyst—full partner undermined its own role, and ours, by alternating between a spectator stance and the role of self-appointed guardian of Israel and Israeli interests. The PLO negotiating strategy was deliberately devised to demonstrate that no progress or agreement was possible unless they were the legitimate agent to carry it out. Many "outside" Palestinians were hostile and defensive, suspecting or accusing us of taking their place; the Arab coordination charade was all appearance and no substance, but an intricate power game. Such a powerful combination of forces could not help but bring the PLO officially into the negotiations and the international arena. The irresistible inevitability of such a convergence was already in motion as Faisal and I made our way to Washington.

Airborne, I looked at the colorful handmade birthday cards Amal and Zeina had painted for me and wondered whether they found the little presents I had left under their pillows before my departure. The ritual of leaving that we had developed invariably included the silent kiss on the cheek, the whispered "I love you," and the surprise under the pillow for when they awoke. I always tried to make sure they knew ahead of time, the memory of their hurt still alive on the occasions in which I had had to leave at short notice and their waking up to find me gone. It was my mother, living upstairs alone since my father's death, who cried at every leave-taking and prayed for my safety. My share of guilt was a vise tightly gripping my heart wherever I went. I realized the extent of my mother's anxiety only later when after Madrid and several death threats she confided in Emile that she prayed for my imprisonment. The same mother who, since my return from the University of Virginia in 1973 and my trial on Christmas day of that year, had prayed daily for me not to go to prison was now wishing for my incarceration. "I always worried about the cold and deprivation," she told my husband. "Now I'm scared for her life. I think prison is safer." Is there a warm safe place for me, for my daughters, for my mother, for my four sisters, for all the women who are themselves the archetypal warm safe place for others? Where is our sanctuary, if prison is our refuge? Do we have a peach robe of our own?

We met yet again in Washington for another battle of wills. On October 10, 1991, Faisal, Zakariyya and I were joined by Sari Nusseibeh for a long meeting with Baker, Dennis Ross, Dan Kurtzer, Aaron Miller, Margaret Tutwiler, and the newly appointed assistant secretary for Near Eastern affairs, Ed Djerejian. We had heard a lot about him—he had been the U.S. ambassador to Syria, the Arabic-speaking Armenian-American who had gained Syrian President Hafez al-Assad's confidence and brought him on board.

Once again, we took up the "joint Jordanian-Palestinian delegation" construct that the Americans had concocted to appease the Israelis and create the illusion that there was no Palestinian identity separate from the nation of Jordan. This was exactly the position the Israelis preferred. If there were no Palestinian identity, there was hardly any need to make concessions to it. The Jordanians had agreed to provide us with the umbrella of the joint delegation, but we wanted to be out in the open with the recognition of our own national selfhood. We were seeking to disengage from Israel, not to be subsumed by Jordan. We were willing to consider a confederation with Jordan, but only on the basis of parity and the recognition of the separate national identity and sovereignty of each side, and as a result of the free expression of the wills of the two peoples. Baker insisted on having us return through Jordan to conclude the deal: we insisted that only the PLO can conclude such bilateral political agreements.

The Israelis held to their position that they would not meet with Palestinians from East Jerusalem. Baker told us point-blank that Faisal and I would not be part of the official negotiations because the Israeli delegation must not be subjected to Palestinians carrying Jerusalem identity cards.

"We will continue to meet with you. Everybody will know who is leading and directing the negotiations, but the Israelis cannot be forced to meet with people they find unacceptable." Baker's argument sounded hollow, and not only to our ears.

"We're kosher enough for you but not for the Israelis? We have to take all the risks and undertake all the responsibility, and then self-negate?"

"You'll be officially invited to the White House to meet with President Bush."

"We don't want consolation prizes, and we're not interested in ego gratification. The real issue is the status of Jerusalem. According to international law and your own policies Jerusalem is occupied territory. What you're asking us to do is illegal."

"It's only temporary. Right now, you may have a Palestinian residing in Jordan from a prominent Jerusalem family on the Jordanian part of the joint Jordanian-Palestinian delegation in order to finesse the issue of Jerusalem. The Letter of Assurance will state that clearly and we will reiterate our policy on Jerusalem."

"The convolution is quite tortuous and unsatisfactory. The Baker suit is a worse fit than we thought. But in effect, you're willing to distort the law and your policy to appease Shamir. Even West Jerusalem by law is not Israeli; according to U.N. Resolution 181 of 1947, all of Jerusalem is a *corpus separatum*."

Baker hit the ceiling. "You're pulling out a forty-five-year-old resolution now and telling me it's valid?"

"Of course. That resolution created the state of Israel. All countries, including the United States, abide by its provision on Jerusalem. Why else do you think no single state has moved its embassy even to West Jerusalem but kept them in Tel Aviv?"

"Is that true?" Baker turned to Dennis Ross for verification.

Dennis hemmed and hawed but had to admit the truth.

"We also think that what you're asking us to do is illegal. According to the Fourth Geneva Convention, a people under occupation cannot be made to sign an agreement with their occupier that would prejudice their rights and land. The PLO is the only legal body empowered to negotiate and to sign, and Israel—as belligerent occupant—is obliged to talk to them and not to us."

Baker desperately tried to control his temper, but we could almost see wisps of smoke begin to rise. "After seven months you've decided that the whole thing is illegal! The PLO is out for now. We have suspended our dialogue with them and Israel won't talk to them. You're all we have and you may not even mention the PLO in any way, shape, or form. Are you in or out?"

"We can't tell you now. We have to get the decision from the PLO. What about the flag? If there are any flags, we should have ours as well." I could almost sympathize with Baker's frustration and exasperation.

"No, no, no. No PLO, no flags whatsoever!"

"Do we also get to choose the Israeli delegation, since they're choosing ours by categories of acceptable and unacceptable Palestinians? To us a settler is an unacceptable Israeli who's living on land stolen from us. Any Israeli who has been involved in the torture or killing of any Palestinian is also unacceptable."

"You cannot do that. There are no preconditions. Shamir has told us that his delegation will walk out if there are any PLO members or Jerusalemites on your side. You may walk out if there are Israelis you don't want to sit with, but you'll have to bear the consequences. We can't afford to have them walk out, and you can't afford to walk out."

"We still haven't said we're in, in order to walk out. Who's going to pay the expenses if the PLO is out? We suggest you try to find a neutral body like the U.N. to foot the bill. A popular delegation of academics and professionals cannot fund its participation in such a costly venture. The PLO is willing to pay, but if it does, we'll have to acknowledge the fact publicly."

"You mustn't do that at all! The U.N. does not have the mandate to cover such expenses, and it's not in the negotiations anyway. We don't mind the PLO paying, but you can't admit that in public."

"Do we get immunity? What kind of passport would we have? Who will guarantee our safety and that of our families? Will you ensure our freedom of movement and expression? What about Israeli censorship of our telephones and interference in our papers? Can you guarantee parity with the other delegations?"

"We cannot guarantee anything, but we'll try our best. Why don't you talk to the Israelis directly about these issues?"

"We are supposed to represent a people in these negotiations; we're not petitioners before our occupiers. Twenty-four years of occupation have not broken our will or turned us into favor-seekers. The peace process will not either."

"But the Israelis are willing to consider Confidence Building Measures as the talks progress." CBMs was Baker's standard expression to describe steps that would create an atmosphere conducive to peace.

"These are not CBMs or favors. They're substantive political requirements and rights."

As the situation became more painful than humorous, we got on the plane to Tunis with the realization that the moment of truth was at hand. The Baker suit not only did not fit but was unbefitting. How many disadvantages and handicaps could we bear to bring with us to a process whose scales were already weighted in favor of our adversary? I felt the onslaught of serious misgivings. Could we afford the price of no? And if we said yes it would bring not only serious suffering, but also a certain amount of negation and denial. Were we paying the full price of the Gulf War? Or were we atoning for the guilt of the West and the horror of a slaughter of their making, not of ours? The evil of the Holocaust in Europe could not be redeemed by injustice in Palestine. If ours was the "promised land" and they were the "chosen people," we had never promised to give away our birthright nor committed ourselves to be outcasts. As Walid Khalidi (the famous Palestinian scholar residing in Jordan who comes from a prominent Jerusalem family) once said: If their Jehovah told them that, our Allah did not tell us.

CHAPTER SEVEN

"It's true we are objectively weak. We may not be able to impose a solution to our liking, but we can prevent a settlement that is unfair to us. We have negative, not positive, power; hence to use it effectively we must employ our power positively." After another circuitous, clandestine journey, Faisal was presenting his analysis and recommendations to the Executive Committee in Tunis.

"The picture is becoming clear. We have enough to go by, and an equally persuasive argument either way," I said, adding my assessment. There were justifications for either agreeing to the peace conference or not, at this point; there was no clear answer. "The conditions are unjust and painful, more than enough to justify a negative answer to the people, if we can afford the consequences. We also have enough to justify a positive answer if we are confident that we can transform the process itself into an instrument of change, and to gradually modify the framework. Either way, we need a majority backing."

"If we hold out longer, do you think we can improve the conditions?" Abu Ammar asked.

"I doubt it, but there's no harm trying. We could keep trying to the last minute. The Americans are committed to an October date, and that gives us a few days. Baker is coming to the region next week, and he wants the names of the delegation."

"Stay with it, then, and don't make any commitments. What pains me most is that you, Faisal and Hanan, who've done so much and carried out all the negotiations on my behalf are now excluded from the negotiations. How can I accept that? We must set up a structure to circumvent the ban."

"We must urgently seek support from the other Arab countries, at least the ring states that have borders in common with Israel. Hanan and I could visit Arab and Islamic countries to get political support and coordinate a joint strategy. It would be particularly helpful on the Jerusalem issue," said Faisal, trying to persuade Abu Ammar.

"Don't you think we've tried? But the Americans have already cautioned their Arab friends against any coordination with us. It seems we are to go stripped to the peace conference. If there are any visits to Arab and Islamic countries, we are to undertake them as the legitimate political leadership of the Palestinian people. You cannot do that. I have already sent letters to the nonaligned, Arab, and Islamic leadership. They're too intimidated by the Americans to even respond."

"Then you can send us as your envoys," Faisal persisted. "Make a public announcement and we'll try to coordinate on your behalf. We have to go to Jordan soon anyway."

"No. The only way you can do that is if we get prior official coordination between the PLO Executive Committee and the Jordanian government. King Hussein and Taher al-Masri have already agreed to such an arrangement. We'll carry it out discreetly. You, Hanan and Faisal, will go publicly to Amman. Abu Mazen, Yasser Abd Rabbo, and Suleiman al-Najjab from the committee will be there ahead of you. You will attend all official meetings together, even though only the two of you will appear before the press. The Jordanians cannot afford to antagonize Baker, although they do want to help us. We must finalize a bilateral Palestinian-Jordanian political agreement before we enter the process or form a joint delegation."

Despite the umbrella of the joint delegation and the oft-repeated "distinctive historical ties" between the Jordanians and us, the Jordanians feared the "alternative homeland" theory perpetuated by the Israeli Likud and other right-wing parties who volunteered Jordan as the Palestinian homeland. Given the fact that the majority of the population of Jordan was Palestinian, the demographic argument became a source of real anxiety for the Jordanians. In an ironic parallel, the Israeli Labor Party also defined us as a "demographic problem" and used that argument in order to sell the peace process as a way of preventing the Palestinian population time bomb from undermining the Jewish character and majority of the state. Labor also traditionally advocated the "Jordanian option," either in the form of annexing the West Bank to Jordan, or setting up a form of Jordanian-Palestinian relationship that would ensure Jordanian control over the West Bank and Gaza. The right wing also sought to solve the demographic problem by advocating Palestinian "transfer," the forced or voluntary, visible or invisible, mass expulsion of the population. On the other side of the river, the Jordanians saw in the transfer idea the materialization of their worst nightmare. We were intensely resentful of all arguments that attempted to determine our fate as an abstraction or an impediment to other peoples' designs. To us, the right to self-determination was nonnegotiable.

Thus when the option of a Palestinian-Jordanian confederation was proposed and adopted by the Palestine National Council, it was done on the basis of parity and the mutual respect for the sovereignty and national identity of each side, and only with the free consent of both peoples. At an earlier meeting in a San Francisco conference, when Jordan's Prince Hassan raised the question of reviving the PLO-Jordanian Amman Accord, I responded by alluding to the confederation as a means of creating a future rather than resurrecting the past, particularly on the basis of the above principles. Later, in Amman, at an informal dinner with King Hussein and Queen Noor, both Faisal and I stressed the pragmatic, forward-looking approach. We should not be trapped by the pain and mistakes of the past, nor remain captive to harbored resentments and recriminations. That, obliquely, was as close as we could get to any silent reference to the darkest phase in Palestinian-Jordanian relations—the fateful Black September of 1970 and its fury of violence and massacres. Also, the memory of the Jordanian rule of the West Bank from 1951 to 1967 had left a complex legacy of resentments and conflicting claims. King Hussein, both Faisal and I felt, was quite sincere in seeking new relationships based on candor and trust in order to meet the challenges that lay ahead for both peoples—particularly the challenge of peace to which we were both committed. We relayed our impressions and conclusions to Abu Ammar. One issue, however, that was endemic to the geopolitical and demographic realities of the Palestinian-Jordanian relationship was the fact that both Abu Ammar and King Hussein addressed the same constituency—or at least one with a sizable overlap. The implicit rivalry would persist despite our best efforts, particularly as territorial claims, both imaginary and real, had the habit of hovering in the background. The issue of Jerusalem later became the most contentious expression of this rivalry following the Jordanian-Israeli peace treaty in 1994 and Jordan's claim of custodianship over the religious sites in the city.

"Hanan and I will do that," Faisal said. "But what about the rest?"

"We were told that an Arab coordinating meeting will be held only after we give our answer."

"I found it particularly distasteful that Baker had to ask us if we wanted to send any messages through him to our Arab brethren. We told him we didn't need American intercession between us and the Arabs," I said.

"What's worse are the threats I read in the minutes." Abu Ammar was visibly upset. "You have a good memory, Hanan. What did he actually say?"

"He did say flatly that if we did not participate then Israel would not only get the $10 billion in loan guarantees, but would get $20 billion or more. The settlements would not be restricted, but will increase. And he added, 'If you're so worried about the PLO now, name me one country that will host them—let alone a PNC meeting.' Things turned nasty in that meeting."

"We must not be intimidated, but we must play this right."

Faisal and I left Tunis for Jerusalem, and from there to Amman, desperately trying to "play things right." The Palestinian-Jordanian agreement was finalized, awaiting official signatures. In Jerusalem, we met for three nights in a row at Faisal's house trying to work out a pool list of the Palestinian delegation to be sent to Tunis. Representatives of all political factions as well as independent nationalists were suggesting alternative compilations. We tried to no avail to get the PFLP to join. The People's Party, FIDA, Fateh (rather, the Fateh majority), and independent figures were committed. Tunis had agreed to a complex structure to circumvent the constraints imposed on the nature of our delegation's composition. We had obtained from Baker the "concession" that we would have a full fourteen-member delegation; at least the numerology was proper, even though only seven ended up sitting at the table at one time. Given the imposed constraints as well as our political, social, and geographic realities, we knew that we faced a supreme and intricate balancing act. We thought it wisest to recommend categories and expanded lists, and leave the final selection to the PLO.

Our structure, like the Baker suit, was awkward and unwieldy. We had set up a category called the "Guidance Committee" (Executive Office, Steering or Leadership Committee), to be comprised of Jerusalemites and "outsiders" who were not PLO officials. Faisal, myself, one FIDA, and one People's Party representative would be on it, in addition to three from the outside. The fourteen-member negotiating delegation would all be from the West Bank (excluding Jerusalem) and Gaza, in addition to three substitutes in case of absence. The administrative team would have a director, assistants, an accountant, secretaries and computer specialists, press officer and media specialists, translators and archivists. The category of legal advisers would be separate from the broad and amorphous group of "experts" and "advisers." The Follow-up Committee of PLO officials was later set up in Tunis to supervise and direct the Palestinian negotiating strategy and performance.

While in London, Faisal, Akram, and I had worked out an elaborate chart of criteria to guide the process of selection. These included: region, political affiliation, religious affiliation, training and expertise, profession, social status, gender, city or village or camp dweller, 1948 refugee or not, prison record, languages and special skills, and so forth. The hundreds of names were placed on the chart in their appropriate compartments to make sure that all criteria were met. Abu Ammar already had the list, but he also had his own priorities and special considerations. As we sent different configurations, combinations, and alternatives, Abu Ammar was working out his own. In the meantime Baker was sending frantic messages asking for our unofficial response and for the names. We had neither.

Baker arrived in Jerusalem the third week of October. His visit was tempestuous. The Executive Committee in Tunis had promised to finalize the list of names by the morning of the Baker meeting, but at 6:00 A.M. they still had not decided, although we did have a tentative though incomplete list of some who were supposed to participate in the upcoming meeting. One name that we were sure of was that of Dr. Haidar Abdel-Shafi, who would be head of the delegation. I had described him earlier to Baker as a "grand and venerable gentleman from Gaza, a grandfatherly figure who was among the founding members of the PLO and to whom you cannot and should not object." At 7:00 I picked up Sameh Kan'an, who was a candidate for the delegation, and headed toward Jerusalem. Sameh, the son of a Jewish mother and Palestinian father, had spent twelve years of his life in Israeli prisons and thus enjoyed popular support, particularly in his hometown, Nablus. But that also meant that he was carrying a green identity card, as part of the elaborate system of identification and discrimination (Jerusalem blue, West Bank orange, Gaza red) whereby green identified the bearer instantly as a released prisoner, hence a major target and "security risk." At the Israeli military checkpoint, we were stopped and made to wait by the side of the road. The soldiers refused to listen to reason, and our explanation that we were heading for a meeting with Baker merely inflamed them further; one actually gave me a rude signal as his private message to the U.S. secretary of state (which, of course, I was too polite to convey). I used the cellular phone to call Molly Williamson, who immediately got in touch with the U.S. embassy in Tel Aviv, who then contacted the military authorities. The soldiers stubbornly refused to give us their names and numbers and would not respond to their officers' messages. Half an hour later, a jeep pulled up and two officers gave the soldiers direct orders to let us through. We arrived at Faisal's house after 8:00 A.M. already late for the meeting at the U.S. consulate, but as it turned out the meeting had to be postponed even further.

Faisal and Sari Nusseibeh were clearly agitated. It appeared that there was a serious disagreement about the names and whether we should give Baker any list, given the fact that we had not yet expressed our initial intention pertaining to the whole process. As I walked in, somebody handed me the phone. Abu Ammar was on the line.

"This is mutiny. I will not have it. It's up to me to decide who's on the list."

"Of course it is. But what's happened? I'm afraid I'm not familiar with the problem. Did you talk to Faisal or Sari?"

"I did, and I don't want to talk to them. They think they're the leadership, and they refuse to add the names I chose. This is outright rebellion, and I won't put up with it. It's unbelievable! Are they telling me I don't have the authority to add the names I want?"

"I'm sure they don't mean it that way. Maybe they're looking at things from a different perspective; we need credibility for the delegation members, and we've already received petitions from some constituencies—"

"What credibility? I know what is required and I will decide what's best."

"Nobody thinks otherwise. Without doubt the decision is yours. But we must have the list soon. The meeting has already been delayed."

"There will be no list today. Don't give Baker anything official."

Everyone fell silent. Faisal and Sari had certainly not intended to provoke a confrontation. Saeb Erakat immediately sat down and started the damage-control process by drafting a petition of loyalty to be signed by all present expressing our allegiance and unquestioning support for our leadership and their decisions. He faxed it immediately, and we attempted to resolve our dilemma. Some of those on the initial list were already present and ready to go with us to the meeting—in what capacity now? We had also postponed two deadlines, and had to think of a quick excuse for the third.

"Did Abu Ammar tell you not to take the new people to the meeting?" Faisal asked.

"No. He just said not to give Baker any official list."

"Good, and we won't. We'll introduce the people as possible members, and we'll discuss the list with him unofficially."

We went to the meeting with serious misgivings, but as it was the first one in East Jerusalem at our insistence, we did not want to cancel. It took place at the East Jerusalem consulate, an old building with dark corridors and worn stairs. I was already in a bad mood and a no-nonsense mode. Following the introduction of the potential delegation members, Baker asked for a full list.

"We are willing to give you a tentative and unofficial list at this time," I said.

"What do you mean tentative and unofficial? You guys had better get your act together, or you'll prove Abba Ebban true: 'The Palestinians never miss an opportunity to miss an opportunity.' Everybody's on board except you, and if you don't accept, we'll go ahead without you."

Baker had chosen the wrong tone and diction, and I reacted vehemently. "If you cannot find your own words to communicate with us, we would thank you not to use Israeli sources and expressions. We've had enough of their racism and domination and prefer not to have them quoted to us by you. And even if all the rest agree and we don't, you won't have a legitimate and comprehensive peace process. Besides, we are the side most handicapped, since you have accepted Israeli restrictions on our delegation by excluding our leadership and Jerusalemites. You also have not given us any assurances on the CBMs [Confidence Building Measures] and the settlements, which we badly need as a people under occupation. And we're still dealing with a two-phased approach without any projection as to the objectives."

"These are the conditions, and if you think you can change them now by holding back to the last minute you won't succeed. The *souk* is over; the bazaar is closed—finished."

"Here you go again using racist language. We are not haggling over the price of merchandise; we are fighting for our lives and for the future of the whole region. I read the Israeli description of our approach in today's paper; they're the ones who described us as having the bazaar mentality, and that kind of stereotyping is entirely unacceptable."

Needless to say, the meeting was far from diplomatic. Months later, over dinner in Washington, Margaret Tutwiler told me that she had never seen me so angry or short-tempered before. After the dust settled, we agreed to give Baker an informal list.

"I'm relieved to have the list now," he said. "I have a meeting with Shamir at noon and I needed the list before then."

"I hope you're not thinking of giving him the list. I thought we agreed that 'only the Palestinians have the right to choose their own delegation' and that there will be no vetoing or vetting of the names by Israel."

"I won't give him the names, but we have to look into them and be assured ourselves that the names will not be problematic. Then I can tell Shamir in all honesty that I am satisfied with the list."

"Do we get to do the same with their list?"

"Each side will present its list to the other before the meeting. But you must make sure that you never mention the PLO or that you were appointed or selected by the PLO. We don't want an Israeli walkout."

"Is that sword to remain constantly hanging over heads? Let them walk out. Let them bear the consequences; we cannot be held responsible for their actions as well."

"We've got to get them there and keep them there. Trust me; things will change once the process gets under way and develops a momentum of its own. How else are you going to stop the settlements? How else would you end the occupation?"

He did have a point. Or a weak point, which was always the absence of an alternative. Besides, we had plans of our own for making the peace process evolve into an instrument for our own empowerment and for the neutralization of the imposed constraints. We had to use our negative power positively.

In the afternoon, we had a meeting at the National Palace Hotel with the other co-sponsor, the Russian foreign minister, Boris Pankin. He tried to sell us the American argument, and Faisal almost gave him a heart attack by going out to the press and hinting that we might walk out. Palestinian mischief making was at its zenith then. Shamir had announced to the press that he was vetting the names of our delegation to ensure that there were no "undesirables" on the list. Pankin went out and called Baker on the hotel phone and reported (as a Palestinian eavesdropper told us) that the Palestinians were angry and that he was having a hard time mollifying us. Baker asked him to reassure us that the reports were untrue and that he had not submitted any list to Shamir. He relayed the message. We urged him to play a more active role; he promised to be more effective. We never saw him again except briefly at the opening session of the Madrid Conference.

At a press conference in Jerusalem that day, Baker surprised us all by announcing that the peace conference would be held in Madrid—a place never mentioned before as an option, although we had spent many an hour and many a meeting discussing different potential venues. Back at Faisal's we were still wrestling with names—hundreds of them. Akram and Abu Ammar had devised the two official posts of head of the team and official spokesperson to get public recognition for Faisal and me and to get us into the process if not in the actual negotiations. At first, I resisted the title, as I had no intention of becoming a media person. I have always thought that real spokespersons, especially for a people and a cause like ours, grew into and embodied the role rather than being appointed to it. I was assured that in our case, the choice was based on political considerations and needs as well as on merit. The responsibility was policymaking as well as official representation. (I had no idea then that I would be making policy on the spot, and often on my feet!)

Predictably, the opposition singled me out for attack, thinking I was most vulnerable both as a woman and as an independent. Some extremists took cheap shots at my being Christian (in addition to my gender), and therefore unrepresentative. Those who had political aspirations and were entangled by a macho power struggle resented me for taking what they thought was their place—the "Why her?" syndrome as a euphemism for "Why not me?" The petty-minded cynics had the ready answer: "It's her English" or "She's a media star/creation/darling" or "Baker chose her." Needless to say, I had my work cut out for me. Most of the time I did not pay attention, but once in a while it would get to me and I would feel really hurt. Throughout it all, Emile and the girls were always there for me, as were many solid friends. My greatest gratification came from the people whom I did not know but who would come up to me and express support and encouragement. I discovered that public opinion was much more objective, fair, and sympathetic than that of the vocal political aspirants.

Molly Williamson called a few days later. She wanted to bring over the Letter of Invitation and the Letter of Assurance. We started a long negotiation by phone on whether the documents were to be on official letterhead paper; whether they would be signed; whether they would have a cover letter; whether they would be addressed to Faisal Husseini in his capacity as head of the Palestinian team; whether it would explicitly state his address as Jerusalem; whether Molly's Russian counterpart would be with her. Molly was trying hard to be patient and polite although the frayed edges of her nerves would sometimes show in a trembling voice or a shaky hand. The worst was when I would go "over [her] head" to Dennis or Ed or Dan in Washington. As we worked out the seeming technicalities, I finally asked her to wait till the afternoon before coming to Faisal's house. I called Akram.

"It looks like the invitations are being given out today. They'll be handed over simultaneously to all the parties."

"Did you check the format?"

"We took care of everything. But I asked Molly to wait till the afternoon. I have an idea what's in the LOI and I know the LOA by heart. There are many things there that we mustn't accept. I want to write a response detailing our position in a letter of acceptance and treat the others as American policy, not ours. At least, we must do that for the record."

"That's a good idea. I'll tell Abu Ammar. Do you have time?"

"I have two hours provided I'm not disturbed. I'll get Akram Baker to type as I write. Just don't expect me to send you any drafts."

"You rarely do, anyway! You're probably the only one who knows what should go into the letter and who can write it at such short notice."

I finished writing as Molly and Alexei (the counselor from the Russian embassy) came in. Faisal signed it and handed it over. Molly was elated to get such a quick response. She called the next day to inform us that Baker was upset at the contents of our acceptance letter (it reiterated our position, including the basic right of statehood) but that they had decided to proceed. She asked for the name of our advance person, who was to leave for Madrid the next day, as well as the names of our staff and advisers. We were stunned. We had not finished setting up the structure or filling in the names. An emergency meeting was called on the spot, and we started the frantic search for qualified staff. In the meantime, Abu Ammar was giving out promises and commitments to hundreds of people who felt they had the right to be on the delegation.

The category of "advisers" was swelling out of recognition with all of the political personalities and activists who needed to be recognized and placated. Abu Ammar knew that anyone who felt excluded would then be negative, another voice for the opposition. Consequently we had to get permits and make special arrangements for a continuously expanding list of people, most of whom had no clear functions—and who were supposed to leave in two days. Thus with advisers galore and administrators by chance, we still had the task of assembling and briefing the delegation. Many of the delegates, at this point, resented the last-minute nature of our work.

To add to the complications, at one point Saeb Erakat announced on CNN that we were the PLO delegation, appointed and directed by Tunis. The full force of American wrath descended upon us. Saeb instantly became an "undesirable" and, according to Baker, had to be dropped from the delegation. Yet another battle ensued. We succeeded in rescuing Saeb, but he was asked not to make any public statements.

Miraculously, we managed to put together our lists, documents, delegation, thoughts, and luggage. We were to meet early Friday morning at the National Palace Hotel in order to take the bus and cross the Jordan River to meet with our PLO leadership and join the Jordanian delegation. Sunday, the rest of the staff and advisers were to catch up with us. All in all, we reached the enormous number of 130. A standard joke then was that once the whole Palestinian delegation was assembled to leave for Madrid, all the rest of the Palestinian population could get on a minibus to wave them good-bye.

Actually many people did come to bid us farewell. Families, friends, supporters, well-wishers, and the press showed up very early the next morning to see us off, give us last-minute advice, or interview us—as the case might be. I felt the excitement and emotional intensity of the crowd reach out to me and wipe away the tension and misgivings that had taken over my mind and replace them with a strange and comforting quietude. Listening, smiling, speaking, hugging, moving incessantly, I was buoyed and embraced by well-being. As we walked down the main stairs, some women began calling out encouragements in between back slapping, embracing, kissing, and handshaking:

"May Allah grant you victory. *Allah yunsurkom.*"

"Our hearts go with you."

"Bring us back our freedom. Don't forget we want a state."

"Stay firm, *samdeen* (steadfast), don't give in!"

"You're our hope, our *amal,* we're proud of you. Hold your heads high."

But the one admonition that resonated in my head and heart and seemed to haunt my soul as only a pure, sharp, and agonizing melody could was presented to me calmly and directly, almost dispassionately:

"We are a trust, *amanah,* that we place in your hands. We have entrusted our future to your care. Don't let us down."

Amanah is a word redolent with meaning and suggestion, evoking a chain of echoes beyond the audible: a valuable possession placed in the care of a trusted person; a sense of trust and integrity; honesty and trustworthiness; a haven and sanctuary; safety and safe passage . . . and on. Only such a simple, ascetic word could have the audacity to convey such an overwhelming sense of hope, pathos, and responsibility all at once. I felt the enormity of its implications, and I cried. Not hesitantly or apologetically, I cried shamelessly and with abandon. I cried for a whole people longing for a safe haven, for a people who thought that I, that we, could bring the realization of that dream even one step closer or one second sooner. I cried for myself for having taken upon me a mission capable of enslaving, or even destroying, me in its spiritual snare. I cried for the delegation, ambushed by history and circumstance to bear a flame that would in all likelihood devour them. I was also simply touched by trust, and I absorbed this *amanah* like our parched hills take in the first gentle autumn rain, and it seeped down into the roots of my being, where I had come from and who I had come to be.

My name means "tenderness." True to the Arab, and generally Semitic, tradition, we Palestinians attach a great deal of significance to names—their meaning and music, historical allusion and authenticity, identification and identity. More often than not, our names are a form of indulgence in wishful thinking rather than descriptive accuracy, as in the case of rather homely daughters called *Hilweh* or *Jamileh* for "pretty" or "beautiful," and rather tame and timid sons called *Nimr* or *Laith* for "tiger" or "lion." Sometimes, a name could be a direct message to God or fate, as in the case of parents who call their daughters, once they begin arriving in a series, *Tamam* or *Kifayah* or *Nihaya* for "sufficient" or "enough" or "the end." In most cases, infants are burdened with impossible roles to fulfill, to live up to and earn identities in a tradition reminiscent of ancient Greek epics: How does one console *Nasr* (victory) for a lifetime of defeat not of his own making? Who can convince *Khaled* (eternal) that immortality in this world is beyond his grasp? And how does *Niʾmeh* (the gift of grace) understand the disgrace of discrimination deliberately exercised against her gender? More cruel yet are the allusions to historical figures or attributes of divinity and prophecy in an unheroic and profane age of denial. But most important, our long series of names are proof of lineage, of roots for a people uprooted, of continuity for a history disrupted, and of legitimacy for an orphaned nation. Ancestral verification, combined with unfulfilled longing for all that we had been denied, has created a uniquely Palestinian semantic epistemology—a secret code of instinctive recognition that threads together the tapestry of a reality rent by injustice. Thus, *Falasteen Muhammad Abdel-Rahim Barakat Nusseirat* is the cryptic narrative of Palestine, the daughter of Muhammad (named after the Prophet), who is the son of the Servant of the Merciful (reference to God) from the family of Blessings (which also indicates regional origins) from the larger family or clan or tribe of Victories. Such is the history of the Palestinian nation, an ironic fusion of the security of a recognizable past with a future molded in yearning for all that which has been denied us in the present.

True to the Semitic tradition as well, the giving of a name is a sign of power, an exercise of authority. When God created the animals, it was Adam who gave them names, thus establishing a relationship of domination and a hierarchy not unrelated to the uniquely human quality of language and verbal creativity. To me, the power and mystery of language has been a source of constant fascination. To place the Palestinian experience and reality within that verbal domain as a manifestation of both humanity and truth has been my endeavor at validation, particularly of the Palestinian human dimension.

The semantic dimension has also been an essential component and expression of the Palestinian-Israeli conflict. Mutual negation was the underlying component of the public discourse of both sides. While the Israelis went so far as to explicitly deny our existence, consistent with the myth of "a land without a people for a people without a land," we refused to extend to them the verbal acknowledgment of ever mentioning the word "Israel" or "Israelis" in any public or formal speech or tract. Willful negation, on the one hand, and willful omission on the other, created an absurd head-in-the-sand ostrich politics, resulting in a history of mutual exclusion and a highly stilted and artificial linguistic domain. To us, the mere mention of the name "Israel" meant an admission or a legitimization of an unmentionable reality. We treated dread diseases and fatal afflictions the same superstitious way; thus cancer was "that disease" and any mention of it was immediately followed by the incantation B'id ash-sharr or "May evil be kept at bay." To the Israelis, the word "Palestine" was taboo because it also meant an admission of guilt and historical culpability, as well as a recognition of a national identity that might one day be translated into the dreaded Palestinian state. Euphemisms, abstractions, and circumlocutions prevailed. While in our discourse Israel was the evil "Zionist entity," in Israeli discourse we were the "terrorist Arabs" or "inhabitants of the territories." Only when we began the necessary linguistic transformation, and started sending each other signals of admission rather than negation, did we make the indirect announcement that we were ready to make contact of a nonmilitary nature. Verbal confrontations were not only the beginning of dialogue, but an admission of realities that neither side had hitherto found admissible. Negative recognition was the first step toward negotiations and resolution.

Hanan Daud Khalil Mikhail (Awwad)-Ashrawi is my personal and collective narrative. I am Tenderness, the daughter of David, who is the son of Khalil (Abraham) from the family of Michael (also the name of an ancestor), which is of the clan of Awwad (the one who inevitably returns), which is one of the original seven clans who are the descendants of the founding fathers of the town. I hyphenated "Ashrawi" when I married Emile Ashrawi, since the name was acquired by the act of marriage rather than the genetics of lineage, although our daughters will claim the latter. The Ashrawis (from *Ashra*—ten or the tithe levied by tax collectors, or from *Ishra* meaning companionship) are originally from the Palestinian Christian city of Nazareth or its vicinity, and their few remaining descendants are scattered, mainly outside Palestine. But theirs is another narrative.

To us all, Palestine is a composite of history and myth, of memories and dreams, of nostalgia and visions, of possession and loss. Its loss has touched us all and imprinted us with an indelible melancholy and fierceness. We wrote poetry and composed songs, fired bullets and threw stones; we claimed the law and broke the law, stayed on the land and went into exile; and in the fullness of our pain we lashed out and inflicted suffering on others. With one hand the world covered its eyes, and with the other shoved us aside lest we display our unseemly sores. And yet we dared assault the world with the discourse and vision of peace that only the victim can offer as the quality of redemption, and we gained an audience. And we have been offered back fragments of our dismembered land, to be pieced together slowly, and to be transformed into the quality of healing.

I was born and raised in the gentleness of healing, cradled in the short-lived certainty of parental infallibility and protection. My father, a doctor who took his calling seriously, and my mother, a nurse turned homemaker, produced five daughters. I was "number five," as my father used to refer to me with a smile whenever anyone dared refer to him with the cultural cliché "father of girls." He also displayed a deliberate pride at having fathered such progeny. My parents chose our names for their music as well as for their meaning and assertive nationalism. When many Palestinian Christians set themselves apart by choosing foreign or biblical names for their children as a sign of social, religious, or cultural distinction, my parents insisted on specifically Arabic names. (Many a George or

Giselle I know had spent much of his or her life trying to live down his or her Georgeness or Gisellehood.) All my sisters' names were made up of two syllables, ending with a long open vowel as if signaling more to come: Muna (aspiration, wish); Abla (the heroine of an oral romance narrative); Huda (the righteous path, guidance); and Nada (Nadia's actual name—gentle dew)—all preceded me as the daughters of Daud and Wadiᵓa. When I was born, they declared completion with a sense of finality; thus my name ends with a voiceless stop.

While in Arabic Hanan is a feminine name whose meaning is often associated with maternal affection, in Hebrew it is a masculine name pronounced with a hard (kh) initial sound and alluding to a biblical military leader. I have often wondered at this polarized dualism. Was fate from the beginning sending me a not-too-subtle message of historical confrontation? Perhaps it was the appropriate fusion of the dimensions of a conflict whose resolution demanded the accommodation of opposites and the reconciliation of primeval urges. Despite the phonetics of my name, I was never voiceless, and I have not stopped. History has never left me to my own devices and time has evolved its own sardonic sense of memory in which the meager grains of privacy and the expansive dunes of communal terrain intermingled.

• • •

We took our seats on the bus with not a dry eye in sight, the women and men who for the first time in history were going to present the case of a people long denied, long maligned. We were going to intrude, to intervene, and make a place for our people at the feast of nations. I was spokesperson, and I vowed to speak in my people's voice, to put on the mantle of their visibility, and to unfurl before the eyes of the world images of both their melancholy and joy. I would capture their spirit in language, and set it free before witnesses. I would be the speech-bearer of our human reality, to unlock the chest of our silent words and with them unlock the hearts and minds of men and women. And I would do that with *amanah*. We were on our way, ready to cross the River Jordan, already cleansed, and seeking safe passage.

From tears to laughter, we exchanged jibes about the "Baker bus" that replaced the "train" that Baker had urged us not to miss. We took the winding road to Jericho, the lowest spot on earth, stopping on the way to buy the famous Jerusalem *kaᵓk bsumsum* (sesame bread), *zaᵓtar* (thyme), and falafel—a ritual instituted by my assistant, Nuha Awadallah-Musleh, and maintained throughout our collective travels. We are very proud and possessive of our foods, and this is why we feel resentful when it is presented as Israeli food; it is cultural robbery.

The gray road to the Jordan Rift Valley was a simple ribbon carelessly circling the bizarre gift of barren hills and pockmarked moonscape. Suddenly, a break in the barrier of hills revealed the Dead Sea, and to its left stretched the lush green strip of fertile valley land in the midst of which the deceptive sparkle of the ancient town of Jericho seemed to beckon. Neither the salt in the soil nor the ghost town quality of the deserted refugee camps was visible from this distance. Was the peace we were seeking the mythical Dead Sea apple, golden and luscious on the outside and filled with ashes within? As the pressure of our descent increased, we felt the ponderous weight of untold layers of history bear down on us.

Amman, the Roman Philadelphia, city of brotherly love, became our second home base. We held long meetings to design strategies and formulate policy. King Hussein, Crown Prince Hassan, and Prime Minister Taher al-Masri (later Zeid Bin Shaker) also hosted us for numerous (often interminable) meetings in the service of joint coordination. Only when the issue of sovereignty was raised did the atmosphere turn tense; we maintained that sovereignty is inherent in the people and the Palestinians had never relinquished sovereignty although we were prevented from exercising it. Some Jordanians believed that the implementation of U.N. Resolution 242 required the context of sovereign states to effect Israeli withdrawal, hence Jordan would hold the legal responsibility over the West Bank regardless of the disengagement of July 31, 1988.

While in Amman and in the middle of a busy schedule, Faisal calmly made another revelation. "We have to go to Egypt today, Hanan," he said. "President Mubarak wants to see us."

"Akram told me and we agreed," I responded, "that you and Haidar Abdel-Shafi would go as head of the team and head of the delegation, respectively. Besides, we have a full joint delegation meeting with the king at noon and a Guidance Committee meeting this evening. We have a great deal to do in preparation for Madrid."

"I know, but Mubarak called Abu Ammar and specifically asked for you. We'll leave right after the meeting with King Hussein, and we should be back in time for the evening meeting."

I was surprised by Mubarak's insistence. The king offered to lend us his private plane to fly us to Cairo for the meeting, and then return us to Jordan immediately. I consented.

I could not help thinking on the way that the three of us, Faisal, Haidar, and myself, were a strange parody of the Flight to Egypt. From the special landing place at Cairo airport, we were driven straight to the Nile Hilton where Abu Mazen was waiting for us. To our surprise, we were given rooms at the hotel.

"But we're leaving today right after the meeting with Mubarak," I objected.

"I'm afraid that's not possible," Abu Mazen said. "President Mubarak is in Isma²iliyya, and he's holding all his meetings there. You have to go to him tomorrow morning; but you have appointments with the Egyptian president's political adviser, Osama al-Baz and with Foreign Minister ²Amr Moussa this evening. You must plan to spend the night in Cairo."

"But we have important meetings in Amman, and we're unprepared for an overnight stay. Can't we see him in Isma²iliyya this afternoon?"

"We'll send word to Amman that you're unavoidably delayed."

Osama al-Baz received us in a cluttered office, overflowing with books, newspapers, and documents. Removing some files and papers from the couch and chairs, he made room for us. I felt at home in the disorder. Peering at me intently with his big round eyes, he seemed to say, "I have nothing to hide, do you?" He did, of course. While appearing to hold nothing back, he gave nothing away—a politician of the first degree. His disarming candor, sharp sense of humor, and tone of self-indulgent irony combined with a quick, dissecting analytical intelligence produced a force to be reckoned with. Egypt, he stressed, was willing and eager to play a facilitating role in the peace process, and would place at our disposal all the relevant documents and experience of the Camp David negotiations. He also gave us tips on Israeli negotiating strategies: "They're tough bargainers and will use any advantage they have in the negotiations. Hold firm and don't give up. You must always be prepared with counterarguments; better yet, come prepared with your own proposals and make the first move. Their opening bid is never their bottom line." From bitter experience, we discovered later that he was right.

We then proceeded to the meeting with ²Amr Moussa, who was sanguine about the prospects for peace, and enthusiastic about the Egyptian role and coordination with the Palestinian side; this was particularly important since Egypt was the first Arab country of the Gulf War alliance to restore relations with the PLO and to receive Abu Ammar officially. Egypt also became a channel to the Americans and the rest of the alliance and, at a later date, to Israel following the Labor Party's victory in the elections. We held a joint press conference, then prepared to go to dinner at Osama's invitation to a floating restaurant on the Nile.

The Nile was a shimmering jewel, breathtaking both in its sparkle and setting. Dinner involved a dazzling introduction to the political and intellectual leadership of Egypt with its rich and diverse facets. Faisal, Haidar, and I were treated to a veritable feast for body and soul alike. To us, Egypt was an essential ally, but one that evoked conflicting responses from the Palestinians.

The PLO in general, and Abu Ammar in particular, felt close to Egypt and looked to its leadership as a model to be emulated and as a reliable source of political advice. One of Arafat's oft-repeated statements was, "I am Egyptian by temperament and inclination." The dialect of his spoken Arabic was Egyptian rather than Palestinian—a fact that provoked many comments among the Palestinian people. Most of the "inside" Palestinians, however, were still smarting from the Camp David Accords and blamed Egypt for breaking rank with the other Arab countries and concluding a separate peace that weakened the Arab position as a whole. Many felt that Egypt was manipulating the Palestinian question for its own ends and to its advantage—mainly to curry favor with the United States and to consolidate its regional position as the major force in the Arab world. Hence, we were repeatedly warned by the Palestinian public during our popular meetings not to allow Egypt to deliver us to the United States or to appear to speak on our behalf.

The drive to Isma'iliyya was unforgettable. Our motorcade, with blaring sirens and flashing lights, hurtled into and out of the insane Cairo traffic as if bent on a suicide mission. We felt as if our daredevil drivers had decided to take on every single vehicle and pedestrian in Egypt. The three of us had a separate car each, preceded and pursued by security vehicles out of whose windows dangled almost to the waist young officers brandishing their weapons, shouting and screaming at any moving object. Suddenly, the mad motorcade came to a halt. Saved, I thought.

Frantically trying to breathe again, and willing my pulse to slow down to a reasonable rate of 100, I asked in a hoarse whisper, "Are we there?"

The disdainful reply of our aspiring stuntmen put me in my place: "We've barely started. We're still in Cairo."

"Then why stop?" I croaked bravely.

"It seems the car behind us needs help."

That was Haidar's car. I was horrified, imagining their driving must have given him a heart attack. Despite my wobbly knees and the very vocal protests of the security men, I got out and headed back. I saw Haidar walking toward me looking very much alive and indignant.

"They're going to kill us all," he said. "And to add insult to injury, my driver said he couldn't keep up with your cars. So I asked him to stop and told him I'll ride in your car."

We sat in the back seat, eyes closed tight, holding on for dear life, and crying out only occasionally. We were sure that this was our last journey anywhere. By the time we got to Isma'iliyya, Haidar and I felt that we had courted and tempted death to the limit. Whenever we found ourselves in a dangerous spot, all I had to do was remind him of the motorcade in Egypt.

The meeting with Mubarak was unusual, to say the least. Known for his explicit language and direct undiplomatic approach, he still surprised us with his candor. "That Shamir is a liar and a thief," he exclaimed. "You can't trust him with anything." He added, "Imagine, that man wants to come to Egypt. I won't have him. I keep stalling him, but there's no way he'll be invited to Egypt or I'll visit him in Israel." He also repeated his famous statement about the best way to negotiate with the Israelis: keep up an uninterrupted stream of one proposal in the wake of the other (though not quite in the same language). He urged us to learn from the Egyptian experience, and bade us farewell. Having no other way of returning, we took our chances with the suicide squad and made it to the airport, and from there back to Amman.

Our leadership meetings in Amman before the Madrid conference were a letdown. We discovered that the PLO had no clear strategy for negotiations, let alone defined objectives. Farouq al-Kaddoumi (Abul-Lutof), head of the Political Department of the PLO, told us that they had put the delegation together haphazardly since, in the absence of the PLO, it didn't matter who was on the delegation. Without the direct and official participation of the PLO, the whole process would be meaningless and would accomplish nothing. Many of us smarted at the insult, but in retrospect Kaddoumi was accurately forecasting the fate of the delegation and the negotiations. Nevertheless, we took our responsibilities seriously and prepared assiduously—from strategy papers to scenarios, from simulations to talking points, and from objectives to options.

The most pressing and challenging task facing us was that of preparing our speech for the Madrid conference. The first issue to be resolved was whether it should be in Arabic or in English. During the heated discussions in the home of our ambassador, Tayyeb, two schools of thought emerged: those who chose Arabic as an expression of our national identity and pride, and those who chose English as a universal language of communication and a means of addressing the world directly. Abu Ammar favored the Arabic option, telling me on the phone that we had to address the world in our own language "as an expression of our national dignity." I said that our national dignity is in the substance and that the media would relay our speech directly in our own voice and words rather than filtered through an impersonal interpreter. Several writers had prepared drafts in Arabic, some of which were powerful but culturally biased, hence untranslatable. Haidar had prepared a preliminary draft in English but he decided against it. In the course of the intense debate, he came to me and said, "Regardless of what happens here, you must promise me to have an effective speech ready for me to read in Madrid." I promised. We got on the chartered plane to Madrid. I had not written a word.

Madrid was by then a magical word, a code word, a cryptic message about an enormous undertaking. We had been too busy rolling the rock uphill to notice that we were at the end of one stage in the steep incline. Whether we could successfully reach a plateau, a station on the way to help us catch our breath, or whether the rock would roll downhill and destroy us all was still an open-ended question. I knew that the effort needed to give that final push would be a real test of endurance and ability. As it turned out Madrid was a miracle, defying credibility even with immaculate hindsight, but a place where illusion and reality, fact and fantasy, exhilaration and despondency intermingled enticingly to claim both our attention and our souls.

CHAPTER EIGHT

We strode out of the plane and into the terminal with a bounce in our gait and olive branches in our hands. Heads held high, eyes shining with purpose and anticipation, and radiating confidence in our historical mission, we collided head-on with the brick wall of petty bureaucracy. Very official-looking Spanish officials informed us that the official list supplied by the Americans included only the fourteen names of the "legitimate" negotiators. The rest of us were unofficial, hence somehow "illegitimate," thus undeserving of any special consideration or official treatment. That, of course, applied to the whole Guidance Committee—including Faisal and myself. Even in Spain, Israeli preconditions prevailed via the Americans. I vowed to wage the battle for legitimacy and to win in Madrid.

With literary allusions, we had chosen the Victoria Hotel with its echoes of Hemingway and the Spanish Civil War. As our motorcade pulled up to the entrance, we heard chanting in Arabic and saw a crowd of men, women, and children waving olive branches and Palestinian flags. We ran to the crowd, embracing, kissing, shaking hands, exchanging greetings, and wiping away tears. A little girl came up to me and shyly handed me a large bouquet of white flowers. I embraced her, thinking of Amal and Zeina, and I felt as if I were embracing all the Palestinian children—those we had left behind and those who had never seen Palestine. It was on behalf of that little girl with flowers and for all our children that I was committed to speak out and to act in *amanah*.

As a child, I used to play the game of stepping over the cracks in the sidewalk and placing each foot squarely on the tile in a universal innocent dance all children seem to develop instinctively. "Step on a tile and you eat chocolate, step on a crack and you eat cat shit!" In my hometown, Ramallah, the sidewalks of my childhood were of uneven stone tile in a variety of shapes and sizes, worn to a slippery and rounded smoothness by hundreds of years of pedestrians. Now, Ramallah has sidewalks, dull gray, symbols of universal metropolitan unimaginativeness. We played hopscotch and devised *dabke* dances on the patterns of these tiles, and at times we concocted stories of mystery and horror as suggested by their composition. On wet winter days, the sidewalks became unpredictable obstacles. A loose tile would send up splashes of mud to smear our blue school uniforms, or a smooth and slippery tile would send us flying into puddles in embarrassing and ungainly positions.

The course of peace was proving to be similarly precarious. Historical tiles were footholds, though slippery and treacherous, and cracks were ominous fissures that could turn into voracious chasms. Somewhere along the line, our passage turned to concrete and the cement-gray dullness of expediency and narrow self-interest replaced the luster of our dreams. Loss of innocence and idealism is inevitable, but it can be fatal if it saps vitality and hope. We have grown in anticipation of the missing vibrancy of color and the music of the *dabke* as an attribute of reconciliation. Peace must contain the quality of authentication and the diversity of all seasons.

Whether I have lived my life or life has lived me is a question yet to be resolved. We as Palestinians have always felt that we are simultaneously shapers and victims of history—the scribe and the script—interchangeably the affliction and the cure. Now that we were in Madrid, in danger of actually attaining what we were led to believe was our goal, we were in mortal fear that someone had altered the rules of the game. Such discoveries generally should have been wrapped in redemptive humor— a smile, a shrug, or even a swagger as we began training for a new game. But Palestinians have always been excessively prone to tragedy and dark nights of the soul, never beyond a bit of mischief making.

"Hanan, come quick. There are hundreds of reporters outside asking to speak to you, and the security won't let them in." Albert Agazarian was speaking excitedly. "You must go out and speak to them."

"I will. Just give me time to get ready. We barely got here."

"Look out the window. They're a mob. They won't go away, and the security people are giving them a hard time."

Albert and I rushed out. It was already dark. The Spanish security went berserk. I was suddenly surrounded by a sea of faces and microphones, and the noise was deafening. They calmed down, and I spoke, explaining that we had come to take up the challenge of peace, to assert ourselves directly as a people.

A few hours later, around midnight, another crowd gathered in the park across the street. Spanish security had decided not to allow any of the journalists to come up to the hotel entrance. Surrounded by colleagues Penny Johnson and Albert, assistants Suhair Taha and Nuha, and many of our staff, I made a mad dash to the park for a repeat performance. The press, I decided, would be a partner in my battle for legitimacy and the truth. I peered into the darkness.

As we lined up later for official accreditation, we were stopped by Molly Williamson, who had already arrived with her luggage and State Department instructions. "You can't have accreditation, and you're not allowed into the Palace of Nations," she declared.

"We have been accredited by our leadership and our people. I don't see why we can't go anywhere we want." Our great moment, it seemed, was coming down to plastic name tags.

"The security personnel have orders not to allow anyone inside the palace except the official delegates accredited by us. I'll tell you what, though. I'll give you a press card that will allow you to enter the press center, the Efema."

"You can keep the press card. Baker promised to accredit the Guidance Committee, and now you're reneging. Even in this you can't stand up to the Israelis and keep your word. But we'll find a way around it. We've created facts before."

That night, I went to the palace in a CNN car and gave a long interview to signal the beginning of the public debate. Later we had our first meeting of the Madrid season with Baker and his team, with the Arab foreign ministers, and with the European Community representatives. The Israeli veto, it seemed, did not extend to them. Also that night, Albert, Penny, and I decided to hold the first official Madrid press conference at the Efema and to issue our first press release the next day. The next few hours were spent in internal meetings, and as with everything else we did, the issue of legitimacy loomed large.

The PLO in Tunis had sent a number of officials from all over the world to form the leadership in the background and to ensure our legitimacy and that of our political decision making. Nabil Sha'th, our leader designate; my good friend and ally Akram Haniyyeh, another adviser to the chairman; Nasser al-Qidwa, the PLO representative at the U.N.; as well as many others all descended on Madrid. Some came to work, others to prove a point, still others to make sure that we would not start forming an "alternative leadership." Add to that more than one hundred "advisers" with no clear function other than to make long-distance calls, drink coffee in the lobby, and bitterly criticize those of us who did have work to do, and the picture of the internal handicaps would emerge almost as grim as that of the external ones. The PLO was treated as a guilty secret, kept away from the public eye. With the exception of Akram, who was surreptitiously smuggled into the hotel and who spent all his time ensconced in his room, all the PLO officials stayed in different and distant hotels, adopting all manner of subterfuge and disguises to make contact with us. We were different, and we were made to feel the difference. The Baker suit had set us apart, and we decided that the occasion called for a whole new "dress code," one of substance and authenticity. Our strange "attire" was to become a symbol of creativity and defiance as opposed to the other guests' traditional dinner suits. We had to exploit the difference and turn our disadvantages into strength. To do that, we had to take bold and daring initiatives and to harness all our skills. And I started the very next day. It was important that we go first, but if we waited for the official format to be worked out, then we might be last, if at all. Knowing that all the press had arrived, Albert sent out notice of our first conference for that afternoon. Neither Faisal nor I had official escort as illegitimate delegates, and Haidar had half a motorcade as head of half a delegation. The three of us made it to the press center only to be told that there were no press rooms ready and no facilities available. We walked through unfinished hallways and around exposed wires until we reached the main staircase. We stopped right there. More than a thousand reporters gathered around us—the stairs and banister nearly gave way under their weight. Suhair screamed as someone almost pushed her into a gaping construction hole. Finally, Albert, ABC producer Ali Qa'dan, and some Palestinian reporters formed a protective chain around us.

I began by announcing that, unlike all the others, we were a people's delegation made up mainly of professional people and academics, and that we had come here to present the cause of our people. If we behaved differently and dispensed with diplomatic niceties, it was precisely because none of us were professional politicians or diplomats. I asked them for their patience and indulgence, and then proceeded to explain the kind of peace we were seeking. It was hard for all the reporters to hear us, but they had heard enough to make them want to hear some more. We moved to the basement and completed the briefing standing on a wobbly table. As the throng moved closer, Haidar and I looked at each other and exchanged the "we survived the Cairo drivers" look.

I announced that our briefing would be the first one tomorrow, at 2:00 P.M., and we reserved that time slot every day for the duration of the conference. Whether they liked it or not the organizers knew that there was nothing they could do about it, having just heard me announce it before the world. Our improvised escapade, however, did not go down well with the Israeli spokesperson, Benjamin Netanyahu, or with Prime Minister Shamir. Both had arrived in Madrid at the time of our press conference and found their press reception at the airport sadly lacking. I was adamant about staying one step ahead.

The next day, Faisal and I had a hard time getting to the press center, and we arrived a few minutes late for the briefing. Without a police escort, it was almost impossible for us to get anywhere in Madrid. I decided to take care of that. The press was aware of the assassination threats against Faisal and myself that had come out of Iran, so I calmly stood up onstage before thousands of reporters and journalists from all over the world and apologized politely for being late. I explained how we had had to make way for every motorcade and to stop at every red light, since we were neither provided with police escort nor given official recognition. A horrified breath was drawn from the room in disbelief. No sooner had we left the briefing hall than we found ourselves surrounded by two dozen civil guards who had miraculously materialized to protect us. As soon as we got back to the hotel, we found the head of Spanish security and other senior officials waiting for us. They would be more than delighted to supply us with full escort each, they announced. They also had more information on the nature of the planned assassination attempt: they had received a tip that a black Seat was booby-trapped and set to go off by remote control as soon as we were close enough to it. As it turned out, every other car in Madrid was a black Seat. After a short while, we gave up looking, but no one would ride with either of us after hearing that warning. A small battle, but a battle won nevertheless.

We still had no speech, and I had had no sleep in two nights. Sitting on the floor, I set up the bed as a desk and wrote out the speech by hand on Suhair's "Embassy of Palestine" memo pad, while Penny typed it on the laptop. My room became a busy station with people walking in and out, checking progress and consulting on issues. I was so completely absorbed that I hardly noticed. I was driven, possessed by the urge to capture in language the essence of the Palestinian experience and to distill it in such a way as to render it a compelling and irresistible force of change. Only when I saw the pages begin to show damp spots did I realize that I was crying. Penny kept urging me on, "It's powerful, it's real. Keep at it." I worried that the emotions were too raw, too painful. "Don't worry. Finish the first draft and then go over it for the politics. At all costs, you must preserve the honesty and immediacy."

I wrote on. By morning, the draft was finished. Faisal, Haidar, Mamdouh, Nabil Shaʾth, and others came for the first reading.

"It's wonderful, but I don't know if I can read it tomorrow. I'm afraid I will cry." Haidar's voice was trembling and his eyes moist.

"Never mind, maʾlesh, go ahead and cry. Heaven knows we have the right to cry; we have enough to cry about." I was touched by Haidar's sincerity.

"It's a raw cry from the heart," Mamdouh said. His eyes were tearful too.

"That's the speech we need," Faisal confirmed. "But how do we go about convincing the leadership?"

"I agree with Faisal," Nabil said. "It's a great speech. I'll fax it to Abu Ammar and get his immediate reaction."

"It's only the first draft. We'll go over it for the political imperatives and add the appropriate formulations to make it politically accurate. But the last thing we need is a speech full of political slogans and clichés. The human dimension must be the vehicle for transmitting political realities." I was worried that the human integrity of the speech would be sacrificed for the recitation of the frozen politically correct formulae of the past. "The voice of the people must come through without manipulation or contrivance."

"Leave it to me," Nabil said. "Prepare a second draft and I'll send it to Tunis for approval. I'm willing to work on it to ensure that it meets the political requirements."

Abu Ammar's first reaction was one of outrage, even though we had sent him the amended draft, which we felt had incorporated all the political requirements. Mamdouh met with Nabil secretly to follow up on the suggestions and countersuggestions. Many of the "outside" intellectuals and politicians also had their input. The cut-and-paste operation brought back to me a mangled draft that had lost much of its coherence and spirit. Once again, I stayed up all night with Penny trying to restore a natural flow and life to the speech. At 6:00 A.M. the speech had been revived with its integrity and dynamics intact, and its political dimension faultless. Half an hour later, I received a call from Nabil saying that Tunis wanted another reference to the PLO in explicit, unambiguous terms and that an allusion to Chairman Arafat must be added. I agreed.

Having turned one corner, I knew Baker had promised Shamir that the opening of the conference would contain no reference whatsoever to the PLO. Shamir had threatened an Israeli walkout. I called Baker, who was already in the conference room. "We have to have a clear reference to the PLO," I announced. "And it's going to be in our speech."

Dennis Ross, Molly Williamson, Ed Djerejian, Margaret Tutwiler, and Baker himself, all participating in the opening session of the conference, took turns whispering on the phone. I was in my hotel room, wrapped in a towel, balancing different telephone conversations, while Suhair was dealing with the media. I changed a reference to "our leadership" to the PLO and I concluded the speech with the "olive branch" quotation. The speech was finished at noon, and Mamdouh and Taisir Hammad (head of the Languages and Translation Department at Birzeit University) immediately began the translation. I took a clean copy and rushed to the press center with Faisal. There we made copies. I sent the original by courier to Haidar. We left Albert and Rashid Khalidi, a Palestinian-American academic and delegation adviser, to handle the press and went down to the CNN studios.

The moment Faisal and I sat down before the monitors, the whole hectic pace of the preceding day caught up with me: I felt drained and vulnerable, and I was tempted to close my eyes and lay my head down. This was supposed to be the moment of Palestinian revelation, yet Faisal and I were sitting in the basement of a prefab temporary structure watching it from a distance through the eye of the camera. The festival had begun, but there was no room for us in the palace. We were there through the speech, through our delegation—the whole Palestinian nation was there—I tried to convince Faisal and myself.

Look up. Look them in the eye, I willed Haidar as he began the speech. These were the words that had come straight from the heart coming straight back to my heart. Although I repeated them silently within, it felt as if I were listening to them for the first time. A strange transformation had taken place, and instead of speaking for the people I found myself listening with their ears and on their behalf. I was touched by magic. So was Faisal.

"We come to you from a tortured land and a proud, though captive people, having been asked to negotiate with our occupiers, but leaving behind the children of the *intifada,* and a people under occupation and under curfew who enjoined us not to surrender or forget. As we speak, thousands of our brothers and sisters are languishing in Israeli prisons and detention camps, most detained without evidence, charge, or trial, many cruelly mistreated and tortured in interrogation, guilty only of seeking freedom or daring to defy the occupation. We speak in their name and we say: Set them free. As we speak, the tens of thousands who have been wounded or permanently disabled are in pain. Let peace heal their wounds. As we speak, the eyes of thousands of Palestinian refugees, deportees, and displaced persons since 1967 are haunting us, for exile is a cruel fate. Bring them home. They have the right to return. As we speak, the silence of demolished homes echoes through the halls and in our minds. We must rebuild our homes in our free state. . . ."

And when we were asked by the reporters later about our feelings, both of us said we were thinking of the people back home. We had borne them with us, and they had spoken in Madrid. We were all there in the fullness of our humanity laid bare before the world, and we were ready to begin the process of redemption. But our pain was acute.

We had explored the possibility of the whole delegation wearing the *hatta,* the traditional Palestinian headdress, as a symbol of the distinct Palestinian identity, but we had discarded the idea as being too flamboyant. Saeb Erakat, however, decided to put on his *hatta* for the official meetings. Shamir received two blows to his sensitive psyche; he had to listen to the articulation of the name PLO and to look at a Palestinian *hatta*—a fate worse than death. He reported our outrageous behavior to Baker and demanded retribution for the rude shock his finely tuned sensibilities had received.

Baker summoned us to a private meeting, of a sensitive nature. Saeb must not appear before Shamir for the duration of the conference, Baker confided, or before any of the Israeli delegates, as that would have serious consequences. I had visions of Shamir, Netanyahu, Elyakim Rubinstein, all of them, in flowing silks reclining on velvet art deco sofas, wiping their brows with scented scarves and swooning delicately. It was hard to keep a straight face. Baker was asking us to spare them the horror, and he thought that *we* were hung up on symbols. In fact, he was so concerned he had recruited Saudi Prince Bandar and the Egyptian and European delegations to support his request. Prince Bandar extended an invitation to Saeb to visit Saudi Arabia immediately. Saeb, of course, saw through that and was devastated. The pressure reached Arafat, who called and asked us not to send Saeb to the next sessions to avoid an international diplomatic incident. Baker and his team were pursuing the subject with vigor. The fate of the whole peace process was hanging on a Palestinian *hatta*.

Later that evening, Nabil Sha'th informed us that Abu Ammar wanted to see us—the whole delegation. Used to clandestine meetings under the cover of darkness, I could not visualize the one hundred plus people skipping out of Madrid unnoticed and returning to resume meetings with an innocent business-as-usual demeanor. So far we had practiced brinkmanship with bravado and had created facts with flair. But a disappearing delegation might be a difficult trick to pull.

But that night, Arafat sent us a Moroccan plane and smuggled a hundred human contraband out of Madrid. Nabil got up and announced with a deadpan face and in a serious tone that the plane was heading toward the Caribbean for a well-earned day in the sun, and that each of us was to be issued a swimsuit and a beach towel for the duration. Our laughter bordered on the hysterical. We landed in Algiers instead, and headed straight for the amphitheater.

Only then did I realize why Abu Ammar had insisted on taking the risk of holding such a meeting. It turned out to be a marathon grievance session for all those "advisers" and hangers-on who felt excluded or neglected. He played the supreme magician, turning himself into a gigantic sponge to absorb all the anger and pettiness. He joked about the massive phone bill of the idle who sat in their rooms all day and made long-distance calls. "Of course, many of you went to Madrid precisely so that you could call your parents or children, your best friends and acquaintances, and you might even discover long-lost relatives whom you absolutely must call all over the world and tell them you're in Madrid. I always described ourselves as the 'zero-zero people' [the international access code]. So go ahead and call." He defused the aspiring politicians who complained that we were not including them in the decision making: "You should see the problems I have. I am leading a nation of leaders, just like a big sack of onions. No matter where I dip my hand I come up with heads [of onion]. So don't feel left out. Every Palestinian feels he or she should be leading." He then repeated his famous story of the Palestinian in India.

Indira Gandhi called Arafat one day complaining about a Palestinian who was making trouble for her and for the Congress Party. Abu Ammar went to India to investigate. It turned out that the Palestinian was a "god" with a rather large following who refused to vote for the Congress Party and was agitating against it. Arafat sent for him.

"Why are you making trouble for Mrs. Gandhi, who is a good friend of the Palestinian people and cause? And how come you're passing yourself off as a god? Don't you know I could have you recalled or deported?"

"I came to India to study and became the disciple of a famous guru. When he died, his followers chose me to replace him. I do not want to leave India and I promise not to make trouble for Mrs. Gandhi if she will leave us alone."

"Done!" said Abu Ammar.

"You think you're an important leader, but I have seventeen million followers. How many Palestinians do you command? Six million?"

"True, you may have seventeen million adherents and I may have only six million nationals. But the difference is that every one of those six million, like you, thinks that he's a god."

Onions or gods, a placated Palestinian delegation returned to Madrid under the cover of darkness having witnessed a master director at work. I still had to meet press demands, hold daily briefings, participate in all diplomatic meetings, continue the American dialogue, and attend leadership and strategy meetings while continuing to prepare official documents. Having gone without sleep for four nights, I was ready to drop. I literally started seeing stars while waiting for a Guidance Committee meeting to start. Holding on to the table, I whispered that I absolutely had to get some sleep and that I was going to my room. Kamil Mansour, a good friend and brilliant colleague from Paris, apparently unaware of my insane schedule, announced that he was not prepared to wait for a meeting while I slept, and that if I went he would also leave. I was speechless. All my exhaustion and anger seemed to swell up inside me and I felt gagged. I stood up, and with the last remaining surge of energy I hurled my papers and files across the room, then walked out and banged the door behind me. I sobbed for an hour, slept for another, then got up to give several interviews.

Dan Rather, Charlayne Hunter-Gault, ABC, NBC, BBC, TF1, German, Dutch, Spanish, and all the television stations in the world seemed to have an appointment with me that day. But since the stringent hotel security conducted thorough and prolonged searches of every person, bag, and piece of equipment that entered the lobby, there was no way that I could meet all my commitments. Suhair and I had the brilliant idea of having the different crews set up in the park across the street and I would just move from one setting to the other without losing any time. The Spanish security had fits. They also knew that I was crazy enough to do it. Suddenly the park was cordoned off with yellow tape and scores of civil guards; helicopters hovered overhead. I strode out of the hotel, walked into the park, and began to give my interviews as if the park were my own backyard. The Palestinians had done it again! First we had laid claim to the press center and prime-time briefings; now we had confiscated a public park for our special interviews. Between the park and the Efema, Suhair counted more than twenty-seven long television interviews in one day, not counting the briefings or the questions in passing.

That night I was supposed to prepare the rebuttal speech (after the initial speeches each delegation was supposed to present a response to the conference). Slouched on the bed, I first prepared an outline of the major points, then my mind went blank. I called Nabil and told him that I could not function anymore. He was adamant that I try and informed me that he was sending two people secretly to help me with the writing and to stay up with me. The two envoys turned out to be Ilan Halevi, my old-time militant Israeli colleague, and Elias Sanbar, another old-time friend from Paris with whom we had started preparing the negotiations file back in 1989. Both settled down on the floor, and within a few minutes stretched out and fell into a deep sleep. Penny and I continued working, but I kept drifting off. Penny would wake me up at regular intervals with "You can't fall asleep now, just a few more paragraphs, you're almost done," and I would wake up, write a few more lines, and sink back into my slumber. When I heard our rebuttal the next day, it was as if for the first time, as if having written the whole speech in my sleep.

Friday afternoon, an impromptu Arab coordination meeting was called. From the Guidance Committee, I could find only Ghassan al-Khatib; the rest were in different meetings all over Madrid. Ghassan and I went up to the suite of the Jordanian foreign minister, Kamel Abu Jaber. The head of the Jordanian delegation, Abdel-Salam al-Majali (later to become prime minister), the Syrian foreign minister, Farouq al-Shara, the head of the Syrian delegation, Muwaffaq al-Allaf, and representatives of the Lebanese side were all waiting for us. The subject was whether to commit ourselves to begin the first round of bilateral talks in Madrid on Sunday or not. The Americans wanted the bilateral talks to begin immediately but there were some who were dragging their feet. I was puzzled; since we had agreed with the Jordanians to start on that date and had informed the Americans accordingly, I felt that the question was irrelevant. It gradually dawned on me that the Syrians had not given their response yet, and that they had a specific purpose in mind. They must not separate us, Shara insisted. The Arab delegations wanted us all to meet at the same place and the same time because if we were separated Arab coordination would be weakened. After a lengthy discussion, Shara went into the bedroom to speak to Baker on the phone.

We waited. I was then asked by the group to go and see what was holding him up. As soon as I knocked and entered, Shara handed me the phone while still speaking into it, and I heard him say, "Here, speak to Hanan." I picked up the phone entirely unprepared for the harangue that followed, with Baker literally shouting on the other end.

"Don't tell me you're in on this too. The Palestinians had given their word. You all start on Sunday or the whole thing is off."

"What's the problem?" I asked innocently. "I thought it was only a technical question that could be easily solved."

"Technical question! The man wants all delegations to meet simultaneously and in one location. We could manage one building, but the meetings must be held sequentially. That was the agreement," Baker yelled.

"Look at it this way," I said, trying to appear calm, injecting an Aristotelian note into the conversation, "he wants unity of time and unity of place. You say you can provide unity of place. Let's deal with that as a compromise and see how close we can get to the time element." I was glad I did not inject unity of action there. I could visualize the fumes coming out of the receiver.

"You just tell Mr. Shara that the whole thing is off. I'm going home. I'm taking the plane this evening and he can go back to Syria. As far as I'm concerned, it's finished!" And he hung up on me. (I must add that I have paraphrased much of Baker's conversation for the sake of decorum.) Baker later wrote an article on diplomacy and peacemaking, saying that part of it was also knowing when to hang up. I got the message.

I went out into the living room and reported the gist of the conversation to the Arab group. Everyone was convinced that Baker was serious, and we urged the Syrians to accept an Arab compromise. That was how the Aristotelian unities became part of the political discourse of the peace process. Unity of place was more important than unity of time, we said, since we could not guarantee the pace of negotiations but could ensure coordination by sharing the same venue and the same broad time frame. I was asked to inform Baker that such was the nature of the Arab-proposed compromise and that we would do our best to persuade the Syrians, provided the Americans would accept this proposal. I relayed the message and assumed that the crisis was over, particularly in view of the fact that the Americans had already accepted the principle of one venue for all the bilateral meetings. We were supposed to start in Madrid on the third of November.

During the Palestinian leadership meeting, the issue was considered resolved and we worked out both the list of negotiators for the first session and the major policy positions to be presented. As usual, I had a briefing scheduled for 2:00 P.M., before anyone else. I arrived at the press center at 1:00 to give some private interviews and was handed urgent messages from Baker and Ross. Suhair asked if we could use the phones of the MBC (Middle East Broadcasting Corporation), and they gave us full use of their office. Baker was on one line asking if I was going to announce our acceptance that day, and confirming that the Jordanians had already given their affirmative response. I called Nabil Sha'th on another line and told him that I suspected a problem with the Syrians since Baker was on the other line insisting on a public announcement that day. Nabil said that he was not aware of any problem, and confirmed our agreement with the Jordanians; he stayed on the line and kept trying to call the Syrians to investigate. On a third line, I called Abu Ammar, who was keen on a unified Arab position and was sure that we had one, as he had not been informed otherwise. Dennis Ross called on the fourth line (since Baker had already left for the Efema) and asked me to meet him in the waiting room backstage. I told Nabil, who still did not have any response from the Syrians, and we agreed that if he had any news he would call me at the waiting room or during the briefing. In the meantime we agreed that I would go ahead. After seeing Baker and assuring him that our position had not changed, I walked out onstage and gave my briefing.

I described Shamir's speech as absolutist and regressive, a throwback to the past rather than a future-oriented speech, an expression of a closed and anachronistic ideology rather than of an expansive and pragmatic leadership. In his speech he had been accusatory and attacking, holding the world responsible for the Holocaust. Elaborating on our speech, which looked forward rather than backward, I called for the recognition of the human dimension and for a responsible exercise of candor and foresight in the service of peace. In response to a question about beginning the bilateral talks on November 3, I announced that we were ready to start talks in Madrid on that date. Asked about a permanent venue, I responded that we would accept a neutral one outside the region, one that would not exert a negative influence on the talks or place the Palestinians at a disadvantage.

On the question of venue, the Israelis wanted to stay in the region.

None of the Arab parties would accept that, as that could get the process embroiled in complicated regional politics. The Syrians and Lebanese wanted to conduct negotiations in Washington on the turf of the American co-sponsor in order to ensure U.S. involvement and interest in making the process succeed. We were hesitant about Washington because the United States had suspended its dialogue with the PLO, and most of our leadership were either not allowed to enter the United States or were required to get a special visa with a congressional waiver. We also felt that the United States was not neutral territory, given its special relationship with Israel and the extreme bias of the Congress. The Americans wanted to make sure that the process was a winning proposition before moving it to Washington and running the risk of getting saddled with a dud. The Jordanians were upset that I had made the Palestinian announcement before they made theirs.

On the question of timing, Israel wanted to have a separate time frame for each bilateral negotiating track, in addition to different venues, to make sure that there would be no Arab coordination and that the divide-and-conquer strategy would prevail in the negotiations. All the Arab sides wanted coordination, but for different reasons and in different ways. Palestinian-Syrian suspicions loomed large here. In the Arab world, Syria was always perceived of and presented itself as a major player and a regional leader. The Assad-Arafat hostility was no secret, and Syria was playing host and patron to Arafat's opposition. Abu Ammar, though, wanted to play the Palestinian card himself under the heading of "the independent Palestinian decision," and to prevent Syria from using it to improve its own negotiating position. Israel, of course, was constantly trying to play one side off against the other. To put it mildly, Arab coordination was a minefield through which one had to maneuver with extreme caution.

Once I was asked how many audiences I had in mind when I gave public briefings or responded to official questions. I began counting. The strata of listeners became a host of internal ghosts fighting for my soul and speech. Was I expected to keep them separate, to identify each one and address it in its own parlance? Would I speak to our constituency, a people under occupation, the same way I would address Israeli public opinion? Did I excercise self-censorship when targeting the ears of the leadership in Tunis? Which Arab constituency or government did I envisage when speaking the language of our torn world? As a woman was my discourse gender-based? Was I slipping into Western garb and an Occidental mind-set when I faced the foreign media? What messages was

I transmitting to governments and world leaders as opposed to the signals I was conveying to their people? Could it be that I was guilty of making the speaker more famous and important than the speech?

Suddenly, I felt captive of the Word, which I had revered and savored for so long. The *logos,* formidable as an enemy and overwhelming as a friend, had become both master and slave. I began to resent the original question, how many audiences I had in mind, which had opened up such a Pandora's box of linguistic and existential self-consciousness. Then I remembered *amanah*—as an instinctive guide and human compass. Too often described as a people prone to passion and hyperbole, as a people of extravagant tragedy, this was time to let the Palestinian people convey their simple truth. I realized then that it was not so much the pluralism and diversity of the audience as the unity and integrity of the message. In this drama time and place were mere technicalities.

As a child Amal had developed an intense attachment to a children's television program about Maya the Bee roaming the world in search of her lost mother. The bee's name in Arabic was Zeina (which explains her sister's name). Amal got to the point where she would cry at hearing the theme song of the program. Gradually, we realized that she was turning off the televsion set the moment before *Zeina the Bee* came on. Puzzled, we inquired why. Amal's reponse was that she loved the program so much that she couldn't bear the sadness she felt every time it ended. She would rather deprive herself of the pleasure of watching it than have to go through the sorrow of its loss. Was that a child's version of the story of a people and their land? Had our sorrow over the loss of Palestine deprived us of the joy of its existence?

We left Madrid with a combined sense of euphoria and loss. We felt that we had staked a place for ourselves in this public forum, that we had spoken out as Palestinians. But we also knew this was only the beginning, that the hardest part was yet to be; we knew that in Madrid the bilateral talks had not actually produced anything, that there was still no concrete engagement.

Recognition and peripety had simultaneously brought the plot to new heights. I began to worry about the letdown. We were going home to a people whose hopes were raised beyond realistic expectations. Would they be able to bear the sorrow of the end of this episode, or should we have turned it off even before it began?

CHAPTER NINE

Our homecoming was a festival. Thousands of Palestinians were planning on coming to Jericho to receive the returning delegation. The Israeli authorities immediately declared Jericho a closed military area, not open to the public. Closure notwithstanding, Jericho became a human celebration of hope and peace. Zeina and Emile met us on the way, and Zeina climbed in the bus with me. We embraced in laughter and tears amid cheers and shouts of welcome and encouragement. Waving olive branches and chanting excitedly, hundreds of exhilarated well-wishers met our bus at the bridge and accompanied it on foot through town. Some jumped on the bus and others hung on to any handle they could find. Pieces of the bus started coming out in people's hands as if it were made of cardboard. By the time we got to Jerusalem, our bus looked like a mechanical skeleton.

Jerusalem was a frenzy of excitement. All the energy and exuberance that had lain dormant during the years suddenly erupted. Faisal was borne on the shoulders of the crowd and I was swept along. At the National theater, Al-Masrah, we were hoisted up on the stage, which groaned under the sudden weight. The theater was so tightly packed that I was worried about ventilation and the crush of bodies. I shouted and gestured desperately to Emile to take Zeina out. Finally, things settled sufficiently for us to speak and be heard above the din.

True, we had made a place for this nation among the assembled nations of the world; true, we had gained global recognition as a people with rights and aspirations; true, we had defied Israeli lies and constraints and won the day; but all these were just the beginning of a long and arduous journey. The real challenge still lay ahead. While attempting to buttress the people's sense of vindication and joy, we were trying to deflate the monster of excessive optimism and unrealistic expectations, which I knew could result in a great letdown. In Gaza, Haidar conveyed the same message even more brutally: "It is premature to celebrate," he cautioned the crowds. "We still have a long and difficult road ahead." They were true words.

The polls showed an unprecedented high of 87 percent support. While we were in Madrid Palestinians had started going around giving out flowers to soldiers and placing olive branches in the barrels of their guns. Some Palestinians, demonstrating for peace, were shot, and killed, but others, carrying Madrid in their hearts, persisted, believing it was possible to bring about an overnight reversal. I remembered a 1974 visit with Joan Baez in Ramallah in which she advised Palestinians to distribute flowers to the army. We asked her if she had ever lived under military occupation. Flowers wither and die in the sight of a gun, just like our children. Perhaps now, I thought, Joan would understand. Never again did Palestinians hand Israeli soldiers flowers and olive branches. Like Amal, we collectively turned off *Zeina the Bee* before it started, unwilling to undergo the pain of its transience.

From town to town, from camp to camp, the members of the delegation trudged the length and breadth of the Occupied Territories to unfold before the people the contents of our heavy burden. In the absence of a free press or any type of media facilities, such as television and radio, we resorted to the most primitive and direct means of communication: the oral tradition. Ignoring the security risks, we held open-air meetings, town meetings, and special seminars and debates. We became the minstrels of peace, the evangelists of a new type of Gospels. Applauded, reviled, questioned, and advised, we took on a mission of advocacy and laid ourselves bare for the most immediate and honest form of accountability. Our homes became stations for numerous delegations who came to find a way of involving themselves directly. They felt they had the right to seek and obtain information, and to have an immediate say in the conduct of the talks. And they did. Rarely had any delegation brought to its mission such an immersion in the concerns of its constituency. Such was the source of our credibility and strength, but also of our vulnerability —our public Achilles' heel. As the saga—or soap opera—of negotiations played on, we would spend each interval between episodes analyzing the last one and preparing for the next. We were, after all, the people's delegation.

We also had another type of accountability—to our leadership, the backstage directors who had not been allowed onstage, the PLO. During and in between rounds we would rush off to Tunis for sessions of consultation, reporting, discussion, and decision making.

It was the middle of November, and the question of time and place had not been entirely resolved. There was discussion that Washington would be the next venue, and I was busy negotiating with the Americans the question of PLO visas and parity of status and treatment. Shamir had embarked on his stormy U.S. visit, and I was talking to Rowland Evans in the CNN Jerusalem studios. I had received a call from Washington that morning inquiring whether December 4 would be acceptable as a starting date for the first Washington round. Following consultations with Tunis, I had said yes. Right after the interview, I received a call from Molly Williamson asking for an official meeting to extend invitations for the next round. "Washington, December 4?" I asked. "How did you know?" she said. So when the ABC reporter asked me as I was leaving the station if I had any news, I blithely announced the time and place of the next round and created a major diplomatic crisis with Shamir in Washington. Between the White House and the State Department, no one had informed Shamir—and Shamir had not given Israel's agreement. Besides, we discovered later, the U.S. government had promised to coordinate first with the Israelis any proposals or decisions and not to surprise them with any sudden revelations. I surprised them—I had not promised.

On December 1, a delegation of about thirty-five Palestinians embarked for Washington. Once again we were stopped at the bridge, and the crossing was made difficult. With repeated delays, searches, humiliations, and plain obnoxiousness, Israeli officials deliberately challenged our sense of mission and dignity. In Amman, we discovered that the U.S. visas that we had requested for a number of PLO officials, including Nabil Sha'th, had not all been granted. A whole new negotiation commenced to get Nabil and a revised list approved. Abu Ammar arrived in Amman at 2:00 A.M. and we decided not to leave until we received all the required visas. The Jordanians had chartered a plane for 11:00 A.M. By 6:00 in the evening we got four out of five names approved, and Abu Ammar decided we could go ahead minus Nabil, but stressed that I should continue negotiating with the State Department in Washington so Nabil could catch up with us. When we arrived at the airport we discovered that no one had informed the Jordanian delegation of our predicament. They had been waiting at the airport since morning; one could safely assume that they were not in the best of spirits. Actually, Abdel-Salam al-Majali was so put off that when he finally found his voice he just went on and on about how impertinent and inconsiderate we were and how we were always springing surprises on them. That was only the first in a series.

Having weathered the Israeli, American, and Jordanian episodes all in one day, we got on the plane and headed for Washington. On the way, I prepared our official statement and press release, and worked on some position papers with other members of our delegation. Just before landing, I asked that we organize ourselves in a way that would show two separate delegations, and requested that the Jordanians go first. That did not go down well with Majali. At the airport, Haidar tried to calm him down with an old Arabic song: "You and I cannot do without each other!" That succeeded partially in making up for some of my offensive behavior, as he described it: "She decides and tells everybody what to do." I breathed a sigh of relief.

But the day was not over yet. We were met at the airport by a large number of reporters firing questions. I had stayed behind a bit, talking to some women who had received us with flowers. The reporters called me by name and I came forward and started responding to the questions directed at me. Then they asked, "Doesn't anyone have a prepared statement for the press?" I looked at the Jordanian side and waited, but they had none. So I pulled mine out of my handbag and read it. All the networks carried it. Majali was livid. "Not only does she boss everybody around, but the press ask for a statement and she just pulls one out of her handbag. She never even bothered to tell me ahead of time!" That did it, I thought. I was sure I had inadvertently made an enemy for life. However, as it turned out, Majali (al-Basha) and I became very good friends, and would look back and share a laugh at our turbulent early encounters. His generosity of spirit and genuine warmth were as engaging as his candor.

To prove a point, the Israelis refused to start the negotiations on the agreed date. Instead of sending their delegation, they pulled out their master of the sound bite, Benjamin Netanyahu. Armed with studied charm and rehearsed lines, the erstwhile "darling of the American media" called a press conference for 11:00 A.M., the day on which negotiations were supposed to start. The nonnegotiations were supposed to start at 10:00, so I decided to go to the State Department and wait for the delegation there, to meet the reporters who were on a stakeout at the entrance, thereby preempting Netanyahu.

Dennis Ross was furious. "You will not be allowed into the State Department," he flatly announced. "It's against the rules, and the Israelis will cry foul."

"Regardless of American hospitality, I have no intention to enter the building. I will just wait outside for our delegation and chat with the press in the meanwhile," I answered. "Besides, the Israelis don't intend to show up, so you can relax. They won't be subjected to the indignity of actually having to set eyes on me in person." He was not amused.

Five minutes later Baker called. "Dennis told me what you intend to do. I'm asking you not to approach the C Street entrance of the State Department," he said.

"Why? Is there a curfew on, or don't you believe in freedom of movement?" By then I was beginning to get impatient. "Is there a law against my standing on the sidewalk?"

"You know that's not true, but I want to avoid an incident with the Israelis." He tried to explain. "I'm asking you not to show up."

"That's your problem. You know I don't take my instructions from you. I'll consider what you asked as well-meaning advice. I'll think about it and do what I think is best for the Palestinians—not for the Americans or the Israelis."

Akram and I discussed Baker's request. I picked up my walkie-talkie, got into my car and headed for the C Street entrance where the press seemed to have nothing better to do than talk to me. I verified that the negotiations had not started on the agreed date because of the Israeli no-show. "Instead of sending their spokesperson to hold press conferences, they should send him to negotiate. They're supposed to be here to negotiate with us, not to score points with the press," I said. "We're ready, willing, and able. But where is the Israeli delegation?" Then I asked the rhetorical question that no one dared to answer publicly: "I want to know who calls the shots in this peace process, who decides? Is it the Israelis or the co-sponsors? When will the United States stop allowing the tail to wag the dog?"

To get back at us, the Israelis announced that they were ready to start negotiations on the ninth of December, the anniversary of the *intifada,* knowing that we would not break the Palestinian tradition of strikes and prayers that day. That night we decided to maintain the Palestinian strike that was called in the Occupied Territories, and to hold memorial services for our dead at the Washington Cathedral and the Mosque. The Interreligious Dialogue Committee, a Washington-based group made up of Christians, Muslims, and Jews, undertook to make the arrangements and to work out the program. We informed the rest of the Arab delegations and they decided to join us in solidarity.

At the last minute, that morning, the committee decided to hold the services half an hour earlier, but neglected to inform the Jordanian delegation. They arrived half an hour late and we had to make room for Majali in the front row with us. As he squeezed in next to me he whispered, "You've done it again. I hope you don't have any more surprises up your sleeve!" I could not convince him that I had had nothing to do with the arrangements. Two minutes later, the organizer got up and announced that I was going to address the congregation, and that each head of delegation would make a presentation. The look in Majali's eyes was worth volumes! I put my hands up helplessly. Someone was determined to prevent a beautiful friendship from blossoming. It took months for me to convince Al-Basha that I was as much a victim as he.

With all that out of the way, we thought the negotiations would finally take off. But that was not to be. The Israeli delegation refused to meet with ours; that is, they would not meet with us separately but only as part of the Jordanian delegation. The battle over "separate tracks" began. At one moment we were treated as a sub-part of the Jordanian delegation, at another as an item on the agenda. I protested: "We are neither a subhuman species, nor a sub-delegation or appendage to the Jordanian delegation, nor an ad hoc committee, nor a subject for discussion in somebody else's negotiations. We came to negotiate on the basis of the two-track approach, Arab-Israeli and Palestinian-Israeli, not to fall between the tracks." The State Department refused to open the door to a separate room for the Palestinian-Israeli negotiations, so we had another battle on our hands. By locking the door, the United States had begun by taking sides. Armed with the Letter of Invitation and the Letter of Assurance, we challenged the Americans to honor their own commitments, but were flatly told to "work it out with the Israelis." The two-track approach remained a mono track and we refused to enter the one room left open by the State Department for simultaneous Jordanian-Palestinian-Israeli negotiations. This merging of the tracks meant a merger of national identities, and we were not prepared to abandon ours. "All we're asking for now is a separate track, not a separate state. We demand the opportunity and our right to sit face-to-face with our occupiers and address them directly as equals. We want to look them in the eye and say, 'We're a people with rights, with a national identity, and we demand our freedom,' " I declared, but to no avail.

Thus the whole first round was spent in the hallway, giving rise to the concept of "corridor diplomacy." Our delegation would dutifully proceed to the State Department every morning and head for the locked meeting room, then turn to the waiting room and wait. The heads of delegations would meet in the corridor and play a rerun of the irresistible force–immovable object drama. When they sat down on the couch in the hallway, a new variation of the corridor diplomacy emerged—couch negotiations. Haidar Abdel-Shafi and Elyakim Rubinstein, the head of the Israeli delegation, had locked horns, and they continued to do so for the next two years.

Haidar, a gentleman of the old school, was a man of strong principle and firm convictions. Behind his bushy eyebrows and guileless smile lay an unyielding iron will. Tall, thin, and well-dressed, he carried his seventy-two years gracefully; but his eyes were those of a young man. We all had problems keeping up with him, and he waited for no one. As soon as he was ready, he would take off. The moment his car stopped, he would dash out without looking back. He had an intense aversion to being late and disliked it in others. He would take any type of sloppiness —physical, intellectual, or procedural—as a personal offense. His rigor, discipline, and correctness often offset Nabil Sha'th's more relaxed, unstructured attitude. However, his subtle and often sardonic sense of humor, as opposed to Nabil's more jocular wit, struck target with accuracy.

I called him *Hakeemna,* our doctor or our wise man, and I felt possessive about him even when he was at his most stubborn and exasperating. And I did have enough cause to make that claim. Our family friendship dated back to the days before I was born. He and my uncle Ishaq Mikhail (my father's brother) had gone to medical school together and had been roommates in Beirut. I would often entreat him to share with me some memories of those days. "Your uncle," he said, "had an eye for the women. He was more daring and adventurous than I was." At dinner one night he told me: "Do you know why I really enjoy good food? As poor medical students on a strict allowance, your uncle and I would often go hungry. We filled up on starch and carbohydrates, and fantasized about all the rich and scrumptious gourmet feasts that lay in waiting for us after graduation. Ishaq would actually wake me up at night to talk about food. He was always hungry." My uncle, who had gone into surgery and had acquired a long list of letters trailing behind his name, died in a plane crash off the Saudi coast thirty years ago. My father had always talked about him as being brilliant and exceptionally talented. Haidar brought him back to life in my imagination; but he did much more. By just being himself, Haidar gave me glimpses of my father. That was enough to place me forever in his debt.

Both had the habit of absentmindedly twisting upward their eyebrow hairs when absorbed in their own thoughts. They also shared the habit of stroking their bald heads as if patting their nonexistent hair in place. "The question is not being bald," my father always said. "It's just a matter of having the largest forehead in the world." They shared the habit of speaking the formal English of the British mandate with its hints of Victorian propriety and emphasis on correctness and careful diction. Their straight-backed gait and squared shoulders conveyed not so much a military discipline as dignity and self-confidence. Both were medical doctors and graduates of the American University of Beirut, and both had played a role in Palestinian national politics although Haidar's was a more active, public role. Their progressive socialist backgrounds formed another historical bond. My father died in December 1988, just before his eightieth birthday, and I always wished Haidar, who was ten years younger, an even longer life.

Three days before Christmas, during the most violent storm of the year, my father got out of his bed, found an open door, walked out of the house, and disappeared into the night. Over the last few years, we had watched helplessly as Alzheimer's disease ravaged his memory and his brain, despite all our efforts and the best medical attention. I could see the struggle in his eyes as he tried to find the right word and make the right connection with a world that was rapidly becoming incomprehensible. I am not really like that, his eyes seemed to say. The hardest part for me to cope with were the rare moments of lucidity that enabled him to realize the futility of the struggle. I am going under, his eyes seemed to say; help me.

Nevertheless, his good nature and sense of humor prevailed. They seemed to find the means to surface and to save his humanity despite his sinking memory and tortured mind. He and Emile developed a language of their own, and they would spend hours communicating and laughing. They radiated a warmth that thawed the bitterness which gripped my heart at the senselessness, the injustice of it all. I watched them in silence, pretending to read or write as they wove their spell and restored my sanity.

It was this goodness—both Emile's and my father's—that shone through and healed me even at the darkest times. Though I had not married a man like my father, they grew closer and more like each other with time. Coincidentally, they shared the same birthday. Emile, the city man from Jerusalem, with his rock band and contemporary theater group, and my father, the man of nature, intellect, and medicine, became inseparable—father and son by choice. Surrounded by women, the two men of my family, of my heart, were strong enough, confident enough not to feel like they had to compete with or repress their women. Rather they relished our independence. And they had the necessary courage to be sensitive, to make emotional commitments without feeling weak or guilty.

So how did Daud, the Palestinian rebel and peasant doctor, come to marry Wadiʾa, the aristocratic Lebanese and rebel in her own right? The young doctor had sent an employee on a donkey to the train station to pick up the hospital's new scrub nurse. Later he asked the orderly what the new nurse looked like. "She has magnificent large, black eyes, like those of a wild heifer," he replied. "Then send her in," came the quick response. It was love at first sight. Daud broke off his earlier engagement to a more appropriate woman and pursued his new love. Her family at first protested—he was a "Palestinian peasant." But she had already defied them by going to college and getting her degrees in ophthalmic scrub nursing, and then by actually going to work in Palestine. His family protested, for she was older and a "stranger" to boot. Till now, Ramallah people use that term to refer to anybody else who did not descend from the founding fathers of Ramallah—the seven brothers who founded the original seven clans, *hamoulahs,* more than five centuries ago. Besides, she was Episcopalian and daughter of a minister and missionary, while his family was historically Greek Orthodox, like the rest of the "real" Ramallah people. They married Episcopalian, set up a clinic together, and proceeded to have five daughters.

He joined the Palestine army under the British and became a medical officer, moving from one city in Palestine to another every two years and having a daughter with almost the same regularity.

Just as I had learned from the Jewish gentleman who had visited our home to thank my father for his kind treatment when he had been a POW in 1948, I became privy to a similar revelation regarding my father from an opposite source. During the days of the great Palestinian rebellion against both the British and the armed Jewish gangs, my father used to help the rebels hiding out in the mountains with the freedom of movement afforded him by his medical permit, smuggling them food and supplies. "We owe him a lot," I was told by Mustafa Geith, a lifelong friend of his who was one of the mountain rebels, and later became a male nurse. "He took risks and almost got himself blown up several times." I remarked, "But he never told me." Mustafa answered, "Well you know how he was. He never talked about himself or his achievements. In some ways, he was too shy."

However, he did tell me how the family escaped Tiberias in 1947. Stationed there, my father and family thought they had found the earthly paradise. I was just a baby. Violence shortly interrupted their idyllic life. The British were incarcerating or hanging the Palestinian rebels, while the Jewish gangs were growing stronger with arms smuggled under the very eyes (and often with the collaboration) of the British. Acts of terrorism, like the blowing up of the King David Hotel, were on the increase. As the fighting got worse, a Jewish doctor and neighbor of ours informed my father that an armed attack was going to take place against the Palestinians in Tiberias. He helped secure a truck. After my father smuggled the family out to Amman, he went back to Palestine. In time, the family found its way back into Palestine and our ancestral town of Ramallah.

Just before I turned three, I stopped eating meat. No amount of coaxing, threat, or punishment could get me to swallow one bite. With my stubborn streak, I remember sitting in my chair till evening while all the other children were out playing. I was being punished for not swallowing that one piece of meat. My mother thought it was sheer defiance and stubbornness. My father suddenly remembered the reason. "She must have seen the slaughter of the little white lamb we got her." I must have, but could not recall the horror. I simply could not eat meat. My mother then had to prepare alternative meatless dishes for me until I went to college. The lamb was killed under the mulberry tree in the garden of our old home. That tree had been planted by my grandfather the day my father was born, and as such gained mystical significance for the whole family.

As children, my sisters and I would climb its broad and sturdy branches, pick its delicious white mulberries, engrave our symbols and secret messages on its trunk, hide our little treasures in its crevices, and generally treat it as our second home. My mother in particular felt very protective and superstitious about the tree. "It's your father's age, your father's life. No one and nothing must harm it." One summer, my father was quite insistent about my mother going to Beirut on her annual visit to her family. When she came back, she found the tree gone and a large apartment building looming at her in its place. That was one trauma I had witnessed in their marriage. Did she later connect Alzheimer's as the felling of the mulberry tree? I never asked her.

What I did ask her was how she could reconcile such two seemingly disparate cultures and traditions that seemed to coexist in our house. Brought up in the strictest literal Victorian tradition, my mother had inherited a distinct class consciousness and culture that she maintained faithfully, even to the point of refusing to eat with us if the housekeeper was allowed to sit at the same table with us. My father, of course, was a socialist, an egalitarian who thought of himself as a peasant first and doctor second, and who had forged undying friendships with people of all classes and social backgrounds. Most of the time he did not even charge his patients, or would accept payment in baskets of tomatoes, grapes, figs, or whatever produce was in season. While she was a devout, practicing Episcopalian who never missed a service, his church visits were limited to rites of passage such as weddings, baptisms, and funerals. When he had his heart attack, our church minister came to pray with him. My father jokingly told him, "We can talk about amusing issues to lift the spirits of the patient rather than pray for his soul. I've taken care of that department with God and I have many people doing the praying on my behalf." Actually, ours was the archetypal ecumenical family: my father had two sisters who were Catholic nuns, one who was a Quaker, one Greek Orthodox, a brother who was a Baptist, a daughter who was married to a Muslim, a wife who was Episcopalian, and a variety of other relatives of all persuasions.

Both my mother and father had their distinct codes of hospitality. Every afternoon, and in the best of all British traditions, my mother would have guests over for afternoon tea. We would come home from school to a living room full of friends partaking of delicate little crustless sand-wiches and a delicious variety of finger food rolled out on a linen-covered trolley. When it came to wearing white gloves, we all rebelled.

My father's hospitality went back to the ancient madafah tradition, or the hospitality–guest house that each hamoulah or clan maintained to house and feed travelers and guests. My grandfather had maintained the madafah of the ʿAwwad clan and my father upheld the tradition in our house. No guest would be refused food or shelter, and it would be unforgivable had anyone been allowed to leave the house without having joined us for at least a meal. I got used to seeing my mother and her assistants preparing meals for scores of people, never knowing who would show up. We rarely spent a night at home without having guests. Between my mother's afternoon teas and my father's *madafah,* we learned not only what a double dose of hospitality could mean, but also what a complex process of mutual accommodation marriage could be.

When he built the new family house in 1960, my father must have thought that we would stay together forever. The upstairs was for my sisters Huda and Nadia (Abla and Muna having married by then), the main floor for my parents and myself, the downstairs for banquets and receptions (where I now live), and the ground floor for Huda's sculpting studio, his emergency clinic, and for the gardener. But he continued to do almost all the gardening himself. He supervised the terracing of the garden, chose each tree himself and knew exactly where it belonged, and planted the bouquet of fragrant flowers that formed the festival of color at the entrance of our home. It was a Palestinian and Mikhail tradition to drape a shawl of jasmine over the front gate as a scented sign of welcome. On one side of the front wrought iron gate my father had planted a jasmine bush that framed the gate like an aromatic tiara. On the other side, he planted English lavender that my mother regularly picked, dried, and formed into miniature, tulle-wrapped bundles she carefully placed in all our wardrobes. Palestinian jasmine and English lavender were the scents of my childhood, and although my father was born without the sense of smell, he made sure that ours was nourished with a distinctive heritage. When, after my father's death, one careless gardener inadvertently uprooted the two bushes, I felt robbed. Emile found the same species and replanted them, restoring to me and to our daughters the comfort of continuity and beauty. He also tended my father's rose garden with devotion and restored to its previous splendor the brilliant bougainvillea that had withered after my father's death.

At times during the peace process I would feel despair. It was then that I would actually see my father through the window strolling in the garden, his hands clasped behind his back, and nodding in encouragement and approval. I would also hear his words silently reverberate in my mind, "Be daring in the pursuit of right." As his daughter, as a Palestinian, I would dare to undertake the challenge of transforming our tortured reality into a version of his garden, of turning minefields into meadows, and to maintain the *amanah*—the trust—throughout. Having gone through many minefields, my father knew, as I had come to realize, that meadows were the domain of women.

Would we leave the next generation a legacy of failure as we had often, and perhaps unfairly, accused my father's generation? You tried. You failed. It was our turn to take over on our own terms. Armed struggle and pan-Arab nationalism had led us from one disaster to another. Innocent lives were lost and sacrificed. Perhaps, I hoped, our generation could make the supreme effort to divert its course, and leave our children the legacy of living, and redefining the future, rather than joining the danse macabre of the past. Our vehicle for change, this peace process, we knew was flawed, for it had incorporated precisely those self-destructive mechanisms that would make it implode. And I knew that the defeat of peace could be much more lethal than any military defeat.

Back in Washington, we still had not succeeded in opening the door to direct negotiations. The pressure mounted on us to concede to joint negotiations, as part of the Jordanian delegation, and we resisted. If we surrendered before the first encounter, the process would be doomed. A separate track and a separate delegation would mean the first, so important recognition by Israel of a separate Palestinian people rather than the "inhabitants of the Territories" or the "Arabs of Judea and Samaria and Gaza" or the standard "demographic problem" of Israel. It would also mean the first reversal of the Zionist myth of "the land without a people for a people without a land." We wanted them to negotiate "with a people" rather than "without a people," and we refused to disappear for their convenience.

My father, one of the people of the land, often narrated tales of Jewish-Palestinian friendships and neighborly relations before the *nakba,* the disaster of the loss of Palestine. "We were horrified at the cruelty and discrimination of the West toward our Semitic brothers and sisters and felt it incumbent upon us to offer them refuge and hospitality—but that was before they started taking over." Did legendary Arab hospitality contribute to our dispossession? It would be too simplistic to assume that. Anti-Jewish sentiments did arise and translate themselves into political movements, particularly as armed Jewish gangs began a reign of terror against what was quaintly described by the infamous Lord Balfour as the "indigenous population" of Palestine. Massacres, forced expulsions, and a war of propaganda and rumors led to the exile of the majority of the population and its replacement by a rapidly increasing Jewish minority. The fleeing Palestinians carried with them the keys to their homes, the deeds to their lands, and indelible memories of their identity and past, thinking that their exile would be temporary. Now, half a century later, Palestinians who, like their parents, were born in refugee camps in Jordan, Syria, and Lebanon or in the suburbs of Washington and Los Angeles or in the metropolitan centers of London, Bonn, and Paris would still tell you that they came from Haifa, Jaffa, Lydda, or a long obliterated village in Palestine. With such a historical memory, we have become a people who refuse to be eradicated from the memory of history.

The search for my father took place during the worst storm of the year. For three days and three nights we combed the hills of Ramallah calling out his name, but the mist and howling winds absorbed and distorted our voices. The rain was merciless. Torn, bloody, chilled to the bone and numb with exhaustion, we trudged on. I had first gone to the police for help, but the Palestinian police had resigned at the call of the *intifada* leadership. The Israeli officers flatly told me to go to the *intifada shabab* (youth) for help. I did, and all the neighborhood committees of Ramallah formed volunteer search parties. But the army began intercepting the young men and arresting them, particularly at night. My sister Nadia and I went to the military governor and informed him of the purpose of the nocturnal *shabab* excursions, and he promised to issue orders to the soldiers to leave them alone. Again, I went to the police, but with Leah Tsemel this time, and asked at least for an official declaration that my father was missing so that we could make public announcements in Arabic on Israeli radio and television. The police told us it would take some time. So we went to the printer's and had thousands of leaflets made displaying his name and picture and asking for any information. The *shabab* distributed them all over town and we had them printed in the papers. No one came forward with any information.

From house to house, hill to valley, we kept up the search. Never had I known the cruelty of our terrain as intimately as I had experienced it in those three eternal days. As the winter of Palestine unleashed its full fury on the rescuers, the land seemed to develop a will of its own to thwart us. This was the land he loved, the landscape he had experienced as an inseparable aspect of his own life, so why was it concealing him and fending us off? As I scrambled up the harsh cliffs clutching at needle-riddled thistles and blinded by the hail and rain, it occurred to me that our lives were as harsh as our landscape—stark, uncompromising, jagged, and subject to extremes. Had it been mellow, with rolling green plains and gently rippling rivers, with watered lawns and spring showers, would we have been gentler, milder creatures, more willing to compromise and less heroic in our stance? Would we have fewer demons and gods fighting for our souls? One thing I knew: our land would have produced fewer poets and prophets but a more contented race untortured by the mere fact of its existence.

On Christmas day, we were home between search trips to change our drenched clothes, when we heard the phone ring. It sounded different, and I refused to pick up the receiver. Lisa Taraki, a close friend, picked it up, then quietly handed it to me. I knew. It was the chief of police telling me they had found my father. In answer to my silent question, he added, "Dead." I screamed. Someone else got the details I was too horrified to speak. Where, when, who found him, and in what condition? Did he suffer? I would not go to identify him. Emile and my cousin George went. They came back quickly and Emile insisted that I go see him. "I don't want you living with ghosts and visions too difficult to endure." I went.

Suddenly the storm subsided. We walked down a narrow winding trail on the western hills of Ramallah. With every step, the view revealed itself to us gradually, gently admitting us into the mystery of vanishing mists and magnificent valleys sparkling with the freshly washed silver-green of olive trees. A small waterfall had formed a sheltered pond surrounded by natural rock formations and wild growth. My father lay beside the pond, his head resting on a stone, his body partially blanketed by a thin transparent layer of snow. I forced myself to look at him, at his face. He looked beautiful. With a serene smile on his face, and his body lying in calm repose, it was as if he had finally found himself. The ravages of Alzheimer's had disappeared. I felt the tension, fear, and anger of the last three days drain out of me, leaving me with a profound sorrow. I could grieve in peace. "That's why I wanted you to see him," Emile whispered. I was grateful.

It turned out that the land belonged to his mother's family; it was the place where he used to go hunting with his father as a child. Nature had made room for him, created a shrine for the man reunited with the child, and embraced him. We buried him three days later after my sisters Muna and Huda arrived from the United States and the rest of the dispersed family returned. For the eulogy, Bishop Samir Kafʔity read selections from my father's own writings. Every Christmas we make room for him at the head of the table and remember how he used to carve the turkey making jokes about his surgical precision. Every January 22, we celebrate his birthday with Emile's. But now, Emile alone blows out the candles on behalf of both of them.

After much soul searching and discussion, my sisters and I chose the following epitaph and had it engraved on my father's tombstone: "Dr. Daud Khalil Mikhail. January 1909–December 1988. He was true to humanity and people loved him/He loved nature and it embraced him. God is love." That was how my father had lived and died.

I have learned to live with the fact of his death. But I carry his absence with me everywhere, along with the indisputable fact of his existence. The tapestry of my father's life, like that of Palestine, is still unfolding.

• • •

The saga of the Washington nonnegotiations played on. Corridor diplomacy and couch negotiations persisted throughout the round. So did our struggle for "separate tracks" and American "open-door policy." On the way home from Washington, we stopped in Tunis for the standard report and consultations. Opinions were divided: some thought we had been inflexible, though the majority supported our decision. Akram and I held a meeting with Abu Ammar, and we agreed to keep pursuing the same policy. Once home, I called Ed Djerejian and told him that unless we got our separate track we were not prepared to return for the January 7 round. Ed, as usual, insisted that we discuss this directly with the Israelis. As usual, I answered that we do not conduct negotiations under occupation and outside the context of the official rounds. He insisted that the United States would not interfere in Palestinian-Israeli bilateral talks, and I answered that their inaction (except for locking the door) was adverse interference. From the first round, it had become clear that the United States was determined to be self-effacing and to deliver us to Israel by applying pressure on the Palestinian side to carry out Israel's wishes. Then I reminded him the peace process had started out with two cosponsors: the Soviet Union and the United States; one disappeared and the other became a spectator.

The Palestinian call for a more active and effective American involvement started there, and it continued unheeded except when Israel needed bailing out. This ineffectuality undermined the official negotiations and was a contributing factor leading to the alternative back-channel negotiations in Oslo between the PLO and representatives of the Israeli government, as well as to the continued stalling of the talks and implementation of the agreements after the Washington signing ceremony. "If the judge is your opponent, to whom do you appeal?"

On the way to resolving the two-track issue, we were confronted with another Israeli-created obstacle. Shamir decided to deport twelve Palestinians from the Occupied Territories. The delegation held an emergency meeting at Faisal's house, and we made a decision on the spot: we would not negotiate under duress, with Israel exercising a systematic policy of human rights violations against a captive Palestinian population. We asked for a U.N. Security Council meeting to stay the hand of the Israeli authorities and to prevent the deportations. "Deportation—the forced expulsion of Palestinians from their own land—is the worst nightmare of the Palestinian people. The policy and practice must cease immediately if there is to be any viable peace process."

We had occasion to repeat almost the same words at the end of that same year when the newly elected Rabin, with persistent blindness, decided to repeat Shamir's mistakes by deporting more than four hundred Palestinians on December 18, 1992. Add to that Israel's ongoing policy of confiscating land and building more settlements, and the ingredients for the collapse of the peace process were already in place. Baker used to complain that every time he visited the region during his shuttle diplomacy trips, the Israelis would welcome him with another new settlement as a gesture of spite—you can say what you want and we'll do what we want, they seemed to say. On each of his trips, the Israeli authorities would impose a curfew on the Palestinians and declare the Occupied Territories "closed military areas." It got to the point where I announced that we were on the verge of asking Baker not to visit us anymore—we could not afford to pay the price of his trips!

We were making little progress, it seemed. Our decision not to go to the January round caught both the PLO and the Arab sides by surprise. Once again, we had succeeded in creating a political crisis. "Stop springing surprises on us and coordinate in advance," the Arabs said. But at that time, we were earnestly "otherwise engaged" trying to neutralize at least some of the damage of the deportations.

Akram was sure that eventually the PLO decision would be to return to the talks. "Then let's prepare beforehand a list of demands that are achievable, otherwise we'll be asked to go back with nothing gained." We worked out a list that included Israel refraining from deporting the twelve, the United States granting a visa to Nabil Sha'th, the U.N. Security Council taking a resolution on deportations and other human rights violations without an American veto, the talks to begin in Washington on two tracks with Jordanian presence in the Palestinian track and vice versa. As a result, we got the unanimous UNSC Resolution 726 on January 6, 1992, which contained the most strongly worded condemnation of Israeli violations of the Fourth Geneva Convention, particularly its deportation policy. The United States did not veto, and Israel did not deport the twelve. Nabil Sha'th received his visa and we got the promise of a separate track.

We went back to Washington, and on January 13 began "negotiations." On January 15, we submitted our plan for a Palestinian Interim Self-Government Authority (PISGA), and optimistically thought that we had engaged. But the Israeli delegation had received instructions to discuss only technical issues—the time and venue for the next meeting. I called that the beginning of an "infinite exercise in futility." If we were to meet only to discuss when and where to meet next, then we might accumulate a lot of travel mileage, but no movement on substance. Shamir's blockade was setting in. We sent out warning signals, but no one took notice.

We also started presenting the Israeli delegation with a daily list of human rights violations at the beginning of every meeting. They refused to accept the lists. So I decided to start every briefing by announcing these human rights abuses, attempting to bring home to the media the human substance of the talks under way. Penny Johnson and our press office team had set up an efficient system of communication with human rights organizations at home, and they provided us with an accurate updated account on the spot. I gave names, not statistics, hoping to keep the priorities of the world straight—people's rights and lives rather than ingenious political arguments in the abstract. "We must never lose sight of the end purpose of every political endeavor, the well-being of the human being."

That did not work either. The Americans felt that reminding the Israelis of their cruelties was not in the service of the peace process. We felt that the Israeli measures themselves were in direct violation of the principles and objectives of peace. Israel continued to feel free to use our captive people as hostages, as a bargaining chip to be traded in for political advantage in the negotiations. The Americans were interested in the process itself; we were committed to a means of achieving justice. The Israelis were stalling until they would render the process irrelevant. Many PLO elements were still suspicious of the "people's delegation" and were working against our achieving any progress that might undermine the status of the PLO. The convergence of all these attitudes and their persistence with such predictability rendered the PLO-Israeli talks a farce and the 1994 crisis inevitable.

CHAPTER TEN

Who was that Palestinian delegation that seemed to defy definition while giving the world a global political headache? Were we, as Abul-Lutof had described us, an "arbitrary fistful"? Or were we the best and the brightest as had been depicted by the press? True, ours was a people's delegation, designated by its leadership (at that time still backstage) and sent off to negotiate on its behalf and on behalf of the Palestinian people with the seasoned politicians and diplomats of Israel and the world. In addition to the distortions of the Baker suit, and the constraints of multiple accountability and diversity of tasks, we were thrown together literally overnight and were expected to function as a coherent team, a smooth and well-oiled machine. To our amazement, we did. Inevitably, personal, professional, political, and regional factors intruded on our internal dynamic, creating not only complications and problems but also an expansive wealth of experience and breadth of outlook. Despite our differences, however, we managed to form a cohesive unit bent on achieving the goal it was created for.

In addition to Faisal, Haidar, and myself, the Leadership Committee at first included the reluctant Sari Nusseibeh, head of the Technical Committee set up to provide the delegation with data and alternatives to assist in the negotiations. Sari was neither entirely in nor entirely out of the delegation. As a Jerusalemite (who could trace his lineage to at least thirteen centuries of continuous presence in the city), he was not permitted into the negotiating room. Simultaneously a Fateh organizational activist and an Oxford-Harvard philosopher, Sari would switch roles without prior notice and surprise us all. I often told him that I was perpetually intrigued by the question of which persona would emerge at any given moment. We had been colleagues at Birzeit University since the mid-1970s, and as political independents then had been active in setting up the Employees Union and in negotiating with the different political factions to ensure fair and representative elections. He joined Fateh and became embroiled in factional politics while I continued my work with the Legal Aid Committee and the union.

It was during the early days of my tenure as dean of arts that Sari was beaten up by a group of hard-line student activists from his own faction for conducting talks with the Israeli Likud Party and signing an agreement with Moshe Amirav, a Likud member. Faisal, who had been part of the talks, was placed under administrative detention by the Israeli authorities. Moshe Amirav was expelled from the Likud Party. Sari got the beating. I immediately called an Arts Faculty Council meeting and we issued a statement defending freedom of expression and political activity and denouncing the use of violence, singling out violence on campus. We urged Sari to return to the university and take up his classes in philosophy and cultural studies. As member of the University Council, I also subscribed to the public statement published in the papers, and became a member of the investigation committee set up to look into the matter. I visited Sari at the hospital and relayed the council's support, while assuring him of protection and respect. When he later returned to the university, I made a point of meeting him at the gate and escorting him to class. What made matters worse was the fact that the Likud contacts had been carried out at the behest of the PLO, and the leadership took its time issuing any official statement that would have exonerated the Palestinian participants.

But that was not the last nor the least of his worries. During the Gulf War, and on the strength of a casual phone call, Sari was accused by the Israelis of spying for Iraq and was placed under administrative detention. We tried to attend the hearing, but were made to wait outside while Sari responded to the charges. His term was reduced from six to three months. As a founding member of the Political Committee, Sari maintained an ambivalent relationship with it, similar to his on-again off-again relationship to the negotiations. At times he would propose creative and daring political initiatives, and at others he would go by the literal factional book. Sometimes he would propose taking bold unilateral decisions, and at other times he would insist that we were only an information committee not empowered to deal with politics. He often displayed the same ambivalence in working with me, whether in branding me as a media person in line with the opposition and some insecure male politicians, or in supporting and defending my political work and decisions. Throughout, I maintained an unwavering attitude of friendship and respect for one of the most enigmatic Palestinians in our group.

That was the reason I was not surprised at Sari's evasive tactics when Abu Ammar designated him in November 1993 as deputy to the director general of the Palestinian Economic Council for Development and Reconstruction, PECDAR. As a Woodrow Wilson scholar in Washington, Sari chose to wait out the turbulent period of transition and to update his academic credentials instead. I had occasion to play the intermediary when he found it difficult to refuse or hedge a direct request/instruction from Abu Ammar. From my perspective, the chairman had always held Sari in high esteem despite the ups and downs of their long relationship, and often gave himself the right to take the controversial philosopher-politician for granted, as he did others in Fateh whom he considered to be "his men." Twiddling his lighted cigarette between thumb and fore-finger, with his salt-and-pepper hair and sardonic smile and demeanor, Sari would yet play a major role still lying in wait for him in the Palestinian political tapestry of the future. Typically, he managed to avoid appointment to the Palestinian National Authority (PNA), preferring to work in his investment counseling group. He may surprise us yet.

Zahira Kamal, the other woman on the Leadership Committee, decided to leave the negotiations a few months into the talks, not because of any change of heart or political turnabout (she continued to be one of the staunchest supporters of the peace process), but because she decided that she would be more effective at home, working at the grassroots level to serve the cause of women. I respected her for making such a move when many others saw in the peace process a chance to advance their political careers. She was another whom I had met in the mid-1970s after I returned home from the United States and she was under town arrest. It was then that a group of women started forming study groups and holding consciousness-raising sessions to work on a gender agenda that would be intrinsically Palestinian, stemming from a real assessment and understanding of Palestinian women's needs, while simultaneously reaching out to women all over the world who shared the same concerns. Some of the women from her own political faction (then the Popular Democratic Front for the Liberation of Palestine, now FIDA—the Palestinian Democratic Alliance) brought Zahira's name up as an activist and a pioneer. Only in the late 1970s did we get the chance to work together on establishing the women's committee, which would transcend political factionalism and place our concerns at the top of the national agenda. Social work and internal organization were among our priorities. Zahira also joined the political committee as a representative of her faction and was active in promoting the Palestinian-Israeli dialogue, particularly among women. In presenting political arguments, Zahira and mainly the women of the PDFLP first proposed the political program in 1988 that we sent to the PLO in Tunis asking for a Palestinian peace initiative-offensive on the basis of the two-state solution. Its impact was clearly discernible in the Palestine National Council's resolutions of November 1988. (Historically, it was the PDFLP that first proposed a negotiated settlement and the phased approach in 1974.)

Zahira and I worked closely together within the context of the Palestinian-Israeli women's dialogue, often representing the Palestinian side together, as we did in many international conferences. We formed a good team, presenting both the organizational and the theoretical dimensions of the Palestinian women's movement. Like me, she was in the direct line of fire by the political opposition and antifeminist circles. In some ways, she was protected by her overt political affiliation so her political credentials were not questioned, but working directly with women from all social backgrounds and on highly controversial gender issues set her on a collision course with the more traditional and religious elements in our society. Patient, persistent, and unfazed, Zahira pressed ahead determined not to be intimidated or deflected. Not once did I see her lose her composure or good-natured tolerance, even when severely provoked. She is currently dedicated to the establishment of a women's council within the PNA with sufficient authority to ensure nondiscrimination and to empower women.

Haidar gradually acquired two deputies who formed the opposite poles of the delegation—the reserved, curt, and strictly proper physicist Nabeel Kassis, and the outgoing, voluble, and unrestrained political scientist Saeb Erakat. Nabeel was a childhood friend of mine, from the same town of Ramallah and the same clan of ʿAwwad. His trimmed beard and receding hairline projected an image of a Middle East version of Lenin. But he was no revolutionary. Correct, contained, and capable, he brought his brilliance and rigorous scientific approach to the often sloppy task of negotiations. His precision and drive for perfection sometimes made him impatient with the more lackadaisical attitudes and work habits of others, but never to the point of intolerance. I used to call him the "porcupine," and whisper "Your prickles are showing" during meetings or encounters in which he would bristle at provocations or slights. He dealt with the task of drafting position papers and analyzing texts as if he were conducting an experiment in nuclear physics. Underneath all that lurked a mischievous and biting sense of humor. During one serious meeting at the State Department in which we were discussing Israeli intransigence on the issues of settlements and human rights, Ed Djerejian was trying to persuade us not to allow these measures to derail the talks. "You mustn't let them become a *causus . . . [belli]*" he wanted to say. But Nabeel interjected *"interruptus"* before Ed could find the word he was looking for, and despite the solemnity of the occasion, we all burst out laughing. There was nothing like puns in Latin to liven up negotiations. Nabeel usually spoke in staccato, and with the utmost economy, but his brief volleys were always on target. He now heads an economic think tank, while serving as a member of PECDAR's Board of Governors.

Saeb Erakat, the nemesis of James Baker, was Nabeel's foil. He would cast before you his hoard of words and expect you to do the selecting and ordering. A political creature by instinct, he actually enjoyed games of intrigue and political virtuosity, particularly when challenged to pit his wits against others. "Do we play this dirty or clean?" He would ask Akram, his mentor and friend and to whom he gave the loyalty he bestowed on no one other than Abu Ammar. Big, burly, and brash, he would charge first and rationalize later. "There are two misleading characters on this delegation," I once said. "Faisal is not as innocent as he looks and Saeb is not as mean as he looks." Actually Saeb was extremely vulnerable, despite his blustering show of bravado and his bushy beard. Only people he cared for could really hurt him; the others he would either attack mercilessly or simply ignore. But even when hurt, he put up a brave, often macho, front. During one famous meeting in which the delegation defied Abu Ammar and announced its intention to boycott the talks, the chairman lashed out at Saeb as someone on whom he felt he could vent his wrath. Saeb was devastated, and it took a lot of persuasion to reconcile him. Yet when Abu Ammar and Faisal created and repeated the joke about Saeb's memoirs, he reacted in good humor and a positive spirit. Saeb was reported as having announced that if Abu Ammar were to take the decision to go back to the talks, he would withdraw and write his memoirs. When he showed up the next day, someone asked him, "What about your memoirs?" and Abu Ammar answered, "He finished them overnight! What he has to put down on record wouldn't take long to write." Sometimes he would embellish the joke by adding, "I looked at the memoirs and they're all blank pages!"

It was Saeb who always volunteered to help me with my heavy carry-on bag from one airport to another. But he was also not beyond resorting to public displays of bad temper. The first to take offense, he was also the first to forget a slight. When he was assigned the task of coordinating with the other Arab delegations at membership level, he threw himself into it with a great deal of devotion and no small amount of game playing. He had found his platform. After the signing of the Declaration of Principles, and when skepticism among the "inside" Palestinians prevailed, he agreed to head the delegation that was to conduct negotiations on self-government to be held in Washington. Abu Ammar also appointed him head of the official committee charged with preparing for elections. The outcome of both tasks would remain dubious. Saeb's previous academic work at Al-Najah University and his editorial work at *Al-Quds* newspaper would, in all probability, remain in the realm of the past. When the Palestinian National Authority was formed in 1994, Saeb joined it as minister for local government. He remains one of Abu Ammar's most loyal supporters.

Ghassan al-Khatib looked younger than his age, but was a seasoned politician, a graduate of both the Israeli prisons and the Communist (later People's) Party. When I first met him at Birzeit University, he had just joined the undergraduate student body, having completed a different four-year sentence in an Israeli jail. He had horrific tales of beatings and torture to relate, but what I found most impressive was his lack of bitterness or vindictiveness, which could have distorted his soul more than any physical torture. Calm and understated, Ghassan's composure concealed deeply held convictions and an iron will. But it was his sophisticated irony that saved him from succumbing to the dual temptations of wrath and self-pity. As faculty adviser to the student council, I observed both his political astuteness and manipulative powers from a front-row seat, particularly after he was elected to the council. As chairperson of the English Department, I supported granting him a faculty development scholarship although his academic record was not the highest. His leadership qualities were his strongest asset, and the university was committed to furthering such qualities and supporting their development in the student body. When he returned to the university with a degree in agronomy, I was the dean who observed his first faculty presentation in the Cultural Studies Department.

Throughout, he remained a party activist—mainly underground since the Israeli occupation authorities had banned all political parties and activities. When he joined the Political Committee, it was as representative of his party, and all his subsequent activities also stemmed from that commitment. Even when not entirely convinced of or pleased with a party decision, he never failed to conform. The proper politician screened from view a human side that avidly sought the latest movie, play, or concert and equally enjoyed a good meal and a good laugh. But one had to know Ghassan well to catch a glimpse of this. "How do you feel sitting across from the enemy and negotiating when you still carry the physical scars of your prison years?" I once asked him over dinner. "That's how it should be," he answered. "First, we have withstood and survived their worst, and we cannot be intimidated. Second, they cannot hide anything from us. And third, if the victims negotiate, then no one can question our commitment to peace. Actually, it would be difficult to find any Palestinian who has not been victimized at one time or another." On a more personal note, he added, "Sometimes I do remember and I wonder if they realize what it costs or what it means at the personal level. Do you remember when I was beaten by the Israeli army on campus?"

The soldiers had dragged a number of students from the dorm in the aftermath of a student demonstration and had begun kicking and beating them with their fists and the butts of their guns. We tried to intervene but were unable to stop them; we succeeded however in preventing the arrest of the students, pulling some out of army jeeps. Ghassan then was a bloody mass of cuts and bruises. At least in negotiations I would not have to come to his rescue, nor would he acquire visible scars.

Another ex-student and prison graduate was Nathmi al-Ju'beh, Zahira's replacement on the committee, who also held a Jerusalem identity card and hence was a "nonnegotiator." Originally from Hebron, this soft-spoken, warmhearted archaeologist tried to keep his eyes focused on the silver lining, which was not the case with "the good doctor" Zakariyya al-Agha of Baker fame. Coming from Gaza, Zakariyya tended to reflect the skepticism and lack of trust in the Israelis that the Gazans had acquired as a result of their long and bitter ordeal under the occupation. The Gaza Strip had become the embodiment of unmitigated suffering and deprivation, hence the more rebellious and militant. No one could look less militant than Zakariyya, with his ruddy complexion, ready smile, comfortable paunch, and round bald head. He was later chosen as the Fateh leader in Gaza, and as such had to face the challenge of the street leadership, the activists who had emerged and gained their credentials during the *intifada*. In 1994, Zakariyya joined the PNA as minister of housing. Haidar and I completed the "inside" membership of the committee.

Two supposedly "outside" members of the committee, like Akram, were really "insiders." Taisir Aruri of the People's Party and Azmi Shuᵓaibi of FIDA both hailed from the West Bank and had lived in Ramallah until they were forcibly deported by the Israeli authorities in the 1980s. Taisir was a lecturer in physics, who joined Birzeit University faculty the same year I did. Actually, we attended together the concert at which I first saw Emile. Taisir was the only communist at the time whom my mother not only talked to but for whom she developed a deep fondness; she was genuinely pained when he was detained and later deported. Only one year after he joined the university, Taisir was suddenly placed under administrative detention. This type of detention was a leftover of the British mandate Emergency Regulations, which even the British had revoked when they left Palestine. On the basis of this regulation, a person may be imprisoned for renewable and continuous periods of six months without charges, evidence, or trial. When we asked the military governor about the reasons for Taisir's arrest, he answered, "Because we think that he was thinking of doing something." And for that thought which had crossed some Israeli military official's mind concerning what Taisir may or may not have thought, Taisir spent four tortured years of his life in an Israeli jail. After his release, he stayed free long enough to get married and have children before he was deported in 1987, thus dislocating the whole family. When I saw him in Tunis in 1988, he looked so heartbroken and misplaced as to bring tears to my eyes. "One day at home is worth a lifetime of exile," he said. I had heard that from many other deportees. He, and they, were living for the day of their return. Having moved to Amman, Taisir and the others waited impatiently. On April 6, 1994, with the blossoming of green almonds and plums, Taisir and forty-five other deportees returned to their homes as part of the first stage of the implementation of the Declaration of Principles signed by the PLO and the Israeli government on the White House lawn on September 13, 1993.

Azmi Shuᵓaibi, on the other hand, was allowed to return in 1993 at the beginning of the ninth round of negotiations and as part of the agreement to begin the return of deportees and resume the talks. Until then, he had been a member of the Leadership Committee, and quite famous for his high spirits and dedication to the peace process. He had known both jail and exile and, like many other deportees, preferred the former. He had been elected a member of the al-Bireh municipal council, which was disbanded by the Israelis following the Jewish terrorist attack on three of the elected mayors. As a successful dentist, he had participated in a housing project sponsored by the dentists' union. When I asked him why he was fixing up the basement so carefully, he answered, "Suppose I get deported by the Israelis, I want Suheir to be able to rent out the basement to get some income for her and the children." He was deported a month later. His wife, Suheir, an old friend of mine and a member of the early women's study groups, took the children and joined him in Amman soon after. They had to rent out the whole house. Azmi is now minister of sports and youth in the PNA.

Haidar's "outside" foil was Nabil Sha'th, whom Abu Ammar had placed in charge of the Palestinian team in the bilateral negotiations. "Rosy glow" Nabil, as opposed to "gloom and doom" Haidar, consistently presented the most optimistic version of reality. Jocular and voluble, he was addicted to puns and Egyptian jokes with a talent for stand-up parodies that Haidar received with a tentative smile or an incredulous frown. His work capacity was monumental, with boundless energy and drive. At all hours, he could be seen drafting options, conducting meetings, giving interviews, reporting to Tunis, and juggling his different "contacts" and "informers." As head of his Egyptian-based management company, called Team, he seemed to have a hard time with our hard-to-manage team. He himself tended to blur the structural lines of any organizational or functional chart that he had enthusiastically designed. His problem was that he tried to please everybody. We had an inside joke that in round one thousand and one of the negotiations, of all the Palestinian delegation only Haidar and Nabil would be left. Haidar would walk out of the session and address the geriatric press on their State Department stakeout announcing solemnly, "I'm sorry to say that we have achieved no progress in the talks; they appear to be deadlocked, and I recommend suspension." Nabil, on the other hand, would call a press conference and cheerfully announce, "I am confident that by the end of this round we will reach a mutually agreed Declaration of Principles. We've had many hints of concessions and between-the-lines suggestions of progress from the Israelis." Nabil became head negotiator and minister of planning and international cooperation in the PNA. He remains one of Abu Ammar's most senior political advisers.

Akram Haniyyeh was Nabil's "outside/inside" foil. As another adviser of Abu Ammar's, Akram was appointed Nabil's deputy. Private, self-effacing, and a firm believer in verbal economy, Akram shunned the limelight, avoided crowds, and spoke only when absolutely necessary. While Nabil reported mainly to Abu Mazen as head of the follow-up committee and sometimes talked to the committee's secretary, Hassan Asfour, Akram reported directly to Abu Ammar. At first, Abu Mazen wanted the Washington talks to succeed and adopted flexible policy positions and negotiations guidelines since he had no "alternative leadership" preoccupation. Later on, however, as the back-channel negotiations took a serious turn and showed signs of genuine progress, Abu Mazen began to issue more hard-line instructions in a deliberate attempt to block the Washington talks and to clear the way for the Oslo backstage negotiations between representatives of the Israeli government and the "official" PLO. This, of course, had been Abu Ammar's strategy all along. Abu Ammar had wanted to demonstrate that without the PLO no talks stood a remote chance of success. He pulled the strings and was determined to leave no doubts as to who was in charge. I had often talked to both, though separately and privately, about this issue.

"If this is your purpose, at least tell the delegation," I urged Abu Ammar. "They're your best people, and they've taken their responsibilities very seriously. You can't burn them politically."

"The Israelis have not given us any indications of seriousness. They're not negotiating in good faith. When they present anything remotely acceptable we'll see."

"Just don't let the delegation feel they're being used. Be frank with them, and if you want them not to bring the talks to a close tell them. Don't worry, we'll work out the strategies to suit your purpose."

"I can't now, but we'll see how things develop."

"The options are clear: either you want these talks to succeed and we'll sign an agreement at the proper time, or you want them to reach a deadlock that only the PLO can break so we'll mark time until the PLO is in and then the serious negotiations will begin, or you really don't want the peace process and just want us to go through the motions, or you want the talks to fail entirely. Each option requires its own strategies and work plans. All you have to do is tell us. But we need clear political directives."

"We have made a commitment to the peace process, but that involves many factors—internal Palestinian, Arab, and international. Many things must fall in place in due course."

These factors were the minefield through which Arafat was steering with exacting precision and caution. He had the Palestinian opposition to contend with and to balance, while he also wanted to maintain his constituency, particularly in the Occupied Territories. Arab politics were also a complex and intricate quicksand territory with shifting sets of checks and balances. On the one hand there were the ring countries that neighbored Israel and were involved in the talks, including their internal rivalries and changing alliances as well as competition for the leadership position. Did Syria call the shots or was the Palestinian side the difficult card? Would Syria continue to play host and patron to the opposition and how would that play out in the balance? Would Jordan make a deal behind our backs? Would it lay claim to the West Bank? How would Egypt use its political weight, particularly in the larger Arab context? And in that larger Arab context, the PLO's priority was to mend fences with Saudi Arabia and the Gulf states following the havoc wreaked by the Gulf War. Would Egypt use its good offices there and how would it balance that with its Syrian alliance as well as the unstable Syrian-Jordanian relations and equally unpredictable Jordanian-Egyptian relations? The North African Maghreb countries could play a balancing role.

But in the regional context, Iran was stepping in following the weakening of Iraq in the wake of the Gulf War. It used its patronage of radical rejectionist groups including Hamas and the other extremist organizations as leverage, having gained entry through its Syrian connection. Turkey controlled the water sources but was a member of NATO and maintained other Western alliances. With the dissolution of the Soviet Union, Turkey's role in the former Islamic republics, now independent nations, gained significance, also in view of Iran's overtures to gain influence in that direction. The Arab world as a whole was ringed by three non-Arab countries with different designs and relations with the various Arab countries: Iran, Turkey, and Israel. Nevertheless, each Arab country had its own economic and political domestic problems to contend with, even in the midst of this turbulent regional map. All, however, saw in the peace process one way of resolving not just regional but domestic problems. All saw in it an offer they could not refuse, and each played it for its own advantage.

Such was the case with the PLO. To get back into the Arab and international political arena as a major player, and in order to rescue the organization from the financial and political annihilation that had been planned for it after the Gulf War, the peace process was a "compulsory track," as Farouq al-Kaddoumi, head of the PLO Political Department, used to describe it. It was, indeed, an offer they could not refuse. At the same time, it also could spell their doom. If played right, the process could be the lifesaver the PLO needed to extricate itself from the morass of the aftermath of the Gulf War and following the collapse of the Soviet Union and the end of the Cold War. But if mismanaged, the peace process could spell the end of the PLO if we agreed to form the "alternative leadership" (which was never even remotely contemplated by us). Or the rescue of the PLO could be temporary—to be thrown back once it fulfilled its purpose of signing (and implementing) the agreement. The analogy used by Abu Ammar was that of the drone used to fertilize the queen bee and then left to die. Another analogy was that of reviving the patient long enough to make him sign his will and then leaving him to expire, or even finishing him off. The question was how to revive the patient and to maintain him in good health. Abu Ammar was acutely aware of all these complexities and scenarios and was struggling for the survival of the PLO, and not just its temporary revival. We knew that without the PLO we would be political orphans, and the nation of Palestine would fall into disarray. Yet some Palestinians accused the PLO of generating this fragmentation itself and of weakening if not selling out the national cause. The opposition accused it of sacrificing the people for the sake of its own survival.

During the Washington talks and days of blissful ignorance, we were still driven by a sense of mission, enthused by the loftiness of our calling, and unsullied by premonitions of the outcome. We had dedicated people on the delegation, such as the architect Suad al-Amery, who joined the negotiations later. In addition to her intellectual and political skills, she made sure that there was no gender bias in the talks. Mamdouh al-Aker, the urologist, also brought to the talks a human dimension and a sensitivity for the concerns and public mood of the people. The dean of the faculty of engineering at Birzeit University, Abdel-Rahman al-Hamad, and an English teacher, Jabr Fadda (I was on his master's thesis committee), completed the Gaza contingent. From Hebron, we had the deposed (by the Israelis) elected (by the Palestinians) mayor, Mustafa al-Natshe. He was reappointed mayor after the al-Ibrahimi Mosque massacre on the basis of a PLO-Israeli agreement. For some time we were joined by the dentist and head of the board of trustees of Hebron University, Nabil al-Ja'bari. Nabil was the one who after his administrative detention answered when he was asked what he missed most: "My face. I missed my face." After six months of living without mirrors, an exclusively internal self-image could become another form of confinement; one was bound to wonder what one looked like from the outside. From Nablus, we had both Sameh Kan'an (the longest-serving prisoner) and Sami al-Kilani, another ex-prisoner but a practicing writer. We often found moving poems or short stories in our mailboxes, particularly when the going got tough and Sami needed catharsis while we needed to be reminded of the existence of a different language and reality.

A mobile population of advisers converged on Washington when the talks were in session. Gradually, it narrowed down to a number of outstanding academics. All formed the loosely termed "strategic committee," which ultimately formed smaller specialized groups joined by members of the negotiating delegation. These specialized groups prepared position papers, talking points, and detailed analyses of Israeli texts. Such a mobilization of Palestinian brains and skills produced an impressive and comprehensive body of negotiations literature and strategies. We also accumulated a wealth of experience that could have served the Palestinian leadership well in future negotiations. At one point we advised Abu Ammar: "Once you get the official recognition for the PLO your best choice would be to keep the same delegation. This would drive the national unity message home, the fact that all along the delegation had been the PLO delegation, and would give the negotiations the benefit of their experience." But that was not to be. With recognition later came a whole overhaul of the "inside" Palestinians and an attempt at reinventing the negotiations wheel. The consequences were not to be negligible.

Ours was a pilgrimage in reverse—a motley gathering of Palestinians setting out in the cold of winter, away from the Holy Land and into the uncharted terrain of Western diplomacy and peacemaking. What trials lay ahead were still part of an external quest for recognition and vindication. Not until our journey completed its full cycle and took us back to where we began did we turn our mirror inward and recognize that grace and redemption were factors of our internal reality and that the penitential journey took place within the self. That was the face we had missed.

The question of whom we did represent was a recurrent theme. What was the relationship of those pilgrims of peace to the tortured people of the refugee camps, to the besieged people of the towns, and to the land-bereft peasants of the villages of Palestine? Where in our myths, in our recited narratives of epic and romance, in our memories of lost homes and dreams abandoned by the wayside on the path of exile, was there historical mention or prophetic forecasts of a fearless band of warriors who had set out in pursuit of peace as only dreamers could?

With my legacy of jasmine and lavender, my modest cachet of interrogation and arrest, and my adamant insistence on retaining the privacy of my pain, where did I come in? The continuum of the life I had lived in phases had inevitably, yet unpredictably, brought me to this latest phase.

How "typical" was a Christian woman, the daughter and wife, respectively, of advocates of women's rights, a Western-educated academic and human rights activist, the mother of two daughters who voted in favor of my accepting the position of dean in spite of my own reservations because they had wanted their mother to be the first woman to fill that post, and a medievalist caught up in contemporary politics but with the firm conviction that the poetic human vision was the source of legitimate awareness and action? I was determined that the legitimacy of my representation and advocacy should stem precisely from those disparate elements that were proof of the richness and plurality of the Palestinian fabric of existence.

We were the people who had unmellowed with age, whose denial had gradually depleted our storehouse of joy. Locked within the pain to which we had claimed exclusive rights, we became prisoners of our sorrow and captives of our own version of unyielding destiny. We had taken on the attributes of our landscape, rugged and rough, sharp-edged with the absence of our diverted and dried-up springs, longing for rain in the uncompromising glare of a brutal sun. Thus our tenderness was scorched, and we substituted uncompromising passion for compassion.

Our peasants used to embroider as an organic celebration of color and form, and not as a nationalistic compulsion. We used to dance the *dabke* with abandon as the fertility rite it had the right to be and not as a deliberate statement of folkloric revival. Our love songs, then frivolous and now forbidden, had no need to claim political didacticism. Laughter was permitted then, welling up from our depths without censorship or embarrassment, unhampered by the propriety of pain or the decorum of the bereaved. We did hold weddings and ululate unreservedly before guilt locked up our sensuality and we were silenced by shame. Once our children tinkled and tingled with anticipation and discovery before they took up the instruments of justice and became self-righteous in the presence of death.

I wanted to lay claim not just to a lost land, but to a lost life as well. We had to lay claim to our soul. How else could we put an end to the violence and to the slaughter of the innocents, to heal oppressor and oppressed alike, and to stop rationalizing away our iniquities and transgressions? Self-inflicted wounds could be more hurtful than those of outrageous fortune. We owed ourselves forgiveness before we forgave others. Such was the real mission of our circular penitential journey.

CHAPTER ELEVEN

F or three days and three nights we were kept in a state of alert
awaiting the PLO decision as to whether the Palestinian side would participate in the multilateral negotiations to be held in Moscow on January 28,
1992. The Leadership Committee deliberated in my living room, while
keeping in constant phone contact with Tunis. Although we had been the
ones to insist on Palestinian inclusion and equal participation in the talks,
the equation had shifted with Syria's and consequently Lebanon's refusal
to attend. Lebanese decision making was directly linked to and dependent
upon Syria. The bilateral Palestinian-Israeli and Arab-Israeli talks were to
supply the political basis for the resolution of the conflict, while the
multilaterals (which originally involved more than thirty countries and
steadily grew) would provide the inducements for regional participation
and development in order to create the context of cooperation and pros-
perity for peace on a regional basis. It was perceived that if the Israelis
would give at the bilateral meetings, on the basis of the famous "land for
peace" formula, it would receive at the multilaterals—mainly regional
acceptance and international recognition, and the rewards of sharing in
the economic pie (diplomatic relations and recognition with countries
with whom it previously had none, as well as global development plans
for the whole region from which Israel would benefit). The Syrian camp

argued that the multilaterals were premature "normalization" that should not be attempted unless Israel paid its political dues in the bilateral talks. The Jordanian side saw the multilaterals as the spur that could goad the difficult bilaterals forward with the promise of the fruits of peace. We were somewhere in the middle. Political and economic "normalization" prior to the attainment of our objectives would significantly weaken our negotiating position. But not participating in the international endeavor to reorganize the region would perpetuate our exclusion and undermine our capacity to claim equal status. We all agreed that no progress in the multilateral talks was possible unless there were concrete achievements in the bilaterals.

We began the countdown. Abu Ammar, later joined by Faisal, had gone to Morocco for an Arab meeting that refused to let him off the hook. Kaddoumi adopted the Syrian position. Abu Mazen was wholeheartedly advocating participation. At 1:45 A.M. on the morning of January 27, the phone rang with jarring persistence.

"Guess what!" Amjad, the Cyprus contact, said.

"I know and I'm not going," I replied.

"*Al-Waled,* the Father, wants you to call the following people and ask them to head for Amman first thing in the morning."

"I'm not calling anybody. I'm going back to sleep. The others can yell at you, not at me."

"But this is different. The delegation will be made up of Jerusalemites and outsiders. We need you to tell the leadership committee; get Zakariyya, Saeb, Zahira, and Ghassan ready. You'll cross the bridge to Amman where you'll be joined by Anis Fawzi Kassem [a legal adviser to the delegation] and then take a chartered plane to Moscow."

"We're not ready. Tell Abu Ammar that we're not luggage to be dispatched here and there at whim. Put your act together first."

"I know and I agree with you. You can tell him that yourself later, but now we have an urgent task ahead."

"How can we go without a strategy, without a speech, without official statements? The question of to go or not to go consumes all our energy and time, and we end up ignoring what to do or say once we get there."

"Don't worry. You'll write the speech and statements on the plane. You can manage. You've done that before."

"Please feel free to take me for granted! Perhaps the best medicine would be for you not to have anybody to bail you out. Maybe then you'll change the way you make decisions."

"Maybe you're right. But right now our participation in the multilaterals is at stake. Akram, Yasser Abd Rabbo, Suleiman al-Najjab, Nabil ʿAmr, and other PLO officials will meet you in Moscow. We have no visa problems there."

"That itself could be a problem. Anyway, I'm not telling anybody. You call them, and I'll get ready. Who needs sleep anyway."

"I'll call Saeb, and will get back to you later."

"I need Penny and Suhair. If we're going to do a month's work overnight, we need a good team."

"Places on the plane are restricted. See if you can work it out with Akram and the Old Man."

I waited until 5:00 A.M. to call Penny to tell her that she had less than two hours to get ready and pack for a few days' trip to Moscow. She was at my house before 7:00. We picked up Ghassan (who insisted that their party was not participating but that he was there to help out with the press) and Zahira, then met up with Saeb in Jericho. We crossed the bridge and met with the others at the Palestinian embassy in Amman. At the airport, Tayyeb, the Palestinian ambassador, pointed to what looked like a miniature toy plane parked at the edge of the runway and informed us that it was ours. Between incredulity and horror, we tried to figure out whether it would be physically possible for eight fully grown adults, with no acrobatic skills to speak of, but with a sizable amount of luggage, to fit into such a limited space. The chartered Arab Wings jet, we found out later, was designed to accommodate five passengers with minimal luggage.

Half jokingly, we asked whether the PLO had found the perfect solution to its participation dilemma: send a delegation that was not destined to arrive. We started imagining search parties in the Alps hopelessly looking for the lost Palestinian delegation. We could envisage members of the Executive Committee shaking their heads in profound sorrow. "A tragic loss" was the least tribute we could expect. Recklessly, and somewhat suicidally, we wriggled, twisted, and contorted ourselves onto the plane only to discover that our luggage was piled up in and in front of the lavatory. We knew we were in trouble then, with a new version of "the battle of the bladder." But our resolve was not shaken. Saeb and Zakariyya, the heavier of the group, claimed the only two armchairs, and we begged them throughout not to move, particularly during the bumpy part of the ride. Anis and I sat on a work chair each facing each other and separated by a tiny tray, but with no leg space whatsoever. Zahira, Ghassan, Penny, and Suhair sat on a narrow bench that was normally reserved for the stewardess. They literally slipped and slid their way to Moscow. The shocked stewardess could neither sit nor move, so she spent the entire time in the cockpit shouting instructions at the bench team about how to locate the cooler and get to the snacks and soft drinks. As the plane valiantly tried to take off, we did our best to look nonchalant, while Penny whispered, "Are you sure this thing is made to fly?"

It flew, but we had to land in Ankara, Turkey, at a snowed-in airport. After we emerged from a mad rush to the rest rooms, I was amazed to see a long line of U.S. Air Force officers waiting for us. They had seen me on television and wanted to take the opportunity to shake hands and wish us luck! They must have been just as surprised at seeing the Palestinian delegation appear suddenly as we were at seeing the unusual American reception committee in the middle of nowhere. The Turkish officers, who had received no official notification of our unexpected visit, were the most surprised, but somehow gracefully managed to find two high-ranking officials to receive us. As for us, we managed to pile back into the plane, and as soon as I sat down, Penny said, "Write," and I did.

Had I deliberately conjured a situation less conducive to serious writing, I could not have done a better job. Yet somehow as soon as I embarked on the journey into the world of words, my surroundings receded, replaced by a universe in which the magic of language reigned supreme.

My fascination with words began at an early age. As the youngest of five, I had to watch from outside as my older sisters entered a world still closed to me. At the age of three, I gave my mother an ultimatum: either she gave me a baby brother or sent me to school with my sisters.

"Why this choice?" she asked.

"My cousin Maha has a baby brother and my sisters go to school," I answered. "Either one will do."

"You're too young to go to school. They don't accept three-year-olds. And Maha prayed hard for her baby brother."

"I can pray too," I announced confidently and proceeded to kneel down and pray right there and then. But no baby brother materialized.

"You have to be patient," my mother explained. "Maha prayed for nine months before her brother was born."

"Then you have to send me to school."

As a compromise, my sister Abla volunteered to tutor me. I remember my sister and I sitting on the ledge of the recessed arched window of our old home engrossed in deciphering the mystery of books. With me, it was an instant and mutual possession. I knew that I had solved the mystery and was privy to the secret of language, and I recognized that I was captive for life. I was accepted at preschool before I turned four, and when my teachers discovered that I could read and write both Arabic and English, they promoted me to first grade. During reading class, our teacher would hand out picture storybooks for silent reading. I would devour one after the other and go back for more. At one point, the teacher gave me a quizzical look and announced that the books were to be read and that I should not just look at the pictures. "But I did read them," I protested. "Don't lie to me," she said sternly. "You couldn't have read them all in such a short time." I was shattered. I was being accused of lying for the first time in my life, the shock of being disbelieved for stating the simple truth. More significantly, I learned that in this new world, achievement could be a double-edged sword. I began to understand the need to put up defenses and to be wary of standing out. Throughout school, I always understated my grades. The discrimination of success was even more biting than the pity brought on by failure. "Very few people take kindly to being made to look inferior by comparison," my father cautioned me. "The worst you can do is to take it personally." He then told me that he had opened an account for us at the bookshop we passed every day on our way to and from school. "The one thing you can never have enough of is books. There are no limits."

I began my first attempts at writing at the age of eight. My father told me, "Keep a notebook with you at all times. Write down anything that you read or hear that is of particular interest to you. But you must also jot down any observations or ideas you may have. It will be your own personal record, and you will have occasion to refer back to it often." I did keep this record and my father took the time to read and comment on my writing. He particularly appreciated one short story about a street beggar and his internal narrative. "It shows sensitivity and compassion, for both language and substance," he told me. That was my first critical assessment. Although I tried hard to return the favor by listening critically to the speeches he and his political colleagues made from the balcony overlooking the town *manarah*, I did not succeed. Like the rest of the crowd, I was too carried away by the music, by the fervor of the rhetoric, by the significance of the moment, by the electricity in the air to maintain an objective distance. Besides, the pride of an eight-year-old in her father did not leave much room for words.

On the plane to Moscow, as in the cramped hotel room in Madrid and in our Jerusalem meeting rooms, the language I was grappling with was the literature of politics and the politics of humanity. My Palestinian perspective shaped my language—but was guided by universal feelings.

After a precarious landing on the icy runway of the Moscow airport, a disheveled and exhausted group of Palestinians tumbled onto the tarmac. The Russians insisted that I get into the official limousine to be escorted to the hotel. Sirens blaring and lights flashing, we arrived at the huge American-owned and operated hotel. From the toilet paper to the daily menu everything was a well-known American brand. Suleiman al-Najjab and Yasser Abd Rabbo from the Executive Committee and Akram Haniy-yeh and a variety of PLO ambassadors and officials were waiting for us. None had been given official escort. They joked to Abu Ammar that they had had to arrange their schedules around mine to be able to use the motorcade and get around. During one telephone conversation he asked me with some amusement if it were true. "Of course," I said. "These Russians are very smart. Normally, escort and security are provided to protect the government from the people. In this case, they took one look at the members of the committee and decided to protect the people from such a government. And I was the only people there." He laughed, and this remained one of our private jokes.

From the hotel, we set off for a series of meetings. Secretary of State Baker, almost as soon as we arrived, informed us that our delegation was not acceptable.

"You've presented us with a list made up mainly of Palestinians from Jerusalem and from outside the Occupied Territories. This is against the rules. I'm afraid we can't accredit this delegation," he said, acting as if we had committed a crime.

"There are no rules governing the composition of our delegation except that which states that only the Palestinians can choose the members of their delegation, and we have chosen," I replied.

"But you know very well that no side will be made to sit with anyone it does not wish to sit with and the Israelis would not accept Jerusalemites and outsiders."

"Let them walk out then. We tried to be accommodating in the bilater-als because it was only the two sides alone. But now there are over forty countries participating in the multilaterals and not a single one, including the United States, shares Israel's conditions. Are you going to impose Israeli constraints on the whole world?"

"We cannot afford to have the Israelis walk out. You have three people who qualify—Zakariyya, Saeb, and Ghassan. We'll accredit these three and you can participate as such."

"That's unacceptable to us. If you extend Israeli restrictions to the multilaterals, you'll be reneging on your promise. You said that when we began discussing regional issues the nature of Palestinian participation will change. Not only will you place us at a severe disadvantage, but you will be giving Israel the advantage of defining for the whole world how they should deal with the Palestinians. We view this as a dangerous precedent."

"It's only temporary. Things will change. It's to your advantage to participate in the multilaterals, and the only way you can do that is by sending only those three people. Neither you nor Faisal nor the 'outside' Palestinians can be part of the delegation."

"Our delegation is made up of eight Palestinians, and no one should vet or veto the delegation members. We either all participate or none will."

"Then it has to be none."

Variations of this conversation took place in meetings with the Europeans, who were trying to find a compromise solution. The Arab foreign ministers offered moral support, but no action. They wanted to participate, but they also wanted the assurance that we would not attack them publicly for doing so. We would not back down. Following a Palestinian meeting to prepare for the opening ceremony, we headed back to the hotel at 3:00 A.M. I still had to finalize the speech and to prepare the official statement and press release. Penny stayed up with me working away on her laptop. At 7:00, Akram walked in and found me dozing in my chair. "Caught in the act of sleeping!" he exclaimed. "Watch out or this might become a habit. Before you know it, you might start expecting to sleep every night."

The Russian Foreign Ministry called at 8:00 A.M. to inform us that we had only two hours to send in the names of the three delegates to be accredited. We replied that we had eight, and gave them all the names: "All or nothing, and we're not bluffing."

"Are you planning to hold a press conference?"

"Of course."

"You need accreditation as an official delegation to make use of these facilities."

"Then give us the required accreditation and we're all set."

"We can't. The Americans gave us only three names and yours isn't one of them." My interlocutor was beginning to sound frustrated.

"Then we'll hold our press conference in the hotel. Get me Mr. Kozyrev [the Russian foreign minister], or tell him that yourself."

Suhair and a few of our press volunteers informed the hotel and began putting up crude hand-written posters and sending out notices directing the press to our new location. The fever of excitement was reminiscent of Madrid; once again we were being tested.

An hour later the deputy foreign minister called. "We've agreed to give you press credentials so you can hold your conference at the ministry," he announced.

"No, thank you," I replied. "This has been tried before. It didn't work in Madrid and it's not going to work here. We're pressing ahead with our plans and I don't want any accreditation from you."

"You can't. The press are already calling and asking questions about the reason for your unusual venue. You've already created quite a stir."

"I don't mind. When they come to the press conference, I'll explain to them why we had to resort to such venues and means. It seems that the Russians have a problem deciding for themselves whom to accredit and whom to admit into the Foreign Ministry. I thought you were a sovereign state."

It took only five minutes for him to call back.

"You're more than welcome to hold your press conference at the ministry. We'll have a full official reception for you, and all the facilities will be at your disposal. Just give me the names of the delegation that's coming with you. We'll expect you before 1:00 P.M."

Whether the Russians had declared their independence or the Americans had given them the green light was never revealed.

The entire delegation walked into the Foreign Ministry's press center. Suhair and I climbed up to the podium in good cheer, as though we had actually had some sleep the last two nights, and with the confidence of those who had the full right to be there. As Suhair began to introduce me, I gazed at the many faces before me and felt comforted. The press never intimidated me and I never suffered from stage fright. They were after the truth and the truth was my ally. Theirs was to challenge and mine was to take up the dare. In a sense it was a perfect relationship. At the final briefing in Madrid, I had ended by saying, "You have given me and the Palestinian people a fair hearing, and for that I'm deeply grateful." They had given me a standing ovation then.

Now, they were looking up expectantly. "We came knocking at the door, but were turned away. In this gathering of nations, it seems there is no room for a people who do not fit the imposed mold. We are ready, but the world is not prepared to receive us. Israel must not be allowed to continue deciding for us and for the world who the Palestinian delegation should be. We have embraced peace willingly, but we are not prepared to surrender our will in the process." We distributed copies of the press release and the speech, "which we would have given had we been admitted."

Nobody even remotely suspected the improvisational last-minute nature of our work. One reporter actually told me, "It's remarkable how the Palestinians are always on time and fully prepared." The Israelis had sent in an advance team of scores of professionals to prevent a repetition of the creaming they had received in Madrid. They had clearly come out the losers in that round, their aggressive attitude and huge team working against them with the press. With two volunteers, we managed to steal their thunder again. Discriminated against, defiant and unpredictable, we were the maverick people's delegation that broke the rules and got away with it.

Over the course of our meetings with the Americans in Moscow we extracted a U.S. commitment to admit "outside" Palestinians into at least two working groups, on refugees and economic development. We failed, however, to obtain approval for the two working groups we had proposed (and continued to stress) on human rights and Jerusalem. Israel opposed both, and many countries in and outside the region were sensitive in the area of human rights. Moscow had not only given us a platform, but an opportunity to meet and coordinate with the representatives of scores of governments. Rushing from one appointment to the next, I tried to catch glimpses of the city.

To me the Russians were also a people of extravagant tragedy. The terror and drama of their literature and existence imbued even the mundane. Yet driving through the streets of Moscow, and later taking long walks through Red Square and the street markets, I was struck by the slow-paced lethargy that seemed to make their feet drag and their shoulders sag. A sense of shock seemed to have sapped their vitality and color. Neither Dostoyevsky nor Tolstoy had prepared me for the immobility of the long queues frozen in hopeless anticipation or the listless shuffle of aimless pedestrians with nowhere to go and no urgency to get there. What would happen when the effects of the stupor wore off, I wondered. When the heroic urge to rebel grips the Russian soul once more, what shape or substance would it acquire, and whom would it identify as its adversary?

Wandering the icy, fog-wrapped streets of Moscow, I was also haunted by a childhood fantasy of the city. Our family version of Santa Claus started with my great Uncle Nicholas (*Ammi Nqula*), who used to huff and puff his way into our living room each Christmas eve, laden with gifts and good humor. He would stomp his feet, cup his hands and blow into them for warmth, and exclaim that he was tired and cold, having trudged all the way from the frozen land of *Mascobia* just to bring us children our Christmas presents. We would cluster and dance around him, before we settled down on his knees and all around him to sing Christmas carols and bombard him with questions about *Mascobia*. At the ripe and peaceful age of one hundred and six, and having decided that he had lived long enough, *Ammi Nqula* took to his bed and died in his sleep. My father and Uncle Jad took turns replacing him as Santa Claus from *Mascobia* and kept up the tradition of spinning a magical web of fantasy about that frozen enchanted world which produced such warm, generous, and humorous miracles as Santa. Thus, with the eyes of the child of long ago, I searched the streets of contemporary *Mascobia* trying to recapture both the lost image and the lost experience of my innocence. Had I finally reached the home of all those good people who came alive each Christmas in a flurry of activity for no other purpose than to bring joy and gifts to children all over the real world? Would I be able to reach out and lift the veil off the face of this Moscow and reveal what I had known all along to be its genuine *Mascobia* visage? The pain of Moscow's transformation touched an exposed nerve in my own irretrievable loss of my childhood. Was this what lay in store for the Palestinians?

• • •

In Tunis, the leadership felt that the ambivalence of the "nes" answer (a fused form of yes and no) regarding participation, had saved the day for both the pro and the con camps. Abu Mazen, however, had gone into one of his boycott phases in protest at our pseudoparticipation, saying that the politically sound decision would have been a clear yes, since we had consented, or rather insisted, from the beginning that we participate in the multilaterals. Abu Ammar, in his typical way, stressed the negative with the rejectionists and the positive with the participants, and managed to extricate himself from a sticky polarized situation. We knew he would do that from the moment he asked us to recommend participants for the different working groups.

After all the corridor diplomacy in Washington, it seemed like we had also secured a separate track for Palestinian/Israeli bilateral talks. We went back to Washington in January 1992 to resume a series of negotiating sessions with the mercurial Likud delegation, but to no avail. No common grounds could be found. Our PISGA (Palestinian Interim Self-Government Authority) proposal was countered by an Israeli version (the word "Palestinian" being taboo) on the general concept titled "Ideas for Peaceful Coexistence in the Territories During the Interim Period" and an "Informal Draft for a Joint Agenda." We presented an "Expanded Outline" and proposed internationally supervised general elections for Palestine, as part of a complete timetable. The Israeli delegation offered us municipal elections and the administration of our schools and hospitals. While the world applauded this sudden generosity, we were left to explain that we already had the run of our health and educational institutions. We also had to explain that it was Israel who had refused to allow us to hold municipal elections since 1976, when PLO-supported candidates had scored overwhelming victories. The fate of the elected councils and mayors had become, for us, a textbook lesson in Israeli democracy: An Israeli settler terrorist organization attempted to assassinate three mayors by planting bombs in their cars and garages; two of them were maimed. Two others were deported by the Israeli authorities. The elected municipal councils were dissolved and replaced by Israeli appointees. The Israeli terrorists were released on parole and later granted pardon.

Our daily Human Rights Status Reports continued, as did the Israeli refusal to receive them in written form, so we resorted to reading them at the beginning of each meeting as well as at the beginning of each press briefing. The Israeli delegation tried consistently to transform our delegation into petitioners interceding on behalf of individual cases, while we insisted that we deal only with categories and issues on the basis of the Fourth Geneva Convention. In the meantime, we kept up a continuous flow of memoranda to the Israeli and American sides on issues such as settlements and land confiscations, deportations, torture and maltreatment of prisoners, administrative punitive measures, the de jure applicability of the Fourth Geneva Convention and The Hague Regulations, different forms of punishment, summary executions, and the activities of the undercover units (death squads), as well as concrete proposals and plans for implementation. They went unheeded.

Thus, the first five Washington rounds became a battle for "engagement." No matter how hard we tried to get the Israelis to "engage" on substantive issues, they remained "slippery." We decided to re-present our proposals in legal segments dealing with specific Israeli Military Orders in the four areas of land registration, town and village planning, water authority, and access to public information. We got nowhere. Instead, the American State Department blamed us for the stalemate, claiming that our "inexperience" in negotiations and our inability or unwillingness to deal with specific concrete issues rather than with principles was the cause of the deadlock. "They have no intention to engage or negotiate," we protested. "It is time the co-sponsors got involved to get the talks on track and inject them with some momentum." The response was an unwavering negative. It was our responsibility to get the talks moving, and the Americans would not intervene in the talks or put any pressure on the Israelis.

The hands-off policy of the United States and its automatically pro-Israeli stance fueled the flames of Palestinian exasperation and contributed directly, though incrementally, to the back-channel direct talks between the PLO and the Israeli government. The back-channel talks had started in late 1992, but it wasn't until the summer of 1993 that they took on a serious bent. Although I had helped set up several back-channel talks between the Israelis and the PLO I did not know which were working and which were not. All the while I continued participating in the official negotiations, knowing full well they would lead nowhere. It was clear that without the PLO nothing substantive could happen.

At the same time an anonymous American "senior administration official" was reported to have "launched a blistering attack on Palestinians in the Middle East peace process," accusing us of lack of seriousness and of "posturing for the media" instead of negotiating. A group of reporters brought me the tape of the anonymous official's briefing, and I went on the warpath when I recognized the voice of Ed Djerejian. I called him and accused him of foul play, bias, and misleading representation. I also sent him a memorandum, copied to Secretary Baker, reminding him of all the concrete proposals we had presented including the most recent one on elections, and questioning the accuracy of the American evaluation of the course and conduct of the negotiations. Ed promised to rectify the situation officially.

Later, State Department spokesperson Margaret Tutwiler and I agreed on the wording of her statement for the next day's briefing in which she stated that the unofficial comments of an unidentified State Department official did not represent official policy or assessment nor did they reflect Secretary Baker's position. On several occasions, Baker had turned to his assistants in astonishment at concealing information from him. Once, I had been sent to Washington to discuss a Palestinian proposal on holding

PNC elections in the Occupied Territories, and after extensive talks with Dennis Ross, Dan Kurtzer, Aaron Miller et al., I was told that they would consult with Baker and let me know. At a meeting later in Jerusalem, Baker was visibly surprised at the idea and asked his team why he had not been informed. In another instance during a meeting in Moscow, Faisal and I had begun detailing the latest Israeli human rights abuses and their effect on the credibility of the peace process and on Palestinian public opinion. Again Baker was surprised, and he asked us to send him corroborated reports of these measures. We had to remind him that we had already sent these reports and that we had repeatedly detailed their impact on the talks and requested intervention. Baker was obviously angry at having been kept in the dark. From then on, I made a point of getting information to Baker directly whenever we felt that the issue warranted his personal attention. Margaret Tutwiler played a very constructive and honest role preventing misunderstandings and communication gaps. Of all the Baker team, Margaret was the one who seemed not to be involved in a personal political power struggle or to be working on a career agenda that could be served by the peace process. Our friendship continued to be based on the human agenda.

The talks were rapidly displaying symptoms of paralysis and inertia. The Israeli delegation lacked the will and the instructions to actually negotiate; Elyakim Rubinstein was intent on wearing Haidar down, keeping up a semblance of participation without addressing the real issues. At home, there was a studied escalation in human rights abuses, most effective given the absence of any accountability or intervention. At the table, they dealt only with the delegation of administrative tasks rather than with any genuine transfer of authority. Digressions into trivia, circumvention of substance—these became the key nonmoves of Israel's evasive tactics.

All this had become painfully clear to the Palestinian delegation in the course of the talks, but was vehemently denied by the rest of the world until Shamir lost the elections in the summer of 1992. Then Shamir confessed that he had intended all along to draw out the negotiations for ten years or until Israel filled the Occupied Territories with settlements and rendered the talks irrelevant. Once again, I had to tell the Americans and the world, "Don't wait to believe us till we're proven right; it might be too late then and the price could be too high."

Following the fourth round in Washington, Nabil Sha'th and I were invited to Stockholm by former Foreign Minister Sten Andersson (who was a close personal friend as well as a major player in the Palestinian-Israeli peace arena) and the Socialist Party and to meet with the new foreign minister, Margaretha af Ugglas. At the time it was a Palestinian policy that no "inside" Palestinian would accept any official invitation unless accompanied by a PLO official. Partly to bring the PLO back to international diplomacy, and partly to deflect any accusations of creating an alternative leadership, we adhered to this policy rather strictly. Faisal suffered most from this restriction, and our recurrent joke was that nobody had turned down as many official invitations and meetings as the Palestinians had. "No wonder they're against the idea of a Palestinian state," he would add. "If we behave like this without a state, can you imagine how insufferable we'll become when we have it?" My response was, "Then we cannot afford to be that impertinent."

At that time, Nabil Sha'th was the internationally accepted face of PLO diplomacy, or the least objectionable to many Western governments. Hence we formed a "dynamic duo" symbolizing the inside and the outside, the people and the leadership. Although he had the infuriating habit of introducing me as "our star" and of minimizing my political role, he always succeeded in creating a pleasant and informal atmosphere and in raising those issues that had special appeal to each particular host.

In April 1992 we went to meet Margaretha af Ugglas against the backdrop of a long and solid personal and political friendship with her predecessor, Sten Andersson, and a long-standing Swedish-Palestinian relationship. We had been warned that Swedish policy had changed with the new administration, and that a cool reception was to be expected. We braced ourselves for a meeting comparable to the Scandinavian weather. The warmth and generosity with which we were received, however, immediately thawed the hypothetical ice, and nurtured the seeds of a new and lasting friendship. While Nabil was working at the official level, Margaretha and I instantly developed a very special understanding that, in my experience, was exclusive to women. An invisible thread of communication and shared perceptions seemed to weave its way beneath the surface of overt discourse, and to form a unifying bond. Women in politics, unless they adopted male postures of domination and exploitation, tended to bring to their endeavors this hidden dimension and to form a gender community without frontiers or national barriers. And for the sake of that vision, we dared to take the necessary risks. To such women I could reveal the secret that, despite our harsh and uncompromising terrain, the land of Palestine concealed in its folds the largest variety of wildflowers that defied the rocks and thorns each spring and dared to blossom with impunity. They too shared the mystery of wild-flowers.

Margaretha af Ugglas and I exchanged gifts of Swedish crystal and Palestinian embroidery, and when she visited Jerusalem at our invitation, she and I shared a private Palestinian lunch, to the chagrin of some Palestinian male politicians. When she walked through the squalid alleys of refugee camps in the West Bank, she took time to eat corn on the cob off a street cart. With that picture she won the hearts of the Palestinians, and Abu Ammar on our visit to Stockholm more than a year later made special reference to it. Some men, like Australia's Foreign Minister Senator Gareth Evans, also shared this vision when he took his jacket off and played a game of football with the children of a refugee camp in a Godfor-saken alley. In spite of our persistent invitations, no American secretary or high-level official ever really walked our land or met us on our own grounds. But Foreign Minister Willy Claes of Belgium (now secretary general of NATO) promised to conduct the first Palestinian philharmonic orchestra, while Norway gave us the priceless gift of the friendship of the late foreign minister, Johan Holst.

Nabil and I ended our meetings in Stockholm and were preparing to leave for Norway the next morning. We got back to the hotel just before 1:00 A.M. from a lively and politically charged dinner with the Arab ambassadors to Sweden, to find urgent messages waiting for us. Each one of us got on our phone to return them. Swedish security officials in the hallway then saw the silent and simultaneous opening of the doors to the three rooms that Nabil, Suhair, and I occupied. We emerged and stared at one another in shock and utter disbelief—the message was the same: Abu Ammar's plane had crashed somewhere in the Libyan desert and he was missing.

It was an endless night. Palestine without Abu Ammar was inconceiv-able, and the possibility of his death beyond the realm of imagination. Nabil remained positive, as was Kaddoumi on the phone, firmly con-vinced that Abu Ammar would be found safe and sound. Suhair, to whom Abu Ammar was the father who had cared for her and her sisters after her own father's martyrdom, was in tears, on the verge of collapse. When-ever I caught her about to succumb to grief, I reminded her, "Keep up the hope. Now is the time for work, not for tears. So long as there is a chance that he's alive, we cannot give in." Gradually the hotel lobby filled with reporters; our phones never stopped. Akram, who had been the first to call me, sounded so unnaturally subdued that I was terrified he knew something he was refusing to tell me. "He will be found," was all he said.

At one point Ted Koppel called and wanted a live interview. The whole thrust of Nightline that night was elegiac, as though Arafat were dead. I kept insisting that there was hope. Koppel asked me, suppose he were dead, did that mean the beginning of a power struggle and the death knell of the PLO? I replied that Arafat was irreplaceable and that although his death would be a tragic blow to the PLO and to the Palestinian people as a whole, the PLO would continue and that there would be elections for a successor. Neither Nabil, Suhair, nor I saw any problems with that answer. I was asked to seek the help of the Americans in a satellite search of the desert. I called Ed Djerejian after we heard press reports of a downed plane sighted by American intelligence. Ed denied the reports, but promised to assist.

At dawn, Suhair answered a call from Amman announcing that the operations center in Cyprus had received a garbled message about the plane being located by trackers and the Waled being safe. It took us two hours to verify, but the facts confirmed he was safe. We announced this at the PLO office in Stockholm, then called Norway and apologized for canceling our visit, as we had to proceed directly to Tunis to meet Abu Ammar. We got on the plane to Tunis via Paris. Stress and exhaustion brought on a laryngitis attack, and I was rapidly losing my voice. We got to Charles de Gaulle Airport in the evening and received two urgent messages from Emile and Faisal to call back. After numerous attempts, we finally got connected.

Emile was furious. "Israeli radio and television in Arabic are announcing that you had called for elections even before you knew whether Abu Ammar was dead or alive."

"That's ridiculous. I was responding to a hypothetical question about the end of the PLO. This is obvious and deliberate distortion, and quotation out of context. I never called for elections."

"They're not using your own voice and words. It's all reported speech. What's worse is that some people have started responding to what you were reported to have said without actually asking to listen to you directly."

"I can't believe that somebody could be so gullible and irresponsible as to fall into such an obvious Israeli media trap. They've been after me for a long time, and it seems that Yossi Olmert [in charge of information, in the prime minister's office] finally got his chance to get even. He's been trying to discredit me for some time now."

"Don't take things lightly. This place is in an uproar. You're being accused of all sorts of horrible things. A man called Bassam al-Sayeh was on TV launching a vituperative attack on you and asking for your removal from political work."

"I guess that's his chance to replace me! He's not the only one to feel that my work is a direct threat and affront to him personally and to the male ego collectively."

"The Israelis know that, and they're using him and others like him to try to discredit you. You must speak out. People here should hear you in your own voice before this thing snowballs."

"I'll try and do something about it from here."

By that time, my voice was a hoarse croak. While Suhair was trying to reach the Monte Carlo radio in Arabic to arrange for me to make a statement, I finally got in touch with Faisal.

"Don't worry about it. I've issued a written statement already exonerating you and cautioning against such irresponsible accusations by Bassam and the likes of him. The statement will be in all the papers tomorrow."

"But in the meantime, how will the record be set straight before there's even greater incitement and damage?"

"You didn't know? Fortunately, Israeli television finally broadcast your full interview, and Bassam's statements sound totally unfounded and personally vindictive. Jordanian television also had you on giving different interviews, so damage control has already begun."

After my interview on Monte Carlo radio, I called Akram and found out that the PLO had already issued an official statement through its news agency, Wafa, defending me and accusing my accusers of hasty and unjustified statements. I had always maintained that the trust, loyalty, and support of both Akram and Faisal formed the mainstay of my political activity and once again I was proven right. By then, I was not only exhausted but also thoroughly disgusted. Those who had come after me with sharpened knives taught me an unforgettable lesson about treachery and envy, and about the precariousness of political life, particularly for a woman. To those women in the West who shared with me their painful experience of the "glass ceiling" I always pointed out that our confines in the East sometimes looked like stone cells. Whether invisible or concrete, the opposition we face is less painful in defiance than in acquiescence. If we manage to make wildflowers grow out of the crannies of stone walls, we can grow tall enough to smash glass ceilings and let the fresh air in.

The secret journey that followed from Paris to Tunis was another surrealistic experience. I was smuggled out of the plane and into Hakam

Bal'awi's house to receive Abu Ammar upon his return from Libya. Hakam, the PLO ambassador to Tunisia, played the role of minister of the interior for the Palestinians and was always a most generous and gracious host. I could not join the reception committee at the airport because of the very visible nature of the event and the presence of the press. Contact with the PLO was still illegal then, although we were trying to "naturalize" the connection. As I waited, I heard the distant sounds of jubilantly blaring horns drawing closer. Then the trill of ululating resonated in the garden, and I knew that it was time. I stood at the gate of the house as the convoy of cars drew in enveloped in cheers and chants. Suddenly, I heard the quiet discordant sound of bleating sheep, and right in front of me I saw three white lambs tethered to the post. With a sinking heart, I knew what was coming; this was certainly not the first occasion I had witnessed the Arabic ritual of slaughtering lambs to commemorate a homecoming or inauguration. As the door of the bulletproof limousine opened and Abu Ammar, al-Waled, emerged, the bleating was instantly silenced with the sweep of three sharp knives. I refused to look down. I kept my gaze steady and at eye level on Abu Ammar. As he took the three long strides over the corpses, his eyes met mine and he smiled.

At the gate he embraced me and drew me inside. He sat down in his usual seat and insisted that I sit right next to him. The room was filling with well-wishers and the top Palestinian political leadership. Following the usual small talk, Abu Ammar addressed the crowd in a loud voice. "It was the hand of God that saved me and my companions. My heart is filled with sorrow at the loss of my three brothers, the pilot and crew who had given their lives to save mine. I shall tell you the whole story of this miracle in due time. But first I want to tell you that of all the statements and comments that came out in the last twenty hours, those of our beloved sister Hanan were the most responsible and intelligent. As usual, she makes us all proud, and as you know she is not only a dear sister but the crown on our heads, taj rasna." He then looked at me and winked. I knew then that some people had already been up to mischief, and that Abu Ammar had chosen this moment to silence them once and for all. I was touched.

I also remembered the early days when ill-wishers protested my work and told him that I smoked, wore pants, and crossed my legs at official meetings. "Our women should be demure and unobtrusive," they said. His response had been, "We need more women like her, with her confidence and brains." That was when he first used the term taj rasna, and would add in my presence "whether they like it or not."

Although resurrection is a familiar theme in the Holy Land, when it came to a leader emerging from the ashes of his crashed plane, the impact on the popular imagination was astounding. Those thirteen hours of his disappearance became proof of Abu Ammar's power over his people. The phoenix had always been one of the Old Man's favorite mythical creatures. He had used it to describe the Palestinian people; now they were using it to describe him, the survivor.

CHAPTER TWELVE

---◆·◈·◆---

Toward the end of April, all talks were put on hold, pending Israeli elections. Abu Ammar was suffering from painful headaches and dizzy spells. The delegation was meeting and monitoring events and Israeli public opinion for indications about the outcome of the impending elections. Presidential elections were also coming up in the United States. The peace process, it seemed, was suspended in an external time frame. The mood was turning darker, less hopeful, imposing its own pace and priorities.

Even Easter was losing its festive atmosphere; our processions had turned into dispirited meanderings of haunted and distracted pilgrims. When did we start paying more attention to crucifixion than to resurrection? Sorrow held us in its grip like an afterthought, and we had become too listless to notice or resist. At home, Zeina was in tears desperately missing her sister, Amal, who had gone to England for a year as an exchange student. We were determined to keep up our family's tradition of celebration. For days we prepared the sugarcoated Easter cookies— date-filled rings symbolizing the wreath of thorns, and nut-filled domes symbolizing the sponge soaked in vinegar, ka᾽k and ma᾽moul. The egg hunt, which had been the high point of Easter for the girls, lost its excitement that year. It was as if the hiatus in the peace process and the loss of hope in any alleviation of the pain of the occupation had cast a dismal spell on us as individuals and as a people. We were unable to savor the transformation of thorns and vinegar into the exquisitely sweet sensation of hope.

I made the trip to England several times that year to visit Amal at her boarding school near Bristol, and I could hear in her voice, even in the very first phone call after arriving, that she was homesick. She called us upon getting there in absolute misery.

"There's something wrong with the British, Mumsy," she said. "I don't think they're normal kids here at school."

"What's wrong, *habeebty?* Children are the same everywhere."

"No," she said. "Here the kids say nasty things about their parents. They actually don't love their mothers and fathers. I can't stand it."

My heartbreak slowly turned into a warm glow of utter bliss. What greater testimonial does a mother need?

"I don't approve of what they do, either," Amal added. "They smoke and drink and they're only fourteen or fifteen. I don't want to be judgmental and be rejected, but I can't be like them."

With that I could hear the voice of the woman emerging from the innocence of childhood.

"If you're unhappy, Amal, you can always come home." I was convinced that she was still too young to be away from us. "You will still have the opportunity to travel later. You're right, you don't have to be like them. You can maintain your own principles and the attitudes with which we brought you up, but I applaud your tolerance and willingness to suspend judgment."

"No, I will not come home now. It would be like admitting defeat. It's become a challenge and I will see it through. But their priorities are different also. They don't know anything about us or about the *intifada.* To them, life is parties and having fun. But I keep worrying about you and trying to catch you on TV. Is everybody safe at home?"

A heavy melancholy took hold of me, wrapping itself around my heart like a sticky shroud. I cried for the lost childhood of my daughters and the children of their generation. Instead of going to parties in their early teens, they worried about the safety of their families and friends, or were dodging Israeli bullets. When Amal was eleven and Zeina seven, Emile and I took them to America to visit relatives. The first thing they noticed was the absence of the occupation: "There are no soldiers and checkpoints here!" they had exclaimed. Then they noted that the shops did not go on strike and that they stayed open late: "You can actually go shopping at night here, and you can walk in the streets after dark." Only after they had registered the fact of nonoccupation did they begin to look at the country for what it actually was. When a reporter asked afterward whether they would prefer the United States to Palestine, Amal answered: "I would live nowhere in the world but Palestine. It's my home, where I belong and where I know who I am." Asked about her opinion of the States, she said: "Everything is too easy there. They take everything for granted and everything is available and in too much quantity. Nothing comes easy for us. We have to struggle hard and earn everything. That's why we appreciate even the smallest things." What a source of inspiration I found in a child's theory of value and surfeit. After agreeing with her sister and singling out Palestine as her place in the world, Zeina retracted partially and exclaimed, "There is one other place I might choose to live in—Disney World!" Our children's world was never an amusement park, and they did not grow up in freedom. They were weighted down with a knowledge that should not have been theirs and an experience that did not spare their childhood. To whom would we present the reckoning and the claim for a lost childhood?

· · ·

In May 1992 I was in London giving speeches and holding talks on the peace process. In addition to the full political and public program that my close friend and PLO representative Afif Safieh had arranged, he had also put together a package that included theaters, movies, and restaurants to which we took Amal as a special treat. We went out to dinner with Vanessa Redgrave after seeing her play. She is a faithful and longtime friend of the Palestinians, and she and Amal struck up an instant friendship. During this incredible trip I got an urgent call from Amman. It was the Palestinian ambassador, Tayyeb Abdel-Rahim, telling me that Abu Ammar had been hospitalized and would be undergoing surgery. I had heard rumors about his health earlier, but Tayyeb had denied them. Akram insisted that I return immediately, and I took the next plane to Amman. Heading straight to the hospital from the airport, I found Abu Ammar recovering from the surgery, which had relieved the pressure in his head. The physical pressure, anyway.

"The time has come to end the charade," Akram confided in hushed secrecy.

"We'll send after the rest of the delegation and have them meet Abu Ammar in public."

"So it is time to lift the veil, or stop the mirror negotiations." (We had often described our talks as negotiations through mirrors and veils.) "Do you think we'll get away with it? It will have an impact on the Israeli elections next week. That's the objective, I assume?" The implications of an open admission could be enormous.

"That, plus the fact that this could be the most suitable time to publicly announce the relationship between the delegation and the PLO. We have to make sure it doesn't backfire, though."

"I agree. This needs very careful planning and assessment. Maybe we should conduct some discreet inquiries with the other side. It is in our interest and the interest of the peace process to see the Likud lose the elections and have Labor come to government in Israel. Would such a move help or upset their internal balance? The polls predict a very close race and we need to give it a push in the right direction. But we cannot be seen to interfere in internal Israeli politics."

"Get in touch with your contacts, and we'll do the same. But we have to be very careful that this does not come out. Only Abu Ammar knows, and we'll consult with Yasser Abd Rabbo and Tayyeb Abdel-Rahim."

"What about the delegation?"

"We'll tell them when they get here. This is not just a political issue, it's also humanitarian. The delegation cannot be prevented from visiting the chairman after his operation and wishing him long life and good health."

The delegation arrived the next day, and on June 18, 1992, exactly one week before the Israeli elections, we were officially and publicly received by President Arafat. For the first time since June 1967, Palestinians from the Occupied Territories conducted a public disclosure of their connection with the PLO. It had taken a quarter of a century for the people to lay claim to its leadership not just verbally but demonstrably and before the eyes of the world. As we filed in one by one to be embraced by Abu Ammar and members of the Executive Committee, the ritual of public avowal turned into an emotional experience of recognition and unification. When my turn came, I walked up to Abu Ammar and he gave me the symbolic three kisses—on the forehead and cheeks—then in a warm embrace he lay my head on his shoulder and patted my back gently, reassuringly. The moment was so strangely restful, suspended in time and place, as to create the illusion of peace at last. To look at the photograph that had captured and frozen that mood, one would not remotely suspect the turmoil that lay ahead. The turning point of recognition had brought only transitory and deceptive relief.

. . .

"What do you think you're doing?" Dan Kurtzer asked in suppressed fury with the deliberate articulation and measured pace of someone who was on the verge of blowing up. "Have you all gone insane?"

"I don't know what you're talking about. We've been doing many things. What in specific are you referring to?"

"You're on every TV station and on every headline with this embrace between the delegation and the PLO. Why did you do that? You really blew it!"

"We're naturally affectionate people! What's more natural than for the delegation to visit the president and wish him a speedy recovery. He's just emerged from an operation; it's only human."

"The elections are less than a week away. Have you thought of the effect this will have on the outcome?"

"We certainly have! That will teach Shamir to play ostrich politics. All along he knew that this was the PLO delegation. He just wanted to pretend otherwise and bury his head in the sand. Maybe it's time he faced facts. At least Rabin says he doesn't care whom we meet with and who gives us our instructions. It's time to deal with facts, not Israeli-manufactured fiction."

"But why now? This will be a free elections gift for Shamir. You promised not to meddle in the Israeli elections."

"Because now is the most appropriate time. And if this is a gift for anybody, it certainly is not for Shamir, quite the opposite. We haven't meddled in Israeli elections; have you heard any comments from us? Any expression of preferences? If the Israeli electorate want to draw any conclusions from this embrace that's their business, but it seems to me that the most obvious conclusion is that the Likud has been pulling the wool over their eyes. The big lie has been exposed. Maybe they would prefer to deal with an honest alternative, if there is such a thing."

"But now they will have to arrest the whole delegation, or at least the three key people, Faisal, Haidar, and you. What do you think this will do to the peace process?"

"Here we go again. This certainly sounds familiar. Let them arrest us —we want them to. It's about time we blow this whole thing wide open. The law preventing contact with the PLO is undemocratic and unjust. Besides, we're Palestinians, not Israelis, and the PLO is our leadership. We refuse to obey such a law, and now it's all out in the open."

"Just don't try to go back now and force their hand. There's a lot of damage control to be done, and we'll see what we can do."

"That sounds familiar too. Don't worry about us, we know what we're doing. We'll go home when we finish our work and meetings here in Amman."

. . .

I followed the Israeli elections from Jordan. When the Labor Party won, the airwaves were filled with optimistic forecasts as if peace were around the corner. In my statements I cautioned against euphoria and unrealistic expectations. "The real test is yet to come, whether Rabin the bone-breaker can become Rabin the peacemaker." No one knew better than the Palestinians the dark side of the moon when it came to the Israeli Labor Party. "Likud is a much easier adversary," I said. "Their ideological bias and extremist policies and practices are easily exposed and debunked. Labor, on the other hand, knows how to sugarcoat the pill and present a civilized veneer even when reality is anything but civilized. Besides, there is already an international predisposition to look kindly on Labor, particularly as a refreshing antidote to the rigid Likud ideology and in view of Labor's long-standing relations of friendship with the West." We had no illusions about Labor being difficult and demanding negotiators—having been on the receiving end of its human rights abuses and settlement drive, we knew that we were in for a difficult time. But we also realized that Labor had won on a peace platform and that in coalition with Meretz (a coalition of three left-wing parties and the most vocal of Israeli peace advocates), it might try to deliver to its peace constituency. At least we looked forward to the end of ostrich politics and mercurial negotiations, and to the beginning of genuine engagement on the basis of respect for the terms of reference and underlying principles of the peace process.

To our dismay, even those modest and restrained expectations were quickly shattered. Instead of announcing the expected settlement freeze, Rabin began a whole process of equivocation on "political" versus "security" settlements. Instead of a rational discussion on Jerusalem, Rabin reiterated the absolutist ideological prophetic position: "the eternal capital of Israel forever and ever." Instead of human rights, we got the "security of Israel." And instead of a new delegation to signal a new phase and policy, we got Elyakim Rubinstein and his crew again. As the frosting on the cake, when we crossed the bridge home, we were slapped with summonses to police headquarters for interrogation.

As it were, we already had enough on our plate, trying to maintain our own peace constituency and preparing for what we thought would be a new and accelerated phase. We had a variety of visitors and visitations of a haunting and disturbing nature. Baker came in August on his first visit after the formation of the new Israeli government to inject the process with momentum and invite us for a new round toward the end of the month. The Republicans were in trouble with their own presidential election and needed all the help they could get. With Israel as a domestic issue in the United States, it was standard election policy to court the American Jewish community through Tel Aviv and to try and win congressional favor by promising Israel unlimited support and a large chunk of the American taxpayer's money. Bush and Baker were no exceptions. Having waited (and not very passively) for Rabin's election, they were bending over backward trying to please him. Baker was full of praise for Rabin's "new policies" and was trying to sell them to us wholesale as the answer to our prayers, turning a deaf ear to our misgivings and concerns, particularly on the issues of settlements and human rights. Bush invited Rabin to the United States and immediately approved the $10 billion loan guarantees.

These did not translate into votes; Clinton had made Israel a better offer: Jerusalem. Such munificence, we felt, was not unusual in an election campaign, but did it have to be at our expense?

During a break in the meeting at the Jerusalem consulate, Baker told me of his dilemma whether to move to the White House as chief of staff to run President Bush's campaign or to stay in the State Department and deal with foreign policy, including the peace process. His reluctance was difficult to disguise. I expressed my concern about the sporadic and politically opportune attention he had been giving the process. But at the same time I acknowledged the fact that he appeared to be needed in the campaign. I was sure it was not my advice he was after, but the opportunity to think out loud even to the last possible moment.

• • •

My house was host to numerous visitors of different kinds. At one point I received a woman from Al-Am⁏ari refugee camp. One of her children had been deported, the other imprisoned for life, another was wounded and detained, and the fourth was missing. The third and fourth needed immediate intervention. I got a lawyer for the third child and tried to get him medical attention. We located the fourth in Ramallah hospital, in the morgue, a corpse denied burial. Word got to the *shabab*, his youthful colleagues, who stole the body from the morgue. Somehow it found its way into the back seat of our car and was delivered to the family (or what was left of it) to legitimize their grief and his death with proper burial. We had, it seemed, sanctified body snatching as part of the rites of final passage, for the denial of public lament and sanctified burial was more morally repugnant and cruel than this sinister theft. Antigone would have approved.

One woman brought to my house an even more horrible, searing wound. Her eyes seemed to have permanently lost their focus, shifting and darting incessantly like those of a trapped wild creature waiting for the hunter's knife. She had been accused by some masked Palestinian activists of "immoral behavior" and collaboration with Israeli military intelligence. "How can I prove my innocence? Tell me," she pleaded. "They've turned my life into a living hell. They broke into my home and beat me up before my children." Lifting her long hair off her neck and shoulders, she showed me livid scars and disfigured skin that made my own flesh cringe. I recognized the indelible mark of burning acid. "They came back and did this to me. They said that next time they will cut me to pieces unless I confess the error of my ways and stop my activities. How can I confess when I'm not guilty and stop something I'm not doing? If they will leave me and my children alone, I will confess to anything. Tell me what to confess, how to confess, and I'll do it if they'll let us go. But if I confess I'm sure they'll kill me and feel justified. How will my children live? What kind of memory of their mother will they have?"

Another woman came after the fact. Her husband had already been "executed" by the instruments of "revolutionary justice," but she was like a creature possessed, obsessed with the compulsion of clearing his name so that their children would not inherit a legacy of shame. "I know he was not a collaborator, but he was tortured and killed. How can I prove his innocence? Tell Abu Ammar. Ask him for a public decree announcing him a martyr and clearing his name. We are all outcasts now. What do I tell his children when they grow up—'Your father was a traitor'? He wasn't, and I'll never believe it." Not so much hunted as haunted, she had acquired the otherworldly look of a zealot. Her dark eyes had the glaze of distant vision, peering through the here and now as nothing more than an opaque veil that obscured the future. She clutched my arm painfully, oblivious of my flesh-and-blood reality, seeing in me only a potential instrument of vindication.

The burden and knowledge of their pain, their horror and their fear, were beyond the threshold of my endurance and the scope of ordinary moral reproach. Who could undo their pain? What words, what language, could be created to soothe such raw, exposed wounds of the soul and flesh passed on to generations? Our historical memory had already been disfigured with the legacy of evil and guilt imposed on innocent children, and our collective psyche branded with the scarlet imprint of the unspeakable injustice of such summary "justice." I remembered how in the early days of the *intifada* the underground leaflets would announce Days of Repentance in which collaborators would go to mosques, churches, or town squares to confess and recant before the whole community, and gain absolution and the satisfaction of being readmitted into the fold. What had happened to the quality of mercy, of forgiveness? The more collaborators Israel recruited, the more frantic was the fear and the hunt. Had it finally found the ultimate punishment—turning us against ourselves, watching us clawing at our own flesh? Guilty or innocent, their punishment was ours. Perhaps some innocent lives had been saved, but how many more had been lost in the process? And those uncompromising instruments of "justice," what absolution could they find once they discovered that they too were mere mortals?

My house, our home, built by my father as an offering of love and a pledge of faith, held us all in a safe embrace. Solid stone, built on rock, it seemed to breathe with the life of its inhabitants and with the promise of continuity. Across the street loomed the blind and sinister monstrosity called the Taggart Building. Built by the British during the mandate, it functioned as a prison and military headquarters. The Jordanians had used it as a prison, and added to it an unobtrusive structure that became the officers' club. As a child of ten, I remember my mother dressing me up and putting ribbons in my hair to go visit my father, who had been imprisoned by the Jordanians. We took him food and reading materials, and I was cautioned to look brave and cheerful during the visit. Going through the dark corridors and underground cells, I gave free rein to my imagination to conjure up images of unspeakable horrors taking place in secret. When twenty years later it became my turn to be summoned and interrogated there, but this time by the Israelis, I recalled the child I had been and refused to succumb to the nightmare. On both occasions, though, the place had the distinctive smell of evil.

Bearing the Israeli flag, surrounded by barbed wire, and emitting strange sounds, the place across the street was a place without a soul. When Peter Jennings visited me in my father's house in 1974, he was appalled at the searchlights that pierced the privacy of my home. What went on in the darkness within that place across the street was even more appalling, I tried to explain. It seemed to grow under Israeli control, and in 1982 it became the headquarters of the Israeli "Civil Administration." My mother was always resentful that people used the "Civil Administration" building as a landmark when giving directions to our house. "Dr. Daud Mikhail's house is the landmark. The other is an artificial eyesore," she said. We all agreed that with the end of the occupation, the place should be torn down and replaced by a children's playground. No matter how green or colorful our garden became, and no matter how many Palestinian flags Zeina hoisted on our rooftop or painted on the sidewalk, the coiled barbed wire and the sight of the Israeli flag across the street were a constant reminder of the intrusiveness of the evil of occupation.

The machine of the occupation churned on, gnawing on innocent flesh to fuel its obscenity. It mangled both occupier and occupied. "There's no monopoly on pain, no upmanship on suffering," I once told a reporter who had tried to draw comparisons and contrasts between Palestinian and Jewish suffering. "Each pain is unique and beyond quantifying or justification." Once human rights violations had been sanctioned as an instrument of coercion and a factor of political expediency, innocent lives on both sides became sacrificial offerings to the most profane idols of manipulation and revenge. Routine incantations were demanded in the form of denunciations and condemnations, as if lip service were capable of warding off the invasion of darkness. In the meantime, Israeli policies of using us as hostages and human rights as bargaining chips in negotiations persisted, and extremist Palestinian attempts at exacting revenge and destroying the peace process by targeting Israeli civilian victims continued. Neither the Israeli schoolgirls of Affula nor the victims of Khdeira were guilty of any transgression beyond being at the wrong place at the wrong time. The reckoning to settle scores of desecration was scribbled in human blood. Trapped in this self-perpetuating cycle of mutual delegitimization that turned the official "mutual recognition" into a mockery and a formalistic exercise devoid of substance, we were forced to undergo an unfolding human tragedy without even the catharsis of pity and fear. We were denied the detachment and relative safety of aesthetic distance as the unwilling players haphazardly destined to swell the ranks of victims —the anonymous bodies strewn on the battlefield of "dicing chance."

It was by chance again that I escaped another encounter with violent death at the hands of the same Kach extremists whose dialogue was conducted through the barrel of a machine gun. At the end of Baker's visit, I held the usual press conference at the Palestinian Al-Masrah theater in East Jerusalem. In the middle of my briefing, pandemonium broke out in the theater and some of the volunteer security *shabab* jumped up on the stage and tried to spirit me away. Others rushed toward the door. Reporters followed right behind. Two of the young men, unarmed, grappled with an Israeli who was brandishing a machine gun; twice he pressed the trigger and twice the gun jammed. They finally succeeded in subduing him and handing him to the Israeli police. Despite the testimony of the young men and the foreign press, the would-be assassin was again released. I later saw him while I was being interviewed by the press right after the Hebron massacre. He was giving a parallel interview to Swiss television praising the mass murderer Baruch Goldstein and hailing the slaughter as an act of courage and faith while lamenting the insufficient number of Arabs killed. Slowly and deliberately I turned and looked him in the eye. I found nothing there. He went on as though nothing had happened. I walked away chilled to the bone, having looked into the vacuous space of utter evil.

Other potential assassins remained abstract, anonymous, preparing hit lists of people unknown to them. I read my name on some of these lists, but did not recognize myself. I was warned by the PLO, which was warned by others to watch out for these killers, but I refused to personalize the warnings. And when specific descriptions were given, I refused to internalize the image and look at others around me with suspicion. When some were arrested in different countries and worlds, I would not admit them into my own universe. Neither the image of my own fate nor that of my loved ones included the recognition of such a profane violation.

•　•　•

The peace talks did not and could not effect a miraculous transformation. They proceeded in fits and starts, subject to the dictates of the surrounding political terrain, carrying an unbalanced cargo. Our sixth Washington round dashed any lingering hopes of a qualitative change in attitudes and strategies; Labor picked up where Likud left off. Their "Outline" of the "Administrative Council," presented on August 20, was an offshoot of the Likud proposal, with a total disregard of the territorial dimension. We responded with a revised "Proposal for a Framework Agreement," which fell on deaf ears.

We were battling over the terms of reference. The Israeli offers were in a different language, in contradiction with the principle of land for peace and the objective of ending the occupation on the basis of U.N. Security Council Resolutions 242 and 338. These were, supposedly, the basis of American policy in the region, but the United States ominously refused to reiterate them. Neither Israel nor the United States was willing to assert the interlock between the interim phase and permanent status or to commit itself to the objective of the talks as the implementation (rather than the interpretation or discussion) of Resolution 242. Consequently, we were thwarted in our attempts at holding the Americans to their assurances that no unilateral actions that might preempt or prejudice the permanent-status negotiations would be allowed. Israel continued to confiscate land and resources and to expand the settlements, and we continued our futile protest. Jerusalem was being transformed and distorted with a counterfeit imposed reality, and Israel's illegal unilateral annexation of the Palestinian city was rapidly becoming an irreversible fact.

Toward the end of the second part of the round, we agreed to form informal working groups to probe the Israeli side on detailed aspects of their proposal and to reveal its practical implications and consequences. On September 14, the Israeli delegation finally tabled its most detailed proposal under the heading "Informal Concept of the Interim Self-Government Arrangements: Building Blocks for Agreement." To us it was irrefutable proof that Israel was manipulating the negotiations to fit its own version of reality and that a drastic legal and conceptual gap still separated the two sides. For us it became more urgent to address the issue of territorial jurisdiction in more concrete terms, especially in regard to the settlements and Jerusalem, and to define the genuine transfer of authority (rather than the delegation of administrative functions) within the scope of an elected Palestinian legislative council.

PLO instructions were becoming more rigid and demanding. While we held on to our basic negotiating strategy, the leadership was averse even to creating an impression of progress on technical issues. I began to wonder then whether a back channel was already in operation, and asked Abu Mazen and Abu Ammar. Both denied it. Abu Mazen wanted us to press ahead, but Abu Ammar was immovable on 242 ("and if they refuse then tell them 181"—the U.N. plan for the partition of Palestine). He also insisted that "blue berets," U.N. forces, take over the Occupied Territories from Israel, and limit the interim phase to only six months. Without the PLO, I was convinced, the talks would remain an empty charade, a play in the spotlight, waiting for reality to catch up with it, backstage and in the dark.

• • •

The seventh round, from the twenty-first of October to the twentieth of November, was long and eventful. The working groups conducted extensive informal discussions and exploratory talks on the strength of which we worked out a flow chart and a schematic presentation. The American team declared that it was "impressed" and pronounced us appropriately "serious and skilled" at negotiations. Meanwhile, the American presidential elections were under way, and when Bill Clinton defeated George Bush it did not bode well for us. While we had no wish to interfere in American domestic politics and had no overt preferences, we had no illusions that the outcome of these elections would reverberate all over the world, including our region and particularly the peace process.

On the one hand the peace process was a Republican initiative and a major political foreign policy investment; on the other hand the Democrats were weak on foreign policy and might want to subscribe to a winning proposition if they perceived the process as a successful enterprise. A second-term president might have been confident enough to make bold decisions and initiatives and would be relatively free of the pressures of special interest groups like AIPAC (American-Israeli Political Action Committees). On the other hand, a new president, particularly a Democrat, would have immense political debts to pay back, particularly to AIPAC and the pro-Israeli lobby, which had supported his campaign and those of congressional candidates. Clinton had promised Israel a blank check—strategic alliances, aid in maintaining military strength, and Jerusalem, but Bush had given Israel loan guarantees and tailored the peace process to meet its requirements. Having launched the process, Baker and Bush had abandoned it and allowed Israel to exploit its power to its own advantage. The Democrats had a strong human rights platform that could redress the injustice of Israeli abuses and prevent the manipulation of this issue in negotiations. The bottom line had always been that no American administration would ever stand up to Israel—it did not pay political dividends. Historically, the Palestinians had always been dispensable, both as an alien culture and people, and as a negligible factor in making or breaking political careers on the Hill or in the White House.

Our alternative, nonofficial dialogue with the Israelis outside the confines of the negotiations, continued. The women's groups were the most consistent and persistent, never losing sight of the need to create realities besides the official dialogues, and to venture into no-man's-land with a bold vision and firm strides. Many of the political parties that had been our unofficial interlocutors when Likud was in power had now become part of the government coalition. The three parties Mapam, Ratz, and Shinui had formed the Meretz group and become Labor's major left-wing partner in the new government. Shulamit Aloni, one of the early participants in the Brussels women's conference, was now a member of the cabinet, as were Ya'ir Tsaban and Amnon Rubinstein, while Yossi Sareed, a Ratz member, was in line for a cabinet post. Our first meeting of reconciliation after the Gulf War rift took place unofficially in Jerusalem. Our "Mashov Group" interlocutors, the left wing of the Labor Party, were represented by Yossi Beilin, who had become deputy foreign minister, and by the two academics Ya'ir Hirschfeld and Ron Pundik. It was during a meeting with Ya'ir at my house that the Oslo back channel was launched. A meeting was planned for London, which later was shifted to Oslo and developed into the channel that led to the Oslo agreement.

Rabin had taken over the bilateral negotiations. Foreign Minister Shimon Peres was told to dabble with the multilaterals. Ya'ir had been working on economic development and cooperation projects with the Europeans and was quite involved with the multilaterals. Ya'ir was going to London for a Steering Committee meeting. Abu Ala (Ahmad Qrei'), who was appointed by the PLO to head the Palestinian team in the multilaterals, was also going to London to supervise our delegation there. I suggested to Ya'ir that he meet Abu Ala in London and work out some of the economic issues related to the multilaterals that he had been asking me to clear up for him. He said he would think about it and let me know, although he was still hesitant about direct contacts with the PLO, which, according to Israeli law, were illegal.

For more than three years, we had been attempting to establish a back channel between the PLO and Yossi Beilin's group within the Labor Party, mainly through the "Dutch connection" of Max van der Stoel (the previous Dutch foreign minister) and his assistant Robert Serry, a Foreign Ministry official responsible for the Middle East desk.

Thus the Oslo channel, which developed separately from the official negotiations in Washington, did not emerge from a vacuum. The history of secret talks and channels in the context of the Palestinian-Israeli dialogue is long and complex. I took part in some of it. In the early days of February 1989, the Palestinian Political Committee had made a decision to go public with the meetings it was holding with some of the more "establishment" Israelis, mainly Knesset (parliament) members, rather than our usual activists. Thus the famous Notre Dame meetings took place beginning in mid-February between some local Palestinian political leadership figures and up to seventeen Israeli Knesset members. The

Notre Dame Hotel was chosen as an appropriate venue since it was located on the Green Line separating Palestinian East Jerusalem from Israeli West Jerusalem. From that context, Yossi Beilin and his group, including Ya'ir Hirschfeld, pursued separate bilateral contacts with us similar to the older dialogue we had established with Israeli activists and nonmainstream parties. Consequently, when Robert Serry suggested the idea of "proximity talks" at the initiative of Max van der Stoel, we felt that the conditions were ripe. Both had maintained close relations with us and with the Israeli Labor Party, and had conceived the idea of establishing indirect talks with the PLO with the Dutch as intermediaries. In June of that year, the first proximity talks took place in Holland, with Max van der Stoel shuttling back and forth between Israeli and Palestinian hotel rooms. From the Palestinian side, Abdallah Hurani, a member of the Executive Committee, participated on behalf of the PLO in coordination with Abu Mazen. Afif Safieh was then the PLO representative in the Netherlands, and when the time came for the meeting between Ya'ir and Abu Ala in London, Afif had been transferred to England and as such participated also in that first meeting in London. Back channels had a way of establishing spiral patterns, rising incrementally while maintaining continuity.

By December the one-year time frame for the completion of talks on the transitional phase had been passed with no end in sight. Despite our repeated attempts to get the co-sponsors to renegotiate a new timetable, no response was forthcoming except "Keep at it." Of course, the Israelis deliberately exploited the delays to create facts on the ground and to maximize their political advantage. And they were tightening the vise at home—with more arrests, deportations, and other human rights violations. As a result, our public opinion was increasingly turning against the talks, in some ways blaming us for the escalation of repression. Violating timetables became a repetitive pattern of Israeli negotiating strategy.

Our negotiators (now reduced in number, per the decision of the PLO) rotated among the three working groups on the concept of the interim self-government arrangements, territorial jurisdiction, and powers and responsibilities of the elected council. We continued to present our human rights status reports and pressed ahead with our work on the agenda and on issues of common concern.

On December 15, a number of urgent phone calls from home alerted me to unusual activity by the Israeli army, rounding up supporters of Hamas, the Islamic Resistance Movement, in the aftermath of that organization's kidnapping and execution of an Israeli soldier.

"Buses are moving in the direction of all prisons. There are rumors of an intended mass deportation of Palestinians from the Occupied Territories. A very strict curfew has been imposed," Ahmad Saif urgently reported by phone. He was following up with the human rights watch groups.

"We'll try to intervene from here. Please keep me informed of any developments," I responded.

Minutes later, Nasser, our press officer, who had stayed home for that round and who was also a member of a human rights group called. "Our field workers report that a large number of prisoners are being placed on buses with blackened windows. Everyone suspects deportation."

I called Dan Kurtzer. "Does the State Department have any news of massive deportations? We're getting alarming reports from home." I gave him the details.

"We have no information on any such movement. I'll check and let you know. Are you sure your sources are accurate?"

"They're eyewitnesses. I'm sure your consulate in Jerusalem and embassy in Tel Aviv would know. We're asking you to call Rabin and stop him before it's too late. Haidar had already told Elyakim Rubinstein that if the rumors of the deportations were true, then he should not expect to see a Palestinian delegation tomorrow."

Another phone rang while I was speaking. It was Yoram Binun, the Israeli journalist who had written the book *My Enemy, My Self*.

"I have seen the movement myself. Rabin intends to go ahead with the deportations. My sources verify that. He's called for a cabinet meeting."

I called Leah Tsemel. "Can you do something about this? Get a restraining order or a court injunction to prevent the deportation?" I asked.

"I'm trying. I've called four judges so far, with no response. I've been asked to get a list of the potential deportees and present the request in their names. The army should give us the names but they're not cooperating."

"Check with the families of those recently detained. This has to be done by our side."

Ahmad Sayyad, a Palestinian lawyer working with the Mandela Institute dealing with Palestinian prisoners' rights, was my next caller. "We're trying to get the information, and we'll pass it on to Leah. We'll keep you informed."

I called Saeb at the State Department while the delegations were still meeting and asked him to inform Haidar and to tell Rubinstein to impress upon Rabin the seriousness of this step.

In the meantime, Yazid Sayegh, who was the only other member of our team available in the hotel, had come in to help with the crisis and the communication. Dan Kurtzer called back.

"I'm afraid we cannot verify your information. Both the U.S. consulate and embassy do not report any unusual activity," he calmly announced.

"Either this is a coverup or flagrant inefficiency. May I suggest that you fire everybody there. We have corroboration from Israeli sources as well as ongoing witness reports. Leah Tsemel and other lawyers are already on the case. Please call Rabin and stop him from carrying out the deportations. I cannot begin to tell you what deportation means to us; it's the worst Palestinian nightmare. We cannot negotiate if Rabin carries it out."

Leah Tsemel's husband, Michel Warsovski, whose nickname was the "Mikado," called. "Leah's in court right now. I'm in touch with her on her mobile phone, and I'll stay in touch with you to keep you informed. She wants me to tell you that the government plans to expel them to Lebanon."

I called Tunis. Abu Ammar was out of the country and Abu Mazen was at his son's wedding. I talked to Yasser Abd Rabbo, informed him of the crisis, and asked him to call the Lebanese government. Then I called Suheil Shammas, head of the Lebanese delegation.

"Please get in touch with your government," I urged. "The Israelis are planning to deport a large number of Palestinians to Lebanon. Please ask your government to announce immediately that it will not accept them. This is a violation of your sovereignty. Israel must not impose this on you or on any other country. The Jordanians had already announced their policy of no longer accepting any deportees." Suheil followed up immediately, and the Lebanese government made the announcement. Dan called again.

"The Israeli government is in session, and Rabin is not taking any phone calls."

"I could have told you that. A court hearing is already in session. Get [Secretary of State Lawrence] Eagleburger to call, get Bush. This is an emergency."

"We tried, but as far as Rabin is concerned this is not a lame duck administration, it's a dead duck! They're not listening."

Nabil Sha'th came back and he started calling his Israeli contacts. We were particularly upset when members of Meretz supported Rabin's decision, saying the alternatives could be worse. "Nothing could be worse," we answered. They then came back with the lame excuse that they had had no idea about the numbers, more than four hundred. "What happened to your principles?" we asked. In between phone calls to Palestine, Israel, Washington, Tunis, and any other capital as needed, I launched an information campaign. That night I had been scheduled to appear on *Larry King Live,* and I took the opportunity to announce that if the deportations were carried out, there would be no Palestinian delegation the next day.

"But they're Hamas people, opposed to the peace process," Larry said.

"They're Palestinians and entitled to their own opinions," I replied. "Just because we differ politically does not mean that they're stripped of their human and national rights. Besides, they haven't been tried and convicted. This is nothing but collective punishment of the worst kind. They're taking revenge on innocent people and their families."

I remembered Larry's visit to my home in Ramallah that summer. It had been a different world and a different time then. Larry had come with his family and his friend Tom Wolf (who later fulfilled his promise of sending Zeina an autographed Larry Bird basketball). Over tea, we compared the Ramallah and Brooklyn upbringing. From our veranda, we watched my town reclining peacefully on the curved hills of the Palestinian countryside. Our white stone houses emerging from the earth were at peace with the gardens and trees that seemed to embrace them gently, tenderly, as if promising protection from demolition and expulsion. That was a deceptive idyll, but we had allowed ourselves the luxury of temporary peace. A moment in the sunshine with Larry King's family and mine at home was the invisible backdrop of that painful interview on the eve of deportation.

In Washington the talks were halted without the concluding session. We headed home for another somber Christmas while our compatriots were literally out in the cold, pitching their tents on the snow-covered mountainside in south Lebanon. Daily demonstrations, strikes, and confrontations with the army were the realities of that season of peace. A public outcry and ceaseless protest surrounded our return. The U.N. Security Council met and adopted Resolution 799 calling for the immediate return of the deportees and for Israel's application of the Fourth Geneva Convention and cessation of such forms of punitive measures. As usual, Israel ignored it as it had all other resolutions pertaining to its behavior in the Occupied Territories and with the Palestinian people. We developed a horror of being uprooted, a fear of floating ungrounded and unanchored in inhospitable space. For a people like ours, neither wanderers nor seafarers, the land gave us our bearings and defined our security. We developed memories more tangible than our present of a past that had to be redeemed if we were to lay claim to a future. The ripple effect

CHAPTER THIRTEEN

———◆·✦·◆———

Sundays were our wildflower days. Every spring we took family excursions into the hillsides around Ramallah and on the way to Jericho. To us children, these picnics were the essence of adventure and discovery, affording us firsthand communion with nature at its most promising and vulnerable. In a gentle and shy unfolding, a tentative testing of life in the sun, the tiny buds would wince in the bright Mediterranean glare before exploding into a magnificent lush carpet of dazzling color. Catching this transition into sudden being was to us like possessing the elixir of life, the secret of the land. My parents would show us how to pick wildflowers without damaging the roots, while pointing out the rare unpickable ones, indicating the species with medicinal properties, and narrating tales from the magical world of our people's folk imagination revealing their rich history. Wild tulips, violets, anemones, lilies, and shepherd's staff would nod and sway in the gentle breeze in a red, white, and lilac dance, with green interludes in spicy and healing herbs.

Just as deportations damaged our roots, so did the bulldozers that plowed through our hills to establish Israeli settlements and destroyed the roots of our wildflowers. The landscape around Jericho was filled with invisible, lethal mines, and I could not recapture with my daughters my childhood experience of wildflowers. Armed settlers roamed the hilly of family, community, town, nation formed the concentric circles of our individual security, and we took every deportation personally. Every day, each one of us relived the tragedy of the 1948 expulsion and the transformation of a nation into dispossessed and disinherited exiles. The fate of a refugee was a curse and the status of statelessness a pernicious vulnerability. When my brother-in-law, the president of my university, the bishop of my church, my friends and faculty colleagues, and even total strangers were deported, I took upon myself their absence, and every Palestinian felt the diminution of his or her own inheritance.

tracks, tamed and labeled in Hebrew for the newly arrived Muscovites and New Yorkers who sought to discover our land and claim it as their own. We had known these hills instinctively, every trail and hidden spring an intimate revelation of our shared continuity. We never needed signs in Hebrew to find our way, nor did we ever come across barbed wire piercing the flesh of the earth and barring our entry on pain of death. Such had become our lot, and I grieved for our people, for my daughters who could not gain admission into one of the mysteries of my own childhood nor take possession of those priceless heirlooms that should have been their own heritage.

But my overwhelming grief was reserved for those other less privileged Palestinian children whose deprivation was so complete as to dry up even the springs of hope in their hearts and to shrink the realm of their experience to the desiccated terrain of perpetual loss. These had become the moving human targets for the Israeli occupation, to whom the highest form of heroism was to confront a trigger-happy soldier with their bared breasts. Their toys had become makeshift clubs and wooden guns for those who played the soldiers' role and slings for those who played the *intifada shabab*. A make-believe world of lethal dimensions had usurped their imagination, but somehow could not erase a look of longing in their eyes, a yearning for something unknown and undefined that in other worlds and languages went under the name of childhood. Neither they nor their parents had any memory of wildflowers or restful meadows, for violence had intruded on their most secret and sacred inscapes and nipped their dreams in the bud. They had been forced to witness the violation of their homes, however modest and unassuming, and the humiliation of their parents whose halo of invincibility was immediately erased. Their brothers and sisters had been killed or imprisoned and they took upon themselves the burdens of confrontation, resistance, martyrdom, and revenge. At night, they screamed in terror at their uninvited nightmares. Objective scientific studies had shown that Palestinians had nightmares more frequently than any other children in the world. The same dispassionate studies also proved that they had the highest number of bed-wetting instances. In all other aspects their childhood was submerged beneath a superimposed adulthood of gratuitous cruelty. Picking their way in the minefield of their shattered lives, they never had the luxury of pursuing wildflowers.

Neither did our women. Palestinian women developed the sharp fierceness of a denied but not broken spirit. Subjected to the dual discrimination of gender and national identity, those who did not lash out in defiance adopted the deceptive demeanor of the subdued. Beneath that lay the smoldering embers of a guarded fire. Nourished in secret in its dormant state, it would flare up at the first signs of interference. Since the early days of the occupation, it was the women who took to the streets and challenged the army. The women also had taken the initiative of establishing popular committees and alternative structures. They were the ones who would wrestle with the soldiers to rescue their offspring or the children of other women. Many took up weapons, and others took up political work with the same intensity and single-mindedness. Imprisoned, tortured, harassed, humiliated, or plain excluded and disenfranchised, our women displayed a sense of pride that went beyond victimization, visible in their eyes and bearing. Even those held captive by tradition could be seen looking up in the middle of kneading dough or washing the laundry with that faraway look of someone listening to an inaudible internal voice, of someone hoarding that secret message for a more opportune moment. From all the overt messages I had received, I was assured that that moment was inevitable.

Sometimes, in their anguish and anger, the women would turn against themselves and each other. When the anger and rejection of some women were directed at me, I felt it as being understandable at some level. But my pain and sense of betrayal were also very real to me. In 1992, following the announcement of the intended deportation of twelve Palestinian activists, we set up a meeting with the foreign diplomatic corps and a press conference to present the case against deportations. Lawyers, members of the families of the deportees, and representatives of the political leadership were scheduled to speak. Although I had done much of the preparatory work, I decided not to speak at the press conference and to give greater time for the families to present the human dimension. The wife of one deportee belonging to the Popular Front for the Liberation of Palestine, a major opposition faction, got up and started her presentation with a scathing attack against me personally and against the peace process. "Hanan Ashrawi does not represent us," she started. "If the PLO chose her as spokesperson, we did not." I felt the hurt of her comments like a physical blow to my stomach, but I refused to leave. I stood there and listened with deceptive calm to an outpouring of resentment and spite, then when the press asked me to respond I said, "I can understand her anger and pain." As people tried to silence her saying, "The issue is deportations not Hanan or the peace process," she and the other women of her faction stepped up the attack. I waited till she finished and then addressed the press on the impact of the deportations on the peace process. Her husband, a friend and ex-student, sent me an apology from jail via his lawyer. While it was gratifying to receive his message, it also made my hurt more acute at the gender dimension of the attack.

Hamas (the Islamic Resistance Movement) women were also active and defiant at the deportation of their men, but they never allowed their political convictions to degenerate to the level of personal abuse. Following the mass deportation of December 1992, the women decided to come to my house on one of their demonstrations. Faisal and I, and some other members of the delegation and supporters, went out to meet them in front of the house. They carried their placards and pain in plain sight, but their spirits were not broken. "In the name of your father, the great freedom fighter and martyr, Abdel-Qader Husseini, we ask you not to go to the talks. Bring our men back," they said to Faisal. "In the name of your father, the humane human being who healed people and spent his last days lost in nature, we ask you to withdraw from the talks that allow such an injustice as deportation. Bring our men back," they said to me. "Our men are brave, husbands, fathers, brothers, sons, and we are braver. They will endure and be a lesson to all on how to stand firm and not to capitulate. We will bear their absence, and they will return even stronger." Both their anger and arguments had the strength and logic of unwavering commitment and clarity of purpose. They believed the peace process we were engaged in was capitulation. I respected and admired them, but we disagreed amicably.

The deportations had frozen the peace process but unleashed a flurry of international diplomatic activity—mainly damage control—to get the talks back on track. After the exchanging of memos with Eagleburger and later Clinton's secretary of state, Warren Christopher, I was asked by the PLO in Tunis to go to Washington and negotiate with the Americans ways about implementing Resolution 799 calling for the immediate return of the deportees. We were willing to consider a phased return of the deportees, but only if the Security Council would schedule a speedy timetable for the implementation of its resolution. We were still smarting from the way the Americans had stepped in so quickly and worked out a deal with Israel to shield it from having to comply with the will of the international community; Israel and the United States had agreed bilaterally that the deportees would have their sentences halved and would return by December 1993. Coming immediately after the Security Council resolution, which called for their immediate return, and for Israeli compliance with the Fourth Geneva Convention including the cessation of collective punishments, particularly deportation, and bringing back all previous deportees, the deal was not only illegal but also a clear circumvention of international law and the central issues. What would happen when the time came for the implementation of Resolution 242, which was the basis of the talks? Would the United States step in and work out another bilateral arrangement to permit Israel to evade its implementation?

Early in February 1993 I presented these concerns to the State Department and National Security Council team, which the new Democratic administration had not yet changed with the exception of the addition of Samuel Lewis as director of policy planning and Martin Indyk as the NSC representative. Lewis, an ex-ambassador to Israel, was their staunch ally. The Australian Indyk had hastily been granted American citizenship in time to assume his new post, fresh from an AIPAC-established and funded think tank, the Washington Institute for Near East Policy.

It was ironic to us that the political map of the peace team was becoming a direct reflection of the Israeli domestic political terrain rather than any American political scene. In Washington, there was no question of pro-Israeli versus pro-Arab (or pro-Palestinian) trends and currents, but one had to figure out if the players were sympathetic to Peace Now, Labor, or Likud. Some Arab and Palestinian circles resented the fact that most (and later on all) of the members of the team that represented the United States on issues of Middle East policy and the peace process were Jewish. I did not have a problem. It was evident to me and to others that positions were defined on the basis of what was good for Israel from the different perspectives of the Israeli political spectrum. It was particularly ironic when the U.S. team felt it knew what was good for Israel better than the Israelis did.

At that time, we discussed the major Palestinian requirements for the resumption of talks in the context of human rights and accountability. I also raised the question of the credibility and role of the United States as co-sponsor, in addition to the other recurring themes of restoring the U.S.-PLO dialogue and lifting the economic blockade of the PLO that had been imposed before the Gulf War. During the war the blockade had been tightened, threatening Palestinian institutions with collapse.

The American team raised the issue of the Israeli Supreme Court's ratification of the government's deportation order as a means of justifying its illegality. Consequently, the question became one of allowing the Israeli legal system to override Security Council resolutions and distorting international law in a way that would make it subservient to domestic law however unjust and illegal. It was then that the team asked whether we would be satisfied with having the U.N. approve or adopt the Israeli-American agreement. "That would conclusively prove that the U.N. is an instrument of U.S. policy, and you would be perceived as manipulating the international community and its organizations for your own ends and in the service of Israel. It would spell the doom of UNSC Resolution 799 and consequently 242 and the whole peace process."

When I discussed the American role with the press, one reporter presented the justification that the United States could not intervene to prevent the deportations because of the transitional nature of the post-election period and the lame duck administration.

"For a lame duck administration, sending thousands of troops to Somalia was a pretty loud quack. We are not asking for military intervention, just simple respect for human rights and the terms of reference of the peace process. We want to safeguard its integrity and give it credibility."

Even while we were speaking, I received news that the current head of the Security Council had issued a statement in support of the U.S.-Israeli agreement, describing it as a positive step toward implementing 799, and calling for the resumption of the talks on that basis. I realized then that my quest was hopeless. We knew that the United States would block the convening of the Security Council at Israel's request (they had told us that in advance), but now they turned the Security Council into a rubber stamp for these illegal and unjust bilateral deals. To make matters worse, one anonymous official told the press that I had agreed to such an arrangement on behalf of the PLO. I issued a denial, and went home with an even greater sense of disillusionment and foreboding.

• • •

The newly appointed secretary of state, Warren Christopher, announced that his first visit abroad would be to the Middle East to signal American commitment to the peace process and its priority status on the foreign policy agenda. We put together two delegations, one larger, one smaller, and prepared detailed memoranda and information on deportations and human rights violations in the context of the status of the talks. Our first meeting took a more formal position, introducing Christopher to our priorities and point of view. I tried to study his spoken and nonverbal language closely to gauge his attitudes and policies, but the signals were so few and controlled as to betray no personal involvement. Reserved, with a closely guarded demeanor, he was a man of few words and fewer expressions. Christopher consistently avoided any eye contact; even when directing his words at us, his visual focus seemed to lie elsewhere. With time, we also discovered that his look of perpetual surprise was permanent.

At the second meeting, Christopher began by responding to our lengthy human rights memorandum and survey of Israeli abuses. Perhaps now, we thought, we would begin to see some serious concern and action on the part of the American administration. Perhaps now Israel would become subject to accountability and restraint and we would be treated as a people entitled to protection and recognition. All along, we had accused the United States of dealing with us on the assumption that we were a nonpeople, hence disposable and not deserving of moral consideration. We even had a standard joke that the American administration always sent us "nonpapers" because they looked upon us as nonpeople, and that they did not respond to most of our memos because they treated us as a nondelegation. Our expectations of Christopher were short-lived.

Perhaps because he had been briefed on the open communication and good relations between Baker and Faisal, Christopher insisted from the beginning on one-on-one meetings with Faisal, despite Faisal's and our insistence on larger participation. It was as if he had an invisible Orientalist textbook with stereotyped guidelines on the Palestinian and Arab mentality that seemed to reduce all discourse and interaction to the level of cultural clichés and social ritual. Forget substance was his approach, the transparent ego massage and the ready compliment were the keys to reach the decision makers. I could even envisage the instructions on pride in a shame culture and the ritual of social flattery. Factor in Christopher's well-known aversion to large meetings and his reticence in a crowd, and one would understand the motivation behind this insistence on individual meetings. On the other hand we wanted to protect Faisal from being blamed or accused of concluding secret deals whether by the public or the leadership, and we wanted to maintain a full and accurate record of all our talks and agreements. We also did not want to provide the Americans with the convenient excuse of blaming Faisal or his "weak English" for any later misunderstandings or complications. As it turned out, our concern was quite in place.

Before the large afternoon meeting of February 23, Molly Williamson came to pick up Faisal for a private meeting with Christopher despite his insistence on bringing at least one other person. Faisal later returned and told us that Christopher had made a four-point proposal that, upon examination, turned out to be a replica of the Israeli position worked out with the United States following the deportation crisis.

We proceeded to the meeting determined to get our point of view across. On the procedural issues, we expressed our indignation at Israel's continued refusal to allow Palestinian experts from Jerusalem and outside the Occupied Territories to participate in the talks as well as its refusal to disclose information and records that were supposed to be public pertaining to our lives, including population registers, land registration and zoning, and the budget of the Occupied Territories. On substance, we discussed settlements and Jerusalem in the context of land and territorial jurisdiction and legislative authority while we pressed ahead with the issue of deportation and other human rights violations.

At the end of the meeting, Christopher asked to see Faisal alone. I hastily scribbled six points on a torn sheet of paper and asked Faisal to address only these areas. I stressed the specific terminology:

1. Illegality of deportation—U.S.
2. Binding commitment that Israel will not resort to deportation in the future—Israel
3. In compliance with 799 the Israelis undertake: steps—accelerated, agreed-upon
4. Agreed-upon list of deportees since 1967 to be returned in sizable #s
5. Concrete, broad, effective human rights measures—to be agreed upon
6. Negotiations written reaffirmation 242 land for peace—JERUSALEM

These were points for Faisal to present and expand upon as our requirements for the resumption of the talks. Faisal emerged from his meeting with Christopher and showed us the list, which Christopher had checked with the exception of item 2, which he could not endorse on the spot because the terms "binding commitment" might not be acceptable to Israel. The two items required from the United States were numbers 1 and 6, which dealt with the official American position on deportation and the terms of reference for the peace process. Faisal said Christopher had checked these first. "Did he discuss any alternative formulations or specific wording?" we asked. "When he tried, I told him I need others with me and I specifically mentioned Hanan. But we discussed the wording as is." Thus, considerably encouraged, we went back to the Orient House to report to the PLO in Tunis and to wait to hear from Christopher following his meeting with Rabin.

In a conscious attempt to lay claim to our history, not as orphans of time but as its rightful heirs, we had established our headquarters in 1992 in the New Orient House in Jerusalem. Faisal, a descendant of the ancient Husseini family, whose history in the city continued uninterrupted for centuries, chose this nineteenth-century Husseini mansion as a monument to authenticity and commitment to continuity. It was also a gesture of defiance. We were establishing a seat of government in Palestinian Jerusalem as a center of Palestinian political and diplomatic activity and as the address for the Palestinian delegation/team. Having hosted emperors and kings at the turn of the century, the Orient House was not only the venue for our meetings and political base, but also the official Palestinian guest house in which we received prime ministers and foreign ministers from Germany to Japan, from Portugal to Denmark, from Sweden to Turkey, from England to Australia, and from France to Ethiopia. We hoisted the flag, dressed the security guards in official uniforms, and completed the symbolism with antique furniture and contemporary ritual.

Christopher called that night. Faisal picked up the phone and I listened in, taking down the conversation verbatim. "We can meet your points provided we move tonight," Christopher announced. "In addition to the statement by the Israelis, we will provide you with a high-level letter that will reassure you about the U.S. position and role of full partnership." Faisal responded that we would get back to him with our leadership's response shortly. We were jubilant, but before calling the Executive Committee, we agreed that I should call back and double-check. Molly Williamson answered.

"I would like to speak to Secretary Christopher and reconfirm what he had just told Faisal about the six points," I told Molly.

"There's no need to talk to him again," she said. "I can confirm whatever you need."

"Are you sure you have the mandate to give us the official response? We want this to come from the highest levels before we relay it to our leadership. We want to make sure that there are no misunderstandings." That must have gone a long way toward soothing her ego.

"I am mandated to give you the official and binding answers. But you must give us your final answer tonight on the resumption of talks."

"We will, if you will just confirm to me that Christopher's message was an acceptance of all six points."

"Yes, of course," Molly asserted. "Two items were requested of us and the other four from the Israelis. Christopher said that we can meet all six points. Can you get us the response tonight?"

"Since all six points have been approved, we'll get you the answer soon," I promised, fully convinced that we were on our way to an equitable solution.

"But you realize that the details still have to be worked out tonight if you want us to commit ourselves before Christopher leaves in the morning."

"I understand."

An hour later, I called her back and gave her the official response in the form of a memo to Faisal that Abu Ammar and Yasser Abd Rabbo had dictated to me over the phone. Throughout, we had maintained communication with the Executive Committee in Tunis and Abu Ammar had kept the speaker phone on to enable all the members to take part. We had done the same, with Faisal, Nathmi al-Juʾbeh, Ghassan al-Khatib, and myself taking part. The Executive Committee was satisfied with the six points and the proposed American letter, and asked that the details be finalized in Jerusalem. Molly was pleased with this "agreement in principle" as we called it, and promised to get back to us with the arrangements for the work meetings to conclude the agreement before Christopher left at 7:30 A.M. At 3:00 A.M. we went home.

At 7:00 A.M. Christopher called Faisal and thanked him for the agreement, informing him that Molly would hand him a letter from President Clinton and another from Secretary Christopher that morning. When asked about the Israeli statement with the remaining four points, Christopher said that the Israelis had their wording on item 2 but would not release it till after we announced our acceptance to attend the next round. As for the full statement, Molly would follow that up with us.

Alarmed, Faisal asked me to go over to the Orient House and to arrange for the others to come. He suspected foul play. From then on, everything began to unravel. Clinton's and Christopher's letters did not have a clear reference to Jerusalem. Molly informed us that we would not be able to see the Israeli statement, and that they could not get the wording we had wanted. None of the details or steps of implementation would be followed up until after we gave our public commitment. And to make matters worse, she flatly stated that it had all been a language problem and that Faisal had not understood what Christopher had told him on the phone. I reminded her that there were witnesses and that I had reconfirmed with her the essential facts. After four fruitless meetings, we advised Christopher not to make any public announcements or set any dates for the next round. "Don't issue any invitations that we have to refuse." We sent him a detailed letter with a chronology of events and our interpretation of developments. He never answered.

The evolution of the famous six points episode was a significant fore-shadowing of future Palestinian-American relations and the prejudicial role of the new "full partner." It also signaled a modified American modus operandi characterized by hesitancy and vagueness, in which loose ends would be left to threaten the whole process. We had said repeatedly the process needed a sponsor capable of taking bold, firm steps and in posses-sion of a clear vision and leadership qualities. Anonymous members of the team also began spreading the word around that Faisal had initially agreed, but that I stepped in with a hard-line stance and forced Faisal to back down. I seemed to be a convenient scapegoat for the Americans. They had not yet seen what a tough stance could be. The six points incident had six corresponding possible interpretations; none were any comfort to us. Either the Israelis had initially agreed and then reneged, leaving Christopher holding the bag, or they had misled him all along, or he had misunderstood them and consequently placed himself in this awkward situation with us, or he had been trying to pull the wool over our eyes from the beginning, or he really did not understand us and stumbled his way through on the basis of mistaken assumptions. In any case, the peace team and their textbook advice, we felt, had to shoulder most of the blame. Christopher always came to meetings armed with his trusty talking points and never ventured beyond their confines. Try as we may, we could not provoke a spontaneous response or a creative ex-change. Christopher remained a one-on-one person.

On March 9, following a long silence in which the United States did not respond to our memoranda and démarche on the six points, Jerusa-lem, the economic blockade, and other outstanding issues, I received a call that the American consul general, Molly Williamson, wanted an appointment. At first, the meeting was scheduled for the next day at my house. Later I heard rumors from Washington that a date for the next round had been set, despite the fact that nothing had been settled with us. I called the consulate and asked whether Molly was coming alone. It turned out that Alexei, the political officer from the Russian embassy, was coming with her. I immediately changed the venue to the Orient House and called Tunis.

"It looks like the meeting is official and they'll be making us an offer we have to refuse."

"They're going to spring an invitation on us without resolving the six points?" Akram was indignant. "That's going too far. They're taking us for granted and it's humiliating."

THIS SIDE OF PEACE ■ 237

"Then we should refuse to have the meeting till they respond," I suggested.

"Let me talk to the Old Man and I'll get back to you."

He called back an hour later from Abu Ammar's office. "You should go to the meeting and hear them out, but you must not accept the invitation."

"Are you sure? That would be a real diplomatic slap in the face. Maybe we should cancel the meeting or take the invitation, then write a negative response detailing the reasons."

The chairman got on the line. "I have studied this carefully and you must refuse to receive the invitation. If they think they can ignore us or take us for granted or humiliate us, they are mistaken. We must send them a strong message back."

"I'll prepare for the meeting and call you back tomorrow morning in case you change your mind."

I called Ghassan al-Khatib and Zahira Kamal and briefed them. Faisal was out of town. Saeb was to be on a panel in a public meeting at the time. I checked with Tunis twice, but there was no change of heart. Ghassan, Zahira, and I went to the meeting. Molly gave us a rundown on the proposed multilateral meeting schedule and presented us with an invitation to carry out prenegotiation consultation in Washington. Before she went any further, the three of us excused ourselves and went into the adjoining room to consult. We called Akram on the mobile phone, but the decision still stood.

When we returned, Molly handed me the invitation to the next round of bilaterals. I refused to take it and went into a lengthy explanation of why we found their behavior unacceptable. Alexei's eyes almost popped out. (I found out later that he told Molly that had this happened between representatives of their countries during the Cold War the world would have witnessed a nuclear war.) Molly put the envelope on the table, and I handed it back to her. She put it back down and then left. I called someone from the diplomatic office and he raced the envelope to the American consulate and handed it to the officer on duty.

We shocked everybody, including ourselves. "What's the next step? A declaration of war?" Penny asked. We did not want a repetition of *The Mouse That Roared*. "No," I said, "we can't afford to win." However, we did form a small delegation to go to Washington in order to see Christopher and his team to pursue the outstanding issues. They refused to state openly the U.S. position on East Jerusalem and we suspected a change of their policy. The deal with Israel stood, and according to them was not subject to review or amendment. We were promised, however, that once we declared our commitment to return to the talks, Israel would announce or inform us directly of a series of measures on deportation and human rights, and that these would be implemented immediately upon the resumption of talks. In these talks, the United States would play a more effective role as "full partner" and would intervene on the question of Palestinian experts from Jerusalem and the outside and on access to public records with information pertaining to our lives. And as usual they asked us to talk to the Israelis directly.

By that time we had decided to carry out discreet exploratory talks with the Israelis, and Faisal and I began meeting in Jerusalem with Foreign Minister Peres and with Prime Minister Rabin's envoy, Ephraim Sneh. The question of behind-the-scenes meetings with Israeli officials had always been a delicate and potentially explosive issue, both with the public and with our leadership. Traditionally, only collaborators or people with questionable national credentials had conducted talks with Israeli officials, particularly as popular perceptions represented such meetings as "normalization" under occupation or suspicious secret deals/sell-outs. Even when the PLO sanctioned secretly such talks, the Sari Nusseibeh beating and other similar incidents had taught us that this did not provide sufficient protection. PLO "scouts" of this type were often "disposable" and had been frequently stigmatized or punished for their efforts. Thus when Abu Mazen asked us to start a direct secret channel in Jerusalem for negotiations with the Israelis at the highest levels, we were reluctant to do so, and asked for Abu Ammar's explicit request and approval. He did not sanction any political meetings preventing the establishment of a back channel to the PLO. When Rabin sent word that he was willing to meet with Faisal and myself to discuss the issue of the deportees, Abu Ammar approved on condition that we work out the details earlier and through envoys in order to emerge from the meeting with an acceptable solution and positive results. Rabin refused, and we had to reject the proposed exploratory meeting on the grounds that the political price was too high and the results uncertain.

Peres was pushing a French proposal that involved the return of deportees in two groups beginning immediately, and phasing in a gradual return of 1967 deportees in large numbers. Tunis rejected the proposal, and the American-Israeli deal, which was much worse, took effect. Sneh was given the very restricted and closely defined task of working within that deal, while adding to it the return of twenty-five to thirty previous deportees and the immediate assumption of responsibility for economic projects that would be presented to the delegation prior to their submission to the Israeli authorities. "Once the talks resume, matters would improve significantly," he claimed, but he refrained from giving any details. The deal with the Americans was sacrosanct to Rabin and not subject to review or amendment, according to Sneh. We realized then that U.S.-Israeli cooperation, their special relation, had become a major component of the peace process and a decisive policymaking factor for both sides. I became convinced that American intervention in the talks would be to the increasingly distinct disadvantage of the Palestinian side and to the process. In the meantime, the talks in Oslo between Ya'ir Hirschfeld and Abu Ala were progressing quietly behind the scenes, although their nature was still unofficial and their substance tentative. The United States was not yet taking the back channel seriously, believing they were just two academics talking to each other.

After a meeting in Washington we left for Tunis with a grim account of both the Israeli and American positions on the deportation crisis and their implications about behavioral patterns for the future. April 20 was the date set by the co-sponsors for the ninth round of talks in Washington. The foreign ministers of the Arab countries participating in the talks were meeting in Cairo to coordinate and give a unified response. Abu Ammar was waiting for the results of our Washington talks, but at the same time was apprehensive that the Arabs might accept invitations to resume talks without us. We urged Abu Ammar to stand firm and not commit us to the next round unless we received the assurances we had asked for, and unless the negotiating table was more leveled. Abu Ammar decided to ask the Arab parties for a postponement. At 3:00 A.M. he announced that he would pay a visit to the foreign ministers in Cairo and to the Syrian President Hafez al-Assad in Latakia. He turned to me and said, "You're going with me, of course. Meet me at the airport at 6:00." He then gave instructions to have the whole delegation proceed from the Occupied Territories to Amman for a full meeting the next day. "We will take the decision together," he announced.

The small private jet took off from Tunis airport just after dawn and landed in Cairo in time for an urgent meeting with the Arab foreign ministers in the government VIP lounge. Osama al-Baz arrived with a message from Egyptian President Mubarak. Abu Ammar spoke to Mubarak on the phone. I called Ed Djerejian with the message that a postponement seemed inevitable. The foreign ministers agreed to a two-day extension. We took off for Damascus in Syrian Foreign Minister Farouq al-Shara's plane accompanied by the larger delegation that had been participating in the Cairo meetings. Faisal had been in Cairo for a meeting with the Saudi foreign minister, Prince Saud al-Faisal, the beginning of fence-mending with the Gulf states and the end of the economic blockade. Prince Saud had promised Faisal a Saudi contribution of $10–20 million to the Jerusalem Fund (which offered aid to various Jerusalem institutions and to religious structures in need of restoration) to be released with the beginning of the talks, and other funds on the basis of specific projects and feasibility studies. The transformation of Faisal into a fund-raiser and the linkage of all assistance and moves to the resumption of talks had begun to rankle with many on the Palestinian side. The economic blockade and the suspension of the U.S.-PLO dialogue in addition to Israel's human rights abuses had become the pressure points and bargaining chips to be exchanged for Palestinian political concessions. The first two were the Achilles' heel of the PLO, and the third was ours.

From Damascus we took a helicopter to breathtaking Latakia to President Assad's residence, perched on top of steep cliffs overlooking the Mediterranean. It took almost six hours of political chitchat, reminiscing, humor, and hidden messages—without getting up—to get us to the issue at hand. (Although I must admit that after four hours I announced that I would do the undoable and I got up and walked around the couch to restore some circulation to my numbed limbs.) "What's the matter with your delegation?" Assad asked. "Just give them their instructions and send them to carry out their tasks." Then he turned to Saeb, whose family had just been threatened by unknown intruders, and said, "If you're afraid, bring your family here and go negotiate. This is a political process we're involved in. The occupation by definition is difficult. True revolutionaries resist and negotiate." Ultimately, we got Assad's agreement for a brief postponement: "We are committed to a comprehensive peace and we must stay with it no matter how long it takes. We're in no hurry."

Following a lavish dinner we were driven to the airport where Assad's plane was waiting to take us back to Amman. We arrived in Jordan after midnight and began preparing for the meetings to follow. The rest of the delegation had been meeting at home, and had evolved a position against returning to the talks. Thus when Arafat convened that evening's meeting with the whole delegation, he found out that he had a full-fledged mutiny on his hands. For eight hours he sought to convince the delegation members to return to the talks but they refused. "Mandela suspended talks for four months on issues of principle," Mamdouh al-Aker said. "We can afford to suspend for a while until the Israelis demonstrate respect for human rights and the legal basis of the negotiations." Haidar Abdel-Shafi was adamant: "We must respect our people's feelings and take our public opinion into account. I already announced that I will not return to the talks unless the deportees are returned. My integrity is at stake." Most were indignant at being summoned to take part in the decision making, only to find out that Abu Ammar had already decided. He was furious. "Other leaders just issue instructions to their delegations and they obey. I have to cajole, persuade, and argue with you. It's my credibility that's at stake here—whether I can give my word and deliver or not. Are there two leaderships here?"

Faisal and I tried to play a conciliatory role: "We cannot on the one hand claim that the PLO is our sole legitimate leadership, and on the other undermine Abu Ammar's ability to deliver. We can continue pressing for the return of the deportees within the overall context of human rights, maintain Arab coordination while working on ending the economic blockade and for the recognition of the PLO, and test both Israeli and American intentions on the conduct of future negotiations." At one point, Haidar announced that the delegation would like to deliberate alone and reach its own decision. Abu Ammar stormed out. We followed, trying to convince him to return. The press was congregated in corridors and side rooms trying to make sense of the loud noises coming from the meeting room. Every once in a while, I would walk out to take a call from the State Department or to convey a message from the chairman. Different world leaders called urging Abu Ammar to be firm with us and to bring the meeting to a positive conclusion. The Russians called with a deadline. Abu Ammar was furious. "Who do you think I am?" he thundered. "Now I have two ultimatums, both from the Americans and the Russians. I'm not suicidal. What do you think will happen to the leadership? Where will the PLO go? Which country will host us? Can you imagine what will happen to the Palestinian refugees at the mercy of their host countries. If we leave the talks and your exiled compatriots are expelled, where will they go? Don't just think about yourselves. Think about others—this is a responsibility you have undertaken, and you must continue. If you're afraid for yourselves and your families, we'll protect you and them. I have to think of all the Palestinian people, and I know we can't afford the price of walking out." Other members of the Executive Committee and Central Council who were in Amman also presented the same argument. Gradually, we began to see how we may be perceived as being cowardly and selfish instead of people of integrity and courage. At dawn, we gave our consent and I was asked to inform the Americans. Abu Ammar took off for Cairo to address the Arab foreign ministers, and we went home to prepare for the next round. All the while Rabin was quietly and closely following events. The Israelis had finally repealed the law preventing them from meeting with the PLO, and now the next inevitable step for the Israeli government would be to establish official contact with our leadership. The long, stormy meeting in Amman was both an eye-opener and an incentive in that direction.

• • •

Following another stormy meeting with the whole team at my house in Ramallah, we prepared to go to Washington for the ninth round, which had been postponed from April 20 to the 27th. The collective cry of "Oh no, we won't go" gave way to a reluctant "We'll see what can be done." However, an unmistakable shift had taken place not just in the mind-set and mood of the delegation but also in the political calculations of leaderships on both sides. Further developments reinforced this trend as the peace process demonstrated that it was rapidly going nowhere. At the same time, we stepped up our call for the reassessment and amendment of the Madrid framework, and for an even-handed and more involved U.S. role. With the faint echoes of a saxophone in the distance, we could discern a knight in somewhat tarnished armor approaching on a white charger with a halting gait, and bearing a banner emblazoned with the legend "Full Partner."

The Americans began to roll up their sleeves and try their hand at negotiations, Middle East style. They decided to negotiate with the Israeli and Palestinian delegations separately and then play the role of intermediary in a new type of table tennis diplomacy. Each delegation was assigned a specific team member to serve as contact and to ease the passage into this new partnership. Ours was Aaron Miller, often accompanied by Dan Kurtzer and sometimes by Molly Williamson. Automatically, the focus gradually shifted from negotiations with the Israelis to the daily negotiations with the Americans. At first we saw signs of progress and flexibility. The Israelis returned thirty early deportees, began discussing issues of land and territorial integrity, expanded their concept of Palestinian self-government to include legislation, and seemed closer to the Palestinian position on linking the interim phase with permanent-status negotiations in a way that would ensure the implementation of UNSC Resolutions 242 and 338. We responded by forming working groups (which included Palestinians from outside the Occupied Territories), by drawing up a flexible draft Declaration of Principles and potential agenda items, and by beginning an exploratory exercise on issues in common. This lasted for one week. Suddenly, and in an unexpected reversal, the Israelis refused to pursue other steps on human rights as promised earlier, and presented us with a draft declaration that reflected none of the points conceded earlier in the discussions of the working groups. In response, we got frantic calls from Tunis protesting the "optimistic tone" of my briefings of the first week, and instructing us to suspend the human rights working group and recalling Faisal to Tunis. In addition, we were asked to decrease our already shrunken delegation (the People's Party having already taken the decision not to participate after the eighth round). The earlier path to compromise seemed to be rapidly turning into a collision course. We turned to our "full partner" for intervention, but were told to work it out with the Israelis, whether on human rights or on negotiating positions. The Americans even claimed their hands were tied as to the promise to end the economic blockade—it was a matter to bring before the Saudis. Even after Faisal held another meeting with Prince Saud al-Faisal in Washington, there were promises but no funds. We publicly accused both the Americans and the Israelis of reneging on their promises and commitments. There was worse in store.

During the third week, I received a call one night that the Americans wanted to set up a trilateral Palestinian-American-Israeli meeting to present us with a draft of a Joint Statement that they had prepared as a result of their extensive consultations with both sides. Nabil Sha'th received information from his American and Israeli sources (whom we jokingly referred to as Nabil's "birds") that the document had already been discussed with the Israelis beforehand and had been sent to Rabin for his approval. I called the team several times for verification, but they all denied it. We asked to see the document in advance as well and to have the opportunity of discussing it with them and commenting on it before the official presentation, but they refused. We were to send the head of our delegation to meet with the head of the Israeli delegation in the presence of Aaron and Dan. The Americans would hand each side a copy of the statement, without discussion or negotiation. Each side would then meet separately with the Americans to discuss the draft. After these meetings, the text was supposed to evolve into a final document.

Abu Ammar and the follow-up committee sent us instructions to refuse the meeting unless we held a preparatory meeting with the Americans first and got the same opportunity as the Israelis to review the document in advance and to send it to our leadership for its response. The Americans refused. We declined the invitation to the trilateral meeting (which was not a meeting at all but a handing over of documents). Three members of the team showed up at our hotel that night and gave us the document. It was obvious from the first glance that the Joint Statement was in no way joint, but had the clear "Made in Israel" stamp on every page. We reacted to it with outrage; not only had it adopted Israeli priorities, diction, and attitudes, it had also regressed to the point of presenting Israeli positions that the Israeli delegation itself had modified or conceded in the bilateral negotiations. We immediately prepared a comprehensive response based on a thorough text analysis of the American document, and began the presentation of our response in a meeting with Aaron, Dan, and Molly. In the middle of the meeting I received a note with a message from Abu Ammar that we were not even to discuss the American document but to declare unequivocally that it was unacceptable and therefore did not even constitute a basis for discussion. Yasser Abd Rabbo had already issued a public statement to that effect. I had already made a statement that we would study the draft and respond to it at the proper time and to its authors.

Conflicting messages were not unusual for us, due to our unusual circumstances. But they also betrayed different mind-sets at work. We were pushing for more emphasis on substance, less on technicalities. "Disagreements, protests, and rejections should be expressed in the text and in negotiations, not by reducing the delegation or rejecting documents and meetings or dissolving committees." However, the language of Tunis was becoming more strident in direct proportion to the quiet progress made in the secret talks under way in Oslo. The delegation was coming under increasing pressure, whether from public opinion at home, whose support for and confidence in the talks was eroding, or from the leadership, whose unpredictable and often erratic instructions prevented a coherent strategy.

While the Israeli leaks developed further leaks, "anonymous" Palestinian sources developed the habit of divulging documents as the need arose, and the negotiations went public. Even minutes of meetings, both carefully doctored or accurate, were published in newspapers and magazines. Thus the negotiations took on a double vision, with one eye on our constituency and another on our counterparts, all under the scrutiny of Tunis. Our press briefings became debates by proxy, and the substance of our talks the public property of all interested parties and individuals. I became even more convinced of the need to change the negotiations framework and to get serious and discreet negotiations going between the PLO and the Israeli government away from the limelight. Ironically, it was at that time in May that the Oslo talks were beginning to take a serious turn, while we, in retrospect, had taken our task too seriously.

We also found out then that we had taken the American Letter of Assurance too literally. When we pointed out that the American position and drafts were in violation of their letter, we were bluntly told that it could not be brought to bear on negotiations. It was merely a statement of American policy that had no direct bearing on the talks and could not be made applicable even to the American "bridging" attempts. We also discovered that our leadership in Tunis was adamant about staying in the talks but not addressing any American bridging proposals. During a trip to Tunis at this time, I was informed by Hassan Asfour that a back channel had been successful and was fully functional. "That's good," I responded in passing. Abu Mazen expressed his disappointment at our refusal to hold secret negotiations with Rabin at home. "We couldn't," I replied. "We lacked the proper mandate."

On the plane from Tunis to Amman in order to cross the bridge home, I was haunted by the question of our mandate and our mission. We had launched a grand quest for peace through historical vindication and redemption and yet were gradually becoming captives of an ever constricting vortex of petty manipulations and self-interest. Sucked into this downward spiral, we were in danger of losing our bearings. A group of professionals and intellectuals, we were plucked from our offices, clinics, and libraries to wrestle with history and chart a blazing course of glory in full *amanah* for our people. The intricate machinations of the politics of sterility were not only alien to our nature but were also equally incapable of nourishing dreams on wildflowers.

Mahmoud Darwish, our national poet, had once sadly lamented the loss of our collective memory. "What we need is a memory for the future," we had both agreed. Some of us saw our reflections in cracked or splintered mirrors, while others (like Mahmoud) held the magic of going through mirrors beyond the reflected image and into the substance on the other side. What I lamented then, and even more so now, was the diminution of our dream and the shrinking of our heritage to pass them through the eye of the needle of contemporary necessity and survival— the prison of pragmatism. Repeatedly admonished not to lose ourselves in singing the glories of the past or in weeping over its ruins, in relinquishing its hold over us many ended up denying it even before the cock crowed once. In our haste to prove that we were of the future, we had abandoned our priceless heirlooms including the keys to the kingdom. We could not claim a future as the orphans of time, nor could we renounce its claims on us. Perhaps as the tapestry of peace unfolded, we could reveal the continuum of our narrative—I tried to console myself. But all the while the shears of fate were busily clipping away at the fabric, detaching the panel of our present from its frame, and threatening to unravel the threads that held the embroidery together.

CHAPTER FOURTEEN

Jerusalem was being altered before our very eyes, its people evicted and dispossessed, its ancient walls studded with soldiers, its rolling hills violated with settlement fortresses, its open roads blocked with military checkpoints, and its spirit soiled by possession as the conqueror's spoils. It lay stifling under siege, slowly strangulating, bereft of the lifeblood of its own children, groaning under the boot of military occupation. And we mourned Jerusalem instead of reveling in its magnificence. We watched the city that had been our core and cornerstone become a city without a soul.

To me Jerusalem was cobbled streets and covered walks, infinite variations of domes and cupolas, hidden courtyards and fountains bathing in the sudden sun concealed behind stone walls and deceptively closed facades. A Byzantine church and an ancient mosque, implacable in their harmonious communion, looked on impervious to our transience but exuding a timeless benevolence.

I always felt small in Jerusalem, but never petty or diminished. As a child, I was awed and annoyed at the timeless mystery and the incense of faith as well as the press of bodies. Jerusalem was a place where a child held fast to her mother's hand for fear of getting lost in the maze and human swell. It was a place where people went to dark, obscure churches to light candles in fulfillment of vows, where incense and miracles were facts of life, where the lips and knees of the faithful wore down the stones to a curved smoothness. There we conducted elaborate rituals with processions and symbols, brandishing crosses, icons, Korans, and passions with obsessive routineness. Hundreds of thousands answered the call to prayer every Friday filling the mosque and the courtyard kneeling in unison before the majesty of Allah. Equal numbers responded to church bells with a timeless devotion before the Lord.

Jerusalem was where Emile was born, in a modest room in Christ's Church, where his family had taken refuge following the 1948 war. He was brought up in a simple home in St. George's Convent with an open courtyard where the residents held their parties, prepared their pastries and preserves, and watched their children grow. Emile and I used to meet there; we got married in Jerusalem; and both our daughters were born there. Later on, we would bring Amal and Zeina to visit their grandmother and play in the courtyard. From there they went on their first Palm Sunday and Easter processions, and from there we saw the first Jewish settlers come in and redo the neighborhood adjoining the convent and the Armenian Quarter. Orthodox Israelis became the neighbors of my mother-in-law. After a while, I stopped going there; my face had become too familiar and often provoked the Israeli settlers in the neighborhood. Gradually many Palestinians stopped going to Jerusalem, whether having lost their homes and property to the Israeli government and settlers, or prevented by the siege, or driven into bankruptcy by the taxes and fines.

In Palestinian peasant dialect Jerusalem was the *Mdineh,* the City (*Madinah*) of all cities, beyond further definition. There was no other. In my family's oral tradition there is a story of one of my ancestors who on his way to Jerusalem met a man with a boat ticket to the United States but who got cold feet at the last minute. He asked my ancestor if he would like to go to America in his place. "Only if you take my donkey home to my wife and tell her that on my way to the *Mdineh* I stopped in America." He was rumored to have made many riyals, dollars, which he sent home and with which he bought property and sent his children to college. My hometown, Ramallah, was less than ten miles north of Jerusalem but never perceived itself as a suburb. Like Bethlehem, ours was a town with its own lineage and traditions that stood on their own. It was said that Ramallah people found it easier to go to America than to Jerusalem. More than thirty-five thousand Ramallah people created mini-communities in the United States, living on distant memories of the old country and faithfully preserving traditions. The seven clans had moved West, taking their cultural and tribal luggage with them, but with a constant eye on the East "back home" as the unifying principle of their identity, both past and future. Two thousand were left in Ramallah itself in a town that was rapidly becoming not their own, swelling with refugees and a flood of residents from neighboring villages.

As a Ramallah-Jerusalemite, I inherited the legacy and deprivation of both, and as a Palestinian I felt the eye and weight of history as a personal intrusion. The Palestinian people as a whole habitually exacted a heavy toll from those who dared intrude on the course of their fate, particularly from those who presumed to lead or speak on their behalf.

I felt a sort of maternal protectiveness for the whole delegation, particularly those innocents who had been thrust in medias res as unwitting agents of a particularly complicated and merciless destiny. Faisal, the most political of all of us, was also the most vulnerable. A visible and credible leader, he was accountable both before the people and the leadership, and was often held responsible by one for the decisions and actions of the other. He had chosen the Gordian knot of Jerusalem as his personal challenge and responsibility. On May 24, Christopher invited Faisal to Washington for consultations before the tenth round. We sent Christopher an eight-point memorandum with ten specific questions. Again, we knew we were risking a political confrontation. The response to these questions would determine whether the meeting was to take place. "We send you an invitation and you send us back a test," was the indignant American response. "We want to deal with substance, terms of reference, and objectives, and you are interested in the technicalities of the process itself," was ours. "You want to start building a house from the roof down, and we want to start with the rooms and walls," they countered. "We have to inspect the site, prepare the architectural plans, and check the foundations first," we responded; "we are still not sure that we have the right blueprints, or if the foundations can support the proposed structure." They never responded in writing to our "test," and were evasive regarding it when we met.

The tenth round began on June 15 and lasted through July 1, 1993. Our "full partner," though still smarting from the Joint Statement boomerang, was quite determined to present a bridging document, and we were consumed by talks with the Americans. The Israeli delegation hung up its hat, put its feet up, and waited for the results of the American-Palestinian negotiations. We rolled up our sleeves and decided to give it our best shot. We tried every possible means to influence the American position and persuade our interlocutors that our "red lines" (basic rights of national consensus we could not compromise) could not be crossed and must be incorporated within any draft. We used all our powers of persuasion, in a combination of legal arguments and tenacity, repeating the substance ad nauseam in various forms. At the core lay Jerusalem and the land with territorial jurisdiction and settlements as textual signposts. We still saw the end of the process bringing the resurrection of the Palestinian state with the return of the exiles and the eclipse of the evil of occupation. To get there, we insisted on the implementation of UNSCR 242. Our efforts proved fruitless.

• • •

Despite numerous meetings with the team and several with Christopher, and despite our admonishments that any American text would gain a life and legitimacy of its own and form a reference for the process, the new American "preliminary, nonbinding, thoughts and ideas" for a Declaration of Principles ended any remaining expectations of American evenhandedness. Haidar and I went to receive the document; when we returned the whole delegation experienced a collective letdown. The PLO declared it inadequate even as a basis for discussion, despite the assurance that we had given the Americans that we would not "throw it into the garbage can." Faisal and Nabil Sha'th went to London, and the British started work on redrafting the document. I stayed in Washington. Abu Ammar asked us not to discuss options during the meeting with the Americans. Faisal came back for the Christopher meeting and we tried to undo some of the damage, but to no avail.

After the meeting Dennis Ross asked me about the rumors of back channels.

"Which ones?" I replied. "Some are decoys, others are real, but I can't tell you which is which." I added, "You were the first to be asked to set up a back channel. I personally asked Ed and you several times on behalf of the chairman to host or participate in serious and discreet trilateral talks, but you refused. Without the PLO, nothing can happen. We know it and you know it, but you're too hung up on the PLO taboo to do anything about it. I have already told Dan and Aaron that if American positions continue to be so rigid and you persist in being an obstacle to peace, the natural conclusion will be to address the Israelis directly without you."

During the concentrated work meetings with Aaron and Dan we became convinced of the futility of expecting the Americans to exert a corrective influence on Israel, let alone to come up with fair formulations consistent with international law or even with avowed American policy. The mere reference to Jerusalem in the Declaration of Principles they said would be taboo, as was the "unmentionable" PLO. They described as "otherworldly" our presentation on security in which PLA (Palestine Liberation Army) units would be brought in to maintain internal security and public order once the territories were returned. After we finished scraping them off the ceiling, they said, "Come back to us with a proposal of this world. If you think that the Israelis would for a moment contemplate such an outrageous prospect, you are sadly mistaken."

I answered, "But they have. I have the minutes of Palestinian-Israeli security meetings in which Israeli security experts explicitly agree to such arrangements. They know there are pragmatic requirements involving necessary concessions; you project, anticipate, and put up illusory defenses that do not necessarily serve Israeli interests, let alone the cause of peace."

They were not amused. "If there are secret talks we know nothing about, you cannot bring their substance to bear on these talks." In the meantime, the Oslo talks were proceeding quietly away from the public eye. During these Washington meetings we made the first official, though tentative, reference to the "Gaza first" option at the explicit request of Abu Ammar, although we still had not formulated a coherent and workable proposal. The idea was to start the devolution of the occupation in phases. With total withdrawal from Gaza, Abu Ammar hoped that that would bring about Palestinian sovereignty while he continued negotiations on the rest of the Occupied Territories.

"We've heard about it from the media," the Americans responded. "But if you have a concrete suggestion, we'd like to see it in writing." I had severe reservations about the Gaza first idea from the beginning, and I was not certain whether Abu Ammar was really pursuing it or whether he had floated it as a digression or a tactical diversion.

With the American draft of the DOP in hand and no small degree of apprehension, we went to Tunis. The body of the PLO leadership had assumed a tone of indignation. The Gaza first option was on the agenda in a preliminary form, with Abu Ammar's addition of Jericho as expression of territorial integrity, as a border with Jordan, and as a link to Jerusalem and the rest of the West Bank. No detailed or workable proposals were presented or discussed. However, in a closed meeting that included Abu Ammar, Faisal, Nabil Sha'th, Saeb, Akram, and myself, we formulated two paragraphs on territorial jurisdiction (which included the issues of Jerusalem and settlements) and the linkage between the interim phase and permanent status. We agreed that these drafts were for internal use only, and not for presentation or circulation, because we wanted to try to get a verbal commitment from the United States and Israel. We headed back to Jerusalem to prepare for the proposed visits of Dennis Ross and the team, to be followed by a Christopher visit.

Dennis Ross and the team arrived July 9 and Christopher was due three days later. We had a six-member delegation and an eight-point agenda faxed to us from Tunis that addressed issues including the Declaration of Principles; defining U.S. positions on the core issues (terms of reference, the West Bank and the Gaza Strip as occupied territories, and Jerusalem); and the economic blockade.

We stuck faithfully to our agenda and resisted all attempts to engage in textual collations or amendments. Even when we were informed that via the Egyptians, Nabil had presented the draft formulation on Jerusalem and territorial jurisdiction to Dennis in Cairo, we refused to go beyond "describing our positions" orally. Nabil called from Cairo in utter shock and anger at our refusal to give Dennis our draft paragraphs, since he already had them. "Those were not our instructions," we replied. "In fact, we were explicitly told in writing not to do that."

After the meeting we checked with Abu Ammar and the position remained unchanged: we had no mandate to discuss the American draft or to deal with written counterproposals. As an internal exercise, we prepared a compilation with variations of our own Declaration of Principles and called it the "Composite DOP." When Nabil Sha'th called from Cairo, I faxed him a copy. He later called and sent a tentative and incomplete version called "The Palestinian Response to the American Draft," which had been worked out with ʿAmr Moussa and Osama al-Baz for Mubarak to present to Christopher. Again I checked with Tunis and again I was told that no documents were to be presented.

Instead, I was to prepare a response to the American-Israeli suggestion of "early empowerment," which was to be the transfer of administrative tasks involving health, education, social welfare, and taxation, without granting sovereignty, thereby making Palestinians mere functionaries of the Israeli government. I wrote a long critique showing why early empowerment was prejudicial to the transitional phase and to permanent status and how it was a consolidation of the Israeli functional approach, which attempted to separate the people from the land. In addition, I wrote an explanation of our concept of an American "side letter," which we felt would be counterproductive unless it was binding on the U.S. position in negotiations, particularly as we saw its potential as a tool for the United

States whereby it could avoid all contentious issues in the DOP and transfer them to an ineffectual side letter that could be negated when the time came to cash it in—as had been the fate of the American Letter of Assurance. At this point several colleagues and I had been asked individually to prepare full proposals on what was now the Gaza-Jericho first option. I started mine reluctantly and the more I thought about it the more concerned I became that such an approach would not be in our best interests. Not only was it technically and procedurally difficult and precarious to implement, but it also contained future self-destruct mechanisms capable of undermining any genuine peace and stability.

Though I did carry out my assignment, I also appended to it my own concerns. I cautioned against the fragmentation of the land and the authority, against the possible apartheid system that might emerge, against dividing the transitional phase into sub-phases, and against allowing Israel to get rid of the areas it found difficult to control while maintaining its hold over areas that had an intensive settlement presence and a strong ideological bias. I sent the paper to Abu Ammar and expected the subject to be discussed during our forthcoming visit to Tunis.

Faisal went to Cairo and saw one draft of the "Palestinian Response" but he told us that without Abu Ammar's signature such a document could not be presented. Our instructions had not changed. We continued our own work in preparation for the meeting with Christopher on August 3. The night before the meeting, we received an official draft of the Palestinian Response, which was identical to the Cairo draft, but now had the signature of Abu Ammar on the first page and instructions to present it to Christopher during the meeting. We immediately called a meeting of the Leadership Committee and the delegation named to meet with Christopher, and subjected the document to a thorough scrutiny.

Without exception, the participants saw the document as flawed and recommended that it not be presented unless amended. We began working on the necessary changes and called Abu Ammar trying to persuade him to delay the presentation. He insisted, saying that we had received our instructions and that we were to carry them out.

"But Christopher is coming back in two days, and with the proper corrections, we can give him the response then." We persisted. "There are not two leaderships here," he replied.

We asked to cancel or postpone the meeting, but he refused. We pleaded: "We cannot have you go down in history as having signed this paper, particularly with the formulation on Jerusalem. We can go over it and hand it to Christopher in two days."

"I already gave my word to Mubarak, and I will not go back on it," he asserted conclusively.

"Then you must accept our resignations," we insisted.

"Hand in the document, and we'll talk later." Abu Ammar had made up his mind.

We went to the Christopher meeting on August 3, but refused to give him the document. Not only did we find the sudden change in strategy and directions inexplicable, we also could not understand the lack of concern over the substance. From an often incomprehensible refusal to deal with any American drafts to an equally incomprehensible lack of concern about form and content was too sudden a shift for our system to accept. The Palestinian Response, we felt, was inconsistent with our strategy and positions thus far, and represented a serious departure from the commitments we had made.

None of us remotely suspected that at that time a draft DOP had been worked out in Oslo. Neither did the Americans.

• • •

Christopher asked us for the draft response, which the Egyptians had promised would be presented in Jerusalem. We said that there was a draft but it was not ready for presentation yet. "I am puzzled by your response," Christopher replied. "Mr. Arafat had approved the response with President Mubarak; he had approved the DOP reactions, but you are not giving them to us. If we were dealing with your leader, we would have gotten the formulations."

We immediately used that opening to launch into our argument as to why he should be dealing with our leader instead of us. "He sees the forest, we don't see it for the trees," Faisal commented.

"He is our president and his commitment will be honored," Saeb added. "We will follow his instructions, but there are some technical difficulties that have to be resolved first."

Christopher arched his eyebrows even higher: "I am surprised by this tactic—that he approved the DOP and you are not ready to give it to us. . . . You describe him as your president and we have to respect that. I am just amazed that you would not serve as his agents and give us the document he approved."

Again we replied, "Then you should be talking to him and not to us. We will carry out his instructions and give you the document as soon as we iron out some issues." Then we raised the Gaza-Jericho first option.

"This has an interesting potential, if we understand in what context," Dennis said. Both he and Christopher asked to see a fuller presentation.

We spent the intervening hours amending, drafting, faxing, arguing, explaining until we emerged with a corrected draft with explanatory notes to justify the suggested changes. Just before the meeting, we received an authorized draft incorporating some, but not all, of our amendments. We had also added the item on Gaza-Jericho as we had been asked to do. Faisal, Saeb, and I tried to persuade Abu Ammar again not to submit the document, or at least to postpone its submission until all the issues were resolved, but he refused. We asked to be excused from going to the meeting, but he insisted. We suggested that Faisal should go alone just to present the document, but he turned the suggestion down. "If we go and submit the document, then you should consider it as a submission of our resignations," we informed him.

"Give him the document, then come to Tunis and we'll talk." It was to be the shortest, most somber meeting of all. We handed Christopher the authorized draft, exchanged a few sad remarks about the cost of this document, and took our leave.

Those of us who had met with Christopher reconvened and drafted our resignation letters. The next day, we met with the whole delegation and informed them of our intentions. Some approved, and others advised us to wait. Abu Ammar sent after us for August 8, my eighteenth wedding anniversary. I tried to postpone the trip on the grounds that we take our family occasions seriously and I wanted to be home with Emile and the girls for the eighth, but to no avail. We had an early family celebration and we voted on the resignation the way we usually voted on every significant decision that affected the family. Amal and Zeina wanted to reclaim their mother. Emile was pressing to bring the moment to its conclusion. "Unless you want to stay in politics for the rest of your life, you're going to have to leave sooner or later. You've given it your best, and you've served above and beyond the call of duty. We're all proud of you. Should you decide to go back to academics, I'm sure you'll also give it all you've got. The choice is yours, and I'll support you either way. The girls also will understand and support your decision."

Amal was more explicit: "Being a teenager is hard enough, and speaking to you on the phone does not take the place of a heart-to-heart talk. I'd like to feel that my mother is home and that I can go to her with my ideas and problems whenever I need her."

Zeina too wanted a more physical presence: "I want to snuggle up to you. I want to feel you're here with me. Even when you're home, we rarely see you. The house is turned upside down, with the phones constantly ringing, people walking in and out, and with your nonstop political meetings. And we can never plan anything together because we don't know when you'll suddenly take off."

Amal agreed: "We've stopped doing things together as a family because you can't go to public places because your face is too well known and it's often dangerous."

The whole underlying tension and the constant threat were coming to the surface. Intellectually, Amal and Zeina understood the historical imperatives and the sense of commitment that had intruded on their lives, but emotionally they were still children who wanted to lay first claim to their mother and to the semblance of a normal life in which absence and fear were not the running undercurrents in an unstable and precarious existence. Was I placing in jeopardy our inner circle of harmony or was I part of the energy that was generating the protective shield of our internal calm? This pressing question was looming in search of an urgent resolution. Part of the answer lay in my impending resignation.

Faisal, Saeb, and I headed for Tunis via Amman the next day, determined to speak our minds and to get a fair hearing. All of us sensed that an era was drawing to a close. The process we had launched held us in a firm grip, and at that juncture we were compelled to decide if, on the verge of achieving our immediate objectives, we would be their first victims or their slightly battered survivors. None of us felt that he or she was slated to be among the victors. But could we still influence the course of this transition? We thought and hoped so. Once the PLO took over, our usefulness would have come to an end. Yet for the sake of *amanah*, we had the duty of ensuring a clear course ahead. The question remained: would we be allowed to, or would the inexorable political machine crush us in its pursuit of fulfillment? We had to try.

Our first encounter was with Abu Ammar alone. He attempted to take our resignations lightly and urged us to withdraw them, but we refused.

"There are structural, procedural, tactical, and strategic problems that must be dealt with now if the Palestinian performance in negotiations is to produce optimal results and do justice to the cause we are defending. All cards on the table, we have to speak frankly. We cannot go on with conflicting instructions, multiple channels, lack of a coherent strategy, inconsistent political decision making, total disregard for our structures, and lack of accountability and openness in our internal work."

He took all this calmly, and seemed to be smiling inwardly all the time.

On September 3, 1993, the Palestinian-Israeli Declaration of Principles was signed on the White House lawn, and the famous handshake between the Palestinian Chairman Yasser Arafat and Israeli Prime Minister Yitzhak Rabin signaled to the world a new beginning. The struggle for peace, however, has been long and difficult—and neither a handshake nor a trio of Nobel Peace Prizes guarantees its outcome.

A meeting with the American peace team.

2

In a panic that morning, I had been called by Arafat to work out the last-minute details. I barely had enough time to get to my seat.

3

My parents, Wadi'a Ass'ad
and Daud Mikhail, at their
wedding in 1935.

4

5

With friends at the American University of Beirut, just before the 1967 War,
which shattered my protected universe and irrevocably altered the course of
history in our region.

My sisters and I at our parents' fiftieth anniversary in Ramallah, 1985.

With my husband, Emile, and our two daughters, Amal and Zeina.

From the outset, the occupation and I did not get along. I became a faculty member and head of the English department at Birzeit University and later Dean of the Faculty of Arts. I nevertheless found myself closely involved with student activities. Following a few demonstrations and protest marches, I received a summons, underwent questioning by the Israeli police, was arrested and fingerprinted—but I did not stop. In December 1987, these student protests took on a whole different character, with the outbreak of the *intifada.*

10

11

We knew we had to confront the Israeli soldiers with defiance, but as the *intifada* gathered momentum, we realized that we also had to confront the world with our reality. The televised "Town Meeting" between Palestinians and Israelis on Ted Koppel's *Nightline* was a major turning point. No Palestinian had ever addressed an Israeli in a public debate, and at the last minute a barrier had to be constructed between the two panels.

In protest of the May 1990 massacre at Ilyun Qara, we went on a hunger strike, which lasted two weeks.

12

Officially, the peace process was launched in Madrid on October 30, 1991. Since we were a delegation of professional people and academics, not politicians and diplomats, we behaved differently and at times dispensed with traditional diplomatic conventions and niceties. We held our first press conference on the stairs of the press center because we were told that there were no rooms ready and no facilities available.

13

14

Our homecoming was a festival. We had gained global recognition as a people with rights and aspirations.

On June 18, 1992, exactly one week before the Israeli elections, we were officially and publicly received by President Arafat. For the first time since June 1967, Palestinians from the Occupied Territories conducted a public disclosure of their connection with the PLO. As we filed in one by one to be embraced, the ritual of public avowal turned into an emotional experience of recognition and unification. When my turn came, Arafat gave me the symbolic three kisses—on the forehead and cheeks—and then in a warm embrace he laid my head on his shoulder and patted my back gently, reassuringly.

15

16

There followed countless
meetings, international
conferences and backdoor
negotiations around the
world—in London, Paris,
Moscow, Washington,
Oslo—that moved the
dialogue of peace along,
step by step.

17

A meeting of
Women Speak Out
with delegations
from Palestine,
Israel, and Belgium.
November 11, 1993.

18

Arafat's return to Gaza, July 1, 1994.

Now, as Commissioner General of the Palestinian Independent Commission for Citizens' Rights, I try to steer clear of the mines. I am not a politician by choice. Instead I try to pursue the objective of institution-building, an essential component of the reconstruction of our nation.

"Things will work out, you'll see," he replied enigmatically, then added: "But I will not have anyone accuse me of giving up Jerusalem or try to cast doubt on my national integrity and commitment. Your resignations have been presented and perceived as a protest against the PLO, as if you're more concerned about and protective of Palestinian rights than we are."

We explained that we had neither intended nor presented such an interpretation, and that we were motivated by the urgent need to put matters right. "We refused to carry out your instructions, and we are morally and politically bound to present our resignations, particularly since we're the ones always calling for professional and responsible behavior as well as respect for our own structures and institutions."

Mollified, he tried to dismiss the crisis. "I know and respect your reasons, and since I approved the second draft, I don't consider this a mutiny. Let's put this behind us. If you don't want to withdraw your resignations, then I reject them and that's that."

"We insist on having a full hearing. This latest incident of the draft DOP did not occur in isolation. It is symptomatic of serious and repetitive problems and flaws in our work. We have to deal with them seriously."

"All right, we'll set up meetings to discuss your grievances. But I know how to turn even your resignations to my advantage." Again, his hidden smile and lack of agitation seemed to be concealing and conveying an unspoken message.

"We have no doubts you can. Let's use it now to solve these pressing problems and to adopt a structure and work plan capable of handling the serious issues facing the negotiations. At the same time, we feel you should come clean with the delegation. The same questions we had raised earlier are still unanswered: Do you actually want the negotiations to succeed? Are the Washington negotiations a front? Are we buying time for the PLO or do you want them to fail? Do you have back channels that are working?" We asked, but we got no answers.

At the first meeting with the leadership, we presented a diagnostic assessment of the issues.

"It's our duty to tell you how things are, frankly and honestly without embellishments," I said. "It's your responsibility to listen to us and to take our presentation seriously. We are not here just to complain or to present a list of grievances. We are going to suggest solutions and present a tentative work plan because we want to be constructive."

Having set the tone and approach for the ensuing discussion, I began from the beginning. "Never before in the history of negotiations had a government formed a delegation and given it all the elements of failure the way you have. You set us the already difficult task of negotiating with an entrenched adversary and with the international community, and you started stabbing us in the back, casting doubt on our integrity and abilities. We are not an alternative leadership and never intended to be. Had we wanted to sell you out, we could have a long time ago. We had a mission to rescue the PLO and bring it into the negotiations and the international political arena, and this has been our constant refrain. We carried out your instructions faithfully, even when they made us appear erratic and unreliable. We held on to the basic tenets of Palestinian national rights and tried to present our people's pain and aspirations faithfully. But all the while you have been trying to undermine us. And when you give us instructions that we feel violate our rights and mandate, we will question them. We are not regimented soldiers carrying out orders blindly. You chose us precisely because we had brains and skills, not because of our mindless obedience. Make use of our abilities, but don't turn us into instruments of political manipulation."

In subsequent meetings, mainly with the Executive Committee, we presented our proposed solutions and work plan, and pressed them for answers to the basic questions of what they were actually seeking from these talks. They approved our plan, and announced the first step in the new "reform" phase as the merging of the "inside" leadership committee with the "outside" follow-up committee, plus the formation of local political "references" in each region comprised of institutions and individuals with political, representative, intellectual, and activist status. We were promised clear channels and consistent messages as well as respect for specialized job descriptions and an integrated structure. They formally rejected our resignations, and affirmed their commitment to a relationship based on mutual respect, professionalism, and openness. Of all the members of the Executive Committee, only Abu Mazen and Abu Ammar were aware of the Oslo channel at that time, or of the fact that a draft agreement had already been worked out. In response to our questions about negotiations strategy, Abu Mazen outlined the main features of the Declaration of Principles, while not giving any indication of the secret talks under way. None of the people in the meeting were enthusiastic about the presentation or saw in it the official Palestinian policy. When I pressed for responses from others, Abu Mazen turned to me and flatly said, "I told you. This is it." I did not take this at face value, perhaps because I did not want to believe it.

Abu Ammar's mood continued to be buoyant and mysterious. At

lunch, I told him jokingly, "You have a mischievous twinkle in your eye. Are you hiding something up your sleeve?"

He smiled and said, "Yes I am. I know where I'm heading."

I immediately replied, "Then perhaps you should tell us. But first tell me, are you really serious about this Gaza-Jericho business? I did write you the proposal you requested, but have you looked at the reservations and drawbacks?"

He then turned to me and spoke in a confiding tone. "I read everything, but I'll tell you how I see things. I will get full withdrawal from Gaza and Jericho as the first step of disengagement, and there I will exercise sovereignty. I want Jericho because it will get me to Jerusalem and link up Gaza with the West Bank. The Palestinian state will start in Gaza-Jericho and from there I will negotiate with the Israelis to end the occupation in the rest of the Palestinian territories on par with the other Arab leaders. I will accept early empowerment in the rest of the West Bank while I negotiate Israeli withdrawal. Trust me, we will soon have our own telephone country code, stamps, and television station. This will be the beginning of the Palestinian state."

The general conversation then turned to a discussion of the symbols of sovereignty, and someone turned to me and whispered, "If he's talking about international codes and television stations, you can be sure he's already working on them. He'll get them, you'll see." I was convinced that he did have something up his sleeve.

With that we went home and worked on documents and strategies for the eleventh round scheduled for August 31 to September 14, 1993. Of all rounds, this was the one that involved the greatest amount of preparation on such issues as the DOP, Jerusalem, the Gaza-Jericho option, and security. Again our delegation was to be reduced in number because of financial constraints. Haidar, Saeb, Nabeel Kassis, Zakariyya al-Agha, Mamdouh al-Aker, Suad al-Amery, and myself from the "inside," and Kamil Mansour and Ahmad al-Khalidi (an academic adviser) from the "outside" were to participate in the round. Haidar was in Europe and Saeb was in Beirut for the Arab coordination meeting, but the rest of the "inside" group were to head for Tunis on the twenty-sixth of August. On the twenty-fourth Akram called and told me cryptically of some developments and drafts of which I should be aware. I guessed. "The back channels have delivered?"

His response was economical, "You'll see when you get here. But be prepared for some significant developments."

I arrived in Tunis prepared for an epiphany. Faisal was at Akram's and we both received a preliminary briefing. Abu Ala and Hassan Asfour, under the instructions of Abu Mazen, had worked out and initialed a Declaration of Principles with Uri Savir and Joel Zinger in Oslo with the help of Norwegian Foreign Minister Johan Holst and the mediation of Foreign Ministry officials Terrye and Muna Larsen.

"You're the one responsible," Akram said to me. "It was the channel you had set up between Ya'ir Hirschfeld and Ron Pundik on the one hand and Abu Ala on the other." I was not surprised by the existence of a back channel or the agreement, only that this particular channel had succeeded. Then I realized that it was precisely because of the inconspicuous, low-key nature of this contact that it had gone unnoticed and succeeded where other high-level channels had come to naught. Nabil Sha'th's more visible and highly leakable contacts had been decoys, encouraged by Abu Mazen. Abu Mazen also disclosed that he had refused to follow up on any proposed channels after Oslo began to produce because he felt that the Israeli side, Rabin in particular, was testing the PLO, Abu Mazen in particular, for seriousness and discretion. Peres had sent Uri Savir, but when Rabin sent Joel Zinger, the proposition turned serious. "I didn't want to jeopardize our work or create multiple channels to confuse the issues. Oslo was the one, and we gave it everything. That's why I avoided meeting Shulamit Aloni and all the other envoys who came with Rabin's blessings. When I was sure that we had a serious channel going, I told Abu Ammar and he was kept informed of every move." Abu Mazen knew precisely what he was doing.

The next morning Faisal and I went to Abu Mazen's office and studied a copy of the initialed agreement. My first reaction was one of shock. "It's clear that the ones who initialed this agreement have not lived under occupation. You postponed the settlement issue and Jerusalem without even getting guarantees that Israel would not continue to create facts on the ground that would preempt and prejudge the final outcome. And what about human rights? There's a constituency at home, a people in captivity, whose rights must be protected and whose suffering must be alleviated. What about all our red lines? Territorial jurisdiction and integrity are negated in substance and the transfer of authority is purely functional." Both Faisal and I were extremely concerned about the gaps, ambiguities, lack of detail, and absence of implementation mechanisms.

"All these will be negotiated," Abu Mazen said. "We got strategic, political gains, particularly the fact that this is an agreement with the PLO and not just a Palestinian delegation and the recognition of the Palestinians as a people with political rights. We got the admission of the return of displaced persons and a commitment to discuss the refugee issue and Jerusalem in permanent status. We're going to discuss boundaries and that means statehood. Could you have gotten more?"

I responded to the challenge. "It's not who makes the agreement but what's in it. I have no ego problems about being excluded or kept in the dark, or even about being used. My main concern is about substance. I think this agreement has many potentially explosive areas and could be to our disadvantage. At least you should have done something about Jerusalem, the settlements, and human rights. Strategic issues are fine, but we know the Israelis and we know that they will exploit their power as occupier to the hilt and by the time you get to permanent status Israel would have permanently altered realities on the ground."

He answered calmly, "You can negotiate settlements and human rights. Talk to them directly in Washington and ask for a freeze on settlement activities, the release of prisoners, the lifting of the Jerusalem siege, and the return of deportees."

I was amazed. "After you had signed? What power do we have? Do you want me to talk to the Israelis as a petitioner?"

"It's your fault," he said. "I had asked you to start secret talks in Jerusalem and you refused. Now we have a DOP and we need follow-up."

"You know perfectly well why we could not do that. Without Abu Ammar's approval, it would have been political suicide. Now I say maybe you were right. We should have done it. It's too late now; let's see what we can do with what you got us. It's difficult enough as it is."

When Nabil Sha'th arrived, he called the delegation together and started an enthusiastic prognosis of the coming round. Suddenly we realized that he still did not know about the Oslo agreement. As soon as he and the other members of the delegation read it, we entered into a heated debate. Nabil saw only the positive aspects and launched an inspired defense and acclamation of the Declaration of Principles. The rest were much more cautious, pointing out the departures from the cornerstones of our negotiating policy and the pitfalls in the agreement. I expressed my concern and reservations as I had discussed them with Abu Mazen, and Nabil accused me of pessimism and cynicism. I responded that it would be wrong and misleading to try to beautify such a flawed agreement and to embellish it in such a way as to create exaggerated expectations. It certainly was not the answer to our prayers nor an airtight or comprehensive agreement capable of easy implementation. I turned to Abu Mazen, "Can we change it? Are there any items in it open to amendment?" He answered frankly, "No." I added, "In that case, let's see what we can do with it. With all its shortcomings and drawbacks, this is what we have. The next set of negotiations will probably be the most difficult and painful, requiring our best experts and top brains. Let's make sure that the DOP doesn't blow up in our faces."

With that we went to Washington for the last round of post hoc negotiations. The process launched in Madrid had come to an end. Was this also the end of our mission? From agents of change would we become instruments of fate or victims of circumstance? Saeb and Haidar were outraged when they heard the news, but while Saeb typically bounced back, Haidar felt deep hurt and personal grievance. Nothing would persuade him to remain for the signing, and an unbridgeable breach had taken place. As for me, I recognized the end of a phase but I was intent on a conclusion with a bang and not a whimper. I had once told a small group of friends, "The real test is to know how and when to exit gracefully." The occasion for the graceful exit was drawing close, but I still had one more mission to accomplish: Washington had to be a success, and the PLO must enter the international arena in a blaze of glory befitting the magnitude and pain of the people and cause it represented. This promised to be a moment of historical vindication, and it was up to us to bring our leadership to enter the moment in a triumphal procession and not as captives on display. The time had come for the orphans of time to become the heirs of history. I owed this to the Palestinian people, whom I bore in my soul and heart as a priceless *amanah*.

It was not time for recriminations, apprehensions, or internal soul searching and accountability. We had to put Palestine on the map. To do that, we had to introduce the PLO, embrace it as the body and symbol of a nation, and then make a graceful exit. The stage was set. A spectacle on the White House lawn was being meticulously choreographed and we had to bring our players stage front while we withdrew to the wings.

I was there in the heart of pandemonium. From endless negotiations with the State Department and the team, to incessant press interviews and arrangements, to intricate talks with Arab-American organizations and the Palestinian community, to complex diplomacy with American political figures, to balancing acts with grassroots organizations, to technical administrative arrangements with the limited volunteer staff, to solving squabbles over security arrangements. By phone, I was also trying to coordinate with Tunis, which had its own internal balancing act to perform. I did not have the time to stop and take stock.

At the first meeting with a rather sheepish Dan Kurtzer and Aaron

Miller, Dan said, "We took a week off and you came up with the DOP. Would you like us to take a month off so you can resolve final status?" His sardonic question had an element of truth in it. Both wanted to know where we were heading from there and how to proceed. "There will be time," I said. "But now we have urgent tasks to attend to. We need to change all reference to the 'Palestinian delegation' in the DOP to the 'PLO.' "

Two of our negotiators had tried to work out the changes, but the Americans had refused with stubborn finality. But that was not the end of that subject. "Who's coming to sign?" they asked. "Will it be Abu Mazen or the chairman?" At that time, the issue had not been resolved.

"I'll let you know soon," I promised.

"Please remember," they said, "no guns, no hugs, no kisses on the White House lawn. Is there any chance of discussing uniforms?"

That was too much. "Don't even think of it," I warned.

Abu Ammar took my question whether he was coming to Washington as an urgent request. "You see," I heard him tell the Executive Committee while I was still on the phone, "my delegation wants me to go to Washington. Isn't that so, Hanan?" My predictable response was, "Of course. You should be here for the signing." He continued, "But Abu Mazen must do the signing. It's only fair that Peres and Abu Mazen sign on behalf of the two sides; after all they're the ones who were behind this agreement. Rabin and I will be there to represent our respective governments."

I knew what I had to do. I called Dennis. "You have to get Rabin to come. The chairman is coming."

So began the process of stage-managing an international spectacle, with a surrealistic cast of world leaders and a flawed agreement worked out in secret for a script. When my old friend Peter Jennings of ABC News saw me running around doing everything at once, he later told me he resented my playing the role of a female manager while the men sat around playing the role of political big bosses. "It wasn't that at all," I said. "The work was so enormous and complex that only a woman could do it."

All decked out and filled with excitement at the coming event, we went to the airport to meet Abu Ammar and his entourage on their first visit to Washington. As we were lining up on the tarmac in a receiving line, we noticed a strange segregation taking place. All the PLO officials and employees were grouped together in one line ahead of us. Nabil Sha'th and Akram Haniyyeh as the PLO officials in the leadership committee were the only two on the reception committee at the bottom of the plane stairway. The delegation looked at the Palestine Affairs Center employees ahead of us and we all started cracking jokes about signs, symptoms, and priorities. "Portents of things to come," some said. "God will have mercy on him who knows his own station," was the proverb of the day. Nasser al-Qidwa, the PLO representative at the U.N., was furious at the division and came to stand with us. We urged him to go back to his place and keep his distance "for fear of contamination." Those few paces separating us at the tarmac as the plane landed seemed like a yawning abyss. We went back to our cars at the tail end of the motorcade, and knew that things would never be the same again.

• • •

The day had finally arrived, Monday, September 13, 1993. The in-house phone rang with a shrill and persistent urgency. It was 5:00 A.M. and I had just gone to bed. Suhair, my assistant at the time, was still juggling two other phones, alternating between Arabic and English as she responded to each receiver in turn, desperately trying to maintain her composure and tone of polite assurance. She too had gone without sleep in Washington the last three nights. We looked at each other and smiled, with the tacit recognition that our longed-for naps were not going to take place that morning either. It must be Abu Ammar, I mouthed the words silently, and she nodded in agreement. We were both used to crises, summonses, and insane hours. I picked up the receiver.

"You must come immediately. We have to talk to the Americans," said the chairman. "Unless the text is changed as agreed, there will be no signing today."

I showered and changed with record speed, and decided to put on my formal suit just in case. Suhair was left with the unenviable task of having to explain to the network morning news shows why they had to accept a substitute. Carrying my shoes in one hand and my papers and purse in the other, I dashed down the long corridor of the ninth floor of the ANA Westin Hotel. Dozens of American and Palestinian security guards looked on with resignation as they tried to make way for me, the barefoot Palestinian spokesperson who was often seen running frantically among suites at all hours of the day and night, shredding documents haphazardly, and exchanging hasty comments with any number of people on the way. Such was the work pattern of most of the Palestinian delegation, with the exception of Akram, who had earned the title of "kosher inspector" by sitting quietly in his suite and allowing documents, delegates, and dignitaries alike to find their way to him. An American security officer hastily opened the door to the chairman's suite with practiced skill, just in time to avoid a major collision, and I rushed in unceremoniously.

Abu Ammar was visibly angry. "I haven't slept a wink all night!" he exclaimed, forgetting that many of us stayed up with him trying to avert the crisis.

"I will not sign unless the text is amended. The Israelis had agreed to the changes, and now they're reneging. This invalidates the whole thing." Turning to his assistants, he issued clipped instructions. "Call Abu Ala. Call Abu Mazen. Find out if Ahmad has returned from Rabin's hotel, and bring him here."

"Have you heard anything new after Rabin's arrival?" I asked, dreading the worst.

"Peres claims that there is no such agreement, and now Rabin supports him. Please call the Americans now and tell them the whole deal is off unless they convince the Israelis to change."

"I have already talked to Aaron, Dan, and Dennis. I'll try talking to Ed again, and if that doesn't work, we'll have to try to reach Christopher."

"This has to go up to Clinton. Tell them that the Executive Committee had endorsed the agreement only if 'Palestinian team/delegation (of the joint Jordanian-Palestinian delegation)' is changed to read 'the Palestine Liberation Organization' throughout the text of the DOP. They are talking to the PLO now, and the letters of mutual recognition must be reflected in the declaration. There is parity now: the Israeli government and the PLO."

As he spoke I picked up the receiver and dialed Dennis Ross's number. The response was the same. For days now we had been trying to incorporate the PLO in the text, and the State Department "peace team" had been adamant, refusing to consider any amendments to the "official" text that the Israelis had given them. "It is already too late," they repeated. "Even logistically we cannot revise an official document." I tried to convince Dennis that the situation was serious and that the chairman really meant business. He responded, "Only if the Israelis agree." I tried hard not to lose my temper. Once again, the Americans turned to the Israelis for their cue. Once again proving that it was easier to talk to the Israelis directly than to try to get the Americans to mediate or to influence Israeli behavior.

As I dialed the State Department's Operations Center number, I heard Abu Ammar issuing instructions to the pilots of the Moroccan airplane lent to him by King Hassan to proceed immediately to Andrews Air Force Base and to prepare for possible takeoff that morning. Even if it turned out to be a bluff, it sounded quite serious.

"This is Hanan Ashrawi. I need to speak to Ambassador Djerejian urgently please. Yes, you can call it an emergency."

"This is Ed. What is it, Hanan?"

"Ed, you must take this seriously. Call Rabin and convince him. If the text is not made to reflect new realities, then the whole Executive Committee endorsement will be withdrawn. The chairman is thinking of leaving this morning."

"Have you talked to the Israelis?"

"We have. Ahmad Tibi, Arafat's envoy, has been playing yo-yo all night between the ANA and the Mayflower hotels. Now that Rabin has arrived, he can make the decision instantly. Ahmad is still there."

"It's good that you talked to them directly. Keep talking, and we'll see what we can do."

In the meantime, Abu Ala, Hassan Asfour, and Abu Mazen (all of whom were key players in the secret Oslo talks that brought us to this signing stage) had come in and were carrying out talks with their Israeli counterparts by phone. They concurred that the amendments had to be carried out as agreed. Uri Savir and Yossi Beilin were trying to persuade their side. Peres was amenable. As usual, all were waiting for the final word from Rabin.

"Hanan, you and Faisal as well as the delegation and the Executive Committee members are to wait here until this is solved. Let the administrators and staff go to the White House and take their seats. I need you here in case we have to leave quickly."

Abu Ammar's sitting room was rapidly clouding with the smoke of scores of cigarettes. Usually health-conscious and disapproving, he didn't even notice. Hayel al-Fahoum of the PLO Political Department walked in. He was to play the role of legal adviser during the signing ceremony. He too was told to sit down and wait.

"It is getting late. We should be on our way," Hayel said.

"Not until we get the answer we need," Abu Ammar responded. Yasser Abd Rabbo and Nabil Sha'th were also trying to solve the impasse. Four or five conversations were taking place simultaneously, some by phone and others directly. Faisal was sitting quietly, taking everything in with his usual equanimity. He too was of the opinion that none should leave until we got our answer. Abu Ammar was urging everyone to stay calm. "Don't lose your nerve. It will happen." Suddenly, and as happens sometimes when I find myself in a situation of intense pressure, I was completely detached.

Abu Ala, soft-spoken and outwardly calm, rubbed his eyes and repeatedly drew on his cigarette with a sense of purpose. He was the main protagonist of the Oslo back-channel drama. Almost a year before, I had put him in touch with Ya'ir Hirschfeld, the Israeli academic from Haifa University and a close associate of Yossi Beilin's, triggering a whole chain of events that brought us here. Looking at Faisal through that same veil of detachment, I was reminded of another chain of events that may have been the real starting point of the whole process. Did it start with that fateful meeting in Jerusalem with the American consul general then, Philip Wilcox, when he told us of Secretary Baker's impending visit to the region and his intention of exploring the possibilities of launching a Middle East peace process? Or did it start almost six years ago with the *intifada* and the setting up of the then illegal Political Committee, meeting in my living room under the very eyes of the Israeli military authorities? Perhaps the real beginning goes back to 1967 when after the June war Faisal set up the first training camp for new Fateh recruits, both young men and women, which I was supposed to join in Lebanon, but did not. Historically, did it start with one of our many disasters—the First Zionist Congress, the Balfour Declaration, the horror of the Holocaust in Europe, the 1947 U.N. plan to partition Palestine, the 1948 war and tragedy of exile and displacement, the war of June 5, 1967, and its terrible legacy of occupation and oppression? Perhaps for me it started on October 8, 1946, in the maternity ward of the Anglican Hospital in Nablus, Palestine, where I was born—the fifth daughter of Dr. Daud Mikhail and his wife, Wadi'a. How fatalistic can one be? Is our Arabic saying true: What is written on the forehead the eye must see.

It was pointless, perhaps irrelevant, to indulge in such speculations then. The man who has loomed larger than life in the Palestinian imagination, often described as the symbol and destiny of the Palestinian national struggle and identity, was right there in a hotel suite in Washington, probably ready to pull another rabbit out of a hat. So much had happened since I first met him in 1969 in Amman, Jordan, when I was an undergraduate student. Now, I recognized the human being, under pressure, called upon to make yet another decision that would inevitably affect the course of history, and my life. Did anybody have that right? Should I just walk out?

The room was suddenly filled with commotion. Rabin had consented to the changes and we had to run. It was already after 10:00 A.M. We piled into the waiting cars, all decorum forgotten, and were driven at breakneck speed, sirens wailing, people gaping, to the White House. Literally tumbling out of the cars, Akram, Faisal, and I were joined by other latecomers of our delegation. But somebody had neglected to give the security officers at the gate a full list of our names for clearance and we were prevented from entering. They thought that perhaps we were at the wrong gate. There was no time. The irony was inescapable, and I almost laughed aloud. Having done the impossible to make this happen, we might end up missing the whole event because of a bureaucratic mix-up. Mine was the one face that the guards recognized, and I was told I could proceed. "What about the rest of the delegation?" I asked.

"Without clearance, they can't."

"What if I vouch for them?"

"It's highly irregular."

I could tell they were bending. Catching sight of Ted Koppel up ahead, I pulled a familiar, though not entirely ethical, trick.

"We all have to go through together. How do you think it will appear to the world if the Palestinian delegation is prevented from attending the signing ceremony because of you?"

"I'll tell you what. Why don't you stand right here beside me and give me the name of each person of your delegation as he or she comes in and I'll make a full list."

"We don't have time. It's 10:35 and the ceremony is supposed to start at 11:00. Why don't I just identify them individually by name as they come in, and you don't need to keep a list. Just take my word for it." Sensing our desperation, or perhaps the volatility of the situation, he agreed. We filed in quickly. I came up last. I hoped he wouldn't get fired. Running up the path leading to the South Lawn, we overtook Ted Koppel, who thrust a microphone in my face and asked how I felt about the agreement. "It's a minefield," I panted and resumed my breathless sprint uphill. It was then; it still is.

We caused a commotion as we ran up to the roped-off guest area. The whole delegation rose and shuffled their seats trying to make room for us. At first, some of us sat awkwardly, two to a seat. Saeb gave me his chair, and Akram pulled it up to the front row. I scanned the faces on the lawn trying to find Hayel. Catching his eye, I signaled to him and he ran over.

"Please check the text of the official documents to make sure that the changes have been made."

"The last time I saw them, about three minutes ago, there were no changes."

"Did you tell them about the agreement?"

"I certainly did, but nothing was changed. Come and see for yourself."

I ducked under the rope and ran across the White House lawn heading straight for the American legal adviser. He was not aware of any changes, he said. I asked him to bring over the Israeli legal adviser. He too claimed ignorance. I was frantic.

"Do you realize that without these changes there will be no signature?"

The gravity of the situation became apparent to them. "Why don't you have Abu Mazen cross out the wrong lines and write in the corrections before he signs?" the American legal adviser asked.

"He can do that only if he signs first and initials the corrections; then Peres will sign after him and initial the same corrections. Otherwise, it would be illegal."

"We can't do that. There's no way we can change the order of the signing."

"Then you have to go back to your leaders and tell them there will be no signing today unless the documents are corrected."

"What are the changes that have to be made?"

"Do you have an extra copy of the DOP?"

He handed me one, and I took his pen and crossed out all references to the "Palestinian delegation" or "team" or "joint Jordanian-Palestinian delegation" and wrote "the Palestine Liberation Organization" or "the PLO." He took the amended draft and ran back inside the White House. Hayel and I agreed that I would go back to my seat while he waited to make sure that the documents to be signed were indeed corrected. If all was well, he would signal me an affirmative nod. If not, we would have to go back and inform Abu Ammar and Abu Mazen. We both knew that there would be no signing then.

Ten fifty-nine A.M. and still no sign of Hayel. My eyes were smarting and the manicured lawn began a slow green dance like a gigantic T-shirt spread out to dry. My one consolation was the thought that the State Department peace team must have been undergoing even greater anxiety fits at the moment: the Palestinians have done it again! I pulled out a copy of the official program, detailed down to the last minute. So much for planning and all that. I found myself smiling inwardly for the second time within one minute. My new shoes were pinching unbearably. After all these years I still catch myself longing for the familiar comfort of my worn sneakers, resentful of the constraints of formal heels. I wondered if I could take them off. Immediately, an image of barefoot Hanan in the front row on the White House lawn flashed before my eyes and they began to tear. I could not afford the third inward smile, so I made do with an inward rebuke as I dabbed at my eyes with a Kleenex. All I needed was for my eye makeup to run. Would the headlines read "Barefoot and tearful on the lawn"? This was no time for frivolity, I silently reprimanded myself. The Declaration of Principles that would or would not be signed that day held the key to the future of many Palestinian and Israeli genera-tions as well as of the region. Actually, a central piece of a global jigsaw puzzle was to be positioned that morning, provided the right signal was given. We had lived with suspense and last-minute reversals all our lives, so what was one more instance? The Palestinians have upset many an apple cart before.

Eleven two A.M. and my eyes began to smart again. It was a toss-up between a cigarette and my worry beads. I dared not pull out either.

Still out of breath, I sat on the edge of my fold-up seat and peered through the glare to catch a glimpse of Hayel. It seemed as if Hayel had been chosen by fate to play this pivotal role precisely on that day and then to exit, leaving the stage to the more prominent players. On my right, Faisal was also trying to catch his breath, his asthma acting up. On my left, Chelsea Clinton was chattering excitedly with a group of teenag-ers all clad in bright green T-shirts with the legend "Seeds of Peace" boldly displayed on heaving chests. Behind me, the rest of our Palestinian delegation, both official (from the "outside") and unofficial (from the "inside"), was jostling for position—their seats having been taken by the green brigade. So much for meticulous State Department and White House planning. It was not the first time in which Palestinians found themselves displaced, I smiled to myself, somewhat sadly. Anxiety leaves very little room for self-pity. Besides, I had discarded that habit a long time ago, although I still allow myself the luxury of moral indignation— even anger—every now and then.

The green lawn and countless faces were in focus again, but the podium with its historical table of Camp David fame was ominously vacant. There was no sign of life at the White House exit from which an impressive procession would or would not shortly emerge. I figured that they must have been in the Green Room: President Clinton, Vice Presi-dent Gore, Secretary Christopher; Foreign Minister Kozyrev; Chairman Arafat, Abu Mazen; Prime Minister Rabin, Foreign Minister Peres; and their wives—with the exception of the Palestinians, of course. Maybe it was better for the wives not to participate in an event that was not of their doing; absence may be less demeaning than attendance as an appendage. Which brought to mind the real question: how many of those world leaders, the main performers in this spectacle, had had anything to do with its actual materializing? The production was spectacular, but most of the real players were waiting anonymously in the wings. The harsh glare of the sun was almost painful. I shielded my eyes, longing for a cool and shady place. Suddenly, I noticed a hand waving furiously as a figure approached. It was Hayel. He looked at me, smiled, then nodded. I sat back and smiled—this time outwardly.

The ceremony started at 11:07. The spectacle on the White House lawn was a huge success. As for me, I knew that the hard part had just started. This whole event was a signal, a passage. The crossing out of "delegation" and writing in of "PLO" had ushered in a whole new phase. Whether Arafat and Rabin got something more than their green T-shirts from the White House ceremony still remained to be seen. So would the passage from Tunis to Washington. A transition of tremendous magnitude was taking place, and I would have to choose a few stations along the way.

With the amendment of the text on the White House lawn, we had come full cycle. The actual denouement was yet to come as we now had to look within. That famous handshake between a reluctant Rabin and an eager Arafat represented to us more of a challenge than a reconciliation, a beginning rather than an end. Both leaders would henceforth be held directly accountable and responsible by their own people. Their future would hang on the success or failure of the tremendous tasks they had undertaken with that loaded handshake. Peace with our historical enemy was not possible unless we proved capable of forging peace among ourselves and with ourselves. The minefield that lay ahead was not only across the border but on our own terrain, and that was the more difficult course to steer. Could we generate the language of our future to shape and express an inner harmony, or would we revert to the rhetoric of strife and self-deception? For years, I had urged Faisal never to use the first-person singular pronoun in political discourse, for ours was a collective mission. For years, I had tried to transform our reality from an adjective to a noun, from Palestinian to Palestine, and to introduce into global discourse the use of the term "people" as a recognition of our humanity in conjunction with our land of Palestine as a contemporary reality instead of a geographical abstraction. Had we succeeded in substituting the PLO for Palestine as our historical noun, and had we accepted the dismemberment of our land along with the fragmentation of our concept of peoplehood? If the PLO, in the fullness of its recognition, could pass the test of wholeness, then it could carry us through to the future. If it could pull together all the different threads of this tormented people's narrative, then it would be capable of weaving an image of our destiny. It had placed itself squarely at the crossroads of external recognition and internal validation, precisely where our past and future would meet and merge to shape our collective memory for the future or would clash and be wrenched apart in sorrow and fury.

CHAPTER FIFTEEN

———◆+◆◆+◆———

The chairman's speech at the signing sent a sad signal to Palestinians all over the world. Rather than touching our hearts and minds as an act of grace and healing, it rebounded like impersonal sound waves etching a vague image of an unidentifiable object. We could not recognize ourselves in it. The world would not know us through it. In Madrid, we had tried to establish our uniqueness and our union with the grand sweep of nations and history; in Washington, Abu Ammar used the language of exclusion to set us apart.

Although some Palestinians read the speech as a foreshadowing of the impending degradation of our language and vision, I tried to excuse it as a temporary relapse. "The choice of this speech was a conscious decision," someone told me. "The implicit message is that your language is over. The next phase is not one for poets and intellectuals. It's the era of hardcore politicians, one in which slogans are the weapons of a struggle for power. Self-interest produces clichés, not humanistic visions." But I knew that no one could banish from our midst the poets and visionaries, those who would continue to form the conscience of a nation with a fear of hope. Edward Said described the signing as the triumph of the "shopkeepers." Mahmoud Darwish told me in anguish, "Our language has been usurped." Akram said it was time for me to go back to literature. "Whatever you do from now on would only diminish you if you do it on their terms. You have set your own standards and your integrity is at stake."

I knew it was time for the graceful exit, but I had a few tasks yet to perform, and I resolved to do them well.

We had to go to Tunis to prepare for the ratification of the agreement by the Central Council (the intermediate representative body between the Palestine National Council and the PLO Executive Committee) and to participate in planning for the next phase. I flew with Abu Ammar on his plane to New York where we held a meeting with Secretary General Boutros Boutros-Ghali at U.N. headquarters, and from there to Tunis. We were in the air when Abu Ammar broached the subject of political positions. I told him, "The way to go about it is to set up a comprehensive structure and work plan, then find the appropriate people to carry out the tasks. It's not a question of finding posts for individual people. I personally do not aspire to a position and I did not get into this for power or benefits. I want nothing, and you don't need to worry about me."

We landed in Tunis with every possible ambassador and diplomat lining up to welcome Abu Ammar back from his peacemaking foray. We met with the Executive Committee, then set off for home to prepare for the Central Council meeting and for the challenge of planning ahead. Abu Ammar began the first leg of his diplomatic world tour to receive the accolades from leaders who a few months earlier had recoiled at the mere mention of the PLO. Before he left, he asked me to consider taking the post of Palestinian representative in Washington. "I need to upgrade the status of the office and the quality of the work," he said.

"I don't want any official post," I replied. "However, if you're serious about beginning a new phase, I'm willing to look into the Washington situation and prepare a full proposal with a rationale, structure, priorities, objectives, a phased work plan and a full budget. This way, regardless of who's there, the work will be done effectively and efficiently." He agreed.

Saeb and I went to Amman on our way home. Abu Ammar had asked me to talk to Abul-Lutof (Farouq al-Kaddoumi) and to King Hussein. Both had been taken by surprise at the Oslo agreement and both had expressed serious reservations about it. Kaddoumi, head of the PLO's Political Department, had refused to attend the signing in Washington and was concerned about the document's divisive effect on Arab coordination, particularly in view of Syria's opposition. King Hussein, our closest partner and patron of the umbrella of the joint Jordanian-Palestinian delegation, was indignant at having been left in the dark, and seriously concerned about the implications of the agreement for Jordan. Saeb and

I held an all-night meeting with Abul-Lutof and tried our best to respond to his reservations, and by lunchtime the next day we had reached a consensus on the strengths and flaws of the agreement and the inevitability of upholding it. Abul-Lutof used the expression he had coined to describe the process as a "compulsory course" but assured us that we would all work together in facing the challenges ahead.

The next day, I went with Tayyeb Abdel Rahim to see King Hussein and had a frank off-the-record talk. King Hussein expressed real concern about the fate of Jerusalem. "Jerusalem is not just the holy places," I said. "It's a living, throbbing city with national, political, and historical Palestinian rights, with institutions, human beings, homes, and land that have to be protected."

I was worried that the perceptual spiritual shift to celestial Jerusalem might undermine our terrestrial city. By granting God sovereignty over the sacred aspects of Jerusalem, we might be sanctioning Israel's actual and illegal exercise of sovereignty in the secular domain. But I was convinced that the king's concerns were deep-felt and genuine. The challenge was where to go from here. His initial suspicions after the revelation of the Oslo agreement had already begun to abate, and I relayed to him Abu Ammar's intentions to visit in a few days and begin a new phase of joint work.

As soon as I got home, I was faced with a deluge of requests and questions of all types. Some had to do with the donors' conference to be held in Washington under American auspices and with the participation of Europe, Canada, Japan, Saudi Arabia, among others, and preceded by a World Bank coordinating meeting; others had to do with European and Asian countries which wanted to set the terms for future cooperation; and others still with the implications of the agreement on domestic and regional political maps, including the need for establishing the Palestinian-Israeli Liaison Committee.

Abu Ammar was in China, Abu Mazen in Morocco, Abul-Lutof in between Amman and Damascus, and Abu Ala in Brussels, while Faisal and Akram were in Paris. Somehow we managed to make decisions and move ahead through an international Palestinian network and numerous overseas phone calls. But the sense of urgency remained for establishing a coherent system capable of discharging all the tasks and undertakings of the PLO in accordance with the agreement.

A group of us who had taken the challenge seriously went to Tunis and immediately set to work devising plans and structures for the future. First we set up negotiating committees as required by the Declaration of

Principles, and we described the qualifications and expertise required for each group depending on its area of negotiations. We proposed a leadership/follow-up committee to supervise the talks and devise strategies and coordinate policies. Then we designated internal committees to do the preparatory work for permanent-status negotiations and some of the other postponed issues. Finally, we set to work on the structures of the political authority, its platform, departments, and work programs. Every time we tried to present our proposals and plans to the leadership, the talk would turn immediately to the names of the projected political authority. Abu Ammar wanted to set up a provisional government, but neither the Americans nor the Israelis would accept it despite our repeated attempts at persuading them. Finally, Abu Ammar announced that he would set up the Palestinian National Authority in accordance with the Palestine National Council resolution of 1974, which had called for the establishment of a Palestinian national authority on any inch of Palestine that was liberated from Israel or from which Israel withdrew. All agreed that this Authority should be made up of Executive Committee members and "inside" Palestinians, working within the structures of the PLO. It took us four nights to get our proposals approved on paper. On September 30, and as part of the preparations for the coming phase, Abu Ammar signed the first decree after Washington. It was a commitment to the establishment of a national human rights commission that would enjoy both independence from and access to the offices of the PLO, and be a safeguard against human rights abuses, a guarantee that the executive branch of the coming political system would respect such rights and freedoms within a democratic system. I had plans for that decree.

Again, I went home to do the follow-up. Two nights later, I received another predawn call for an urgent departure. This time it was from Faisal in Cairo. "This had better be important," I warned.

"You are needed in Cairo for the chairman's meeting with Rabin today," he answered.

"There's no way we can make it," I protested. "When will we ever learn to plan, at least one day in advance?"

But of course he had my travel plans all worked out: "If you leave Ramallah at 6:00, you'll find a car waiting for you at the Orient House in Jerusalem. From there you'll drive to the Gaza Strip and cross to Egypt via the Rafah border at 8:00. A car will take you to Al-ʾArish where Abu Ammar's plane will be waiting to fly you to Cairo. A car will meet you at the airport and take you to the presidential palace in time for the 10:00 o'clock meeting. We'll all come back in the evening the same way."

I packed my papers and set off with my co-travelers, Nabeel Kassis and Ziad Abu Zayyad, on another hectic, last-minute mission.

Abu Ammar and Rabin—no two men could be more different. Rabin was a study in sullen seriousness, with a no-nonsense attitude and the demeanor of a school prefect on a mission. His ruddy complexion was betrayed by calculating eyes suggesting a sharp intelligence and instant strategies. The moment I lit a cigarette, he lit one, and that seemed to break the ice. But the moment he started his presentation, the disciplinarian and military commander took over. Abu Ammar, on the other hand, was the incarnation of Arab social decorum and cordiality. At the same time as his eyes smiled with hospitality, they were simultaneously measuring up his counterpart for an immediate sparring contest. He deflected Rabin's direct verbal punches with evasive tactics and attempted reengagement on his own terms. Yet both had one thing in common: they insisted on being the central decision makers and the focal (even omniscient) source of authority. Four negotiating committees were set up: the Liaison Committee at ministerial level to meet in Cairo; the Gaza-Jericho Committee to meet in Taba, Egypt; the Interim Arrangements Committee to meet in Washington; and the Economic Committee to meet in Paris. Faisal was to pursue Jerusalem arrangements with an Israeli counterpart. Rabin refused to consider any human rights steps dealing with prisoners and deportees beyond promising not to transfer Palestinian prisoners to prisons within Israel. All other issues, he said, were "gestures" (pronounced with a hard G) that he was not ready to undertake until negotiations were well under way. With Cairo becoming the most frequented venue for Palestinian-Israeli talks, the two sides had already established a unique pattern of negotiations: sign first, talk later.

Following a delightful late lunch hosted by Osama al-Baz in a restaurant by the Nile, we took the same circuitous route back and arrived home at midnight. I began to notice unusual activity at home, with mysterious phone calls and a conspiratorial mood. Every time I attempted to step out onto the western veranda, I was immediately whisked back on flimsy pretexts. Mikael Dahl, the Swedish consul in Jerusalem and a close friend of Emile's and mine, seemed to be part of the conspiracy. On the evening of October 8, my forty-seventh birthday, I was escorted out through the veranda and into the earthly paradise. Nearly forty of my closest friends were gathered in a garden of brilliant colors and soothing water flowing over porous rocks. Emile had created for me this gift; it was to be our sanctuary, our hidden haven to which ugliness and pain were not admitted. Carefully placed and concealed lights created a subtle interplay of fluid illumination and deep darkness. We sang, and marveled at the renewal of a joy long withheld, surprised at our capacity to resurrect a sense of wonder. We exchanged reminiscences and reveled in our shared expanses of memory. We savored each bite of shish kabab and maza, as if this were a secular communion. Even our jokes took on the power of parables and the fantasy of fables. Flowers seemed to reach out and touch us with careful tenderness, somehow aware of our emotional vulnerability and the tendency of our spirit to bruise easily. The moment enfolded and cherished us as we in turn nurtured it and were nourished by it. Emile and our daughters and friends had worked this miracle on my birthday as a continuous gift of gentle people who knew the art of soothing. This was the world of poets and prophets, of fragile visions and memories. The other world seemed to crumple and devour itself in envy. I knew where I belonged, quietly, irrevocably.

• • •

The Central Council meeting in Tunis, two days later, was a complicated system of political maneuvering, formulaic speech making, and debate. Abu Ammar expected neither unanimity nor an overwhelming majority—a vote ranging from 60 percent to 70 percent would do. The DOP was ratified by a 63 percent majority. Along with that, the council approved setting up the Authority to be headed by President Arafat. We thought that this was an all-systems-go green light for the implementation of the plans we had designed. Instead, we discovered that even then, right before our eyes practically, the political bargaining had already begun, based on a system of quotas and paybacks. Factional favoritism intruded, and personal preferences began to shape the lists being passed among the inner circle.

When Yasser Abd Rabbo and Abu Mazen showed me the proposed lists, I was dismayed. Our lists had included only descriptions of qualifications for each negotiating group, such as "legal adviser," "cartographer," "hydrologist," "geologist," "security expert." Then we had put together lists of all the experts in each field. The names being discussed had no correlation with the areas and lists we had presented, but appeared to be politically motivated either to deliver factional representation or rewards for earlier favors.

"Being on a negotiating committee is not a position of political leadership and it should not be done on a political basis. We need our best experts, technocrats, and legal brains for the next set of negotiations, otherwise the DOP will blow up in our faces," I warned.

The group from the Occupied Territories was of one mind, but we felt increasingly discouraged by the discrepancy between verbal commitments and actual implementation. Nabil Sha'th was placed in charge of the Gaza-Jericho talks to commence on the thirteenth, and by the twelfth he was still engaged in a frantic search for negotiators. A few hours before the plane took off the last of the delegation was hurriedly informed of their impending tasks, and they clambered on still searching for copies of the agreement. Abu Mazen was placed in charge of the Liaison Committee and headed off for Egypt, while Abu Ala was to head the economic talks in Paris. I went home.

In November, I took off for Washington to pursue talks with the State Department on the status of Palestinian representation in the United States, to look into plans for setting up an upgraded and updated Palestinian mission, and to represent Abu Ammar at the National Association of Arab-Americans' convention, while giving a few talks at universities in between. It was no secret that the official Palestinian presence in the United States had been an unmitigated disaster—an embodiment of a common Palestinian saying that ours was a most just and compelling case with the most inept and unconvincing presentation. With the help of a few close friends, I put together a proposal for a Palestinian office that would deal with official political representation, congressional action, media policies, grassroots and community activities, economic cooperation projects, and dissemination of information. It included clear objectives and a work plan, to be implemented in phases, as well as a comprehensive structure and budget. I then headed for Belgium where I joined Abu Ammar on his official visit to Brussels and the European Union. Both he and Abul-Lutof were enthusiastic about the project and endorsed it wholeheartedly in theory, but neither had the funds or the willingness to embark on it.

I was more interested in translating the human rights decree into an institution. This time, I was involved in an act of conviction and commitment—a marker for our future. For years we had struggled to launch a nation into the future, to heal it in peace. But whenever we held the threads to this future we found out that they simultaneously led out to the global community and also inward. Whichever way we turned, we had to look homeward. While Abu Ammar and the PLO were globetrotting, relishing the taste of international recognition and official hospitality, there was restlessness and anxiety at home. With a global embrace the PLO, our exiled revolutionary leadership, lost its immunity from internal criticism and accountability. The transition from the glamour of a national liberation movement to the mundane tasks of building and running a state had begun. When symbols take on substance and become accessible, they turn into the stuff of daily life. When icons lose their mystical aura, they hang on walls like badly drawn portraits, all the more grotesque because of their two-dimensional reductive lack of depth.

Human rights and accountability were the key issues with which we tried to begin the devolution of the occupation and to provide the Palestinian people with the protection they needed and deserved. Now that a Palestinian authority was in the making, these issues would become the test of its integrity and of our consistency and moral fiber. Having been on the receiving end of a complex and systematic policy of abuse and repression, it was our turn to demonstrate that the victim would not turn oppressor and that the same stringent standards that we had applied to the Israelis would be applied to our own system and authority. Besides, the practices of a national liberation movement and its exercise of "revolutionary justice" in exile would have to undergo a drastic transformation into a system of government and governance firmly embedded in the principles and rights of a people on their own land. It was a new social contract. Such a transition, it seemed, would be the most difficult and painful passage. To fuse together a leadership that had undergone the indignities and alienation of exile and a people suffering from the trauma of occupation was going to form the most exacting challenge to the health of our nation and a test of our continuity. In my public speeches, I often made reference to our most pressing challenges, the big "Rs"—rehabilitation, reconstruction, reconciliation, all of which required an overhaul of the political program.

At this juncture, several voices were emerging with increasing urgency calling for democratic reform and for safeguards to protect the pluralistic nature of our society and its institutions.

During the last week of November 1993, I joined Abu Ammar on his official tour of the Scandinavian countries. While in Oslo, the first leg of our journey, I presented him with a proposal for the establishment of the Palestinian Independent Commission for Human Rights, with its own rationale, objectives, structure, by-laws, and budget, which attorney Raja Shehadeh and I had prepared a few days earlier. Abu Ammar immediately approved and signed the proposal, and I took it and ran with it. The Scandinavian countries with their ombudsman tradition immediately grasped the intention behind the project and extended support. Sweden was the pacesetter, with funds and expertise, followed by Denmark and

Norway. Abu Ammar gave it his public endorsement as he traipsed around the world, and I knew that my commitment to the future had already begun charting unknown waters, while clouds were amassing on the horizon promising a turbulent passage.

At the end of the journey, I told Abu Ammar that we had come to the end of one phase and that another needed to be launched. "We have to turn the page, close one chapter and begin another. I will not be part of any political structure, nor will I accept any official post. From now on, I will be pursuing a different vision. I had entered the public political arena to serve the people and the cause, and for the last few years I've given it all I had. Now it's time to move on, for each phase requires its own instruments and vehicles, its own language and people." He understood, or so I thought.

With a studied though quiet deliberateness, I began consultations to select the members of the board of commissioners; there was an impressive list of Palestinians whose credentials and integrity were earned and recognized. The preparatory committee included top legal brains and human rights activists such as Raja Shehadeh, Raji Surani, Muna Rishmawi, Mamdouh al-Aker, and Fateh Azzam. We began a systematic review of potential board members and research into legal formulations to ensure legitimacy and recognition for the commission.

In December, I made the public announcement that I was leaving the realm of official political work and devoting my energies to serving within the institutions of civil society, particularly in the field of human rights and systems of accountability. Since the signing in Washington, I announced, the Palestinian delegation as we had known it no longer existed, and I was no more the official spokesperson. Reactions ranged from shock to relief, but those closest to me had known the inevitability of my move. "It's a question of conscience and conviction, as well as a pledge to a future of nation building," I explained. Many interpreted this as a falling out with Arafat, and others saw in it a political maneuver. Some called it suicidal, others described it as naive idealism. A timely escape, said some; a collision course, cried others. The Palestinian human rights nongovernmental organizations sent out signals of alarm: a political trick to circumvent/sabotage/centralize/control the NGOs. We kept our eyes firmly on the goal and steered a straight course toward the unprecedented objective of establishing the first legally constituted watchdog authority in the Arab world.

• • •

As 1993 melted into 1994, Palestinian-Israeli negotiations entered into a sliding time frame and the talks seemed to diminish in scope and substance. Gradually, Israeli priorities, diction, and approaches began to surface, and to take priority over our conceptual and semantic plan. Substance was ceded for technicalities and procedures; fragmentation replaced the integrated comprehensive perspective; the asymmetry of power was fully incorporated into the process. Israel not only persisted in creating unilateral facts to prejudge the outcome, particularly of postponed issues such as Jerusalem and the settlements, it also placed the PLO on probation, in a never-ending test of good behavior. Many Palestinians, including prominent intellectuals and political leaders, started speaking out in public cautioning against the slippery slope of peacemaking under coercion and duress.

We celebrated the new year with a family reunion. I decided to write this book. An amateur fortune-teller read my coffee cup by chance and saw many signs—portents of change and destiny. Nabil Sha'th called and asked some of us to go to Egypt and help draft texts for the Taba talks. It was too late; he found no takers. As the scope of the talks constricted, the circle of concern widened. The human dimension was submerged beneath a flood of technical details, and the official Palestinian utterance rang hollow. The signing of the first Cairo Agreement on February 9, 1994, sent alarm bells ringing throughout the Occupied Territories and among the Palestinian exile communities, and generated even greater political fragmentation, particularly on the issue of ceding control over crossing points to Israel. Then came the Hebron massacre on February 25, at the al-Ibrahimi Mosque during Ramadan at the hands of Baruch Goldstein, a Jewish settler. The slaughter sent shock waves throughout the land, and, to compound the horror, as the mourners took to the streets in anguish and outrage, the Israeli army shot and killed more of them than Goldstein did worshipers.

During this time, Leah Tsemel, who had throughout her career defended Palestinians—and as a result been threatened, even gagged, by Israeli extremists—shared our pain. She wanted to pay her condolences, accompanying Palestinian lawyers who would be visiting the families of the Hebron victims. But the lawyers told Leah no, and she was terribly hurt. They gave her all sorts of excuses, including that they were concerned for her safety. To this she replied, "How come nobody was worried when I used to go into the middle of demonstrations, during the *intifada,* and defend Palestinians?" And then they said it was because she was a woman and Hebron was a very conservative place. And she said, "I've always gone there, they know me. Why don't you just come out and say it's because I'm Jewish." After much protest finally she was allowed to go. But their resistance to her request was not a good sign.

As a further punishment, we were placed under total curfew and military siege. Once again, the victim was punished. Instead of weakening our resolve, we became more resolute—determined that any agreement must begin the unraveling of the settlements and that immediate steps were needed to put an end to the daily friction and provocation presented by the settlers.

Abu Ammar was clearly under tremendous pressure. Israel and the United States wanted to resume the talks immediately with a total disregard for the public mood or our inflamed public opinion. The Palestinians were calling for "intervening" and corrective steps. First, the settlers had to be disarmed and those who had settled in the middle of populated areas, such as Hebron, had to be removed. Second, international protection must be secured for the Palestinian people. Third, the issue of settlements and the security of the Palestinians must be placed at the top of the negotiating agenda. Rabin formed a legal commission of inquiry and declared the Kach and Kahane Hai extremist movements illegal. But what we needed was a serious and immediate handling of the real source of instability and conflict—the settlement issue itself and the activities of the settlers. Rabin refused under the pretext that according to the DOP the settlement issue was one of the postponed issues to be negotiated in permanent-status talks. "That does not give Israel a free hand to create facts and impose realities prejudicial to the outcome," we protested. "Throughout the Taba talks, they've been discussing settlements from an exclusively Israeli perspective—how to carve out Palestinian land for the settlements, how to maintain the Israeli army in Gaza and Jericho to protect the settlers, how to patrol the roads and which roads to control for the benefit of the settlers, ad absurdum, while the real issue is how to protect Palestinian property and lives from the violence and illegal behavior of the settlers and from the encroachment of settlements. Now that our worst nightmares have come to life, settlements are supposedly not on the agenda." We were outraged.

Abu Ammar faced a dilemma. He was losing support where it counted most—with his own people. At the same time he needed to deliver to Israel and the United States to demonstrate that he was a man of peace and a man of his word. "You used to tell the world you can do and say whatever you want, I have the support of my people," I told Abu Ammar on the phone. "What benefits a leader if he gains the whole world and loses credibility with his own people? Your own constituency is your source of legitimacy and strength."

He had seen on television the people of Hebron tear up his posters and had heard them questioning his leadership, and he was truly saddened. But the peace process was demanding a heavy price of him. So was Israel and the donor countries, including the United States, who were now demanding the price of their recognition, by asking him to make a concession on the issue of rights. "Our will is not broken," I told him. "You can count on the people to withstand even greater suffering if their rights are protected. Hold on and they'll support you." But he went the traditional way of seeking a U.N. Security Council meeting and resolution.

People saw this as a transparent excuse to return to the talks in the face of Israel's intransigence and its refusal to take the real steps needed to put the peace process back on track. The irony was that what Abu Ammar needed to resume the talks without losing his constituency could be delivered only by Rabin. Was Rabin interested in saving Arafat's credibility and hence his ability to pursue the talks and deliver peace, or would he try to weaken Arafat enough to accept any peace, even on Israel's terms, before it was too late? Rabin knew how to hit where it hurt most —the hostage Palestinian population, whose feelings were manipulated by Israeli practices. Ironically also, what Rabin identified as his needs to cater to Israeli public opinion, particularly the hard-line right wing, were exactly those steps and statements that would undermine Arafat—such as protecting Israeli "security" even at the cost of violating the civil rights of the Palestinian people. What Abu Ammar needed to placate public opinion were those statements and positions that would not go down well with the international community and would inflame the Israeli public. After two weeks of haggling and political blackmail exercised mainly by Christopher and his crew, the U.N. Security Council announced its Resolution 904.

"The last thing we need is another resolution to deplore and denounce Israeli actions and then get filed away along with all the other resolutions gathering dust in the archives of the U.N. Without implementation, it will only serve to create the impression of action and to ease the conscience of the guilty and the impotent." We did not mince words; we had been there before. This time, however, UNSCR 904 held more serious implications: that the legal status of Jerusalem was in dispute and thus postponed till permanent-status talks, despite the fact that Jerusalem legally continued to be part of the Occupied Territories notwithstanding the postponement of negotiations on its fate. The resolution was used by the United

States to cater to Israel's position on Jerusalem. It was also used to claim that the Occupied Territories were disputed land whose sovereignty would be determined in permanent-status talks; thus the United States distorted its own policy on Jerusalem and the Occupied Territories, violated international law and all previous relevant Security Council Resolutions, including 242 and 338, and made the Declaration of Principles the supreme legal reference superseding any international legality.

"International Presence" was lifted straight out of the DOP and used as another sop to create the impression of protection without any genuine preventive or interventive power. Representatives of the International Presence were brought to Hebron from other countries, but they were subject to Israeli military restrictions themselves and therefore their protective presence was invalidated. The symbolic value was significant, though, because for the first time Israel had implicitly admitted that Hebron was occupied territory. Having lived under Israeli occupation in the West Bank, Jerusalem, and Gaza for twenty-seven years, we responded with understandable cynicism to this epiphany. And at the first breakout of settler violence in Hebron in May, TIPH (Temporary International Presence in Hebron) was barred from entering the "closed military area" and placed under curfew along with the Palestinians. We were not surprised. With a collective metaphorical shrug and a few wise nods of "I told you so" we went about our business with a compound sense of fatalism and cynicism.

We lost the conviction and the passion. Even massacres were taken in stride by this peace process, incapable of producing genuine peace or of sustaining itself as an ongoing process. Even our "dignity"—such a hard-earned quality of human value—had been pounded by pettiness into a negotiating commodity of hollow shells. The principle of domination and control had been conceded, and we had been handed "dignity" as a soiled handkerchief with which to wipe our public shame and humiliation. The Israeli soldier who would control our entry at the bridge would be "invisible" behind a one-way mirror. Our leaders would cross with "VIP status" and a Palestinian flag would be permitted on the roof of the building instead of inside it. I remembered the days in which people died raising the flag, wearing the flag, earning substance and recognition for the flag. We concealed it in our hearts and wore it as a badge of pride and defiance. It had taken courage to proclaim the dignity of the forbidden flag then. Now we could wear it and bear it with Israel's permission as a consolation at having relinquished control over our land and destiny. We had always lived with the conviction that the Palestinians were very important people because of our human commitment and will, because of our innate dignity as people of courage and destiny in harmony with our history and vision. We had no need of Israeli cards to acknowledge our status.

The first meeting of the Board of Commissioners of the Palestinian Independent Commission for Human Rights (soon to become for Citizens' Rights) took place in Jerusalem at the same time as the Hebron massacre and its aftermath—perhaps as another of history's supreme ironies, or maybe as a particularly humorless retaliation at our having dared to intrude on its oblivious course.

All members were of the mind that the commission had to have teeth, the legal basis and mandate to hold the political executive accountable, even though in a transitional capacity until the election of the legislative council. I spoke out against the deteriorating turn of the talks. In Amman in late April, following a particularly fruitful and uplifting meeting of the Board of Commissioners, I gave a public talk on the loss of vision and volition that seemed to characterize the Palestinian side in the negotiations. Intelligence reports reached Tunis the same day, and news of Abu Ammar's anger began to reach me. I went home and sensed a heaviness in the air, an almost palpable dread among the intellectual and political elite, and a somber almost stony apathy among the public at large. Worse than pain, worse than rage, this loss of spirit immobilized us like a murky hypnotic trance. What happened to the spark, the glimmer, the mischievous twinkle in the dark eyes of children who had been nursed on defiance and the women whose fathomless eyes used to smolder with determination and an agenda for life? That same week Faisal obtained a draft of the Gaza-Jericho agreement being negotiated in Cairo with the "good offices" of the Americans, the Norwegians, and the Egyptians. Christopher was in the area and was badly in need of a foreign policy victory and another international spectacle to bolster his domestic standing. Besides, Mubarak of Egypt was celebrating his birthday on May 4. Popular humor claimed that our leadership gave expensive birthday presents—the Oslo agreement to Israeli Foreign Minister Peres, and the Gaza-Jericho agreement to Egyptian President Mubarak. "Look out for birthdays!" was a common warning when setting up any date. "You never know what they'll give away next!"

We met at Faisal's house in ʿEin Sinia just north of Ramallah. Saeb Erakat, Nabeel Kassis, Nathmi al-Juʾbeh, Ziad Abu Zayyad, Ali Safarini (a legal adviser), Faisal, and I, for the first time since Washington, were able to examine actual negotiations documents. As we waded through the details of the draft agreement, we were horrified. Once again we felt it was time for us to intervene, although we were fully aware that forces beyond our control had shaped the conduct and substance of the talks and were pressing for a hasty signature. We decided to study the documents, prepare written analyses and suggestions, then meet again at my house the next day to collate our responses and relay them to Tunis. Several others joined us the next day, and we were unanimous in recommending that the draft agreement should not be signed.

Once again, we argued, the Palestinian side had failed to get guarantees barring Israel from taking unilateral steps and measures to prejudge the fate of issues deferred to permanent-status talks, particularly Jerusalem and settlements. We also pointed out that Israel retained residual authority on legal as well as territorial issues, and had retained veto power and control over all steps of implementation. The agreement itself, we stressed, was in violation of the Fourth Geneva Convention and UNSC Resolutions 242 and 338, and formed a new and prejudicial legal reference against which all future steps would be measured. Ultimately, the agreement did not provide for actual Israeli withdrawal from Gaza and Jericho or for the gradual ending of the occupation, but had "reorganized" Israel's control of Palestinian land and lives with Palestinian approval and cooperation. In its implementation, the agreement was cumbersome, extremely complicated and unwieldy, and out of step with the specific needs on the ground of the Palestinians. By creating numerous areas of ambiguity and friction, the agreement could backfire or implode at any time.

For the next two days, we were on alert trying to persuade the PLO not to sign the agreement and to do damage control at home. A meeting with Christopher was scheduled for Monday, May 4, but I was reluctant to participate. Our meetings with the State Department had become perfunctory and formalistic, with the Americans dealing directly with Abu Ammar and the leadership in Tunis on any issues of substance that required pressure or decision making. I saw no need to keep up the appearance of serious meetings knowing that they had become a sham, and had no desire to participate in photo opportunities or meaningless press briefings. Although the rest of the delegation shared my reservations, they insisted that we should participate and convey our position directly and with uncompromising candor.

We went to the meeting with a clear agenda: Israel's continued human rights violations, the closure of Jerusalem and continued settlement activities, the imperative of effecting an unconditional release of Palestinian prisoners, and our reading of and reservations on the proposed agreement.

Christopher had been warned and he began with a sales pitch on how for the first time Palestinians would have "a place of their own." It was the only note I wrote down in the whole meeting. We went through the agenda with a distinct sense of déjà vu and ritual. Christopher went through the motions of listening, and we tried our best to be persuasive. Although I had decided not to speak, toward the end I felt I had to try one last time to set the record straight. "The issue is not to find a place of our own as you described it. We have always had a place of our own, Palestine. The problem has always been with others trying to take it away from us. Now we just want to keep it, or what's left of it." I then made a final attempt to reach him with an urgent personal statement. "More than anybody else, Faisal and I feel a sense of historical responsibility for this process. We both have been doing a lot of soul searching and self-questioning. We started with a vision of peace and a dream of freedom, and we took risks in pursuing them. But it wasn't for this that we had placed our lives on the line and endangered the safety and future of our children. We sought justice for our people and a lasting peace for the region. How can we justify such an agreement, such a diminution, such restrictions and constraints? Can you?" He replied in a monotone, "It's a first step," and never looked me in the eye. Faisal made a plea to postpone the signing on Wednesday, and Christopher turned to stone. The process we had participated in launching had changed its course and would in all probability claim us as its first victims. From where we stood, from this side of peace, the future seemed ominous and painful and far from peaceful. We could find no peace of mind.

Abu Ammar and Rabin were to meet in Cairo the next day, on Tuesday, May 3, one day before the official signing. We persisted. In a last-minute attempt to salvage whatever we could to spare the Palestinians further pain, we sent Abu Ammar a letter, signed by Faisal, asking him not to sign unless he could get several commitments from Rabin on the issues we had detailed earlier, and we outlined a few workable steps. We got no response. Abu Ammar had sent word asking us to attend the signing in Cairo on Wednesday, May 4. The other members of the original delegation and myself had neither the heart nor the will.

May 4 was also the second date we had selected to hold a press conference to announce the launching of the Commission for Citizens'

Rights, the first having been obliterated by the Hebron massacre at the end of February. Once again, I canceled and stayed home. Tuesday night, Emile, Amal, Zeina, and I sat outside in the garden and watched the stars stand still. I took time off from my nightly writing ritual, and the girls from their piano and clarinet practice. Emile played our guide in a floral universe of his creation, and we all listened to the gently flowing water chuckling to itself. Zeina was still proud that her picture had been in the paper showing us together at a demonstration for Jerusalem a few days earlier. She had finally persuaded me to take her with me; she had come into her own as a true protester. Amal was writing a poem for the school paper and preparing for exams. In less than two months, they would turn thirteen and seventeen; they had made the crucial passage from the six- and ten-year-old children who had witnessed the beginning of the *intifada* seven years ago. Emile's eyes warmly embraced the women in his life, and he strummed his guitar as he sang the song (usually performed by Feiruz, a female Lebanese singer) that I had chosen on our wedding:

> In my first country
> They welcomed me back,
> And said how much they had missed me.
> In my first country
> I became a little girl again
> Running down the streets
> And marveling at the size of the sky.
> In my first country
> Doves hovered overhead,
> They shielded me from the sun
> And became my parasol.
>
> I have two homelands, whose love made me weep—
> My first homeland cherished and nurtured me
> And your eyes, my love—
> Your eyes, my love, are my second homeland.

Tomorrow would signal a different passage and a difficult transition for all of us. That night we had taken time off, to relish our peace before The Peace broke out.

•   •   •

A few days later Amal showed me the poem she had been working on, one of such searing honesty that only people her age could write. It was about a Palestinian guide in Jerusalem. I accepted it both as a confession and a consolation. I also took upon myself the accusation and the blame:

The Guide
Amal Ashrawi

He used to lead the tourists
Down the cobbled streets.
He used to caress each stone
As friends who daily meet.
Each window a personal promise,
Each engraved door a pledge,
Each olive tree a vow of faith,
A story of eternal truth.
They forged his map
And changed his route—
Whom could he guide without a guide?
He feels the path, his feet are sure,
Despite the chart, the stones endure.
Though nothing but ruins still remain,
Unguidable memories of the past
Linger among the days that be
From house to house, from tree to tree.

CHAPTER SIXTEEN

————◆·•·◆·•·◆————

The sun on the Mount of Olives peered through passing clouds. A cool breeze chilled us, and we sat in a patchwork of light. Behind us, the Dome of the Rock variously shone golden or subdued depending on the interplay between sun and clouds. I assured Maher, our television host, that it would not rain. We sipped strong coffee, and tried to make sense of the blurred images on the small monitor placed on the tiled floor directly facing us. The Arabic commentary was coming through clearly, but the visual image was no match for the bright Jerusalem sun. I had arrived late to the interview site, having been stopped at the Israeli check-post that was part of the blockade on Jerusalem. As I took my seat, I could still hear the jeers of the young men who were made to leave their cars and stand on the sidewalk, barred from entering Jerusalem: "Is this the peace you're going to sign today? Tell the Old Man not to sign. Peace is made here not in Cairo. Let him come and stand in the lineup with us!" Angered and saddened, I made my way to Jerusalem—both the city and I wounded by peace.

We were a strange, yet familiar, gathering—Faisal, Haidar, and I next to the Islamic Movement representative, Sheikh Jamil Hamami, on top of the Mount of Olives against the backdrop of the Old City of Jerusalem, watching a fuzzy image of a signing in Cairo that would determine our future. We were being interviewed by the Arabic satellite station, MBC. Transformed from movers to spectators, we had chosen at this moment to keep our distance and our dignity. When asked why we did not go to Cairo, both Faisal and I replied, "Because our place is in Jerusalem."

Was this an international birthday celebration or a wake? Was this one of Oslo's minefields or the inevitable outcome of the grand quest for peace that we had embarked on with such confidence and hope?

"You and I," I told Faisal during the interview portion not televised, "will be called upon to give an account to history."

He nodded sadly. "We carried out our mission faithfully. Perhaps that was our flaw," Faisal said.

Around us, and all over the hills of Jerusalem, wildflowers were blazing in that last brilliant explosion of color of the season.

Abu Ammar hesitated. The world held its breath. This time, the last-minute drama was enacted onstage. The signing took place. A clearly agitated Abu Ammar rifled through documents and maps, scribbled his addenda, then appended his signature. It was business as usual everywhere else except in this tortured part of the world. We were left to deal with the daily and mundane business of peace as designed for us by others.

In responding to Maher's question of what next, I said, "The agreement is now fact. We can neither change it nor nullify it. It is in nobody's interest to sabotage it. The pressing issue now is how to transform this agreement with all its shortcomings and handicaps into a viable starting point for the building process that lies ahead. The challenge is in its conscious transmutation from a restrictive siege into a liberating and incremental process of reconstruction." The challenge, the enormity of it were overwhelming, and I felt weighted down under its pressure. Palestinian people went around in a daze, still trying to find their bearings.

"Aren't you pleased with the agreement?" one Israeli reporter asked me as I was leaving the Mount of Olives. "Name one Palestinian who is," I replied. Joy had no room in our lives then. We were no longer afraid to hope; we knew too much to even dare to hope.

The first steps of implementation were delayed, and then moved forward only in fits and starts. All eyes were turned toward Gaza and Jericho, looking toward the crossing points for the first signs of the promised Palestinian police. A journalist from the *New York Times* told me she had never seen people approach independence with such a sense of gloom and foreboding. I compared the celebration of democracy in South Africa with our lot: "I find it sad that while Mandela is triumphant in ending apartheid and claiming his people's inheritance, we are legalizing apartheid in Palestine by this agreement and entering a diminished phase of nation building with sorrow and reluctance. The fact that our first sign of independence is the arrival of the police force encapsulates the irony." Mandela had told us not to forget them when we had our state, and now it was our turn to tell our gentle and dignified friend not to forget us in his triumph.

The people, confused, were still shocked. All the traditional factions had faced and failed their historical test and were now called upon to rethink their platforms and structures in light of the agreement. The opposition who sought to sabotage and destroy the agreement had to come to grips with the fact that they had no alternative to offer and that reality was being shaped before their very eyes where their slogans could no longer prevail or apply. Those who wanted to stand by the sidelines and bide their time also knew that they could be abandoned by history, and that a total collapse would destroy them as well. The failure of the PLO would bring the Islamic opposition to the forefront as the strongest alternative, not the left-wing opposition. A crisis of the soul held the intellectuals in its grip, and cries for a new national consensus were being heard with increasing frequency.

The one objective that seemed to offer a means of national salvation was democracy, and everybody latched on to it for dear life. Elections became the rallying point for mainstream and opposition alike as a national safety net.

One consequence of the agreement was that it had created the misleading impression that peace was at hand, and thus gave the whole world leave to wash its hands of the Palestinian question and turn its attention elsewhere. Along with our voice we had lost our moral edge. Those of us who cried foul sounded peevish and petty before the grandeur of the historical moment of reconciliation, at least as it was packaged and presented by the media. And who were we to cloud the image with reality?

Women sensed the danger first. Their sensibilities fine-tuned to impending upheavals, they felt the rumblings and the first tentative tremors of a national earthquake. We began to suffer a creeping disenfranchisement as political deals were being made and institutions of the political authority were being established. PECDAR (Palestinian Economic Council for Development and Reconstruction) did not have a single woman on its Board of Governors, and when the time came for filling administrative posts not a single woman applied. We called for a national program of affirmative action and conscious recruitment. The Legal Review Committee established in Tunis did not have any women members, and the first draft of the Basic Law reflected in clear discriminatory terms this glaring absence. Women legal experts and committees began their own review, and a coordinating committee started work on a Declaration of Women's Rights as a charter to govern the legal and effective definition of women's rights. We began a campaign to empower women and ensure their participation in all political, economic, and social spheres on an equal participatory basis. "We will not go back to the kitchen."

Thus when the issue of participation in the National Authority came up, the women's (and my personal) dilemma was very real. On the one hand the women were critical of the agreement and aware of the implications of its implementation, and on the other hand they stressed participation and nondiscrimination. On the one hand, they were aware of the influential role women could play from positions of power, and on the other, they supported the idea of institutions of civil society as a safeguard for democracy and our basic rights and freedoms. Women knew very well that they could be the first to be sacrificed for political expediency and thus felt the imperative and urgency of claiming their territory immediately. While we pushed for the appointment of women as members of the Authority, I came under increasing pressure to "put my money where [my] mouth is."

When Faisal called me from Tunis and asked me on behalf of Abu Ammar and the Executive Committee to accept my appointment to the National Authority, I told him that I had already made up my mind and that my commitment was to the Palestinian Independent Commission for Citizens' Rights. I did promise Faisal to assist in his efforts at getting credible candidates with the national credentials and abilities to form a strong and capable Authority. He took this to be a positive attitude, which he relayed to Abu Ammar as such. That same evening, Abu Ammar officially conveyed a list of fourteen names, including mine, as potential candidates, to Rabin in order to facilitate the entering of the Palestinian police force, which had been held up at the bridge. Nabil Shaᵓth announced the names and confirmed that they had all been consulted and had accepted individually. That evening I was in Jerusalem attending the opening session of a seminar at Birzeit University. Faisal called me there with the news, and I was taken aback by the use of my name, knowing I had turned down the offer.

Meetings and consultations ensued with potential candidates for the National Authority, representatives of different political factions, and with concerned national figures. At our first meeting, we agreed that the emphasis should be on an agreed platform and work plan rather than on names, and we set about preparing drafts and suggestions to present to the Executive Committee. I promised Faisal to help him persuade individuals with the required credentials—ability, integrity, national commitment, and public support as well as the willingness to undertake such a responsibility. While I was fully supportive of the formation of a PNA on the basis of such criteria, I also felt that our main challenge ahead was an integrated and comprehensive process of nation building and reconstruction, which required more than a police force and a political authority. We had to build the substance of the state, including the institutions of civil society, of participatory democracy and accountability, as well as the systems and structures that would regulate their work and bear the weight of statehood. The independence of the judiciary had to be guaranteed, while free and fair general elections must be held for a separate legislative council. The mentality, attitudes, and work procedures of the past were no longer applicable, and the worst thing our leadership could do would be to superimpose these on a new reality with a human substance that would reject them. It was up to us, I was convinced, to ease the transition and to ensure that the principles we had espoused and defended for so long would be translated into fact as the operative norms and systems of our future. My position on accepting a post in the PNA remained unchanged.

Abu Ammar would not take no for an answer. He was already unhappy with press reports (as well as personal reports of a more malicious nature) detailing my criticisms of the Gaza-Jericho agreement. The letters I had sent him on behalf of the Palestinian Independent Commission for Citizens' Rights had made some people nervous knowing that we took our work seriously.

When Abu Ammar sent for me a second time, I felt I had to go to set the record straight. Faisal and I left on Wednesday, May 25, and arrived in Tunis in time for a late lunch with Abu Ammar. Munib al-Masri, a wealthy Palestinian nationalist and a good friend, had already agreed to join the PNA, and had been the most persistent in trying to recruit people like myself and Mahmoud Darwish to the Authority.

Lunch was cordial. No, Abu Ammar insisted, he bore no grudge at my reported mutiny but rather respected my honesty and forthrightness. I told him: "Even when I was spokesperson, you never interfered or tried to tell me what to say. We look to you to protect and respect freedom of thought and expression."

He was adamant that he did. "You are more than a sister to me and I will always defend your right to speak out."

"Then you understand why I spoke out and still have to speak out about the shortcomings of this agreement. It certainly is not to our advantage, but we have to try to succeed in spite of it. Nation building goes beyond the constraints of this accord, and that is why my work with the commission is important as part of the comprehensive and integrated institution-building process that is capable of laying the foundations for statehood. A nation is more than security and political authority."

His response was immediate. "I was the first to support the work of your commission and I endorsed it publicly on my official trips. I understand your motives and objectives, but I still need you for the Authority."

This became the motif of many subsequent meetings. These meetings were intense and demanding, but we emerged with an "officially approved" statement that included the terms, basic principles, and work plan for the Authority, which was later endorsed by the PLO's Executive Committee. The real test remained in the implementation, and the first signs were not encouraging, especially with Abu Ammar's retention of some people who had been unacceptable to many of the PNA members for reasons of political credibility, personal integrity, or professional capability. My participation in these meetings, plus some deliberately leaked anonymous tips by PLO officials, sent conflicting messages to the media. While I consistently repeated my position on refusing membership in the Authority, press reports were rife with rumors that I had accepted. Emile and the girls were concerned that I might succumb under pressure. Munib al-Masri was still trying to form a strong combination that could lend the Authority credibility and efficiency, and in that context he told Abu Ammar that I would give him my final response in the next meeting of the PNA. When we got down to business, however, I informed Abu Ammar and the whole membership that I would not be joining the Authority.

Faisal had agreed to join, but on condition that this would not prejudice his status and work in Jerusalem. When it later became an either-or situation, he chose Jerusalem over the Authority, and in a subsequent meeting of representatives of Palestinian institutions in Jerusalem we gave him the mandate to take up the cause of the city on all our behalf. Saeb Erakat, after vehemently protesting that he would not join as a matter of principle, came back from a meeting with Abu Ammar having given his consent. Akram, whom Abu Ammar was trying to recruit as the Authority's secretary, refused to even consider the post. The opposition stayed out for the time being. Abu Ammar's cabinet was certainly taking a long time to be formed.

As Faisal and I flew back to Jerusalem, I could not help wondering whether this was a grand gesture or a great escape. As a child I had once run away from home precisely to make a point. I won, but the victory had left me with a haunting wistfulness and a sense of irretrievable loss. With a ten-year-old's conviction of injustice and victimization, I had rebelled against my mother's "cruelty" for making me practice the piano instead of allowing me to go cycling with my friends. After writing her a passionate note, I took off on my bicycle and pedaled all the way to Jerusalem to the hospital where my father was spending the last days of his prison sentence. (My sister Huda insists I had been reading Mark Twain then.) Having sent the nurse out to buy me my favorite comic books (and to call my mother, I suspect), my father listened patiently to my indignant recounting of my tragic plight and promised to try his best. Thus I was spared the torture of piano lessons and practice, and went cycling off into the sunset while my sister Nadia went on to become a pianist, and to teach my daughters later on. Now as I listen to Amal playing with talent and dedication, along with my pride and pleasure I always feel the stirring of an urge like a static impulse that runs through my fingers but produces no music.

I could discern no harmony emerging from the agreement or the formation of the National Authority, and the score seemed to promise jarring dissonance. I had made a promise to serve the people and the cause with *amanah,* and to do so I was convinced that my place lay outside the political domain. Mine was the difficult choice, and I was aware that in all probability it would be a lonely and painful task. But it had to be done, and I was determined to proceed.

The third meeting of the Board of Commissioners of the Palestinian Independent Commission for Citizens' Rights was scheduled to be held in Stockholm during the third week of June at the invitation of the foreign minister, my good friend Margaretha af Ugglas. We studied the Nordic ombudsman institutions and met with their various representatives as well as with international human rights commissioners. Following a brief stop in London to give a speech, I proceeded to South Africa on my first visit to the country, a trip now possible after the elections. Previously, I used to meet with Mandela and African National Congress members outside of both South Africa and Palestine, and I was excited about our first meeting at "home." The magic of "one person, one vote" had brought apartheid to its knees and South Africa to triumph with Mandela at its head claiming the inheritance and glory of his people. I longed to see him again with the innocent yearning of a child for its parent, of the weary for repose, and of the dispossessed for empowerment.

The magic touched me, and as we embraced I rested my head on his shoulder.

"Help us reclaim what is ours. Bring us home too," I implored. And he sensed my sorrow.

"How can I help?" he asked.

"Teach us the secret of your calm, of your dignity and your power, so that we too may share the glory of the moment," I responded. "We have been sadly diminished, but we too can lay claim to you, for you do not belong to only one race or one nation. The whole world has taken comfort and inspiration from your stature and guidance, and we in particular need you."

"I know how you feel. You have had to sign an unjust agreement, and you have a difficult road ahead."

"We tried to stop the signing, at least until we got certain amendments on legislation and territorial jurisdiction plus guarantees on Jerusalem and the settlements while solving the issue of prisoners and deportees. We were unsuccessful," I admitted sadly.

"We also expressed our reservations. But now we have to look ahead, and I would like to be helpful. I have a personal fondness for Yasser Arafat and a deep sense of loyalty and commitment to the Palestinian cause. You were the first to stand by us and support our struggle, and we shall never forget that. I shall be the first to come and visit Yasser on Palestinian soil."

"The Palestinian people as a whole will appreciate that, as would Abu Ammar. All over the world, people look to you for hope and courage, for guidance and leadership. I know it's a difficult burden to bear, but you have signaled a new era in global politics and the discourse of democratic inclusion and genuine empowerment. No one can provide the leadership and vision that you do, and there is no one of your stature and humanity. Your triumph is ours as well, but we still need to take on your patience and your wisdom."

As he embraced and comforted me, I felt a calm spread into my heart like a soothing balm applied to an open wound. Mandela's humility and serenity and his gentleness of spirit created a majesty and splendor throughout the world. I doubted whether he was fully aware of the power he wielded, or of the intense fascination and loyalty he evoked in the imagination of the world at large. He had reached out and removed the veil that had screened our vision to reveal the potential, the very real possibility, of a different future. His black eyes and large hands held the warmth and power of genuine humility stored up over centuries of deprivation in the spiritual coffers of a race long denied. I longed for a similar affirmation, for the miraculous healing of my own people. Having lived in captivity under occupation most of my life, and having spent much of my present wandering throughout the world on a pilgrimage of peace, it was in South Africa that I felt the first intimations of an overwhelming homecoming.

Violent storms ravaged Cape Town, known also as the Cape of Storms and the Cape of Good Hope. I was witness to both attributes, the recipient of two disparate offerings from the edge of Africa where two oceans met and clashed and where ancient travelers feared falling off the rim of the world. I reveled in the raging storm, in the drama of the massive waves lashing at the jagged rocks with the pent-up fury of ages. Fortified by Mandela's calm, I walked out into the storm invigorated by its force, twice humbled by man and nature. This, I felt, was the essence of harmony, the heart of repose.

As gray gave way to silver, a strange sheen seemed to well up from the depths of the turbulent ocean and cast an eerie glow over the long-troubled land. Andre Brink, the South African writer, his wife, and I were sharing a quiet dinner in the midst of the storm. He presented me with a signed copy of his latest book, *On the Contrary,* and pointed out a quotation of exhortation for reconciliation that he had borrowed from our Madrid speech. "I have used your language long before I met you," he gently acknowledged. "We have shared much more than words long before we met," I responded. And we recognized each other in the silvery glow of the storm and the warm candlelight of our communion.

Recognition extended also to embrace many others who formed the South African human tapestry. With former President F. W. de Clerk, now first deputy, who had recognized the magnitude and inevitability of the moment, I shared coffee and revelations. With Frene Ginwala, the Speaker of the National Assembly and a woman with the power of perception, I shared recollections of the past, visions of the future, and the unbreakable bond of womanhood. With the leaders of Inkatha and the Freedom Front, I shared the meaning of inclusion and participatory democracy as harmony in diversity. With Ministers Asmal, Pahad, and others, I shared memories of exile and the challenge of the future. With human rights and legal commissioners, I shared the pain of their past and our present as well as reverence for the rule of just laws. With Jessie Duarte and the other women of the ANC, I shared the absence of fear and intimidation as well as the knowledge of a struggle yet to be won. With the Jewish community leaders, I shared candor and the common definition of the courage required to embrace peace. With the leaders of the Muslim community I shared the realism of relative justice and the imperative of reconciliation. With all, I shared the incredible wealth of human will to triumph and the certainty of an impending calm. But in Soweto, I saw all the Palestinian refugee camps concentrated in a sea of misery yearning for human and historical redemption, and I was reminded of the even more difficult and painful tests yet to come.

When Emile and Akram called to inform me of Abu Ammar's intended return to the land of Palestine at least as it was currently defined within the confines of Gaza-Jericho, I knew I had to be there for his homecoming. After two sleepless nights and a heroic effort on the part of my hosts to get me back on time, I got on a flight to Cairo that landed a mere half hour before Abu Ammar's plane. I stood on the tarmac at the edge of the red carpet in the sizzling heat of the Egyptian sun, along with the Egyptian prime minister and cabinet members as well as Palestinian officials, including Nabil Sha'th. I first saw him through the window, and as he came down the stairs he smiled. Abu Ammar embraced me warmly, then he looked at me directly and said as if with a sense of wonder, "You did come!"

"Yes," I replied calmly. "I did."

He was on his way to a land denied him for more than a quarter of a century, leaving behind almost three million exiles and returning to the two million Palestinians who had languished under a brutal Israeli occupation for close to three decades. His was an ambivalent homecoming, fraught with uncertainty, circumscribed by a flawed agreement, diminished by the dictates of the disequilibrium of power and self-preservation. We had struggled to bring about his recognition and return, but was this the real return and legitimization we had so ardently sought? The PLO was the expression and embodiment of our national identity and unity. Had we brought it back divided and dismembered to rule part of the people on fragments of the land? Or had Israel brought it back only to contain it within restricted terrain under its own watchful eyes and subject to its approval? How did our dreams shrivel and our vision blur? At what price had we bought this homecoming? Was Jericho the Dead Sea

apple seducing the weary wanderer and Gaza the blinding glare for un-
wary warriors? Or had we actually embarked on the first step of a long
journey to peace at the end of which true redemption awaits the pilgrim
whose soul has been seared by longing and pain?

I did go to Cairo to meet him, and I flew to El Arish on his plane,
crossing the border at Rafah to enter the Gaza Strip. I looked for the one-
way mirrors that the Palestinian and Israeli delegations had spent hours
negotiating over, but saw only very visible Israeli soldiers with lethal
weapons in one hand and permits written in Hebrew in the other. They
made an effort to be civil lest we entertain the misconception that we
were still under occupation. But in Gaza, we were met with a human
explosion—thousands of Palestinians with banners in their hands, chants
on their lips, tentative hope in their hearts, and questions mingled with
tears in their eyes. He kept me beside him, and asked me if I had changed
my mind. "No," I said. "I know where my priorities lie." The heat, humid-
ity, and sand lashed at us, ruthlessly, oblivious of the Mediterranean
breeze that was gently blowing from the sea whispering a tantalizing
promise of relief.

Two days later, we drove through burning roadblocks set up by Israeli
settlers to receive Abu Ammar once again, this time in Jericho. As we
descended to the lowest place on earth, our ears ringing with the increasing pressure, I caught myself unconsciously scanning the unfolding Jordan Rift Valley for a long-forgotten pillar of salt, and I consciously willed
myself not to look back.

The homecoming drama was played out once again. Abu Ammar's
Egyptian helicopter landed in Jericho at the "rest place," a transitional
station for travelers who usually cross the bridge from Jordan on their
way to the West Bank. Israeli and American television helicopters hovered
overhead as he inspected the guard, greeted the dignitaries, and headed
for the podium. The expected crowds did not show up; they had been
turned away either by Israeli army roadblocks or by settler violence. The
rest of the West Bankers, still under Israeli occupation, did not exhibit
much enthusiasm for the occasion. But those who did show up displayed
the frenzy and the dazed sense of displacement typical of a crowd suddenly released from a long incarceration. I had been asked to sit in the
front row on the podium, but I found a seat on the side hidden from
view by the speakers and the security guards, and then settled down to
observe this latest spectacle.

Jericho had always been the green oasis of the Jordan Valley, and the
warm refuge for the winter-chilled Palestinians of the surrounding

heights. Despite the helicopters hovering overhead, the television camera towers looming before us, and the unruly throng pressing forward, I mentally lifted the shimmering veil of the heat and saw myself as a child in our Jericho winter home holding my father's hand and setting off on a guided tour of the garden. The trees that my father had planted grew as I grew up, steadily seeking the sun, surrounded by warmth and tended with care. Oranges, lemons, grapefruits, pomelos peered enticingly from their lush green winter nests, while in summer languid date clusters dangled in utter abandon from the palm trees. We inspected each tree carefully, my father and I. His was the peasant pride at making nature respond and yield its splendor, while mine was the wonder and the anticipation of a feast of flavors to be tasted. Such was the substance of the peace and certainty that I spent the rest of my life seeking. I grew up and he died. I never went back to our Jericho garden.

As we proceeded to the hall for the swearing in of the members of the Palestinian National Authority, Abu Ammar asked me for the last time, "And you?"

Again, I replied, "I can't."

Already the offices of the Commission for Citizens' Rights in Jerusalem were receiving a flood of cases and complaints. The test we were all facing was the most difficult of all, for we had come full circle to begin our internal quest. Would he, would we, pass the ultimate test of *amanah* with our people? Abu Ammar, with his military and political authorities, was launching a new phase of the quest for statehood from the confines of Gaza-Jericho. Other Palestinians, including myself, had launched the quest for nationhood and democracy through institutions of civil society. A Palestinian Genesis had begun, launched from the chaos and pain of a past almost beyond time.

My personal narrative is also unfolding. Often when I find the pain of self-inflicted wounds unbearable, as on my inspection of interrogation cells where Palestinians used violence on other Palestinians, or when I investigate cases of dark deals concluded in secret, I am reminded of the words of an Old English poem, "Deor." As the poet catalogues a series of past disasters, whether with the comitatus or of personal import, he repeats at the end of each stanza a formula of consolation for the present misfortune: "All that passed, so may this." Our catalogue of disasters from a past almost beyond time is long, but it passed. So may this.

My pledge to unfolding time is Amal and Zeina, Emile and our garden. From there I drive to Jerusalem every day where I take upon myself the pain of a people still in a state of emergence, still longing for *amanah* and peace, both from the world outside and from their reality within. Thus, once again, we recount an ancient narrative but with a new beginning. Once more we shall undertake a confrontation with history, unrepentant and untamed, but armed with the knowledge of our own sorrow and in possession of the full potential of a joy yet to come.

INDEX

NOTE: HA refers to Hanan Ashrawi; DOP refers to Declaration of Principles.

Abboushi, Nadia Mikhail (sister), 19, 20–21, 32, 34, 135, 167, 169, 297
Abboushi, Sameh (brother-in-law), 32, 34
Abd Rabbo, Yasser, 115, 236, 266, 278: and bilateral talks, 244; and Christopher, 236; and deportations, 223; and Israeli elections, 210; and Jordan-PLO relationship, 122; and multilateral talks, 190, 193; and U.S.-P.L.O. dialogue, 59
Abdel-Rahim, Tayyeb, 96, 99, 139, 190, 209, 210, 275
Abdel-Shafi, Haidar, 157, 177–78, 182, 200, 222; as against returning to talks, 240–41; and Arafat-Palestinian delegation meeting, 240–41; arrests of, 211, 212; and beginning of peace process, 83–84; and bilateral talks, 159, 162, 259, 262; and Cairo Agreement signing, 291–92; commitment to peace process of, 182; and DOP, 250, 262; and Egyptian-Palestinian meeting, 136–139; HA's relationship with, 162–63; and intifada, 49; and Madrid

Conference, 140, 144, 145, 146, 147–148; Mikhail (Daud) compared with, 163; as Palestinian delegation member, 174; and Palestinian delegation selection, 125; personality of, 162
Abu Zayyad, Ziad: 277, 286–87
Abul-Lutof (aka Farouq al-Kaddoumi), 174, 184, 189, 202, 274–75, 279
accountability, 157–58, 230, 232, 279, 280, 281, 286, 295
administrative detention, 181
affirmative action, 294
Agazarian, Albert, 39–40, 41, 42, 142, 143, 144, 147
Agha, Zakariyya al-, 117, 259; and beginning of peace process, 82, 88, 90; and multilateral talks, 189, 190, 194; as Palestinian delegation member, 180–81
Aker, Mamdouh al-, 49, 50, 80, 146, 147, 185, 240–41, 259, 281
Ala, Abu (aka Ahmad Qreiʾ), 220, 221, 239, 260, 265, 266, 267, 275, 279
Aloni, Shulamit, 60, 220, 260
"alternative homeland," 122–23

"alternative leadership," 185
American University of Beirut, 19–20, 25, 28, 69, 70, 163
Amery, Suad al-, 60–61, 185, 259
Amjad (Cyprus contact), 98, 102, 189
Amman, Jordan, 136; and Arafat-Palestinian delegation meeting, 239, 240–41; Mikhail family exile in, 22–24; Palestinian-U.S. meeting in, 95–101
Ammar, Abu. *See* Arafat, Yasser
Andersson, Sten, 59, 200–201
Ankara, Turkey: reception at, 191
al-Aqsa Mosque massacre (1990), 65, 73–74
Arab coordination, 151–52, 154, 172, 259, 274
Arab foreign ministers, 194, 239, 241–242
Arab Summit (Baghdad, 1990), 67
Arab-Israeli War (1967), 9, 19–21
Arafat, Yasser, 54, 193, 202, 257, 275; and Arab foreign ministers meeting, 239, 241–42; Ashrawi family's relationship with, 54; and Assad, 154, 239, 240; and backchannel talks, 183–184, 218, 238; and Baker ultimatum, 110; and Baker's Middle East visits, 95–96, 97, 98–99; and beginning of peace process, 80, 81–82, 92; and bilateral talks, 158, 159, 171, 218, 237, 243, 244; and Cairo Agreement, 288, 292; as charismatic leader, 205–6; and Christopher's Middle East visits, 236, 252; complexities facing, 183–84, 185; "death" of, 202–3; and deportations, 223; and DOP, 250, 253–54, 255, 263, 264–71, 278; and Egypt, 137, 138; and "Gaza/Gaza-Jericho first" option, 251, 253, 259; and Gulf War, 69, 70, 71; HA's first meeting with, 267; HA's relationship with, 27, 28, 104, 183, 193, 205, 210, 258–59, 283–84, 286, 295–96, 298, 300–301; health of, 103, 206, 209–10; on Jordan, 123–24; and Letter of Invitation, 130; and Madrid Conference, 130, 139–40, 146, 147, 148–49, 153; and Madrid delegation, 125, 126, 127, 129; and multilateral talks, 189, 197; Nobel Prize for, 9, 11; official visits of, 279, 280; and Oslo talks, 258; Palestinian defiance of, 178–179; and Palestinian delegation meeting,
239, 240–41; and Palestinian delegation resignation, 255, 256–57, 258; and Palestinian public opinion, 283–84; and Palestinian six-point requirements, 236, 237; and Palestinian-Christopher meeting, 253–254; personnel appointments of, 176; plane crash of, 202–3; and pre-Madrid talks, 121–22, 124; provisional government of, 276; public reception of Palestinian delegation by, 210–11; and Rabin, 11, 53, 271, 276–77; and reception on return from plane crash, 204–6; return to Palestine of, 300–302; and a return to talks, 240–42; secret meetings with, 102–5, 106, 107, 149–150, 203, 204–6; style of, 104–5; and Swedish talks, 59; and territorial jurisdiction, 251–52; and U.N. Resolution 242, 218; U.N. speech of, 59; undermining of, 284; and U.S.-PLO dialogue, 58; Washington welcome for, 263–64; Western image of, 28; and White House Lawn ceremony, 11, 53, 263, 264–72, 273–74. *See also* Palestine Liberation Organization; *specific person*
Asfour, Hassan, 183, 245, 260, 266
Ashrawi, Amal (daughter): birth of, 34–35, 248; childhood of, 36; effects of HA's activities on, 52, 111–12; effects of occupation on, 208–9; in England, 207, 208, 209; personality of, 34–35, 112; as a pianist, 297; as poet, 289, 290; U.S. visit of, 208–9; and *Zeina the Bee*, 155. *See also* Ashrawi family
Ashrawi, Emile (husband), 36, 50, 52, 98, 99, 117, 167, 300; and assassination attempt, 115; birth of, 248; birthday of, 164, 170; courtship/marriage of, 31, 32–34, 248, 289; and Daud Mikhail's death, 170; Daud Mikhail's relationship with, 163–64; family of, 33; as father, 34–35; and HA's birthday, 277–78; and media misrepresentation of HA, 203–4; personality of, 31, 32–33, 112–113; as supportive husband, 112–13, 164, 255. *See also* Ashrawi family
Ashrawi family: and al-Aqsa Mosque massacre, 74; Arafat's relationship with, 54; and beginning of peace process, 92; daily activities of, 289; effects of

demonstrations on, 41, 43–44; and family days, 226–27; and Gulf War, 72–73, 75–77; and HA's appointment to PNA, 296; and HA's birthday, 278; HA's pledge to, 302–3; knowledge of prison life of, 78; and *intifada*, 53–54; and Palestinian delegation resignation, 255–256; and return from Madrid Conference, 156, 157; as supportive of HA, 129

Ashrawi, Hanan Mikhail: arrests of, 31–32, 108–9, 111–12, 113–15, 117, 211, 212, 215–16; assassination attempts on, 114–15, 216–17; birth of, 22, 47, 267; birthdays of, 73–74, 113, 116–17, 277–78; "calling" of, 25; childhood/youth of, 22–25, 35–36, 47, 165–66, 191–92, 297, 302; as Christian, 24; as college student, 19–21; courtship/marriage of, 31, 32–34, 248, 289; cultural legacy of, 29; early activism of, 25–28, 29–30, 43–47; education of, 24, 25, 28–30, 33, 191–92; as faculty member, 31–32, 38–43, 175, 179, 187; guilt of, 117; jealousy toward, 205; as mother, 34–35, 43–44, 52, 62, 111–113, 116–17, 208, 255–56; naming of, 134, 135; negotiating experience of, 39–40; narrative of, 134, 302–3; Palestinian attacks on, 228, 229; personal notebook of, 192; poetry of, 89; self-image of, 34, 35; threats against, 90, 113–15, 117, 145; in U.S. as student, 28–30; validation of, 94; as writer, 191–93

Ashrawi, Ibrahim (brother-in-law), 31, 32

Ashrawi, Zeina (daughter), 207–8, 224; as activist, 289; birth of, 248; effects of HA's activities on, 52, 111–12; effects of occupation on, 208–9; Israeli friendships of, 38; personality of, 35, 112; U.S. visit of, 208–9. *See also* Ashrawi family

Assad, Hafez al-, 117, 154, 239, 240

Awadallah-Musleh, Nuha, 135, 143

back-channel negotiations: beginning of, 199; and bilateral talks, 171, 183, 218; and "Dutch connection," 220; in London, 221; PLO strategy for, 183–84; reasons for, 199; rumors about, 250; spiral patterns of, 221; U.S. views of,

239. *See also* Oslo (Norway) talks; Palestinian-Israeli dialogue

Baker, Akram, 89, 130

Baker, James: abandonment of peace process by, 219; anger at Palestinians of, 127–28, 152; and bilateral talks, 160; and Five-Point Framework, 58; and Gulf War, 11, 74; and human dimension, 59, 89; initiates peace process, 79–94; and Madrid Conference, 59, 147, 148–49, 152, 153; and media, 100–101; Middle East visits of, 79–94, 95–101, 125–29, 172, 213, 216–17; and multilateral talks, 193; and Palestinian acceptance of Letter of Invitation, 130; Palestinian meetings with, 81–83, 95–101, 109–110, 115–20, 124, 126–29, 148–49; personality of, 82; and PLO, 68, 99, 100–101, 119, 128; and PNC secret visit, 111; and settlement issue, 172; team of, 88–89, 199–200; threats of, 124; ultimatum to, 109–10; and U.S. elections, 213

"The Baker suit," 86–87, 118, 120, 144

Baz, Osama al-, 137, 239, 252, 277

Beilin, Yossi, 220, 221, 266, 267

Beirut, Lebanon, 19–20

bilateral talks: and Arab coordination, 154; Israeli demands concerning, 86; and land for peace, 83, 188; letter of invitation for, 237–38; and multilateral talks, 188–89; and Oslo talks, 244–45; and Palestinian delegation, 182; and Palestinian-Israeli dialogue, 238; and PLO, 117; purpose of, 188; and Rabin, 220; rescheduling of, 231–38; and a sense of mission, 185; timetable for, 221; timing of, 154; as two-phased, 83; and U.N. resolutions, 83; U.S. role in, 171, 238; venue of, 153–54. *See also specific round*

birthdays, 73, 74, 113, 116–17, 164, 170, 277–78, 286

Birzeit University: closure of, 42–43; HA as faculty member at, 31–32, 38–43, 175, 179, 187; Israeli army at, 39–43; student arrests/demonstrations at, 37, 39, 40–43

Birzeit University Legal Aid Committee, 32, 37, 78, 175

Black September (1970), 123

Boutros-Ghali, Boutros, 274
Brussels, Belgium, 60–62, 220, 279
Bush, George, 11, 74, 213, 219, 223

Cairo Agreement (1994), 11, 13, 282, 291–92. See also Gaza-Jericho agreement
Cairo, Egypt: Arab foreign ministers meeting in, 239, 241–42; Arab Summit in, 74; and Arafat-Rabin meeting, 276–277. See also Cairo Agreement (1994); Egypt
Camp David Accords, 10, 84, 93, 137, 138
Central Council, 241, 274, 278
children, 23, 53–56, 78, 89, 141–42, 167–68, 208–9, 226–27
Christmas, 74, 114, 197, 224
Christopher, Warren, 265, 270; and DOP, 253–55; and deportations, 229; and eight-point memorandum, 249; and Gaza-Jericho agreement, 286, 287; and human rights issues, 232; Middle East visits of, 231–35, 252; and one-on-one meetings, 232, 233–35, 237; Palestinian meetings with, 231–35, 249, 250, 252, 253–55, 287–88; and Palestinian six-point requirements, 233–36; personality of, 231–32; and PLO, 287; and U.S.-Palestinian relations, 237
Clinton, Bill, 213, 219, 236, 265, 270
co-sponsors: role in peace process of, 86, 199. See also Russia/Russians; United States
collaborators, Palestinian, 214–15
Commission for Citizens' Rights. See Palestinian Independent Commission for Citizens'/Human Rights
"Composite DOP," 252
Confidence Building Measures (CBMs), 120, 127
corridor diplomacy, 162, 171
couch negotiations, 162, 171

Darwish, Mahmoud, 94, 107, 245, 273, 295
Declaration of Independence (Palestinian), 53
Declaration of Principles: and bilateral talks, 259, 262–64; Central Council ratification of, 274, 278; and Christopher, 252, 253; criticisms of,

260–61; draft of, 242, 250, 251, 252, 253, 254; and "Gaza-Jericho first option," 253, 254, 255; HA's views about, 268; and insider-outsider tensions, 179; Jordan's reaction to, 274, 275; last minute changes to, 263, 264–271; negotiating committees for, 275–76, 278–79; and Oslo talks, 254, 260; Palestinian delegation's reaction to, 255–58, 261; and PLO, 251, 260; and side letter, 252–53; signing of, 11, 62, 181, 263, 264–72; and U.N. Resolution 904, 285
Declaration of Women's Rights, 294
Denmark, 280
"Deor" (Old English poem), 302
deportations: and Arafat-Rabin meeting, 277; and back-channel negotiations, 238–39; and bilateral talks, 238, 242; and Christopher, 231, 233; and DOP, 181; and effects of occupation, 89; and feelings of deportees, 181; increase in, 221; mass, 221–25; and media, 228; and peace process, 171–72, 228–29, 250; and postponement of talks, 241; and return of deportees, 181, 224, 229–230, 233, 238–39, 241, 242, 250; and U.N., 172, 224, 229, 230–31; and U.S.-Israeli agreements, 229; and U.S.-Palestinian talks, 229–31; and women, 229. See also specific person
dialogue: need for, 12–13. See also specific dialogue
Djerejian, Edward, 88, 250, 265, 266; and Arafat's "death," 203; and bilateral talks, 171, 199; and Letter of Invitation, 130; and Madrid Conference, 147; and postponing talks, 239; and pre-Madrid talks, 111, 117; and pro-Israeli stance of U.S., 111; verbal attack on Palestinians by, 199
DOP negotiations: criticisms of, 282. See also Cairo Agreement (1994); Gaza-Jericho agreement; specific issue
"Dutch connection," 220, 221

Eagleburger, Lawrence, 223, 229
"early empowerment," 252–53, 259
Economic Committee: creation of, 277
economic development, 13, 196
Egypt, 137, 184; and Gaza-Jericho agreement, 286; Israeli treaty (1979)

with, 10; and Madrid conference, 148; and Palestinian-Egyptian meeting, 136–139; and PLO, 137; Ten-Point Plan of, 58. *See also* Cairo Agreement (1994); Cairo, Egypt

elected council working group, 221

elections: Israeli, 200, 210, 211–13; Palestinian, 13, 84, 179, 198, 199–200, 218, 293, 295; PLO, 203–4; U.S., 213, 219

eleventh round (Washington, 1993), 259–262

Erakat, Saeb, 83, 240, 268: Arafat's relationship with, 178–79; and bilateral talks, 237, 259, 262; and deportations, 222; and DOP, 251–52, 254, 255, 262, 274–75; and Gaza-Jericho agreement, 286–87; and *intifada,* 49, 50; and Madrid Conference, 148–49; and Madrid delegation membership, 126, 131; and multilateral talks, 189, 190, 194; as Palestinian delegation member, 177, 178–79; and Palestinian delegation's resignation, 256; and Palestinian six-point requirements, 237; and PNA, 296–97; professional positions of, 177–78

European Community, 85–86, 143

European Union, 279

Executive Committee (PLO), 80, 236, 274; and Baker ultimatum, 110; and DOP, 263, 265, 266; and Madrid delegation, 125–26; and Palestinian delegation's resignation, 257–58; and PNA, 276, 295, 296; and postponement of talks, 241; and pre-Madrid talks, 121–22; public reception of Palestinian delegation by, 210; and White House Lawn ceremony, 263, 265, 266

extremists, 216, 283. *See also specific group*

Fahoum, Hayel al-, 266, 268–69, 271

Faisal, Saud al- (Saudi prince), 240, 243

Falasteen Muhammad Abdel-Rahim Barakat Nusseirat, 132–33

Fateh, 24, 25–26, 49, 115, 124, 267. *See also specific person*

feda'yeen, 25–26

feminism: in Palestine, 32, 60–61, 176–177. *See also* women

FIDA. *See* Palestinian Democratic Alliance

first round (Madrid, 1991), 151, 152–55

Five-Point Framework (Baker, 1989), 58

flag: Israeli, 21–22; Palestinian, 28, 45, 63, 119, 216, 234, 285

Follow-up Committee, 125, 243

Four Point Plan (PLO), 71

Fourth Geneva Convention, 118, 172, 198, 224, 229, 287

fourth round (Washington, 1992), 197–200

Friends Girls School, 24, 25

funerals, 55–56, 214

Gandhi, Indira, 149–50

gas masks, 73, 76

"Gaza first" option, 251

Gaza Strip: Arafat's return to, 11, 301; and Christopher, 252; closing off of, 12, 13; Egyptian control of, 22; *intifada* in, 37; Israeli occupation of, 9, 21–22; and Jordan, 123; militancy in, 180–81; and Palestinian delegation membership, 125; and return from Madrid Conference, 157; standard of living in, 14; violence in, 12

Gaza-Jericho: DOP negotiating committee for, 279

Gaza-Jericho agreement, 277, 286–87, 291–94, 295, 296

"Gaza-Jericho first option," 253, 254, 255, 259

General Union of Palestinian Students, 27

General Union of Palestinian Women, 60

Golan Heights, 9, 20, 67

Goldstein, Baruch, 217, 282

Great Britain, 165, 250

Guidance Committee, 141, 143, 150, 151

"The Guide" (Amal Ashrawi), 290

Gulf States, 184

Gulf War: HA's comments about, 74–75; beginning of, 69–72; curfew during, 76, 77; effects on Palestinians of, 75–77, 78–79; information network during, 76, 77; Iraq's surrender in, 83; and missile attacks, 77; outcomes of, 11, 78–79; Palestinian preparations for, 72–73; Palestinian "spies" in, 175; and PLO, 71, 72, 78–79, 81, 83, 101, 184–185; as "state of art" war, 74–75

The Hague: women's meetings at (1988), 59–60

The Hague Regulations, 198
Halevi, Ilan, 51–52, 151
Hamas (Islamic Resistance Movement), 11, 12, 13, 115, 184, 221–22, 224, 229
Haniyyeh, Akram, 71, 136, 178, 209, 268, 273–74, 275, 300; and Arafat secret visits, 103, 104, 106; and Arafat's "death," 202–3; Arafat's relationship with, 183; and Arafat's welcome to Washington, 263–64; and Baker, 96–97, 98, 110; and beginning of peace process, 80, 82, 92–93; and bilateral talks, 160, 171, 172, 236–37, 259; and DOP, 251–52; deportation of, 97–98; and early Palestinian-Israeli talks, 58; and hunger strike, 64; and Letter of Invitation, 130; and Madrid Conference, 144; and Madrid delegation membership, 125, 129; and media misrepresentation of HA, 204; and multilateral talks, 190, 193, 194; and narrative from within, 94; and Oslo talks, 259–60; as Palestinian delegation member, 181, 182–83; personal/professional background of, 58, 97–98; personality of, 58, 97, 98, 182–83; and PNA, 297; and PNC secret visit, 106, 107, 108; style of, 264–65; support of HA by, 204
Harb, Ahmad, 40–41, 42
Hassan (king of Morocco), 265–66
Hassan (prince of Jordan), 123, 136
hatta, 148–49
Hebron al-Ibrahimi Mosque massacre (1994), 65, 113, 185, 217, 282–83, 284, 285, 286
Hijjawi, Sulafa, 60–61
Hirschfeld, Ya'ir, 220, 221, 239, 260, 267
Holst, Johan, 202, 260
hospitality, Arab, 166–67, 168
Hull, Edmund, 88, 92
Human Chain (1990), 63–64
human element, 59, 89–90, 153, 185, 228, 282
Human Rights Action Project, 37, 39
human rights commission. See Palestinian Independent Commission for Citizens'/Human Rights
human rights issues, 67, 213–14, 216, 219; and Arafat-Rabin meeting, 277; and Baker, 100, 200; and beginning of peace process, 83, 90; and bilateral talks, 173, 198, 238, 243; and Christopher, 231, 233, 287–88; and DOP, 260, 261; and repression, 116, 200, 221–22; institutionalization of, 279; and Israeli elections, 212; and media, 173, 198; and Palestinian public opinion, 200; and peace process, 200, 221–22, 230; and PLO, 240; working groups on, 196, 243. See also deportations; Palestinian Independent Commission for Citizens'/Human Rights
hunger strike, 64–68
Hussein (king of Jordan), 23, 99, 122, 123–24, 136, 274, 275
Hussein, Saddam. See Gulf War
Husseini, Faisal, 62, 156, 178, 200, 237, 275, 295, 297; and al-Aqsa Mosque massacre, 73; and Arafat-Rabin meeting, 276–77; arrests of, 108–9, 111–12, 113–15, 211, 212; assassination attempt on, 114–15; and back-channel negotiations, 175, 238, 259–60; and "The Baker suit," 86–87; and Baker, 95–96, 100, 110; and beginning of peace process, 79, 80, 82, 84, 87–88, 90, 92–93; belief in peace process of, 116; and bilateral talks, 243; and Cairo Agreement signing, 291–92; and Christopher, 232, 233–36, 237, 249, 254, 255; and DOP, 250, 251–52, 253, 254, 255, 260; demonstrations/threats against, 90, 113–15, 145, 229; and deportations, 171; and disillusionment with peace process, 288; and Egyptian trip, 136–39; and Executive Committee meeting, 121–22; as fund-raiser, 240; and Gaza-Jericho agreement, 286–87; and Gulf War, 71; HA meets, 57–58; and HA's appointment to PNA, 294; and human element, 90; and hunger strike, 64, 65; and Jerusalem headquarters of Palestinians, 234; and Jerusalem issue, 87, 90, 122, 249, 277, 296; and Jordan-PLO relationship, 122; and Letter of Invitation, 129, 130; and Madrid Conference, 129, 141, 144, 145, 146, 147; and media misrepresentation of HA, 203, 204; and multilateral talks, 189, 194; and official invitations, 201; and Palestinian delegation membership, 90–91, 118, 122, 125, 126, 127, 129; and

Palestinian delegation's resignation, 256; and Palestinian six-point requirements, 233–36, 237; and Palestinian-American talks, 95–96, 100, 117–20, 233–36, 237; and Palestinian-Jordanian confederation, 123, 124; Peres's meeting with, 238; personal/professional background of, 57–58; personality of, 58; and PNA, 294, 295, 296; and PNC/PLO secret visits, 98, 100–107, 108; as Political Committee member, 50; and pre-Madrid talks, 95–96, 100–107, 117–20, 121–22, 128; and Saudis, 240, 243; support of HA by, 204; and White House Lawn ceremony, 266, 267, 268, 270

Husseini, Najat, 101, 105

Ibrahim, Muhsen, 105, 107

al-Ibrahimi Mosque massacre. *See* Hebron al-Ibrahimi Mosque massacre

"Ideas for Peaceful Coexistence in Territories During Interim Period" (fourth round), 198

"Informal Concept of Interim Self-Government Arrangements: Building Blocks for Agreement" (sixth round), 218

"Information Draft for a Joint Agenda" (fourth round), 198

insiders and outsiders: and Arafat's welcome to Washington, 263–64; and beginning of peace process, 80, 81–82; and DOP, 179; and Gulf War, 71–72; and *intifada*, 81; and Leadership Committee, 258; and official invitations, 201; and Palestinian delegation, 85, 186, 189, 193; and PLO review, 71; and PNA, 276; tensions between, 58, 97–98, 179; and working groups, 196. *See also specific person*

interim phase-permanent status talks, 242, 251–52, 277

international conferences: purposes/benefits of, 62–63. *See also specific conference*

"International Presence," 285

intifada: antecedents of, 26; beginning of, 36, 37–38, 43; and bilateral talks, 160–161; and children, 53–56; daily living during, 53–54; and Gulf War, 70; impact of, 10; and information

campaign, 48–51; innocence of, 59; and insiders-outsiders relationship, 57–58, 81; leadership of, 49; message of, 43; and police resignations, 169; reasons for, 36; as training ground for activists, 180–81; and visitors to Palestine, 50; and Welfare Association, 69; women's role in, 43, 44–47, 60

Iran, 184

Iraq. *See* Gulf War

Israel: and Clinton administration, 219; effects of immigrants on, 61; establishment of state of, 22; and media, 159–60; normalization of activities with, 11; Palestinian recognition of, 10; and PNC secret visit, 108–9; public opinion in, 284; suffering in, 216; terrorism against, 216; and the U.N., 85, 172; and U.S. elections, 213; U.S. loan guarantees to, 88, 124, 213, 219. *See also* elections: Israeli; *specific person, country, political party, or round of talks*

Israeli Military Orders, 198–99

'Iyun Fara massacre (1990), 64, 65, 66

Jennings, Peter, 25–26, 215, 263

Jericho: Arafat's return to, 11, 301–2; and DOP, 251; and Madrid Conference, 136, 156; Mikhail/Ashrawi family days near, 226. *See also* Gaza-Jericho agreement; "Gaza-Jericho first option"

Jerusalem, 13, 90, 156–57, 291–92, 202; and Ashrawi family, 248; Baker's visits to, 125–26; and beginning of peace process, 87, 90, 93; and Christopher's visits, 252; as city without a soul, 247–248; and "The Guide" poem, 290; and human rights meetings/offices, 286, 302; and hunger strike, 66–68; and *intifada*, 50; as *Mdineh*, 248–49; Palestinian headquarters in, 234; and settlements, 248; and Women's March, 63–64

Jerusalem (as an issue), 13–14, 298; and Arafat-Rabin meeting, 277; and Baker's visits, 100; and bilateral talks, 218, 259; and Christopher, 233, 236, 252, 253, 287–88; demonstrations about, 289; and DOP, 251–52, 253, 260–61, 275, 282; and Gaza-Jericho agreement, 287; as goal in peace process, 250; and Husseini, 87, 90, 122, 249, 277, 296;

Jerusalem (as an issue) (*cont.*)
and Israeli elections, 212; and Jordan, 124; Palestinian delegation membership, 85, 86, 90–91, 118, 127, 189, 193; and Palestinian six-point requirements, 236; and pre-Madrid talks, 100, 118, 122; and U.N. resolutions, 118, 284–85; and U.S. election, 213; U.S. position on, 213, 219, 237–38; working groups on, 196
Jerusalem Fund, 240
Al-Jihad Al-Islami organization, 12, 13
Johnson, Penny, 143, 145, 146, 151, 173, 190–91, 194, 237
Joint Statement (ninth round), 243–44
Jordan, 184; and "alternative homeland," 122–23; and bilateral talks, 154, 159; and deportations, 223; and DOP, 274; Israeli treaty with, 11, 13–14, 124; and Jerusalem, 124; and Madrid Conference, 153; and multilateral talks, 189; Palestinian confederation with, 122–24; and Palestinian delegation, 136, 159, 161; Palestinian mistrust of, 13; and Palestinian political activities, 23; and PLO, 122–23; and U.S., 122; and West Bank, 123, 136. *See also* Amman, Jordan; Hussein (king of Jordan); Palestinian delegation: as joint Jordanian-Palestinian delegation
"Jordanian option," 122–23
Juʾbeh, Nathmi al-, 180, 236, 286–87

Kach movement, 113, 114–15, 216–17, 283
Kaddoumi, Farouq al-. *See* Abul-Lutof
Kamal, Zahira, 50, 80, 176–77, 189, 190–191, 237
Kanʾan, Sameh, 125–26, 185
Kassem, Anis Fawzi, 189, 190
Kassis, Nabeel, 177–78, 259, 277, 286–287
Khatib, Ghassan al-, 236, 237; and al-Aqsa Mosque massacre, 73–74; and *intifada,* 48–49; and Madrid Conference, 151; and multilateral talks, 189, 190–91, 194; as Palestinian delegation member, 179–80; as Political Committee member, 50; torture of, 179–80
Khreisheh, Amal, 45, 46
Knesset, 220–21
Koppel, Ted, 48–50, 203, 268

Kurtzer, Dan, 59, 200, 250, 265; and Baker ultimatum, 110; and beginning of peace process, 85, 88, 92; and bilateral talks, 242, 243, 244, 263–64; and deportations, 222, 223; and DOP, 263–264; and Letter of Invitation, 85, 130; and PNC secret visit, 108; and pre-Madrid talks, 108, 110, 117; and PLO-Palestinian public contact, 211–12
Kuwait. *See* Gulf War

Labor Party (Israel), 84, 122–23, 137, 210, 212, 217–18, 220, 221. *See also* Peres, Shimon; Rabin, Yitzhak
land for peace, 83, 188, 217, 233
Larry King Live (TV), 224
leadership: HA's views on, 107, 271
Leadership Committee, 174–75, 181, 188, 189, 253, 257–58, 263–64. *See also* *specific member*
League of Communist Workers, 51–52
Lebanon, 10, 19–20, 81, 154, 188, 223
Legal Review Committee, 294
legal system, Palestinian, 14
Letter of Assurance, 91, 100, 101, 118, 129–30, 161, 245, 253
Letter of Invitation: for bilateral talks, 161, 237–38; and Madrid Conference, 85, 91, 129–30
Letter of Understanding, 91–92
Liaison Committee (DOP), 275, 277, 279
Likud Party (Israel), 84, 122, 175, 210, 211, 212, 219–20. *See also* Shamir, Yitzhak
London, England, 101, 207, 208, 209, 220, 221
loyalty, petition of, 126

madafah tradition, 166–67
Madrid Conference, 40, 135–36; and Arab coordination, 151–52; and Arafat meeting, 149–50; Baker's speech at, 59; as beginning, 157; and European Community, 143; and language problems, 139–40; and media, 142–43, 144–45, 153, 195; opening of, 129, 141–49; origins and evolution of, 9, 10, 11; outcomes of, 157; Palestinian speeches at, 145–48, 151, 153; and Palestinian-U.S. meetings, 143, 148–49; and PLO, 139, 143–44, 147; preparations for, 130–31, 136, 139–40;

public announcement of, 129; return from, 155, 156–58. *See also* first round (Madrid); Letter of Invitation; Palestinian delegation (Madrid); *specific person*

Majali, Abdel-Salam al-, 151, 159, 161

Malki, Riad, 50, 80

Mandela, Nelson, 293, 297–99

Mansour, Kamil, 150, 259

Masri, Munib al-, 295, 296

Masri, Taher al-, 95, 96, 122, 136

Mazen, Abu, 183, 275; and Arafat secret visit, 103; and backchannel negotiations, 218, 221, 238, 245; and Baker's visits, 97, 98; and beginning of peace process, 81; and bilateral talks, 218, 245; and deportations, 223; and DOP, 258, 260, 263, 279; and Egyptian-Palestinian meeting, 137; and Jordan-PLO relationship, 122; and multilateral talks, 189, 197; and Oslo talks, 258, 260; and Palestinian delegation's resignation, 258; and White House Lawn ceremony, 263, 265, 266, 269, 270

media: and Arafat-Palestinian delegation meeting, 241; Arafat's impression on Western, 28; and Arafat's return to Palestine, 301; and assassination attempts on HA, 216–17; and Baker, 99–101; and beginning of peace process, 88, 90, 92; and bilateral talks, 159–60, 173, 244; and Cairo Agreement, 291–92; and Commission for Citizens' Rights, 288–89; and deportations, 228; and Gaza-Jericho agreement, 295; and HA's arrest, 113; HA's relationship with, 129, 154–55, 195; and human rights, 173, 198; and *intifada*, 48–51; and Israelis, 159–60; lack of Palestinian, 157; leaks to, 100; and Madrid Conference, 142–43, 144–145, 147, 148, 150–51, 153, 195; misrepresentation of HA by, 203–4; and multilateral talks, 194–96; and peace process, 293; and PNC visit, 100, 101, 107–8, 109; and postponement of talks, 241; and pre-Madrid talks, 128; and announcement of Madrid Conference, 129; and public talks, 244; and return from Madrid Conference, 157–58; and U.S. role in peace process,

231; views of Palestinian delegation by, 174. *See also specific person*

memorial services, Palestinian, 161

Meretz Party, 212, 220, 223

Mikahil, Jad (uncle), 197

Mikhail, Abla (sister), 21–22, 43, 44, 46, 135, 167, 191

Mikhail, Daud (father): Abdel-Shafi compared with, 163; birthday of, 164, 170; courtship/marriage of, 164, 165–167; culture of, 166–67; as doctor, 22, 164, 166; Emile Ashrawi's relationship with, 163–64; as father, 33–34, 36, 47, 134; as gardener, 167; on HA's education, 192; HA's relationship with, 47, 163–64, 167, 297; and HA's wedding, 33–34; illness/death of, 163, 169–71; and Palestinian demonstrations against HA, 229; and Palestinian-Israeli relations, 168; personality of, 163–64; political activities of, 23, 24–25, 31, 57, 163, 164–65, 192; and political secrets of children, 23; as a prisoner, 23–24, 215; and religion, 166; as Santa Claus, 197; and women's rights, 47

Mikhail family, 21–22, 25, 165, 197, 226

Mikhail, Hanan. *See* Ashrawi, Hanan Mikhail

Mikhail, Hanna (aka Abu Omar), 25

Mikhail, Huda (sister), 135, 167, 170, 297

Mikhail, Ishaq (uncle), 162–63

Mikhail, Muna (sister), 21, 135, 167, 170

Mikhail, Nadia (sister). *See* Abboushi, Nadia Mikhail

Mikhail, Wadiʾa (mother): culture of, 166–67; and HA's childhood/youth, 22, 23, 25, 35–36, 165–66; HA's relationship with, 117, 297; marriage of, 33, 164; as mother, 134; and religion, 24, 166; and Taggart Building prison, 215, 216

Miller, Aaron, 59, 200, 250, 265; and beginning of peace process, 88, 92; and bilateral talks, 242, 243, 244; and DOP, 263–64; and pre-Madrid talks, 117

minute-takers, 59, 99, 100–101

Moscow, Russia: multilateral talks in (1992), 188–91, 193–97

Moussa, ʿAmr, 137, 252

Mubarak, Hosni, 95, 136–39, 239, 252, 254, 286

multilateral talks: bilateral talks' relationship to, 188–89; in London, 220; in Moscow (1992), 188–91, 193–197; purpose of, 188–89

Najjab, Suleiman al-, 122, 190, 193
names: need for alternate, 27; significance of, 132–33, 134–35
nation building, 278–90; women's role in, 293–94. *See also* Palestinian National Authority (PNA)
negotiating committees (DOP), 275–76, 278–79
Netanyahu, Benjamin, 145, 148, 159–60
"New World Order," 79
Nightline (ABC-TV), 48–50, 203
ninth round (Washington, 1993), 181, 239, 242–45
Noor (queen of Jordan), 99, 123
"normalization," 189, 238
Norway, 202, 203, 280–81, 286. *See also* Oslo, Norway; Oslo (Norway) Agreement (1994); Oslo (Norway) talks
Notre Dame meetings, 220–21
Nusseibeh, Sari, 50, 77, 92, 117, 126, 174–76, 238

occupation by Israel: and the children, 54, 78, 89, 208–9, 226–27; ending of, 217, 250, 251, 287; intrusiveness of evil of, 215–16; and prisoners, 89; psychologizing the, 64–65; and women, 227–29
Omar, Abu. *See* Mikhail, Hanna
Oslo, Norway: Arafat's visit to, 280; HA's visit to, 274–75. *See also* Oslo (Norway) Agreement; Oslo (Norway) talks
Oslo (Norway) Agreement: signing of, 11, 13, 264–72. *See also* Declaration of Principles
Oslo (Norway) talks: beginning of, 220; and bilateral talks, 244–45; and DOP, 254, 260; and PLO legitimacy, 183; progress in, 239, 251; reasons for, 171; success of, 259–60
"Outline of Administrative Council" (sixth round), 217

"A Pair of Shoes" (HA short story), 54
Palestine: Arafat's return to, 11, 300–302; funds promised to, 14; geography of, 169, 170; meaning to Palestinians of, 134; partition of, 218; Zionist myth about, 168
Palestine Liberation Army (PLA), 251
Palestine Liberation Organization (PLO), 67–68, 201, 204, 263–64; accountability to, 158; and "alternative leadership," 185; and Baker, 99, 100–101, 119, 128; and beginning of peace process, 81–83, 88, 92; and bilateral talks, 117, 158–59, 171, 172, 218, 243, 245; and Cairo Agreement, 13; and Christopher, 233, 287; criticisms of, 279–80; and DOP, 250, 251, 260, 282; economic blockade of, 79, 86, 230, 240, 241, 243, 252; and Egypt, 137, 138; elections within, 203–4; emergence of, 24–25; expulsion of, 10, 57, 81; Four Point Plan of, 71; and "Gaza first" option, 251; and Gaza-Jericho agreement, 287; and Gulf War, 71, 72, 78–79, 81, 83, 101, 184–85; and hunger strike, 66; implications of failure of, 293; Israeli bans on contact with, 28, 57, 210–12, 220, 242; and Jordan, 122–23; and Likud party dialogues, 175; and Madrid Conference, 139, 143–44, 147; membership in, 83; and multilateral talks, 188, 189–90, 193, 197, 220; and Oslo Agreement, 13; Palestinian meetings with, 98, 100–107; and Palestinian-Israeli dialogue, 238; Palestinians' relationship to, 13, 84, 185; and peace process, 116, 173, 183–85, 199, 250; recognition of, 86, 186, 241, 260, 271–72; role of leadership of, 107; strategy of, 116, 183–84; as symbol of a nation, 262; and U.S. visas, 158–59. *See also* Arafat, Yasser; back-channel negotiations; Oslo (Norway) talks; Palestinian delegation; United States: PLO dialogue with the; *specific person*
Palestine Partition Plan (1947), 51
Palestinian Academic Society for Study of International Affairs (PASSIA), 70
Palestinian delegation: as against returning to talks, 240–41; Arafat's meeting with, 239; Arafat's public reception of, 210–211; and back-channel negotiations, 183–84; and bilateral talks, 158–59, 161–62, 168, 172, 182, 243, 259; changes to, 186; and Christopher, 287–

288; and DOP, 253, 255–58, 261, 279;
defiance of Arafat by, 178–79; erosion
of support for, 244; financing, 119,
259; and Gaza-Jericho agreement, 288;
HA's resignation from, 281; HA's role
in, 186–87; and insiders and outsiders,
85, 189, 193; Israeli vetting of, 127,
128–29, 193–94, 196; and
Jerusalemites, 85, 86, 90–91, 118, 127,
189, 193; as joint Jordanian-Palestinian
delegation, 86, 96, 117–18, 122, 131,
161–62, 168, 172; mandate/mission of,
245; and multilateral talks, 189, 193–
195, 220; overview of members of,
174–86; people represented by, 186;
and PLO, 118–19, 127, 128, 131, 186,
210–12, 244, 258; resignation of, 255–
258; and sense of mission, 185; and
specialized groups, 186; and "strategic
committee," 186; undermining of, 116,
258; vulnerability of, 249; and White
House Lawn ceremony, 266, 268, 270.
See also Leadership Committee;
Palestinian delegation (Madrid); Political
Committee; specific member
Palestinian delegation (Madrid):
administrative team for, 125; constraints
on, 124; experts/ advisers to, 125, 130–
131; finalizing of, 127–28; and first
round, 152–55; and Follow-Up
Committee, 125; Israeli vetting of, 127,
128–29; and loyalty petition, 126;
membership of, 90–91, 117–18; and
PLO, 86, 118–19, 124–25, 126–27,
128, 131; selection of, 122, 124–25,
126–27, 129. See also Palestinian
delegation; specific member
Palestinian Democratic Alliance (FIDA),
115, 124, 125, 176–77
Palestinian Economic Council for
Development and Reconstruction
(PECDAR), 176, 178, 293
Palestinian Genesis, 302–3
Palestinian Independent Commission for
Citizens'/Human Rights, 276, 280–81,
286, 288–89, 294, 295, 296, 297, 302
Palestinian Interim Self-Government
Authority (PISGA), 172–73, 198
Palestinian National Authority (PNA), 176,
297; appointments to, 182, 294–95,
296; and Cairo Agreement, 13;
challenges to, 13; creation of, 17, 276,

278; credibility of, 13; erosion of, 13;
HA's appointment to, 294–95, 296; and
inter-Palestinian fighting, 13;
organization/responsibilities of, 296;
and Oslo Agreement, 13; swearing in of,
302; and women, 177, 294
Palestinian National Council (PNC):
Algiers meeting (1988) of, 10, 52–53;
and Baker, 100; and early Palestinian-
Israeli talks, 58–59; elections of, 199–
200; Israeli ban on contact with, 98,
100–101, 105–7; and media, 100;
Palestinian meetings with, 98, 100–
101, 105–7; and Palestinian statehood,
10, 53; and Palestinian-Jordanian
confederation, 123; and two-state
solution, 53, 177
Palestinian National Liberation Movement.
See Fateh
Palestinian Question: as personal issue, 25
"The Palestinian Response to American
Draft," 252, 253, 254
Palestinian statehood, 10, 53, 250, 259,
261
Palestinian-Israeli conflict: origins of, 9–10
Palestinian-Israeli talks: and bilateral talks,
197–200, 238; and early contacts, 31,
32, 37–38, 58–59; and Gulf War, 79;
and Israeli political parties, 219–20,
221; and League of Communist
Workers, 51–52; and Notre Dame
meetings, 220–21; and Peres, 238; and
PLO, 238; and violence, 175; and
women, 37–38, 59–62, 219. See also
back-channel negotiations; Oslo
(Norway) talks; specific round of talks
Palestinian-Israeli Women's Network, 62
Palestinian-Jordanian confederation, 122–
124
Palestinians: anger of, 12, 13; Baker's
views of, 90; character of, 187; as
collaborators, 214–15; collective
memory of, 245–46; communication
about peace process to, 157–58; curfew
for, 76, 77, 222, 283, 285; as
dispensable, 219; divisiveness among,
12, 13, 115–16, 185, 228–29, 240–41,
255–58, 279–80, 282; effects of Gulf
War on, 78–79; exile of, 168–69; fear
of Iraq by, 71–72; gas masks for, 73,
76; general amnesty for, 30; meaning of
Palestine to, 134; and narrative from

Palestinians: anger of (*cont.*)
within, 93–94; pain of, 213–15, 216;
PLO's relationship with, 84; recognition
of, 260; stereotyping of, 64, 127; U.S./
Western image of, 28, 30, 110–11
Pankin, Boris, 128–29
PASSIA. *See* Palestinian Academic Society
for Study of International Affairs
PDFLP. *See* Popular Democratic Front for
Liberation of Palestine (PDFLP)
peace: popular celebration of, 63–64
Peace Now movement, 113
peace process: abandonment of, by Bush
administration, 219; and advocacy
mission, 157–58; and "Baker suit," 86–
87; basis of, 83, 93; beginning of, 79–
80, 81–94; benefits of, 184–85; and co-
sponsors, 86, 199; credibility of, 200;
disillusionment with, 242, 285–86,
288; and divisiveness among
Palestinians, 115–16; and domestic
problems, 184; Egyptian role in, 137–
139; erosion of, 13; and European
Community, 85–86; and extremists,
11–12, 216; financing of, 119; and
human element, 89–90; and Israeli-
Palestinian dependence, 14–15; and
land for peace, 217; and media, 293;
nature of Palestinian participation in,
86; and need to make it work, 168;
objectives of, 217–18; observer states
to, 85; Palestinian criticisms of, 228,
282; Palestinian goals in, 250; and
Palestinian public opinion, 200, 221,
224, 241, 244, 283, 292; Palestinian
support for, 157; PLO importance to,
173, 183–85, 250; and pragmatism,
245–46; as preset paradigm, 93;
reassessment of, 13; stalemate in, 198–
199; suspension of, 206; as two-phased
approach, 127; and U.N., 85; and U.N.-
U.S. relations, 231; U.S. as an obstacle
to, 250; U.S. commitment to, 231; U.S.
role in, 116, 173, 230–31, 242, 250–
251; and violence, 11–12, 13. *See also*
bilateral talks; Letter of Invitation;
Madrid Conference; multilateral talks;
settlements; *specific round of talks or
person*
PECDAR. *See* Palestinian Economic
Council for Development and
Reconstruction

People's Party, 48–49, 115, 124, 125, 243
Peres, Shimon, 9, 11, 220, 238, 260, 263,
266, 270, 286
PFLP. *See* Popular Front for Liberation of
Palestine
Phalangists, Lebanese, 10, 25
Pimental, Gil, 48, 49
PISGA. *See* Palestinian Interim Self-
Government Authority
PNA. *See* Palestinian National Authority
PNC. *See* Palestinian National Council
police, Palestinian, 292, 294
Political Committee, 50–51, 115, 174–82,
220–21, 267
political system, Palestinian, 14
Popular Democratic Front for Liberation of
Palestine (PDFLP), 49, 176–77
Popular Front for Liberation of Palestine
(PFLP), 30, 48, 60, 115, 124, 228
pragmatism, 245–46
prison: as an honor, 23; Taggart Building
as a, 215–16. *See also specific person*
prisoners, 77–78, 89, 277, 288, 298
"Proposal for a Framework Agreement"
(sixth round), 217
public talks, 244
public opinion: Israeli, 284; Palestinian,
200, 221, 224, 241, 244, 283, 292
Pundik, Ron, 220, 260

Qreiʾ, Ahmad. *See* Ala, Abu

Rabin, Yitzhak, 62, 242, 283; and Arafat,
11, 53, 271, 276–77, 284; and back-
channel negotiations, 238, 245, 260;
and beginning of peace process, 84; and
bilateral talks, 220, 243; and
Christopher, 233; and DOP, 263; and
deportations, 172, 222, 223; and Gaza-
Jericho agreement, 288; and Israeli
elections, 211, 212; Nobel Prize for, 9,
11; and U.S. relations, 213; and White
House Lawn ceremony, 263, 265, 266,
267, 270, 271
Ramallah, Palestine: HA returns to, 30;
Jerusalem's relationship with, 248–49;
as Mikhail home, 22, 164, 165; Taggart
Building in, 215–16
"red lines," 249–50, 260
refugee camps, 77–78, 202, 213, 300
refugees, 14, 78, 196, 224–25, 260–61. *See
also* deportations; U.N. Resolution 242

Republican Party (U.S.), 213, 219
Ross, Dennis, 59, 111, 200, 250, 265; and
  Baker ultimatum, 109–10; and Baker's
  Middle East visits, 99; and beginning of
  peace process, 88, 92; and bilateral
  talks, 160; and Christopher, 255; and
  DOP, 255; and Letter of Invitation, 130;
  and Madrid Conference, 147, 153;
  Middle East visit of, 252; and PNC
  secret visit, 108–9; and pre-Madrid
  talks, 109–10, 111, 117, 118
rounds: first, 151, 152–55; second 158–
  162, 168, 171; third, 171, 172–73;
  fourth, 197–200; sixth, 217–18;
  seventh, 219–20, 224; ninth, 181, 239,
  242–45; tenth, 249–50; eleventh, 259–
  262; twelfth, 262–64
Rubinstein, Elyakim, 148, 162, 200, 212,
  222
Russia/Russians, 86, 171, 184, 188–91,
  193–97, 241

Safieh, Afif, 101, 209, 221
Said, Edward, 25, 93–94, 273
Salah, Raja, 54–56
Saturday of Light ceremony (1981), 35–
  36
Saudi Arabia, 148, 184, 240
Savir, Uri, 260, 266
second round (Washington, 1992), 158–
  162, 168, 171
security issues, 12, 251, 259, 283
self determination, 100, 123
self-censorship, 14
self-government, 172–73, 179, 198, 221,
  242
semantics, 132–34
Serry, Robert, 85, 220, 221
settlements, 226–27, 298; and Baker, 100;
  and bilateral talks, 218; and
  Christopher, 233, 287–88; and DOP,
  251–52, 260, 261, 282, 283; expansion
  of, 13, 116; and Gaza-Jericho
  agreement, 287; and Israeli elections,
  212; and Israeli-U.S. loan guarantees,
  88, 124; and Jerusalem, 248; and peace
  process, 83–84, 85, 88, 90, 116, 172,
  200, 250; and pre-Madrid talks, 124,
  127, 128; Rabin's policies about, 212,
  213
seventh round (Washington, 1992), 219–
  220, 224

Shamir, Yitzhak, 128, 158; and beginning
  of peace process, 84, 86, 90, 91; and
  deportations, 171–72; and Israeli
  elections, 200, 211; and Madrid
  Conference, 145, 147, 149, 153;
  Mubarak's views of, 139; Palestinian
  views of, 110, 111–12; and PNC secret
  visit, 108–9, 111
Shara, Farouq al-, 151, 152, 239–40
Sha'th, Nabil, 98, 201, 266, 282; and
  Arafat's "death," 202, 203; Arafat's
  relationship with, 182; and Arafat's
  return, 300–302; and Arafat's welcome
  to Washington, 263–64; and bilateral
  talks, 158, 159, 172, 243; commitment
  to peace process of, 182; and
  deportations, 223; and DOP, 250, 251–
  252, 260, 279; and HA's PNA
  appointment, 294; HA's relationship
  with, 201; and Madrid Conference, 144,
  146, 147, 149, 151, 153; and Oslo
  talks, 260; as a Palestinian delegation
  member, 182; personality of, 98, 162,
  182; and Stockholm visit, 200–202
Shin Bet, 114
sixth round (Washington, 1992), 217–18
Sneh, Ephraim, 238, 239
South Africa, 293, 297–300
Stoel, Max van der, 220, 221
students, 32, 37–38, 180
Susskind, Davide and Simone, 60, 62
Sweden, 59, 200–202, 280, 297
Syria, 67, 151, 152, 153, 154, 184, 188–
  189, 274

Taba talks, 282, 283
table tennis diplomacy, 242
Taggart Building (Ramallah), 215–16
Taha, Suhair, 204, 264; and Arafat's
  "death," 202, 203; and Madrid
  Conference, 143, 144, 145, 147, 150,
  151, 153; and multilateral talks, 190–
  191, 195
Ten-Point Plan (Egypt, 1989), 58
tenth round (Washington, 1993), 249–50
territorial jurisdiction, 221, 251–52, 260
terrorism: against elected Palestinian
  officials, 198; against Israelis, 216;
  victims of, 216. See also specific act
third round (Washington, 1992), 171,
  172–73
Tiberias: Mikhail family exile in, 165

trilateral meetings (Washington, 1993), 243–44, 250

Tsemel, Leah, 36, 37–38, 113, 169, 222, 223, 282–83

Turkey, 184, 191

Tutwiler, Margaret, 88, 117, 128, 147, 199, 200

twelfth round (Washington, 1993), 262–264

"Two States for Two Peoples" (peace celebration), 63–64

two-state solution, 10, 32, 53, 177

two-track approach, 161–62, 168, 171, 172

Ugglas, Margaretha af, 201–2, 297

United Nations, 19, 74, 85, 119, 218: Arafat's speech before, 59; and deportations, 171–72; and hunger strike, 66, 67; and Palestinian rights, 284; and U.S. policy, 231. See also specific resolution

United Nations Resolution 181, 118, 218

United Nations Resolution 242: and bilateral talks, 83, 218; and Christopher, 233; and ending of occupation, 136, 217; and Gaza-Jericho agreement, 287; implementation of, 230, 242, 250; and Israeli-U.S. agreements, 230; and Jordan, 136; and Madrid Conference, 10; talks about, 217, 218; and peace process, 10, 85; and U.N. Resolution 904, 285; and U.S. relations, 231

United Nations Resolution 338, 10, 83, 85, 217, 242, 285, 287

United Nations Resolution 726, 172

United Nations Resolution 799, 224, 229, 230–31, 233

United Nations Resolution 904, 284–85

United States: credibility of, 230; double standard of, 68; HA as a student in, 28–30; and hunger strike, 67, 68; and Israeli loan guarantees, 88, 124, 213, 219; Jordan's relationship with, 122; and Letter of Invitation as policy, 91–92; negotiating style of, 242; and Palestinian image, 110–11; PLO dialogue with, 58–59, 67, 68, 81–82, 105, 119, 154, 240; and PLO visas, 158–59; policy of, 217–18, 231; as

pro-Israel, 86, 109–11, 116, 118, 154, 199, 230, 239, 265; role in peace process of, 79, 86, 116, 171, 173, 199, 230–31, 242, 250–51; Shamir's visit to, 158; U.N. as instrument of policy of, 231. See also elections: U.S.; specific person or round

University of Virginia, 28–30

Washington Cathedral: Palestinian memorial services at, 161

Washington, D.C.: Palestinian representation in, 274, 279; Palestinian-American meetings in, 101, 109–10, 115–20; and pre-Madrid talks, 98, 101, 109–10, 115–20. See also specific round of talks

Washington Institute for Near East Policy, 230

Welfare Association, 69

West Bank, 9, 20, 22, 123, 125, 136, 252. See also Jericho; Ramallah

White House Lawn Ceremony (1993): Arafat's speech at, 273–74; last minute changes at, 264–71; preparations for, 262–64; signing at, 11, 53, 271–72. See also Declaration of Principles

Wilcox, Philip, 79, 88, 267

Williamson, Molly: 89, 99, 110, 126; and bilateral talks, 158, 237, 242, 244; and Christopher's Middle East visits, 232, 234–35; and Letter of Invitation, 129–130; and Madrid Conference, 143, 147; and pre-Madrid talks, 99, 110

women: against women, 228–29; in Arab society, 47, 60–61; bonds between, 201–2; creeping disenfranchisement of, 293–94; demonstrations by, 43, 44–47, 63–64; and deportations, 229; effects of occupation on, 227–29; and intifada, 43, 44–47, 60; as Palestinian delegation members, 176–77; and Palestinian-Israeli dialogues, 59–62, 219; in politics, 204; rights of, 294; role in nation building of, 293–94; of South Africa, 300. See also feminism; specific person or organization

Women's March (1990), 63–64

working groups, 196, 197, 218, 219, 242. See also specific group

Year of Peace (1990), 63–64